Pattern Recognition by Humans and Machines

Volume 1

Speech Perception

This is a volume in
ACADEMIC PRESS
SERIES IN COGNITION AND PERCEPTION
A Series of Monographs and Treatises

Pattern Recognition by Humans and Machines

Volume 1
Speech Perception

Edited by

EILEEN C. SCHWAB

AT&T Information Systems
Indianapolis, Indiana

HOWARD C. NUSBAUM

Speech Research Laboratory
Indiana University
Bloomington, Indiana

1986

ACADEMIC PRESS, INC.
Harcourt Brace Jovanovich, Publishers
Orlando   San Diego   New York   Austin
Boston   London   Sydney   Tokyo   Toronto

ACADEMIC PRESS, INC.
Orlando, Florida 32887

United Kingdom Edition published by
ACADEMIC PRESS INC. (LONDON) LTD.
24–28 Oval Road, London NW1 7DX

LIBRARY OF CONGRESS CATALOGING-IN-PUBLICATION DATA

Main entry under title:

Pattern recognition by humans and machines.

   (Academic Press series in cognition and
perception)
     Includes index.
     Contents: v. 1. Speech perception — v. 2 Visual.
perception.
     1. Pattern perception.   2. Pattern recognition
systems.   I. Schwab, Eileen C.   II. Nusbaum, Howard C.
III. Series.
BF311.B316   1986   001.53′4   85-20110
ISBN 0–12–631401–2 (v. 1: hardcover) (alk. paper)
ISBN 0–12–631403–9 (v. 1: paperback) (alk. paper)

PRINTED IN THE UNITED STATES OF AMERICA

86 87 88 89   9 8 7 6 5 4 3 2 1

Contents

7. COGNITIVE SCIENCE AND THE STUDY OF COGNITION AND LANGUAGE
Zenon W. Pylyshyn

Preface

The basic problem of understanding how humans perceive information in the constant bombardment of sensory flux is, without question, one of the most difficult problems facing cognitive science. However, understanding perception is critical to developing a complete theoretical account of human information processing because perception serves to interface the physical world with the mental world. The patterns of energy impinging on sensory receptors must be transformed into representations that are canonical with the structural and dynamic properties of the physical world. At the same time, these representations must be compatible with the cognitive processes that mediate perception, comprehension, and memory. Theories of perception, therefore, need to take into account the physics of light and sound, the structure of objects and language, the neurophysiology of the sensory system, the limitations and capabilities of attention, learning, and memory, and the computational constraints of parallel and serial processing.

Perception will not be understood solely through better or more complete descriptions of the physical stimulus or the neural code that is used to represent the product of sensory transduction. Recognition simply does not occur in the sense organs. Similarly, new algorithms for pattern matching, or theories of memory or attention, or even new basic theories of computation will not, by themselves, solve the problem. Instead, the solution to understanding human perceptual information processing will depend on an interdisciplinary approach that integrates scientific knowledge about cognitive psychology, computation, physics, mathematics, and linguistics.

With this approach in mind, we decided to bring together some of the essential and yet diverse aspects of research on perception. Previous treatments of this subject have tended to consider perception from the perspective of cognitive psychology alone, or artificial intelligence alone, or some perspective in isolation, but there have been few attempts to integrate work on human perception together with discussions of the basic computational issues surrounding the modeling of perceptual processes. Within the limitation of two volumes, it is impossible to deal with all of the interrelated and interdisciplinary issues that must be considered in the study of perception. Therefore, we chose to focus on several basic problems of pattern recognition in speech perception and visual form perception. Our aim in editing this book, then, was to assemble a set of chapters that would consider perception from the perspectives of cognitive psychology, artificial intelligence, and brain theory.

Certainly at a relatively abstract theoretical level, pattern recognition is, in its essence, quite similar for speech perception and scene perception. There are two theoretically distinguishable parts to the problem of pattern recognition: First, how does the perceptual system segment meaningful forms from the impinging array of sensory input? Second, how are these forms then recognized as linguistic or physical objects? It is our belief that in spite of the apparent differences in the processing and representation of information in speech and vision, there are many similar computational issues that arise across these modalities as well. Some of these cross-modality similarities may be captured in basic questions such as: What are perceptual features, and how are these features organized? What constitutes a perceptual unit, and how are these units segmented and identified? What is the role of attention in perception? How do knowledge and expectation affect the perceptual processing of sensory input? And what is the nature of the mechanisms and representations used in perception? It is this set of fundamental questions that we have chosen to cover in these two volumes.

In considering the theme of perception across the domains of speech and visual form, some questions are quite apparent: Why compare speech perception and visual form perception? Why not compare the perception of spoken and written language, or general audition with vision? The reason is that our intention in editing these volumes was to focus specifically on the perception of meaningful sensory forms in different modalities. Previous books on spoken and written language have emphasized the role of linguistics in perception and thus are concerned with the role of meaning in perception. However, the problems of pattern segmentation and recognition for spoken and written language are not directly comparable; printed words are clearly segmented on the page by orthographic convention, while there are no clear linguistic segmentation boundaries in spoken language. Similarly, with respect to the issues that arise in books comparing the perception of arbitrary patterns in audition and vision, the emphasis is generally more on the psychophysical problems of transduction, coding, and detection than on the cognitive psychology of segmentation and recognition.

These chapters have been organized into two volumes—one focusing on speech perception and the other focusing on visual form perception. It is important to note that within each volume the theoretical issues touched on by the chapters are all quite distinct, while between volumes there are a number of similarities in the issues that are discussed. In Volume 1, some of the basic theoretical questions in speech perception are considered, including the perception of acoustic–phonetic structure and words, the role of attention in speech perception, and models of word and phoneme perception. In Volume 2, several fundamental questions concerning visual form perception are considered, including the perception of features and patterns, the role of eye movements in pattern processing, and models of segmentation and pattern recognition.

These volumes would certainly not have developed without the cooperation and contribution of the authors. In addition, we are grateful to a number of colleagues for their assistance. We would like to thank David Pisoni and Barry Lively for their active support and encouragement of our work on this project. We would also like to acknowledge Stephen Grossberg for his constant stimulation to bring this project to fruition despite several problems and setbacks. Finally, we conceived of this book while we were graduate students at the State University of New York at Buffalo, and it developed as a direct consequence of numerous discussions and arguments about perception with our colleagues and professors there. We thank Steve Greenspan, Jim Sawusch, Irv Biederman, Jim Pomerantz, Erwin Segal, Naomi Weisstein, and Mary Williams for providing the scientific climate from which this book could develop.

Contents of Volume 2

Visual Perception

CHAPTER 1

Speech Perception: Research, Theory, and the Principal Issues*

David B. Pisoni and Paul A. Luce

Department of Psychology, Indiana University, Bloomington, Indiana 47405

I. INTRODUCTION

The basic problems in speech perception are, in principle, no different from the basic problems in other areas of perceptual research. They involve a number of issues surrounding the internal representation of the speech signal and the perceptual constancy of this representation—the problem of acoustic–phonetic invariance and the phenomena associated with perceptual contrast to identical stimulation. When viewed from a fairly broad perspective that stresses the commonalities among sensory and perceptual systems, the problems in speech perception are obviously similar to those encountered in vision, hearing, and the tactile system. However, when viewed from a more narrow perspective that emphasizes the differences among sensory and perceptual systems, speech perception immediately becomes more distinctive and unique because of its role in language, thought, and communication among members of the species. Indeed, many researchers have suggested that seemingly unique biological specializations have developed to meet the demands imposed by the use of a vocal communication system such as speech.

The field of speech perception is an unusually diverse area of study involving researchers from a number of disciplines including psychology, linguistics, speech and hearing science, electrical engineering, and artificial intelligence. Despite the diversity of approaches to the study of

* Preparation of the chapter was supported in part by NIH Research Grant NS-12179 and NSF Grant BNS-83-05387 to Indiana University in Bloomington. We thank Beth Greene and Jan Charles-Luce for helpful comments and suggestions.

speech perception, a small number of basic questions can be identified as "core" problems in the field. For the psychologist, the fundamental problem in speech perception is to describe how a listener converts the continuously varying acoustic stimulus produced by a speaker into a sequence of discrete linguistic units, and how the intended message is recovered. This general problem can be approached by examining a number of more specific subquestions. For example, what stages of perceptual analysis intervene between the presentation of a speech signal and eventual understanding of the message? What types of processing operations occur at each of these stages? What specific types of mechanisms are involved in speech perception, and how do these interact in understanding spoken language?

Although the speech signal may often be of poor quality, with much of the speech slurred, distorted by noise, or at times even obliterated, the perceptual process generally appears to proceed quite smoothly. Indeed, to the naive observer, the perceptual process often appears to be carried out almost automatically, with little conscious effort or attention. Listeners are conscious of the words and sentences spoken to them. The speech sounds and the underlying linguistic organization and structure of the linguistic message appear transparent, and a good part of the perception process is normally unavailable for conscious inspection.

One important aspect of speech perception is that many components of the overall process appear to be only partially dependent on properties of the physical stimulus. The speech signal is highly structured and constrained in a number of principled ways. Even large distortions in the signal can be tolerated without significant loss of intelligibility. This appears to be so because the listener has several distinct sources of knowledge available for assigning a perceptual interpretation to the sensory input. As a speaker of a natural language, the listener has available a good deal of knowledge about the constraints on the structure of an utterance even before it is ever produced. On one hand, the listener knows something about the general situational or pragmatic context in which a particular utterance is produced. Knowledge of events, facts, and relations is used by listeners to generate hypotheses and draw inferences from fragmentary or impoverished sensory input. On the other hand, the listener also has available an extensive knowledge of language which includes detailed information about phonology, morphology, syntax, and semantics. This linguistic knowledge provides the principal means for constructing an internal representation of the sensory input and assigning a meaningful interpretation to any utterance produced by a speaker of the language.

In understanding spoken language, we assume that various types of information are computed by the speech processing mechanisms. Some forms of information are transient, lasting for only a short period of time; others are more durable and interact with other sources of knowledge that the listener has stored in long-term memory. Auditory, phonetic, phonological, lexical, syntactic, and semantic codes represent information that is generally available to a listener. The nature of these perceptual codes and their potential interactions during ongoing speech perception have been two of the major concerns in the field over the last 10–15 years.

In this chapter we review what we see as the principal issues in the field of speech perception. Most of these issues have been discussed in the past by other researchers and continue to occupy a central role in speech perception research; others relate to new problems in the field that will undoubtedly be pursued in the future as the field of speech perception becomes broader in scope. Each of these problems could be elaborated in much greater depth, but we have tried to limit the exposition to highlight the "core" problems in the field.

II. THE PRINCIPAL ISSUES

II.A. Linearity, Lack of Acoustic–Phonetic Invariance, and the Segmentation Problem

As first discussed by Chomsky and Miller (1963), one of the most important and central problems in speech perception derives from the fact that the speech signal fails to meet the conditions of linearity and invariance. The *linearity condition* assumes that for each phoneme there must be a particular stretch of sound in the utterance; if phoneme X is to the left of phoneme Y in the phonemic representation, the stretch of sound associated with X must precede the stretch of sound associated with Y in the physical signal. The *invariance condition* assumes that for each phoneme X there must be a specific set of criterial acoustic attributes or features associated with it in all contexts. These features must be present whenever X or some variant of X occurs, and they must be absent whenever some other phoneme occurs in the representation. As a consequence of failing to satisfy these two conditions, the basic recognition problem can be seen as a substantially more complex task for humans to carry out. Although humans can perform it effortlessly, the recognition of fluent speech by machines has thus far proven to be a nearly intractable problem.

For more than 30 years, it has been extremely difficult to identify acoustic segments and features that uniquely match the perceived phonemes independently of the surrounding context. As a result of coarticulation in speech production, there is typically a great deal of contextual variability in the acoustic signal correlated with any single phoneme. Often a single acoustic segment contains information about several neighboring linguistic segments (i.e., parallel transmission), and, conversely, the same linguistic segment is often represented acoustically in quite different ways depending on the surrounding phonetic context, the rate of speaking, and the talker (i.e., context-conditioned variation). In addition, the acoustic characteristics of individual speech sounds and words exhibit even greater variability in fluent speech because of the influence of the surrounding context than when speech sounds are produced in isolation.

The context-conditioned variability resulting from coarticulation also presents enormous problems for segmentation of the speech signal into phonemes or even words based only on an analysis of the physical signal, as shown in the spectrograms displayed in Figure 1.1. Because of the failure to meet the linearity and invariance conditions, it has been difficult to segment speech into acoustically defined units that are independent of adjacent segments or free from contextual effects when placed in sentence contexts. That is, it is still extremely difficult to determine strictly by simple physical criteria where one word ends and another begins in fluent speech. Although segmentation is possible according to strictly acoustic criteria (see Fant, 1962), the number of acoustic segments is typically greater than the number of linguistic segments (phonemes) in an utterance. Moreover, no simple invariant mapping has been found between acoustic attributes and perceived phonemes or individual words in sentences.

II.B. Internal Representation of Speech Signals

There has long been agreement among many investigators working on human speech perception that at some stage of perceptual processing, speech is represented internally as a sequence of discrete segments and features (see, e.g., Studdert-Kennedy, 1974, 1976). There has been much less agreement, however, about the exact description of these features. Arguments have been provided for feature systems based on distinctions in the acoustic domain or the articulatory domain, and for systems that combine both types of distinctions (Chomsky & Halle, 1968; Jakobson, Fant, & Halle, 1952; Wickelgren, 1969).

A number of researchers have come to view these traditional feature descriptions of speech sounds with some skepticism, particularly with regard to the role they play in ongoing speech perception (Ganong, 1979; Klatt, 1977, 1979; Parker, 1977). On reexamination, much of the original evidence cited in support of feature-based processing in perceptual experiments seems ambiguous and equally consistent with more parametric

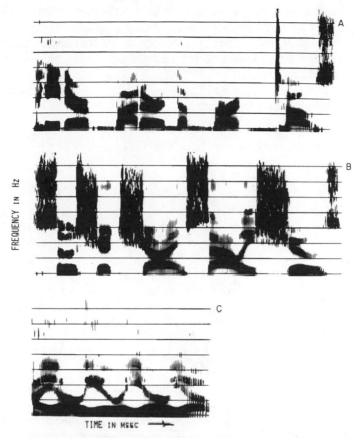

Figure 1.1 Three spectrograms—(A) Peter buttered the burnt toast, (B) Sue should shine Sally's shoes, and (C) I owe you a yoyo—showing differences in acoustic segmentation resulting from differences in articulation.

representations of speech. As a consequence, numerous investigators have begun to look more closely at how speech waveforms are processed in the peripheral auditory system, and at what these more detailed representations may contribute to questions surrounding phonetic processing, particularly the problem of acoustic–phonetic invariance (Klatt, 1979; Searle, Jacobson, & Kimberley, 1980; Zwicker, Terhardt, & Paulus, 1979).

One of these approaches has been to represent speech in the frequency domain as a sequence of magnitude spectra sampled about every 10 ms or so. If these spectral samples are adjusted in various ways to take account of certain psychophysical facts about hearing (such as critical bands, spread of masking, and the growth of loudness), a continuous representation can be obtained that is similar, in some sense, to a "neural spectrogram." Efforts along these lines have directed attention specifically to the problem of the neural representation of speech, and to questions having to do with the psychophysical filtering that speech undergoes during very early stages of processing.

II.B.1. Peripheral Auditory Analysis

Over the last 3 or 4 years, a great deal of new research has been reported in the literature on how the peripheral auditory system processes and encodes speech signals (see Carlson & Granstrom, 1982). The research on auditory modeling of speech signals comes from two different directions. First, a number of important physiological studies using animals have been carried out to describe, in fairly precise terms, how speech signals are coded in the peripheral auditory system (Delgutte, 1980, 1981, 1982, 1984; Delgutte & Kiang, 1984a, 1984b, 1984c, 1984d; Kiang, 1980). These studies have examined auditory nerve activity in response to simple speech signals such as steady-state vowels and stop consonants in consonant–vowel syllables (see also Moore & Cashin, 1974, 1976). The goal of this work has been to identify reliable and salient properties in the discharge patterns of auditory nerve fibers that correspond in some direct way to the important acoustic properties or attributes of speech sounds (Miller & Sachs, 1983; Sachs & Young, 1979; 1980; Young & Sachs, 1979).

Pursuing a second approach to the peripheral analysis of speech, several researchers have begun to develop psychophysically based models of speech processing (e.g., Klatt, 1982). These models explicitly incorporate well-known psychoacoustic data in their descriptions of the filtering that is carried out by the peripheral auditory system (Searle, Jacobson, & Rayment, 1979; Zwicker et al., 1979; Kewley-Port, 1980, 1983b). Searle et al. (1979; Searle et al., 1980) have addressed questions related to the appropriate bandwidth of the filters used (by humans or machines) to process speech signals. Marshaling evidence from psychophysical and physiological studies, Searle et al. propose that the human peripheral auditory system analyzes auditory stimuli with approximately a 1/3-octave frequency resolution. The choice of 1/3-octave bandwidths is motivated not only by the psychophysical and physiological data but also by the properties of human speech. Because bandwidth is proportional to frequency, 1/3-octave bandwidths allow spectral resolution of low frequencies as well as temporal resolution at high frequencies. Spectral resolution of low frequencies enables separation of the first and second formants, while temporal resolution of high frequencies provides accurate timing information for the rapid onset of bursts.

An approach similar to that of Searle et al. has been developed in our laboratory. This approach has been directed at several different ways of modeling the energy spectra derived from the filtering carried out by the auditory system (see Kewley-Port, 1980, 1983b; Kewley-Port & Luce, 1984). Using 1/6-octave bandwidths (which more appropriately model the filtering characteristics of the auditory system than 1/3-octave bandwidths; see Kewley-Port, 1980, 1983b), the speech signal is represented in terms of a three-dimensional running spectral display, examples of which are shown in Figure 1.2 for /pi/, /da/, and /ku/. The interest in using this particular type of display to study the acoustic properties of stop consonants is based in part on the assumption that the perceptual dimensions for speech sounds should be represented in terms of what is currently known about the transformation of acoustic signals by the peripheral auditory system. In this work, special emphasis has been placed on a detailed examination of precisely how the distribution of spectral energy changes rapidly over time for stop consonants, particularly for the distinctive acoustic correlates of place of articulation in stops (see Kewley-Port, 1983b).

The interest in developing new and presumably more valid representations of speech signals derives in part from the assumption that a more detailed examination of these auditory representations should, in principle, provide researchers with a great deal of useful information about the distinctive perceptual dimensions that underlie speech sounds (Mundie & Moore, 1970; Stevens, 1980). It has been further assumed that information contained in these so-called neuroacoustic and psychoacoustic representations will contribute in important ways to finally resolving the acoustic–phonetic invariance problem in speech (see, e.g., Goldhor, 1983a, 1983b).

II.B.2. New Approaches to Invariance of Stop Consonants

One of the most firmly established findings in the speech perception literature is that the acoustic correlates of a number of consonantal features are highly dependent on context. This is especially true for the stop consonants (/b/, /d/, /g/, /p/, /t/, and /k/). The early discovery (Joos, 1948) of the apparent lack of invariance for stop consonants led to a general class of speech perception models in which the context-conditioned variability of acoustic cues was resolved by the listener. In these "active" models of speech perception (e.g., motor theory and analysis by synthesis), perceptual constancy was assumed to arise from perceptual processes that "imposed" phonemes on the encoded speech signal. However, another class of models (e.g., Cole & Scott 1974a, 1974b; Fant, 1967) assumed that the lack of invariance was more apparent than real.

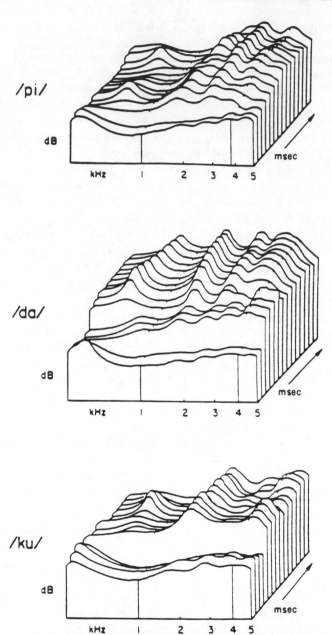

Figure 1.2   Running spectral displays for /pi/, /da/, and /ku/. Frequency is represented on the *x* axis, amplitude in dB on the *y* axis, and time in msec on the *z* axis. Each spectral frame is updated in 5-msec steps. (From Kewley-Port & Luce, 1984.)

These models asserted that a relatively direct mapping of acoustics to phonemes was possible if the speech signal was examined in the "correct" way. Since then, a great deal of interest has been directed at two approaches characteristic of this second class of models—those of Stevens and Blumstein and of Kewley-Port, both of which will now be considered.

Stevens and Blumstein assume that invariant integrated acoustic properties can be found in the acoustic signal that correspond directly to distinctive phonetic features. Following the work of Stevens (1975) and Fant, (1960, 1973), Stevens and Blumstein (1978; Blumstein & Stevens, 1979, 1980) have focused on more complex integrated acoustic attributes of consonants rather than simple isolated cues. By following this strategy, they assumed that an integrated acoustic pattern would show invariance even if each of its components failed to do so when considered separately. For stop consonants, Stevens and Blumstein have examined the gross shape of the spectrum at the onset of burst release. They propose that the spectral shape of the onset at the burst serves to distinguish uniquely and invariantly place of articulation. According to Stevens and Blumstein, labial stops are characterized by a diffuse-falling or flat spectrum, alveolar stops by a diffuse-rising spectrum, and velar stops by a compact spectrum.

This approach can be characterized by an emphasis on a static "snapshot" of the speech signal at abrupt changes in the spectrum. Stevens and Blumstein therefore define their proposed invariant acoustic attributes of stop consonants on the basis of single spectral sections averaged over changes within a given sampling period. Although they acknowledge that formant transitions do provide information for identifying place of articulation, they propose that the gross shape of the spectrum at the onset of the burst constitutes the primary attribute of place. According to Stevens and Blumstein (1981), the primary attributes are those that are first picked up by the child acquiring speech. Later the child learns to attend, on the basis of the primary attributes, to the secondary source of information provided by the formant transitions (see, however, Walley & Carrell, 1983, and Sawusch, this volume, for evidence against this view).

In contrast to Stevens and Blumstein's approach, Kewley-Port (1980, 1983a, 1983b), working in our laboratory, has suggested an account of the acoustic–phonetic invariance problem that is more in line with the spirit of Fant's earlier auditory theory. Kewley-Port's goal was to identify invariant acoustic events that correlate with the articulation of syllable-initial stops. She emphasizes both the auditory transformations of the speech signal and the dynamic changes within the transformations. In this sense, then, Kewley-Port's approach is a "psychophysical" one, as opposed to the more formal linguistic orientation of Stevens and Blumstein (Kewley-Port, 1983a). Although originally the primary contrast between the Stevens and Blumstein approach and that of Kewley-Port focused on the issue of static versus dynamic representations, Blumstein (1983; Mack & Blumstein, 1983) has since proposed that a dynamic description of acoustic information is, in fact, appropriate for describing not only place of articulation but manner as well.

Both of these approaches have made impressive advances in specifying the potential invariant accoustic properties of syllable-initial stop consonants. Blumstein's revised version of the Stevens and Blumstein approach has also made progress in specifying the invariant cues to the stop manner class. Both approaches, however, are only first approximations to a complete theory of acoustic–phonetic invariance in speech. Much work is still needed on the effects of phonetic context (e.g., syllable position). In addition, the issue of how robust these approaches are for fluent speech deserves much more attention. Finally, more detailed perceptual studies are necessary to determine the degree to which the proposed invariants are actually used by the listener in ongoing speech perception. Despite these reservations, both approaches are indicative of a renewed interest in acoustic invariance brought about primarily by more sophisticated analysis techniques and more detailed knowledge of the processing of speech signals by the auditory system.

II.C. The Normalization Problem in Speech Perception

In addition to the problems arising from the lack of acoustic–phonetic invariance discussed earlier, there are also two related problems having to do with the normalization of the speech signal. One is the talker-normalization problem. Talkers differ in the length and shape of their vocal tracts, in the articulatory gestures used for producing various types of phonetic segments, and in the types of coarticulatory strategies present in their speech. As a consequence, substantial differences among talkers have been observed in the absolute values of the acoustic correlates of many phonetic features. Differences in stress and speaking rate, as well as in dialect and affect, also contribute to differences in the acoustic manifestation of speech. Despite the inherent variability in the speech signal due to talker differences, listeners are nevertheless able to perceive speech from a wide range of vocal tracts under diverse sets of conditions. Clearly, then, the invariant properties cannot be absolute physical values encoded in the stimulus but must be relational in nature. Unfortunately, relatively little is known about this form of perceptual normalization, or about the types of perceptual mechanisms involved in carrying out these computations.

A second normalization problem concerns time and rate normalization in speech perception. It is well known that the duration of individual segments is influenced substantially by speaking rate. However, the acoustic duration of segments is also affected by the location of various syntactic boundaries in connected speech, by syllabic stress, and by the component features of adjacent segments in words (see, e.g., Gaitenby, 1965; Klatt, 1975, 1976, 1979; Lehiste, 1970). In addition, there are substantial differences in the duration of segments of words when produced in sentence contexts compared to the same words spoken in isolation. The duration of vowels produced in sentences is roughly half the duration of the same vowels spoken in isolation. Speaking rate also influences the duration and acoustic correlates of various phonetic features and segments. Numerous low-level phonetic and phonological effects such as vowel reduction, deletion, and various types of assimilation phenomena have been well documented in the literature. These effects seem to be influenced a great deal by speaking tempo, dialect, and surrounding phonetic context.

It has been known for many years that duration can also be used to distinguish various segmental contrasts, especially in English. Many phonetic and phonological segmental contrasts are distinguished by redundant differences in duration as well as by their primary spectral correlates. Thus the listener is faced with the problem of trying to ignore certain kinds of irrelevant durational information while simultaneously trying to incorporate distinctive information about segments, stress, prosody, and syntactic structure (see Miller, 1980, and Port, 1977, for reviews).

II.D. Units of Analysis in Speech Perception

Another long-standing issue in speech perception deals with the choice of a minimal unit of perceptual analysis. Because of limitations on channel capacity, especially in the auditory system, raw sensory information must be categorized and recoded into some more permanent form that can be used for subsequent analysis. Is there a basic, or "natural," coding unit for speech perception? Many investigators have argued for the primacy of the feature, phoneme, syllable, or word as their candidate for the basic perceptual unit. Other investigators, motivated chiefly by early work in generative linguistic theory, have proposed even larger units for the perceptual analysis of speech, such as clauses or sentences (Miller, 1962a; Bever, Lackner, & Kirk, 1969). The debate over the choice of a perceptual unit can be resolved if a strict distinction is made concerning the level of linguistic analysis under consideration. The size of the processing unit in speech perception varies from feature to segment to clause as the level of linguistic processing changes. Thus debate over the question of whether there is one basic or primary unit is, in our view, inappropriate since there are, in fact, many units that are used at different levels by the speech processing mechanisms.

II.E. Phonetic and Phonological Recoding of Words in Sentences

One of the major difficulties encountered in speech perception is that each utterance of a language can be realized phonetically in many different ways (e.g., due to dialect differences). It is unrealistic to suppose that human listeners store every possible utterance of the language in long-term memory, since the number of different sentences and phonetic realizations is potentially infinite. While it might be possible to adopt this strategy in the case of machine recognition of speech in very limited contexts, such a strategy seems highly inappropriate in the case of human speech perception. Fortunately, when different phonetic forms or pronunciations of the same sentences are examined carefully, similar alternations and modifications seem to occur at the segmental level, and these have been studied by linguists who have described the operation of various kinds of phonological processes (see Kenstowicz & Kisseberth, 1979). Thus it has been possible to represent a large number of different pronunciations of an utterance by postulating a single base form for a segment from which the actual surface forms can be derived by the application of a set of general phonological rules.

In addition to general phonological processes that may be said to characterize certain uniform dialect differences in pronunciation, there are also sets of low-level phonetic implementation rules that can be used to characterize some of the more specific acoustic–phonetic variations among individual talkers. Thus at least two major sources of variability underlie differences in the observed phonetic realization of words in sentences: general phonological rules and more specific phonetic–recoding rules. Because the number of different phonological phenomena in language is quite large, and because of the idiosyncratic variability of individual talkers sets of decoding rules must be formulated from careful study of the acoustic and phonetic properties of speech in various contexts. Rules such as these must also be assumed to be part of the perceptual strategies used by human listeners in understanding spoken language.

One of the most important findings to come out of the Advanced Research Projects Agency (ARPA) speech understanding project was the realization that even relatively low-level phonetic decoding rules and general phonological rules need to be formulated explicitly for them to be useful in early stages of word recognition (Klatt, 1977). Despite linguists' long-standing interest in phonological processes and the importance they play in the acoustic–phonetic realization of spoken language, little perceptual research had previously been directed toward these problems.

II.F. Specialization of Speech Perception

For a number of years, Liberman and other researchers at Haskins Laboratories in Connecticut have argued that speech perception is a specialized process requiring the postulation of specialized neural mechanisms and processes for perceptual analysis (e.g., Liberman, 1982). Some of the original support for this view came from the early categorical perception experiments with synthetic speech sounds. Categorical perception was thought to be unique to certain types of speech sounds, namely stop consonants. However, later findings demonstrated similar categorical effects for complex nonspeech signals, suggesting that the original interpretation of categorical perception was probably stated too narrowly. Thus the findings observed with synthetic speech were probably a special case of a more general phenomenon involving the coding of complex acoustic signals by the auditory system (see, e.g., Pisoni, 1977).

II.F.1. Categorical Perception of Speech versus Nonspeech Signals

In 1957, Liberman, Harris, Hoffman, and Griffith of Haskins Laboratories reported an experiment that was to have a profound effect on later theory and research in speech perception. Liberman et al. generated a synthetic continuum of consonant-vowel syllables varying from /b/ to /d/ to /g/ by changing second formant transitions in graded steps. When asked to identify these stimuli, subjects perceived three distinct categories of speech sounds corresponding to the phonemes /b/, /d/, and /g/. That is, at certain points in the continuum, subjects abruptly shifted their identification from one phonemic category to another. When required to discriminate pairs of these stimuli, these same listeners were unable to discriminate stimuli drawn from within a category, although discrimination was quite good for pairs of stimuli that straddled the obtained category boundary.

This form of perception, called "categorical perception," was considered at the time to be quite unusual when compared with results obtained in most psychophysical experiments using nonspeech stimuli. Typically, nonspeech stimuli that vary acoustically along a single continuum are perceived continuously, resulting in discrimination functions that are monotonic with the physical scale. This was not the case, however, for the speech stimuli employed by Liberman et al. In addition, Fry, Abramson, Eimas, and Liberman (1962) demonstrated that vowels, unlike stop consonants, show evidence of being continuously perceived.

The finding that certain speech sounds (e.g., stop consonants) show categorical perception, while other speech sounds (e.g., vowels) and certain nonspeech sounds show continuous perception, led researchers (Liberman, 1970a, 1970b; Liberman, Cooper, Shankweiler, & Studdert-Kennedy, 1967; Studdert-Kennedy & Shankweiler, 1970) to postulate a motor theory of speech perception, in which the perception of certain speech sounds is accomplished by a specialized mechanism for processing speech. The categorical perception of stop consonants was thought to be a direct result of reference to articulation in the perceptual process. Because stop consonants are produced in a discontinuous way by a constriction at a particular place in the vocal tract, it was hypothesized that stop consonants are perceived in a discontinuous or categorical manner. Likewise, the continuous manner in which vowels are produced was thought to give rise to the continuous perception of vowels. Finally, the fact that nonspeech sounds modeled after categorically perceived speech sounds show continuous perception was taken as further support for the hypothesis of a perceptual processing mode peculiar to speech (Liberman, 1970a, 1970b).

A number of studies have since called into question the speciality of the categorical perception results for speech. Using nonspeech analogs of speech, these studies have demonstrated that generic psychophysical principles can be invoked to account for the phenomenon of categorical perception. The basic logic behind these studies is that if categorical perception can be demonstrated for nonspeech analogs, there is no need to postulate a specialized speech processor. Instead, these studies have attempted to account for the categorical perception results obtained with speech based on the manner in which the auditory system responds to acoustic stimuli in general, whether speech or nonspeech.

Categorical perception results have been obtained for a number of acoustic–phonetic parameters known to produce categorical identification and discrimination functions for speech. For voice-onset time (VOT), Miller, Wier, Pastore, Kelly, and Dooling (1976) have demonstrated categorical perception for noise-buzz stimuli mimicking the VOT dimension in speech. Pisoni (1977) has also shown that by varying the lead and lag times of two component tones—a manipulation designed to parallel the differences in the onset of voicing in voiced and voiceless word-initial stops—categorical identification and discrimination functions can be obtained that closely match the results obtained for speech. In addition, it has been demonstrated that infants perceive these tone analog stimuli in a categorical fashion (Jusczyk, Pisoni, Walley, & Murray, 1980) and that chinchillas identify VOT in synthetic speech stimuli in a manner similar to humans (Kuhl & Miller, 1975). Although there has been some controversy concerning the perceptual relevance of the timing relations in VOT (Repp, 1983a; Summerfield, 1982; Summerfield & Haggard, 1977), it is clear that the earlier categorical perception results for VOT can be explained, at least in part, by a generic auditory account.

In a somewhat different approach to the question of specialized speech processing and categorical perception, Miller and Liberman (1979) examined the effects of perceived speaking rate on subjects' perception of /ba-wa/ continua. The distinction between /ba/ and /wa/ may be signaled by the duration of the formant transitions, with /ba/ typically having shorter transitions than /wa/. Miller and Liberman demonstrated that /ba-wa/ stimuli having shorter syllable durations tend to be perceived as more /wa/-like and, conversely, that longer syllables tend to be perceived as more /ba/-like. Miller and Liberman argue that this shift in the category boundary was the result of specialized processes that take into account perceived speaking rate (in terms of syllable durations) in the perception of the /b-w/ distinction.

Pisoni, Carrell, and Gans (1983), however, have demonstrated virtually identical results for nonspeech analogs (three component tones) of a /ba-wa/ continuum. Moreover, Jusczyk, Pisoni, Reed, Fernald, and Myers (1983) have shown similar effects for the nonspeech analogs in two-month-old infants. It is therefore doubtful that effects of perceived speaking rate on the perception of /b/ and /w/ are in any way peculiar or unique to speech.

In short, it appears that the evidence from recent studies using nonspeech analogs of categorically perceived speech stimuli tends to disconfirm the hypothesis of a specialized speech processing mechanism. However, the evidence is not completely unequivocal. Not all researchers are sufficiently convinced by the present body of literature on the perception of nonspeech signals to abandon the notion of a specialized speech processor. Although we believe that the present literature on the categorical perception of nonspeech signals tips the scales against the notion of specialized phonetic processing, three other sources of evidence for the operation of specialized speech processing mechanisms deserve discussion:

(1) studies on laterality effects and dichotic listening, (2) studies on audio-visual integration (the McGurk effect), and (3) studies on cue trading of phonetic features.

II.F.2. Laterality Effects and Dichotic Listening

Other evidence often cited in support of specialized neural mechanisms for speech perception has come from dichotic listening experiments in which laterality effects have been demonstrated for competing acoustic signals (Studdert-Kennedy & Shankweiler, 1970). These results have been interpreted as evidence for hemispheric specialization in the perception of speech signals and for the unilateral processing of linguistic information. It has been known for more than 100 years that the left hemisphere of most right-handed adults is the language-dominant hemisphere, specialized for linguistic analysis. The dichotic listening results showing a right ear advantage (REA) for speech signals have been interpreted as behavioral support for this lateral asymmetry *even at the phonetic feature level* and have been used as additional evidence for the assumption of specialized neural mechanisms for processing speech. Unfortunately, little is known about the exact nature of processes or operations that the left hemisphere may perform in perceiving speech and language other than that it clearly differs from the neural processing carried out in the right hemisphere.

Another finding used to support the notion of specialized speech processing that is based on the dichotic listening paradigm is the so-called "duplex perception" effect. Duplex perception refers to a phenomenon first discovered by Rand (1974) in which the same sound may be perceived simultaneously as speech and nonspeech. In one study on duplex perception, Mann, Madden, Russell, and Liberman (1981; reported in Liberman, 1982) presented synthetically generated stimuli dichotically. To one ear, Mann et al. presented one of nine third formant transitions, which are heard as chirps. To the other ear, a base stimulus was presented. The base stimulus consisted of three formants, the first having a rising transition, the second a falling transition, and the third no transition at all. The base was perceived by most of the subjects as /da/.

Upon dichotic presentation of the appropriately synchronized stimuli, subjects reported two percepts (hence the term "duplex perception"): a nonspeech chirp, and a /da/ or /ga/, depending on the isolated third formant transition. Thus the isolated transitions were simultaneously heard as nonspeech and as being fused with the base to render the appropriate cue to place of articulation. Mann et al. then required subjects to attend to either the speech or nonspeech side of the duplex percept and to discriminate pairs of the dichotically presented stimuli. When subjects attended to the speech side of the duplex percept, categorical-like discrimination functions were obtained; when they attended to the nonspeech (chirp) side of the percept, continuous noncategorical discrimination functions were obtained. In the context of the base, the isolated formant transitions are presumably fused by the speech processor to render a phonetic percept. These isolated transitions are also perceived simultaneously in an auditory mode, rendering perception of a nonspeech chirp.

The phenomenon of duplex perception is not without its detractors. For example, Pastore, Schmeckler, Rosenblum, and Szczesiul (1983) have demonstrated duplex perception for musical chords, calling into question the claim that duplex perception is solely a speech-based phenomenon. In addition, Nusbaum, Schwab, and Sawusch (1983) have shown that subjects are able to use the phonetic information in the isolated transition independently of the base, thus casting doubt on the original claim that isolated transitions are perceived as completely nonspeech-like (see, however, Repp, 1984, and Nusbaum, 1984). According to Nusbaum et al., subjects may simply base their phonetic decisions on the information contained in the isolated transitions and need not fuse the transition with the base.

II.F.3. Cross-Modal Cue Integration (the McGurk Effect)

One of the latest findings to be interpreted as supporting the existence of a specialized perceptual mechanism for speech processing has been dubbed the "McGurk effect" (MacDonald & McGurk, 1978; McGurk & MacDonald, 1976; Roberts & Summerfield, 1981; Summerfield, 1979). A subject is presented with a video display of a person articulating simple consonant–vowel syllables. At the same time, the subject is presented auditorily with syllables that are synchronized with the video display. The finding of interest is obtained when the visual and auditory input conflict. In these cases, subjects sometimes report hearing neither exactly what was seen nor exactly what was heard, but some syllable in between. For example, if subjects see a speaker producing a /ga/ and hear simultaneously a /ba/, they may report hearing a /da/.

The McGurk effect has been interpreted as support for the integration of both visual and auditory features in a speech-specific, articulation-based phonetic mode of processing. That is, visual and auditory information are said to converge at an abstract level of processing in which all articulation-based information (from both acoustic and visual sources) is synthesized, giving rise to subjects' perceptions of syllables that are neither what they heard nor what they saw. However, recent work on audio-visual integration suggests that the McGurk effect is not, in fact, indicative of a speech-specific mode of perceptual processing. Massaro and Cohen (1983) have demonstrated that their fuzzy-logical model, which makes no assumption of speech-specific processing, accounts quite well for audio-visual integration effects. In addition, Easton and Basala (1982) have shown that audio-visual integration is eliminated when complete words (as opposed to syllables) are used. It is thus likely that the effects obtained with syllables are due, at least in part, to perceptual biases—and not to true integration—arising from highly ambiguous stimulus situations.

II.F.4. Trading Relations and Integration of Cues

Aside from demonstrations of duplex perception and audio-visual integration of phonetic features, another line of evidence for the operation of a specialized mode of perception for speech (as well as for a revised version of motor theory) comes from a number of studies on cue trading and integration (reviewed by Repp, 1982). It has been well known for many years that several cues may signal a single phonetic contrast (e.g., Delattre, Liberman, Cooper, & Gerstman, 1952; Denes, 1955; Harris, Hoffman, Liberman, Delattre, & Cooper, 1958; Hoffman, 1958; see also Repp, 1982). Thus it is possible to demonstrate that when the perceptual utility of one cue is attenuated, another cue may take on primary effectiveness in signaling the contrast under scrutiny because both cues, it is assumed, are phonetically equivalent. This is called a phonetic trading relation (Repp, 1982). Phonetic trading relations have been cited as evidence for a speech mode of perception primarily for two reasons: First, some demonstrations of phonetic trading relations involve both spectral and temporal cues that are distributed over a relatively long temporal interval. Repp (1982) argues that it is hard to imagine how such disparate cues arranged across relatively long time windows could be integrated into a unitary percept if specialized (i.e., nonauditory) processes were not in operation. Repp proposes, furthermore, that the basis of this specialization lies in the listener's abstract knowledge of articulation. In other words, because we as listeners know (implicitly) how speech is produced, we are able to integrate acoustically different cues that arise from an articulatory plan into a single phonetic percept.

The second line of evidence for the specialization of speech perception involves demonstrations that phonetic trading relations do not apparently occur for nonspeech sounds. Such evidence is taken to be proof that the integration of multiple cues that gives rise to trading relations is special to speech.

The demonstration of trading relations constitutes the latest source of evidence for the existence of a specialized speech mode in which knowledge of articulation comes to bear on the perception of speech. According to Repp (1982, p. 95): "Trading relations may occur because listeners perceive speech in terms of the underlying articulation and resolve inconsistencies in the acoustic information by perceiving the most plausible articulatory act. This explanation requires that the listener have at least a general model of human vocal tracts and of their ways of action." Thus, based in part on demonstrations of phonetic trading relations, many researchers, particularly at Haskins Laboratories, have once again renewed their efforts to argue for articulation-based specialized phonetic processing (see Liberman & Mattingly, 1985).

More recently, however, Repp (1983b) has argued that cue trading results do not in fact support the claim that speech is processed by specialized mechanisms. Instead, Repp (1983b: 132) concludes that cue trading effects "are not special because, once the prototypical patterns are known in any perceptual domain, trading relations among the stimulus dimensions follow as the inevitable product of a general pattern matching operation. Thus, speech perception is the application of general perceptual principles to very special patterns."

Additional support for the specialization of speech perception has come from rational and logical considerations dealing with attempts to communicate language by sounds other than speech. It has been argued (see, e.g., Liberman et al., 1967) that speech sounds are uniquely efficient vehicles for transmitting phonemic information in language because speech represents a complex code rather than a simple cipher or alphabet. The rate at which phonemic information can be perceived in speech is known to be well above the temporal resolving power of the ear if listeners had to process only isolated acoustic segments that stood in a one-to-one relation with phonemes (Liberman et al., 1967). Thus it has been argued that speech sounds are a complex code, since they represent a substantial restructuring of phonemic information in the acoustic waveform.

In conclusion, while there is probably some evidence that can be cited to support the existence and operation of specialized neural mechanisms in speech perception, the exact nature of this mechanism, its mode of operation, and its course of development remain somewhat elusive. Assertions of specialization appear to be generally inconclusive as explanatory principles, especially as more becomes known about the psychophysical and perceptual aspects of speech signals and the physiological mechanisms involved in speech production.

II.G. Prosody, Rhythm, and Speech Timing

Most of the research in speech perception over the last 30 years, as well as the major theoretical emphasis, has been concerned with the segmental analysis of phonemes. One seriously neglected topic has been the prosodic or suprasegmental attributes of speech, which involve differences in pitch, intensity, duration, and the timing of segments and words in sentences. There remains a wide gap between the research conducted on isolated segments and features and prosodic factors in speech perception (see Cohen & Nooteboom, 1975). The role of prosodic factors in speech perception has not been given much detailed consideration. It is clear, however, that this source of linguistic information may serve to link phonetic segments, features, and words to grammatical processes at higher levels of analysis (see Darwin, 1975; Huggins, 1972; Nooteboom, Brokx, & de Rooij, 1978, for reviews). Moreover, speech prosody may also carry useful information about lexical, syntactic, and semantic properties of the speaker's message.

There is also evidence that differences in fundamental frequency can provide important cues to the segmentation of speech into constituents suitable for syntactic analysis. Based on acoustic analysis of connected speech, Lea (1973) has found that a drop in fundamental frequency (F0) usually occurred at the end of each major syntactic constituent in a sentence, while a rise in F0 occurred near the beginning of the following constituent. In more detailed analyses, Cooper and Sorensen (1977) found significant fall–rise patterns in fundamental frequency at the boundaries between conjoined main clauses and at the boundaries between main and embedded clauses. Fall–rise patterns were also found at the boundaries between major phrases.

Lindblom and Svensson (1973) and Svensson (1974) have carried out investigations on the role of prosody in identifying various syntactic structures in the absence of segmental cues. Their findings indicate that prosodic features can convey a good deal of information about the surface syntactic structure of an utterance. They showed that unambiguous identification of the words in sentences can often take place even with an incomplete specification of the detailed acoustic properties of the phonetic segments.

Other evidence on the acoustic analysis of speech indicates that the duration of phonetic segments varies in stressed and unstressed syllables as well as in various syntactic environments, as shown in Figure 1.3. For

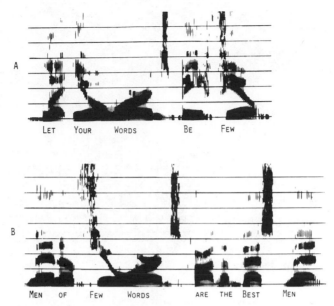

Figure 1.3   Spectrograms—(A) Let your words be few and (B) Men of few words are the best men—showing the effects of sentence position on word duration.

example, in one of the earliest studies, Oller (1973) found substantial lengthening effects for both consonants and vowels in a number of environments. In particular, lengthening occurred in utterances with various intonation patterns, word-final and phrase-final positions, as well as utterance-final position. Klatt (1974) has shown that the duration of the segment [s] is longer in a prestressed position and shorter before unstressed vowels, as well as in word-final position. In another study, Klatt (1975) also found that vowel-lengthening effects occur at the end of major syntactic units, such as the boundary between a noun phrase and a verb phrase.

Durational effects of speech timing provide further evidence against uncovering simple acoustic attributes of phonemes or words that remain physically identical in all phonetic environments and sentence contexts. More important, however, the lengthening and speech timing effects appear to provide additional cues to the identification of lexical items, as well as the higher-order syntactic structure of the sentence. This raises the potential problem that segmental duration may simultaneously cue syntactic boundaries and segmental distinctions such as the voicing of word-final stops, thus introducing a "loop" in the perceptual process in which the listener must identify the presence of a clause boundary in

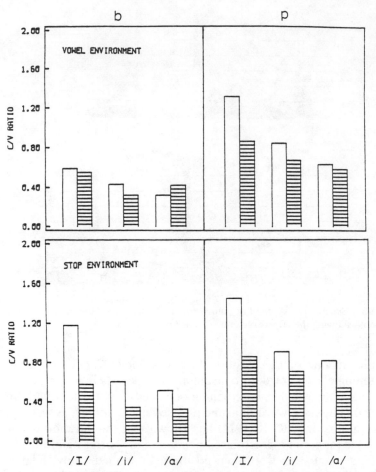

Figure 1.4   Mean C/V ratios for word-final bilabial stops. For each test word, vowel duration and closure duration for the final stop consonant were measured from a digital waveform display. Vowel duration was measured from the onset of periodic energy to a marked
decrease in the periodic energy in the waveform. Closure duration was measured from this
decrease in periodic energy to the onset of burst frication of the word-final stop. The upper
panel shows the mean C/V ratios for test words ending in /g/ and /k/ produced in a vowel
environment. The bottom panel shows the mean C/V ratios for test words ending in /g/ and
/k/ produced in a stop environment. Mean C/V ratios are shown for each vowel (/I/, /i/, /a/)
separately. The open bars refer to the C/V ratios for test words produced in non-phrase-final
position; the hatched bars refer to C/V ratios for test words produced in phrase-final position. Note the consistent difference in the C/V ratios across phrase-final and non-phrase-
final environments (adapted from Luce & Charles-Luce, 1983).

order to adjust his or her criterion for determining word-final voicing on the basis of segmental durations (see Port & Dalby, 1982).

Luce and Charles-Luce (1983, 1985a) have examined three durational correlates of word-final voicing and the durational transformations of these correlates as a function of sentence position. Specifically, they examined the roles of vowel duration, closure duration, and the consonant/vowel (C/V) ratio (Port & Dalby, 1982) as correlates of voicing in production when test words were produced in both phrase-final and non-phrase-final positions within sentences. Of primary interest in their study was the extent to which a relational correlate of voicing expressed as the consonant/vowel ratio would circumvent the problem of segmental duration simultaneously cuing word-final voicing and the presence of a syntactic boundary. The results for the consonant/vowel ratio for test words ending in bilabial stops are shown in Figure 1.4.

Clearly, the consonant/vowel ratio failed to consistently distinguish voicing independently of the effects of sentence position. In addition, Luce and Charles-Luce (1983, 1985a) found that of the three correlates of voicing examined, vowel duration served to most reliably distinguish voicing, although vowel duration was also clearly affected by the effects of sentence position. In a perceptual study, Luce and Charles-Luce (1985b) have demonstrated that listeners do in fact modify their criteria for voicing at clause boundaries when a pause signals the presence of a boundary. The results of these studies underscore the degree to which sentence contextual effects on speech timing and segmental distinctions influence the perception and production of speech.

Much research remains to be done on the role of prosodic variables in speech perception. It would be of interest to explore in more detail the extent to which syntactic and semantic variables influence the duration of phonetic segments and words, as well as the extent to which listeners can and do use this sort of information in understanding spoken language (see Huggins, 1972, 1978; Klatt & Cooper, 1975; Nooteboom & Doodeman, 1980).

III. INTERACTION OF KNOWLEDGE SOURCES

A well-documented finding in the speech perception literature is that words presented in a sentence context are more intelligible than the same acoustic patterns presented in isolation (Miller, 1962b; Miller, Heise, & Lichten, 1951; Pollack & Pickett, 1964). One interpretation of these findings is that syntax and semantics serve to narrow the range of possible response alternatives available to the listener (Miller, 1962b). It is assumed that phonetic segments and features are recognized more or less directly from a set of physical properties in the speech wave and that processing proceeds serially on the basis of independent decisions about discrete speech segments at each successive level of speech processing (Halle & Stevens, 1962; Licklider, 1952).

What role do syntax, semantics, and higher sources of knowledge serve in speech perception? Chomsky (1964) argues on formal grounds that it is not possible to describe a natural language adequately by starting with only a description of the sound system without reference to the function of these sounds as linguistic entities. That is, more information than a phonetic sequence is necessary to establish the identity of a phoneme. This additional information presumably involves the contribution of syntactic and semantic sources of knowledge to the recognition process. Indeed, the great optimism of the initial ARPA study group on speech understanding systems (Newell, Burnett, Forgie, Green, Klatt, Licklider, Munson, Reddy, & Woods, 1971) was based on the presumed ability of machines to make use of higher sources of knowledge in solving the speech recognition problem. The HARPY system "solved" the recognition problem by simply precompiling all the possible "legal" sentences of its 1000-word vocabulary into a finite-state network of words. The words were then represented as phonemic sequences of spectral templates. Such an engineering solution, while elegant for the specifically defined task, provides little new information for models of human speech perception (however, see Klatt, 1977).

Within the general context of the ARPA project, several studies examined the general problem of the interaction of sources of knowledge experimentally. For example, in one study Shockey and Reddy (1974) determined how well phonetically trained listeners could recover the correct phonemes from sentences in the absence of relevant linguistic structures such as syntax and semantics. To accomplish this, the listeners heard recorded sentences taken from unfamiliar and exotic languages and were required to provide a narrow phonetic transcription. The primary basis for the segmentation and recognition of these phonemes was the information contained in the physical signal itself, since the contribution of higher-level information was minimized by virtue of the unfamiliar languages used.

The results of Shockey and Reddy's experiment were quite interesting. As it happened, the transcription task was difficult; only about 56 percent of the segments in the original utterances could be identified correctly.

With an accuracy in this range, it can be concluded that higher levels of linguistic structure must provide a good deal of constraint, even at the earliest stages of perceptual analysis. However, it should be emphasized that exotic languages were deliberately used in this study. A better test might have been to require the phoneticians to transcribe nonsense syllable sentences that had appropriate intonation. In this case, they would surely have done better because they could have used their internalized knowledge of the prosodic features of the language. Moreover, phonetic inventory size, as well as familiarity with the phonology of the exotic languages, were factors that were not controlled in the experiment.

In a similar study, Klatt and Stevens (1973) attempted to recognize a set of unknown sentences by visual examination of sound spectrograms along with a machine-aided lexical look-up program. Although the syllable structure of an utterance could be identified reasonably well from a spectrographic representation, only 33 percent of the phonetic segments could be transcribed correctly. Another 40 percent of the segments could be partially transcribed correctly. Klatt and Stevens (1973) emphasized that the problem of recognizing segments in sentences from spectrograms is substantially more difficult than recognizing segments in isolated words. In sentences, word boundaries are not clearly marked, and coarticulatory effects occur between adjacent words. Moreover, the average duration of segments is shorter in sentences than in isolated words, and the effects of vowel reduction, assimilation, and low-level phonetic recoding are greater. All of these observations led Klatt and Stevens to doubt that accurate recognition from spectrograms could be carried out in the absence of higher-level information. They suggest that these higher-level constraints can be used to verify decisions about segments and predict missing or distorted acoustic–phonetic information based on the generation of some previous lexical hypothesis or search set.

The results of these studies, as well as the findings reviewed earlier on prosody, rhythm, and timing, indicate that the perception of words in connected fluent speech does not relay exclusively on the analysis and recognition of the segmental acoustic features of phonemes. When speech perception is viewed only from the vantage point of the acoustic signal and the phoneme, the task of finding invariant attributes becomes the primary focus of investigation. However, if prosodic information and higher-order variables are included in the perceptual process, the scope of the potential models widens appreciably to encompass broader questions involving the comprehension of spoken language.

The findings we have discussed so far in this section seem to point to a primary role for higher-level sources of knowledge in speech perception.

According to Chomsky and Halle (1968), speech perception should be viewed as an "active process" in which acoustic information is used by the listener to form hypotheses about the structure of sentences. These hypotheses, which are based in part on one's expectations and knowledge of the language, are then subsequently used to generate syntactic descriptions which can be compared against the original input. In this way the listener uses knowledge of phonological principles to determine the phonetic properties of the sentence. Thus a listener's final interpretation of a speech signal depends on a number of variables in addition to the initial sensory-based input. These include the listener's linguistic knowledge as well as extragrammatical factors that limit what a listener may expect to hear at any point in time.

The findings summarized here on the role of higher levels of linguistic knowledge in speech perception have been called into question by a series of "spectrogram-reading" experiments. These experiments have examined the unusual abilities of Victor Zue, an expert spectrogram reader (see Cole, Rudnicky, Zue, & Reddy, 1980). Cole et al. report that without prior knowledge of the specific words present or the sentence context, Zue can produce a phonetic transcription of about 90% of all phonetic segments present. The authors intepret the results to suggest that phonemes can be characterized by well-defined acoustic correlates that are recognizable in a spectrographic display. Moreover, the results indicate that it is in fact possible to read or analyze spectrograms of unknown utterances. Apparently it is possible to learn enough about the visual correlates of the acoustic features of phonemes and the modifications they undergo in fluent speech to enable performance at relatively high levels of accuracy. Thus it seems that we must reevaluate the general and long-standing assumption that the speech signal is so impoverished and noisy that perception can proceed only with overriding support from higher-order knowledge such as syntax and semantics, which are actively used to generate lexical hypotheses.

The findings of Cole et al. have led to numerous claims about the availability of detailed phonetic information in spectrographic representations of speech (see also Greene, Pisoni, & Carrell, 1984). Further, Zue's performance demonstrates that phonetic decoding rules can be derived to identify these features and attributes visually. Several investigators have concluded from these results that accurate bottom-up phonetic analysis of an utterance is actually possible in the absence of prosodic, syntactic, semantic, and pragmatic knowledge. According to these views, the speech signal provides sufficient acoustic information to identify the segmental linguistic content of an utterance, as well as to support bottom-up lexical hypothesization and word recognition (see Church, 1983; Luce & Pisoni, 1986; Nakatani & O'Connor-Dukes, 1980).

III.A. Focused Search and "Islands of Reliability"

There can be little doubt after some 30 or 40 years of research on speech that the acoustic signal contains a great deal of redundant and often superfluous information for human listeners. A basic goal has been to try to locate the most important information in the speech signal and then code it in the most efficient way for transmission over a communications channel. In the same way, investigators concerned with human speech perception have tried to locate and identify the "minimal cues" for phonemes in the hope that once these could be identified, the basic recognition problem of speech could be solved. Unfortunately, there is a great deal more to speech perception and spoken language understanding than simply discovering the minimal cues for phonemes. The speech signal appears to be rich with salient and reliable information that listeners use in understanding messages. As a consequence, the basic problem becomes one of finding "islands of reliability" in the stimulus input that can be used to access various sources of knowledge that listeners have available.

The term *focused search* has been used to characterize one set of strategies that listeners may use for inspecting a signal for information that can be useful at any given point in the perceptual process; focused search also specifically avoids information that does not provide useful support. Put another way, the listener always attempts to look for reliable information in the speech signal on which to base his or her perceptual decisions. Examples of these sources of information include the presence of stressed syllables, the beginnings and ends of words, and the locations of various spectral changes indicating shifts in the source function. Other examples include the presence of reduced vowels, fricatives, nasalization, and voicing during stop closure and aspiration, all of which can provide reliable cues to word recognition and segmentation.

Focused search also emphasizes an important problem—namely, to identify the acoustic correlates of the speech signal on which a listener relies to carry out perceptual analysis of the signal. There can be little doubt that the scope of a listener's perceptual strategies varies substantially with the requirements of experimental tasks; what may be salient and reliable acoustic–phonetic information in one context may not be used at all in another context. Research on this problem has shifted recently from experiments using isolated nonsense syllables which are manipulated in very precise ways to studies directed at how listeners use these cues to perceive words in isolation and in sentence contexts where several diverse sources of knowledge can be used.

III.B. The Principle of Delayed Binding

Human speech perception and spoken language understanding appear to take place very rapidly. Unfortunately, relatively little is known about the specific processes or mechanisms that support such on-line activities. As we have noted, a good deal of the speech perception process occurs automatically and is therefore unavailable for direct, conscious introspection. Do all decisions at all levels of the speech perception process take place immediately or are there selected delays at particular analytic levels pending additional information? What is the size of the scanning window over which low-level phonetic decisions are made? What depth of processing is required before a final and binding decision can be made about the segmental composition of an input signal? These are a few of the questions being pursued by a number of researchers.

An important assumption that emerged from the ARPA speech understanding project was the "principle of delayed binding." According to this principle (also called deferred commitment), decisions at low levels are not forced if the information is unreliable or insufficient to make a final decision (see also Miller, 1962b). Such a principle might be appropriate in computational situations, such as HARPY, where the front-end or basic acoustic–phonetic recognition device failed to perform as well as humans do. However, we know from much of the earlier research on acoustic cues in speech perception and speech intelligibility in noise that listeners can and do make binding low-level segmental and lexical decisions with extremely high accuracy even under very poor listening conditions.

It is possible that a discrete phonetic representation or transcription of the input signal might discard relatively large amounts of parametric acoustic information in order to facilitate processes of lexical access (however, see Ganong, 1980). Nevertheless, there seems to be little reason to adopt a strategy like the principle of delayed binding in human speech perception and subsequently maintain a substantially more detailed or parametric representation of the initial acoustic signal. After all, if the quality of the acoustic–phonetic information is good, as in high-quality natural speech, then phonetic, lexical, and even syntactic decisions can occur on-line quite rapidly. However, in situations where the speech signal is physically degraded or phonetically impoverished, the speed of processing may be substantially slower, and certain low-level decisions may well have to be delayed pending the activation of higher-order constraints (Miller et al., 1951; Miller & Isard, 1963). Clearly, it is important to find out more about the perceptual and interpretative processes in human speech perception that are responsible for the rapid processing and seemingly immediate interpretation of spoken language (see, however, Grosjean & Gee, 1986).

IV. MODELS OF SPEECH SOUND PERCEPTION

For the most part, theories of speech perception have been quite general, vague, and often inconclusive, at least by the standards used in other areas of experimental psychology. It would not be unreasonable to characterize these approaches to speech perception as preliminary attempts at outlining what a *possible* model of human speech perception might look like. Rarely have specific theories been offered. The following quotes should make this point clear:

> Since this symposium is concerned with models, we should say at the outset that we do not have a model in the strict sense, though we are in search of one [Liberman, et al., 1967, p. 68].

> Any attempt to propose a model for the perception of speech is deemed to become highly speculative in character and the present contribution is no exception [Fant, 1967, p. 111].

> Since we are still far from an understanding of the neurophysiological processes involved, any model that can be proposed must be a functional model, and one can only *speculate* on the relation between components of the functional model and the neural events at the periphery of the auditory system and in the central nervous system [Stevens & House, 1972, p. 47].

> We have no models specified in enough detail for serious test [Studdert-Kennedy, 1976, p. 254].

Because speech perception is a very complex process involving many different knowledge sources and their potential interactions, it has been extremely difficult to formulate global perceptual models that can be tested in any careful way through the usual forms of behavioral experimentation. Much of the research on human speech perception has been concerned with specific phenomena in well-defined experimental contexts. Global questions about spoken language understanding have always been important concerns and have often been discussed. However, most of the time investigators work on details of specific phenomena in particular paradigms rather than trying to tackle the complexities of the more integrative questions in the field. This situation is not unique to speech perception research, for the same general situation has been said to characterize the field of experimental psychology as a whole (see Newell, 1973).

Perhaps the greatest shortcoming of research in speech perception has been the conspicuous lack of well-articulated models of the speech perception process. The models that we will discuss below have, at one time or another, enjoyed some special status in speech research. However, they have tended to be rather vague and have uniformly rested on very thin empirical support. The situation remains little improved, although new attempts are being made to construct somewhat more detailed accounts of the speech perception process, two of which we discuss briefly in the conclusion of this section. We will focus primarily, however, on three early models of speech perception—motor theory, analysis by synthesis, and Fant's auditory theory—mostly for historical reasons. Our intention here is to give the reader some flavor for the early attempts at accounting for the basic problems in speech perception. One must bear in mind that none of these models is considered to be adequate. However, each has had a considerable impact on the field of speech research, and some ideas from each may be found in current discussions of speech perception.

IV.A. Motor Theory of Speech Perception

The basic assumption of motor theory as described by Liberman, et al. (1967, p. 452) is that "speech is perceived by processes that are also involved in its production." This view of speech perception was motivated by the observation that the listener is also a speaker, and that it would be more economical to assume that the speaker–hearer uses only one common process for language processing rather than two separate processes. As mentioned earlier, one of the central problems in speech perception arises at the phonemic level of analysis, and the major reason for postulating a motor theory is the lack of invariance between the acoustic signal and its phonemic representation. Advocates of motor theory argue that one possible way of resolving the invariance problem is to assume that the same perceptual response to widely differing acoustic signals arises because the intended pattern is produced by the same articulation or underlying motor commands to the articulators. Similarly, different perceptual responses to fairly similar acoustic signals arise from different underlying articulations or motor commands.

Although motor theory has occupied an overwhelmingly dominant place in contemporary accounts of speech perception, the link between empirical data and theory has not been very strong. Indeed, much of the early support for the theory was based on the finding that synthetic stop consonants tend to be perceived categorically, whereas steady-state vowels are perceived continuously, apparently paralleling the discrete production of stop consonants as compared with the continuous nature of the production of vowels. Subsequent research demonstrated that the categorical–continuous distinction was primarily due to limitations in auditory short-term memory (Fujisaki & Kawashima, 1969, 1970, 1971; Pisoni, 1971, 1973, 1975), thus weakening the claim of motor reference in perception. In short, there seems to be little direct empirical support for some active mediation of articulatory knowledge for information during perceptual processing. Most arguments for some form of motor theory rest on parsimony, logic, and faith rather than a firm empirical foundation. In our view, however, the most serious problem for the theory lies in the failure to specify the level of perceptual analysis where articulatory knowledge is employed in recognition.

IV.B. Analysis by Synthesis

The analysis-by-synthesis model proposed by Stevens (1960; Stevens & Halle, 1967; Stevens & House, 1972) is more explicit than motor theory. Nevertheless, the basic assumption of the model is similar to motor theory: Close ties exist between the processes of speech production and perception, and there are components and operations common to both.

According to Stevens, the perceptual process begins with peripheral processing of the speech signal to yield a description in terms of auditory patterns. In cases where phonetic features are not strongly context-dependent, auditory patterns provide a relatively direct mapping of those features during preliminary analysis. The output of this analysis is a rough matrix of phonetic segments and features that is then transferred to a control system. Recognition of some features is thus assumed to take place by relatively direct operations on the acoustic information output from the peripheral analysis.

When there are no invariant attributes to identify a phonetic feature, additional processing is required. In analysis by synthesis, a hypothesis concerning the representation of the utterance in terms of phonetic segments and features (that is, an abstract distinctive feature matrix) is constructed. This representation forms the input to a set of generative rules that produce candidate patterns which are subsequently compared against the original patterns. The results of this match are sent to a control component that transfers the phonetic description to higher stages of linguistic analysis. In short, analysis by synthesis is simply a more carefully specified version of motor theory, except that the comparison process takes place at the neuroacoustic level rather than the neuromotor level. Like motor theory, analysis by synthesis is quite abstract, and little direct empirical evidence has been found to support it.

IV.C. Fant's Auditory Theory

Fant's theory of speech perception is not well developed. He objects strongly to the "active" motor-type theories on the grounds that the evidence used to support them is not conclusive (Fant, 1967). Fant claims that all of the arguments brought forth in support of motor theory would fit just as well into sensory-based theories, in which the decoding process proceeds without postulating the active mediation of speech–motor centers.

The basic idea in Fant's approach is that the motor and sensory functions become more and more involved as one proceeds from the peripheral to the central stages of analysis. He assumes that the final destination is a "message" that involves brain centers common to both perception and production. According to Fant, there are separate sensory (auditory) and motor (articulatory) branches, although he leaves open the possibility of interaction between these two branches. Auditory input is first processed by the ear and is subject to primary auditory analysis. These incoming auditory signals are then submitted to some kind of direct encoding into distinctive auditory features (Fant, 1962). Finally, the features are combined in some unspecified way to form phonemes, syllables, morphemes, and words. Although much of Fant's concern has been with continued acoustical investigations of the distinctive features of phonemes, the model is much too rough to be empirically tested in any serious way. Moreover, the problems of invariance and segmentation, which are central issues in speech perception, remain unresolved by the model.

IV.D. Other Models of Speech Perception

Although relatively few attempts at modeling phonetic perception have been made since those just discussed, two current approaches are worthy of discussion. The first has been put forth by Massaro and his colleagues (Massaro & Oden, 1980; Derr & Massaro, 1980; Massaro, 1972; Massaro & Cohen, 1976, 1977; Oden & Massaro, 1978). In his "fuzzy logical" model of speech perception, Massaro views speech perception as a "prototypical instance of pattern recognition" (Massaro & Oden, 1980, p. 131). Briefly, this model states that multiple features corresponding to a given phonetic contrast are extracted independently from the waveform and then combined according to logical integration rules. These rules operate on fuzzy sets so that information regarding a given feature may be more or less present or "sort of" present.

The fuzzy logical model stresses continuous rather than all-or-none information. Features are assigned a probability value between zero and one indicating the extent to which a given feature is present in the stimulus input. Subsequently, the degree to which this featural information matches a stored prototype is determined according to a multiplicative combination of the independent features. Massaro's model thus attempts to account for the difficulties of mapping acoustic attributes onto higher-level representations by viewing phonetic perception as a probabilistic process of matching features to prototype representations in memory.

In another model of speech perception, Marcus (1984) attempts to overcome the problems of context-conditioned phonetic variability by postulating context-sensitive units of perception similar to "Wickelphones" (see Wickelgren, 1969). Marcus proposes that "state-pairs" or dyads of phonemes constitute the basic unit of phonetic processing. According to him, these state-pairs provide sufficient flexibility to account for phonetic perception in real time, given that they incorporate considerable coarticulatory information (which helps to alleviate the problem of the lack of invariance) without incorporating information from too long a stretch of speech. In particular, Marcus argues that the context-sensitive coding of state-pairs proves very robust to the local phonetic effects that accompany such manipulations as speech rate.

V. APPROACHES TO AUDITORY WORD RECOGNITION

Among the most important trends in speech research has been the increasing interest in theories of auditory word recognition and lexical access. Although much basic work is still being conducted on fundamental problems in phonetic perception, many researchers have begun to expand their domain of inquiry to include the processes by which words are recognized and meanings retrieved from long-term memory. We view this concern with issues relating to word recognition and lexical access as a healthy trend toward considering speech perception in a broader framework (see Samuel, this volume). In our view, speech perception is not synonymous with phoneme perception, although much of the early work emphasizes this orientation. Certainly, speech perception is a complex operation involving many levels of processing, from phonetic perception to semantic interpretation. To isolate one level of processing for investigation while ignoring the possible contributions of and interactions with other levels is, in our view, somewhat myopic and may actually lead to grossly incorrect theories. What we learn about word recognition, for example, may constrain our theories of phonetic perception, and vice versa. Of course, analysis of the speech perception process is made much easier by the division of our domain of inquiry into autonomous subcomponents. However, investigating one subcomponent (e.g., phonetic perception) to the exclusion of others (e.g., word recognition) would appear to limit our insights into the process as a whole and could lead us to postulate theories at one level that are clearly untenable or unparsimonious given what we know about processing at other levels of analysis.

Many interesting and important problems in speech perception touch on word recognition and lexical access and bear directly on the nature of various types of representations in the mental lexicon. For example, it is of considerable interest to determine precisely what kinds of representations exist in the mental lexicon. Do words, morphemes, phonemes, or sequences of spectral templates represent lexical entries? Is a word accessed on the basis of an acoustic, phonetic, or phonological code? Are high-frequency words recognized "automatically" by a very rapid search through a special precompiled network? Are other, less frequent words analyzed by more general rules for the morphological analysis of sensory input?

Although the theories of word recognition and lexical access that we discuss here are as yet too vague to render any significant insights into the nature of phonetic perception, they are indicative of a growing trend to consider speech perception in a broader framework of spoken language processing. In addition, these theories represent what might be called a new interest among speech researchers—specifically, the way in which acoustic–phonetic information is used to contact lexical items in long-term memory (Pisoni & Luce, 1986). We briefly review six theories of word recognition and lexical access: (1) logogen theory, (2) cohort theory, (3) Forster's autonomous search theory, (4) Elman and McClelland's interactive theory, (5) Klatt's lexical access from spectra (LAFS) theory, and (6) phonetic refinement theory. Summaries of the crucial aspects of each theory are shown in Table 1.1. Each of these theories was proposed to deal with somewhat different empirical issues in word recognition and lexical access, but each addresses a topic of some interest in word recognition—namely, the extent to which higher-level knowledge sources come to bear on the perception of words, which we refer to as the "autonomy–interaction" issue. Another issue addressed by each of these theories is the means by which lexical items are activated in memory. Finally, a few of the theories incorporate explicit processes or structures that attempt to account for word frequency effects. Where appropriate, we focus on each of these issues in our discussion of the individual theories.

Throughout the following discussion, we draw a distinction between word recognition and lexical access. When speaking of word recognition, we refer explicitly to those processes responsible for generating a pattern

Table 1.1
Some Contemporary Models of Word Recognition and Lexical Access

Model	Processing Units	Sources of Knowledge	Primary Recognition Process
1. Morton's logogen	Whole words	Interactive	Passive-threshold devices
2. Klatt's LAFS	Context-sensitive spectra	Direct bottom-up hypothesization of word candidates	Passive-matching to spectral templates stored in precompiled network
3. Marslen-Wilson's COHORT theory	Acoustic–phonetic "sound sequences"	Interactive	Activation of "word initial cohorts"
4. Forster's autonomous search model	Phonetic segments (phonemes)	Noninteractive (Autonomous)	Mediated bottom-up processing
5. Elman & McClelland's TRACE interactive activation model	Distinctive features, phonemes, & words	Interactive	Active-threshold device
6. Nusbaum & Pisoni's phonetic refinement theory (PRT)	Phones, allophones	Interactive	Direct activation of phonetic sequences in networks to develop a detailed narrow phonetic representation

from the acoustic–phonetic information in the speech waveform and matching this pattern to others that have been stored in memory (i.e., for words) or to those generated by rule (i.e., for pseudowords). We use the somewhat neutral term "pattern" to avoid any bias toward postulating a phonemic, syllabic, or word level of representation. When speaking of lexical access, we refer explicitly to those processes responsible for contacting the appropriate lexical information in memory once a pattern match has been accomplished. Lexical access, then, is that process by which information about words stored in the mental lexicon is retrieved (i.e., orthography, meanings, and syntactic class). In our discussion of the theories that follow, we attempt to make explicit where word recognition and lexical access enter into a global theory of spoken language understanding.

V.A. Logogen Theory

In Morton's (1969, 1979, 1982) logogen theory, passive sensing devices called "logogens" represent each word in the mental lexicon. Each logogen contains all of the information about a given word, such as its meaning, its possible syntactic functions, and its phonetic and orthographic structure. A logogen monitors for relevant information, and once such information is encountered, the activation level of the logogen is raised. Upon sufficient activation, a logogen crosses a threshold, at which time the information about the word that the logogen represents is made available to the response system.

One important feature of the logogen theory is that logogens monitor all possible sources of information, including higher-level semantic and syntactic information as well as lower-level sensory information. Thus information from any level can combine to push a logogen over its threshold. In this sense, logogen theory is a highly interactive model of word recognition. For example, a word of high frequency, which has a starting threshold lower than other words of lower frequency, may require very little sensory input if syntactic and semantic sources of information strongly favor the word. Likewise, a word of low frequency with few associated higher-level expectations may require considerable sensory input for the activation level to reach threshold. Thus it doesn't really matter what sort of information activates a logogen, as long as the threshold is exceeded.

According to logogen theory, word recognition is accomplished when the activation threshold of a logogen is reached. As we have seen, logogen theory portrays word recognition as a highly interactive process. In our terminology, lexical access is achieved when the information contained within the logogen is made available to the response system. Thus lexical access is a fairly automatic process once a word has been recognized. It is of interest to note that not only are interactive knowledge sources involved at the level of word recognition, but word frequency is handled at this stage as well, since words of higher frequency have lower activation thresholds than those of lower frequency.

The specific details of logogen theory have changed somewhat over the years, but the basic mechanisms have remained the same. For example, Morton (1982) has broken the logogen system into separate visual and auditory subsystems, and yet the fundamental notion of a passive threshold device that can monitor information from a variety of sources has remained. At the same time, like many of the theories we discuss, logogen theory is extremely vague. At best, the theory may help us conceptualize how an interactive system works and how word frequency can be accounted for, but it says very little about precisely how acoustic–phonetic and higher-level sources of information are integrated, the time-course of word recognition, or the structure of the lexicon.

V.B. Cohort Theory

Marslen-Wilson's (1975, 1980b; Marslen-Wilson & Welsh, 1978; Marslen-Wilson & Tyler, 1975, 1980) cohort theory posits two stages in the word recognition process—one autonomous and one interactive. In the first, autonomous stage of word recognition, acoustic–phonetic information at the beginning of an input word activates all words in memory that share this word-initial information. For example, if the word "slave" is presented to the system, all words beginning with /s/ are activated, such as "sight," "save," "sling," and so on. The words activated on the basis of word-initial information constitute a "cohort." Activation of a cohort is autonomous in the sense that only acoustic–phonetic information can serve to specify the members of a cohort. At this stage of the model, then, word recognition is a completely data-driven or bottom-up process.

Once a cohort structure is activated, all possible sources of information may come to bear on the selection of the appropriate word from the cohort. Thus further acoustic–phonetic information may eliminate "sight" and "save" from the cohort, leaving only words that begin with /sl/, such as "sling" and "slave." Note that word recognition based on acoustic–phonetic information is assumed to operate in a strictly left-to-right fashion. At this stage of word recognition, however, higher-level knowledge sources may also come into play in eliminating candidates from the cohort. Thus, if "sling" is inconsistent with the available semantic or syntactic information, it will be eliminated from the cohort. At this second stage of word recognition, the theory is highly interactive. Upon isolation of a single word in the cohort, word recognition is accomplished.

Cohort theory is a hybrid of autonomous and interactive processes. In addition, it gives priority to the beginnings of words and assumes strict left-to-right processing of acoustic–phonetic information. Cohort theory also embraces the notion of "optimal efficiency" (Marslen-Wilson, 1980a; Tyler & Marslen-Wilson, 1982), a principle stating that the word recognition system selects the appropriate word candidate from the cohort at the theoretically earliest possible point. This means that the word recognition system will commit to a decision as soon as sufficient acoustic–phonetic and higher-level sources of information are consistent with a single word candidate.

Marslen-Wilson's cohort theory has attracted a considerable amount of attention in the last few years, presumably because of its relatively precise description of the word recognition process, its novel claim that all words in the mental lexicon are activated in the initial stage of the word recognition process, and because of the priority it affords to the beginnings of words, a popular notion in the literature (see also Cole & Jakimik, 1980).

The theory is not without its shortcomings, however. For example, it incorporates no mechanism to account for word frequency. Do high-frequency words have higher activation levels in the cohort structure, or are they simply more likely to be selected as candidates for a cohort than low-frequency words? This last possibility seems unlikely, for the system would then be hard pressed to account for the recognition of low-frequency words that may be excluded a priori from the cohort structure. Perhaps associating various activation levels with word candidates would be more appropriate, but the theory as it stands has no means of accounting for differential activation levels.

Another problem with cohort theory is error recovery. For example, if "foundation" is perceived as "thoundation" due to mispronunciation or misperception, the word-initial cohort will not, according to the theory, contain the word candidate "foundation." Although Marslen-Wilson allows for some *residual* activation of acoustically similar word candidates in the cohort structure, so that a second pass through the cohort structure may at times be possible to attempt a best match, it is still unclear how error recovery is accomplished when the intended word is not a member of the activated cohort.

V.C. Forster's Autonomous Search Theory

In contrast to Morton's logogen theory and Marslen-Wilson's cohort theory, Forster's (1976, 1979) theory of word recognition and lexical access is autonomous in the strictest sense. Also, whereas Morton and Marslen-Wilson allow parallel processing of information at some stage, in Forster's theory linguistic processing is completely serial. The theory posits three separate linguistic processors: a lexical processor, a syntactic processor, and a message processor. In addition, the latest version of Forster's theory incorporates a third, nonlinguistic processor, the general processing system (GPS).

In the first stage of Forster's model, information from peripheral perceptual systems is submitted to the lexical processor. The processor then attempts to locate an entry in three peripheral access files: an orthographic file (for visual input), a phonetic file (for auditory input), and a syntactic–semantic file (for both visual and auditory input). Search of the peripheral access files is assumed to proceed by frequency, with higher-frequency words being searched prior to lower-frequency words. Once an entry is located in the peripheral access files, a search of the master lexicon is conducted. Thus word recognition is accomplished at the level of the peripheral access files. Once an entry is located in these files, lexical access is accomplished by locating the entry in the master lexicon, where other information about the word is stored.

Upon location of an item in the master lexicon, information pointing to the location of that item in the master list is passed on to the syntactic processor, which attempts to build a syntactic structure. From the syntactic processor, information is passed to the message processor, which attempts to build a conceptual structure for the intended message. Each of the three processors—lexical, syntactic, and message—can pass information to the GPS. However, the GPS cannot influence processing in any of the three dedicated linguistic processors. Rather, it serves to incorporate general conceptual knowledge with the output of information from the linguistic processors in making a decision (or response).

Forster's theory is autonomous in two senses. First, the lexical processor is independent of the syntactic and message processors, and the syntactic processor is independent of the message processor. Second, the entire linguistic system is independent of the general cognitive system. This strictly serial and autonomous characterization of language processing means that word recognition and lexical access are not influenced in any way by higher-level knowledge sources and are exclusively bottom-up or data-driven processes.

Forster's model is attractive because of its relative specificity and the apparently testable claims it makes regarding the autonomy of its processors. The model attempts to describe word recognition and lexical access in the context of sentence processing. In addition, it incorporates a specific explanation of the word frequency effect—namely, that entries in the peripheral access files are organized according to frequency and that search proceeds from high- to low-frequency entries. However, this model has not yet been used to account for data in auditory word recognition.

V.D. Elman and McClelland's Interactive—Activation Theory, Klatt's LAFS, and Phonetic Refinement Theory

Before concluding this section on theories of word recognition and lexical access, it is appropriate to briefly discuss three additional approaches. The first, Elman and McClelland's (1981, 1983) interactive–activation TRACE model of word recognition, is perhaps one of the most highly interactive theories to date (see also McClelland & Elman, 1986).

The second, Klatt's (1979, 1980) Lexical Access From Spectra model, is a heavily bottom-up or data-driven model. Both models serve to illustrate a basic opposition among all of the current theories of word recognition and lexical access. Phonetic refinement theory (Pisoni, Nusbaum, Luce, & Slowiaczek, 1985) also constitutes a highly interactive theory of word recognition, although it approaches problems in a somewhat novel manner compared with other interactive accounts.

Elman and McClelland's (1981, 1983) model is based on a system of simple processing units called "nodes." Nodes may stand for features, phonemes, or words. However, nodes at each level are alike in that each has an activation level signifying the degree to which the input is consistent with the unit that the node represents. In addition, each node has a resting level and a threshold. In the presence of confirmatory evidence, the activation level of a node rises toward its threshold; in the absence of such evidence, activation decays toward the resting level of the node (see McClelland & Rumelhart, 1981).

Nodes within this system are highly interconnected and when a given node reaches threshold, it may influence other nodes to which it is connected. Connections between nodes are of two types: excitatory and inhibitory. Thus a node that has reached threshold may raise the activation of some of the nodes to which it is connected while lowering the activation of others. Connections between levels are exclusively excitatory and bidirectional. Thus phoneme nodes may excite word nodes, and word nodes may in turn excite phoneme nodes. For example, the phoneme nodes corresponding to /l/ and /e/ may excite the word node "lake," which may then excite the phoneme nodes /l/, /e/, and /k/. Connections within levels are inhibitory and bidirectional. This means that activation of the phoneme node /l/ may inhibit activation of the phoneme node /b/, thus lowering the probability that the word node "bake" will raise its activation level.

The Elman and McClelland model illustrates how a highly interactive system may be conceptualized. In addition, it incorporates notions of both excitation and inhibition. By so doing, it directly incorporates a mechanism that reduces the possibility of nodes inconsistent with the evidence being activated while allowing for positive evidence at one level to influence the activation of nodes at another. Although Elman and McClelland's model is highly interactive, it is not without constraints. Namely, connections between levels are only excitatory, and within levels they are only inhibitory.

Whereas Elman and McClelland's model allows for interaction between and within levels of nodes, Klatt's LAFS model assumes direct, noninteractive access of lexical entries based on context-sensitive spectral sections. This model assumes that a "dictionary" of all lawful diphone sequences resides in long-term memory. Associated with each diphone sequence is a prototypical spectral representation. Klatt proposes spectral representations of diphone sequences to overcome the contextual variability of individual segments. To a certain extent, then, Klatt tries to overcome the problem of lack of invariance by building or precompiling coarticulatory effects into the representations residing in memory.

In the LAFS model, the listener computes spectral representations of an input word and compares these representations to the prototypes in memory. Word recognition is accomplished when a best match is found between the input spectra and the diphone representations. In this portion of the model, word recognition is accomplished directly on the basis of spectral representations of the sensory input. There is a means by which phonetic transcriptions can be obtained intermediate to lexical access, but in most circumstances access is direct, with no intermediate levels of computation corresponding to segments or phonemes.

Phonetic refinement theory (Pisoni et al., 1985) is based on the finding that human listeners do pay attention to fine phonetic detail in the speech waveform and use this information to recognize words even from incomplete or partial specifications of acoustic–phonetic input. According to this view, words are recognized in a one-pass, left-to-right strategy. They are represented in the lexicon as sequences of phonetic segments in a multidimensional phonetic space similar to that proposed by Treisman (1978). Partial or incomplete phonetic descriptions are used to activate regions of the space. As more and more information is obtained, a progressive narrowing occurs in both the specification of the phonetic input of a word and the set of activated word candidates that are phonetically similar to the input signal. A word is recognized when its activation through the phonetic space is higher than for any of the other competing paths or regions through the space. This occurs even when only partial input from the beginnings of words is available to support recognition. If a segment of a word is incorrectly recognized, the process continues to activate more segments of a word until a unique path through the phonetic space is achieved.

Phonetic refinement theory is unique in its approach to word recognition as a process of "constraint satisfaction" in which words are identified within a network of phonetic representations that are activated in memory. Like Elman and McClelland's theory, phonetic refinement theory is also highly interactive. All relevant sources of information may come to bear on the process of isolating a given path through the phonetic space.

VI. SUMMARY AND CONCLUSIONS

Our goal in this chapter has been to identify and elucidate several of the principal issues in research and theory on speech perception and auditory word recognition. Some of these issues, such as the lack of acoustic–phonetic invariance; the problems of normalization, segmentation, and representations; and the specialization of speech processing, constitute long-standing concerns in the field. Although many approaches to these issues have emerged, most notably for the invariance problem, the fundamental complexity of speech perception continues to pose considerable obstacles to speech researchers. In short, we are still far from any comprehensive solutions to these problems, although inroads are being made.

We have also outlined some past and present theoretical approaches to speech perception and auditory word recognition. In particular, we have focused on theories of auditory word recognition that attempt to account for the perception of units of speech above the level of the phoneme. We believe that this interest in the perception of words reflects a healthy trend toward more comprehensive accounts of the speech perception process. Although there has been little definitive work on bridging the gap between research on phonemes and word perception, much of the recent work in auditory word recognition constitutes a substantial broadening of scope in speech perception research.

Much work, of course, remains to be done on almost every level of spoken language understanding. As such, the field of speech perception continues to provide interesting and challenging research opportunities on this unique aspect of human behavior.

REFERENCES

Bever, T. G., Lackner, J., & Kirk, R. (1969). The underlying structure sentence is the primary unit of immediate speech processing. *Perception & Psychophysics, 5,* 225–234.

Blumstein, S. E. (1983, *Oct.*). *On acoustic invariance in speech.* Paper presented at the Symposium on Invariance and Variability, MIT, Cambridge, MA.

Blumstein, S. E., & Stevens, K. N. (1979). Acoustic invariance in speech production: Evidence from measurements of the spectral characteristics of stop consonants. *Journal of the Acoustical Society of America, 66,* 1001–1017.

Blumstein, S. E., & Stevens, K. N. (1980). Perceptual invariance and onset spectra for stop consonants in different vowel environments. *Journal of the Acoustical Society of America, 67,* 648–662.

Carlson, R., & Granstrom, B. (Eds.). (1982). *The representation of speech in the peripheral auditory system.* New York: Elsevier.

Chomsky, N. (1964). Current issues in linguistic theory. In J. A. Fodor & J. J. Katz (Eds.), *The structure of language* (pp. 50–118). Englewood Cliffs, NJ: Prentice-Hall.

Chomsky, N., & Halle, M. (1968). *The sound pattern of English.* New York: Harper & Row.

Chomsky, N., & Miller, G. A. (1963). Introduction to the formal analysis of natural languages. In R. D. Luce, R. Bush, & E. Galanter (Eds.), *Handbook of mathematical psychology* (Vol. 2, pp. 269–321). New York: John Wiley.

Church, K. W. (1983). Phrase-structure parsing: A method for taking advantage of allophonic constraints. Indiana University Linguistics Club, Bloomington.

Cohen, A., & Nooteboom, S. (Eds.). (1975). *Structure and process in speech perception.* Heidelberg: Springer-Verlag.

Cole, R. A., & Jakimik, J. (1980). A model of speech perception. In R. A. Cole (Ed.), *Perception and Production of Fluent Speech* (pp. 133–163). Hillsdale, NJ: Erlbaum.

Cole, R. A., Rudnicky, A. I., Zue, V. W., & Reddy, D. R. (1980). Speech as patterns on paper. In R. A. Cole (Ed.), *Perception and production of fluent speech* (pp. 3–50). Hillsdale, NJ: Erlbaum.

Cole, R. A., & Scott, B. (1974a). The phantom in the phoneme: Invariant cues for stop consonants. *Perception & Psychophysics, 15,* 101–107.

Cole, R. A., & Scott, B. (1974b). Toward a theory of speech perception. *Psychological Review, 81,* 348–374.

Cooper, W., & Sorensen, J. (1977). Fundamental frequency contours at syntactic boundaries. *Journal of the Acoustical Society of America, 62,* 683–692.

Darwin, C. J. (1975). On the dynamic use of prosody in speech perception. In A. Cohen & S. G. Nooteboom (Eds.), *Structure and process in speech perception* (pp. 178–194). Berlin: Springer-Verlag.

Delattre, P. C., Liberman, A. M., Cooper, F. S., & Gerstman, L. J. (1952). An experimental study of the acoustic determinants of vowel color: Observations of one- and two-formant vowels synthesized from spectrographic patterns. *Word, 8,* 195–210.

Delgutte, B. (1980). Representation of speech-like sounds in the discharge patterns of auditory-nerve fibers. *Journal of the Acoustical Society of America, 68,* 843–857.

Delgutte, B. (1981). *Representations of speech-like sounds in the discharge patterns of auditory nerve fibers.* Unpublished doctoral dissertation, MIT, Cambridge, MA.

Delgutte, B. (1982). Some correlates of phonetic distinctions at the level of the auditory nerve. In R. Carlson & B. Granstrom (Eds.), *The representation of speech in the peripheral auditory system.* New York: Elsevier.

Delgutte, B. (1984). Speech coding in the auditory nerve II: Processing schemes for vowel-like sounds. *Journal of the Acoustical Society of America, 75,* 879–886.

Delgutte, B., & Kiang, N. Y. S. (1984a). Speech coding in the auditory nerve I: Vowel-like sounds. *Journal of the Acoustical Society of America, 75,* 866–878.

Delgutte, B., & Kiang, N. Y. S. (1984b). Speech coding in the auditory nerve III: Voiceless fricative consonants. *Journal of the Acoustical Society of America, 75,* 887–896.

Delgutte, B., & Kiang, N. Y. S. (1984c). Speech coding in the auditory nerve IV: Sounds without consonant-like dynamic characteristics. *Journal of the Acoustical Society of America, 75,* 897–907.

Delgutte, B., & Kiang, N. Y. S. (1984d). Speech coding in the auditory nerve V: Vowels in background noise. *Journal of the Acoustical Society of America, 75,* 908–918.

Denes, P. (1955). Effect of duration on the perception of voicing. *Journal of the Acoustical Society of America, 27,* 761–674.

Derr, M. A., & Massaro, D. W. (1980). The contribution of vowel duration, FO contour, and frication duration as cues to the /juz/-/jus/ distinction. *Perception & Psychophysics, 27,* 51–59.

Easton, R. D., & Basala, M. (1982). Perceptual dominance during lipreading. *Perception & Psychophysics, 32,* 562–570.

Elman, J. L., & McClelland, J. L. (1981, Dec.). *An interactive activation model of speech perception.* Paper presented at the 102nd Annual Meeting of the Acoustical Society of America, Miami Beach, FL.

Elman, J. L., & McClelland, J. L. (1983, *Oct.*). *Exploiting lawful variability in the speech waveform.* Paper presented at the Symposium on Invariance and Variability, MIT, Cambridge, MA.

Fant, G. (1960). *Acoustic theory of speech production.* The Hague: Mouton.

Fant, G. (1962). Descriptive analysis of the acoustic aspects of speech. *Logos, 5,* 3–17.

Fant, G. (1967). Auditory patterns of speech. In W. Wathen-Dunn (Ed.), *Models for the perception of speech and visual form* (pp. 111–125). Cambridge, MA: MIT Press.

Fant, G. (1973). *Speech sounds and features.* Cambridge, MA: MIT Press.

Forster, K. I. (1976). Accessing the mental lexicon. In R. J. Wales and E. Walker (Eds.), *New approaches to language mechanisms* (pp. 257–287). Amsterdam: North Holland.

Forster, K. I. (1979). Levels of processing and the structure of the language processor. In W. E. Cooper & E.C.T. Walker (Eds.), *Sentence processing: Psycholinguistic studies presented to Merrill Garrett* (pp. 27–86). Hillsdale, NJ: Erlbaum.

Fry, D. B., Abramson, A. S., Eimas, P. D., & Liberman, A. M. (1962). The identification and discrimination of synthetic vowels. *Language and Speech, 5,* 171–189.

Fujisaki, H., & Kawashima, T. (1969). On the modes and mechanisms of speech perception. *Annual Report of the Engineering Research Institute* (Vol. 28, pp. 67–73). Tokyo: University of Tokyo, Faculty of Engineering.

Fujisaki, H., & Kawashima, T. (1970). Some experiments on speech perception and a model for the perceptual mechanism. *Annual Report of the Engineering Research Institute* (Vol. 29, pp. 207–214). Tokyo: University of Tokyo, Faculty of Engineering.

Fujisaki, H., & Kawashima, T. (1971). A model of the mechanisms for speech perception: Quantitative analysis of categorical effects in discrimination. *Annual Report of the Engineering Research Institute* (Vol. 30, pp. 59–68). Tokyo: University of Tokyo, Faculty of Engineering.

Gaitenby, J. H. (1965). The elastic word. *Haskins Laboratories Status Report on Speech Research, SR-2,* 3.1–3.12.

Ganong, W. F. (1979). *The internal structure of consonants in speech perception: Acoustic cues, not distinctive features.* Unpublished manuscript.

Ganong, W. F. (1980). Phonetic categorization in auditory word perception. *Journal of Experimental Psychology, 6,* 110–125.

Goldhor, R. (1983a). A speech signal processing system based on a peripheral auditory model. *Proceedings of IEEE, ICASSP-83,* 1368–1371.

Goldhor, R. (1983b). The representation of speech signals in a model of the peripheral auditory system. *Journal of the Acoustical Society of America, 73,* S4.

Greene, B. G., Pisoni, D. B., & Carrell, T. D. (1984). Recognition of speech spectrograms. *Journal of the Acoustical Society of America, 76,* 32–43.

Grosjean, F., & Gee, J. P. (1986). Prosodic structure and spoken word recognition. *Cognition,* in press.

Halle, M., & Stevens, K. N. (1962). Speech recognition: A model and a program for research. *IRE Transactions of the Professional Group on Information Theory, IT-8,* 155–159.

Harris, K. S., Hoffman, H. S., Liberman, A. M., Delattre, P. C., & Cooper, F. S. (1958). Effect of third-formant transitions on the perception of the voiced stop consonants. *Journal of the Acoustical Society of America, 30,* 122–126.

Hoffman, H. S. (1958). Study of some cues in the perception of voiced stop consonants. *Journal of the Acoustical Society of America, 30,* 1035–1041.

Huggins, A.W.F. (1972). On the perception of temporal phenomena in speech. *Journal of the Acoustical Society of America, 51,* 1279–1290.

Huggins, A.W.F. (1978). Speech timing and intelligibility. In J. Requin (Ed.), *Attention and performance* (Vol. 7, pp. 279–297). Hillsdale, NJ: Erlbaum.

Jakobson, R., Fant, C.G.M., & Halle, M. (1952). *Preliminaries to speech analysis* (Tech. Rep. No. 13). Cambridge, MA: MIT, Acoustics Laboratory.

Joos, M. A. (1948). Acoustic phonetics. *Language,* Suppl. *24,* 1–136.

Jusczyk, P. W., Pisoni, D. B., Reed, M. A., Fernald, A., & Myers, M. (1983). Infants' discrimination of the duration of rapid spectrum changes in nonspeech signals. *Science, 222,* 175–177.

Jusczyk, P. W., Pisoni, D. B., Walley, A., & Murray, J. (1980). Discrimination of relative onset time of two-component tones by infants. *Journal of the Acoustical Society of America, 67,* 262–270.

Kenstowicz, M., & Kisseberth, C. (1979). *Generative phonology.* New York: Academic Press.

Kewley-Port, D. (1980). Representations of spectral change as cues to place of articulation in stop consonants. *Research on speech perception* (Tech. Rep. No. 3). Bloomington: Indiana University, Speech Research Laboratory.

Kewley-Port, D. (1983a, Oct.). *Converging approaches towards establishing invariant acoustic correlates of stop consonants.* Paper presented at the Symposium on Invariance and Variability, MIT, Cambridge, MA.

Kewley-Port, D. (1983b). Time-varying features as correlates of place of articulation in stop consonants. *Journal of the Acoustical Society of America, 73,* 322–335.

Kewley-Port, D., & Luce, P. A. (1984). Time-varying features of initial stop consonants in auditory running spectra: A first report. *Perception & Psychophysics, 35,* 353–360.

Kiang, N.Y.S. (1980). Processing of speech by the auditory nervous system. *Journal of the Acoustical Society of America, 68,* 830–835.

Klatt, D. H. (1974). The duration of [S] in English words. *Journal of Speech and Hearing Research, 17,* 51–63.

Klatt, D. H. (1975). Vowel lengthening is syntactically determined in a connected discourse. *Journal of Phonetics, 3,* 129–140.

Klatt, D. H. (1976). Linguistic uses of segmental duration in English: Acoustic and perceptual evidence. *Journal of the Acoustical Society of America, 59,* 1208–1221.

Klatt, D. H. (1977). Review of the ARPA speech understanding project. *Journal of the Acoustical Society of America, 62,* 1345–1366.

Klatt, D. H. (1979). Speech perception: A model of acoustic-phonetic analysis and lexical access. *Journal of Phonetics, 7,* 279–312.

Klatt, D. H. (1980). Speech perception: A model of acoustic–phonetic analysis and lexical access. In R. A. Cole (Ed.), *Perception and production of fluent speech* (pp. 243–288). Hillsdale, NJ: Erlbaum.

Klatt, D. H. (1982). Speech processing strategies based on auditory models. In R. Carlson & B. Granstrom (Eds.), *The representation of speech in the peripheral auditory system* (pp. 181–196). New York: Elsevier.

Klatt, D. H., & Cooper, W. E. (1975). Perception of segment duration in sentence contexts. In A. Cohen & S. G. Nooteboom (Eds.), *Structure and process in speech perception* (pp. 69–80). New York: Springer-Verlag.

Klatt, D. H., & Stevens, K. N. (1973). On the automatic recognition of continuous speech: Implications from a spectrogram-reading experiment. *IEEE Transactions on Audio and Electroacoustics, AU-21,* 210–217.

Kuhl, P. K., & Miller, J. D. (1975). Speech perception by the chinchilla: Voiced–voiceless distinction in alveolar-plosive consonants. *Science, 190,* 69–72.

Lea, W. A. (1973). An approach to syntactic recognition without phonemics. *IEEE Transactions on Audio and Electroacoustics, AU-21,* 249–258.

Lehiste, I. (1970). *Suprasegmentals.* Cambridge, MA: MIT Press.

Liberman, A. M. (1970a). The grammars of speech and language. *Cognitive Psychology, 1,* 301–323.

Liberman, A. M. (1970b). Some characteristics of perception in the speech mode. In D. A. Hamburg (Ed.), *Perception and its disorders: Proceedings of ARNMD.* (pp. 238–254). Baltimore: Williams & Wilkins.

Liberman, A. M. (1982). On finding that speech is special. *American Psychologist, 37,* 148–167.

Liberman, A. M., Cooper, F. S., Harris, K. S., MacNeilage, P. F., & Studdert-Kennedy, M. (1967). Some observations on a model for speech perception. In W. Wathen-Dunn (Ed.), *Models for the perception of speech and visual form* (pp. 68–87). Cambridge, MA: MIT Press.

Liberman, A. M., Cooper, F. S., Shankweiler, D. P., & Studdert-Kennedy, M. (1967). Perception of the speech code. *Psychological Review, 74,* 431–461.

Liberman, A. M., Harris, K. S., Hoffman, H. A., & Griffith, B. C. (1957). The discrimination of speech sounds within and across phoneme boundaries. *Journal of Experimental Psychology, 54,* 358–368.

Liberman, A. M., & Mattingly, I. G. (1985). The motor theory of speech perception revised. *Cognition, 21,* 1–36.

Licklider, J.C.R. (1952). On the process of speech perception. *Journal of the Acoustical Society of America, 24,* 590–594.

Lindblom, B.E.F., & Svensson, S. G. (1973). Interaction between segmental and non-segmental factors in speech recognition. *IEEE Transactions on Audio and Electroacoustics, AU-21,* 536–545.

Luce, P. A., & Charles-Luce, J. (1983). Contextual effects on the consonant/vowel ratio in speech production. *Research on speech perception* (Prog. Rep. No. 9). Bloomington: Indiana University, Speech Research Laboratory.

Luce, P. A., & Charles-Luce, J. (1985a). Contextual effects on vowel duration, closure duration, and the consonant/vowel ratio. *Journal of the Acoustical Society of America, 78,* 1949–1957.

Luce, P. A., & Charles-Luce, J. (1985b, April). Perception of word-final voicing in two sentence contexts. Paper presented at the 109th Annual Meeting of the Acoustical Society of America, Austin, Texas.

Luce, P. A., & Pisoni, D. B. (1986). Speech perception: Recent trends in research, theory, and applications. In H. Winitz (Ed.), *Human communication and its disorders.* Norwood, NJ: Ablex, in press.

MacDonald, J., & McGurk, H. (1978). Visual influences on speech perception processes. *Perception & Psychophysics, 24,* 253–257.

Mack, M., & Blumstein, S. E. (1983). Further evidence of acoustic invariance in speech production: The stop-glide contrast. *Journal of the Acoustical Society of America, 73,* 1739–1750.

Mann, V. A., Madden, J., Russell, J. M., & Liberman, A. M. (1981). *Integration of time-varying cues and the effects of phonetic context.* Unpublished manuscript.

Marcus, S. M. (1984). Recognizing speech: On mapping from sound to meaning. In H. Bouma & D. G. Bowhuis, *Attention and performance X: Control of language process* (pp. 151–164). Hillsdale, NJ: Erlbaum.

Marslen-Wilson, W. D. (1975). Sentence perception as an interactive parallel process. *Science, 189,* 226–228.

Marslen-Wilson, W. D. (1980a). *Optimal efficiency in human speech processing.* Unpublished manuscript.

Marslen-Wilson, W. D. (1980b). Speech understanding as a psychological process. In J. C. Simon (Ed.), *Spoken language generation and understanding* (pp. 39–67). Dordrecht, Holland: Reidel.

Marslen-Wilson, W. D., & Tyler, L. K. (1975). Processing structure of sentence perception. *Nature, 257,* 784–785.

Marslen-Wilson, W. D., & Tyler, L. K. (1980). The temporal structure of spoken language understanding. *Cognition, 8,* 1–71.

Marslen-Wilson, W. D., & Welsh, A. (1978). Processing interactions and lexical access during word recognition in continuous speech. *Cognitive Psychology, 10,* 29–63.

Massaro, D. W. (1972). Preperceptual images, processing time, and perceptual units in auditory perception. *Psychological Review, 79,* 124–145.

Massaro, D. W., & Cohen, M. M. (1976). The contribution of fundamental frequency and voice onset time to the /zi/-/si/ distinction. *Journal of the Acoustical Society of America, 60,* 704–717.

Massaro, D. W., & Cohen, M. M. (1977). The contribution of voice-onset time and fundamental frequency as cues to the /zi/-/si/ distinction. *Perception & Psychophysics, 22,* 373–382.

Massaro, D. W., & Cohen, M. M. (1983). Evaluation and integration of visual and auditory information in speech perception. *Journal of Experimental Psychology: Human Perception and Performance, 9,* 753–771.

Massaro, D. W., & Oden, G. C. (1980). Speech perception: A framework for research and theory. In N. J. Lass (Ed.), *Speech and language: Advances in basic research and practice* (Vol. 3, pp. 129–165). New York: Academic Press.

McClelland, J. L., & Elman, J. L. (1986). The TRACE model of speech perception. *Cognitive Perception, 18,* 1–86.

McClelland, J. L., & Rumelhart, D. E. (1981). An interactive-activation model of context effects in letter perception, Part I: An account of basic findings. *Psychological Review, 88,* 375–407.

McGurk, H., & MacDonald, J. (1976). Hearing lips and seeing voices. *Nature, 264,* 746–748.

Miller, G. A. (1962a). Decision units in the perception of speech. *IRE Transactions on Information Theory, IT-8,* 81–83.

Miller, G. A. (1962b). Some psychological studies of grammar. *American Psychologist, 17,* 748–762.

Miller, G. A., & Isard, S. (1963). Some perceptual consequences of linguistic rules *Journal of Verbal Learning and Verbal Behavior, 2,* 217–228.

Miller, G. A., Heise, G. A., & Lichten, W. (1951). The intelligibility of speech as a function of the context of the test materials. *Journal of Experimental Psychology, 41,* 329–335.

Miller, J. D., Wier, L., Pastore, R., Kelly, W., & Dooling, R. (1976). Discrimination and labeling of noise-buzz sequences with varying noise-lead times: An example of categorical perception. *Journal of the Acoustical Society of America, 60,* 410–417.

Miller, J. L. (1980). The effect of speaking rate on segmental distinctions: Acoustic variation and perceptual compensation. In P. D. Eimas & J. L. Miller (Eds.), *Perspectives on the study of speech* (pp. 39–74). Hillsdale, NJ: Erlbaum.

Miller, J. L., & Liberman, A. M. (1979). Some effects of later-occurring information on the perception of stop consonant and semi-vowel. *Perception & Psychophysics, 25,* 457–465.

Miller, M. I., & Sachs, M. B. (1983). Representation of stop consonants in the discharge patterns of auditory-nerve fibers. *Journal of the Acoustical Society of America, 74,* 502–517.

Moore, T. J., & Cahsin, J. L. (1974). Response patterns of cochlear nucleus neurons to excerpts from sustained vowels. *Journal of the Acoustical Society of America, 56,* 1565–1576.

Moore, T. J., & Cahsin, J. L. (1976). Response of cochlear-nucleus neurons to synthetic speech. *Journal of the Acoustical Society of America, 59,* 1443–1449.

Morton, J. (1969). Interaction of information in word recognition. *Psychological Review, 76,* 165–178.

Morton, J. (1979). Word recognition. In J. Morton & J. D. Marshall (Eds.), *Psycholinguistics 2: Structures and processes* (pp. 107–156). Cambridge, MA: MIT Press.

Morton, J. (1982). Disintegrating the lexicon: An information processing approach. In J. Mehler, E. Walker, & M. Garrett (Eds.), *Perspectives on mental representation: Experimental and theoretical studies of cognitive processes and capacities* (pp. 89–109). Hillsdale, NJ: Erlbaum

Mundie, J. R., & Moore, T. J. (1970). Speech analysis using an analog cochlea. *Journal of the Acoustical Society of America, 48,* 131.

Nakatani, L. H., & O'Connor-Dukes, K. (1980). *Phonetic parsing cues for word perception.* Unpublished manuscript.

Newell, A. (1973). You can't play 20 questions with nature and win: Projective comments on the papers of this symposium. In W. G. Chase (Ed.), *Visual information processing* (pp. 283–308). New York: Academic Press.

Newell, A., Burnett, J., Forgie, J. W., Green, C. C., Klatt, D. H., Licklider, J.C.R., Munson, J., Reddy, D. R., & Woods, W. A. (1971). *Speech understanding systems: Final report of a study group.* Amsterdam: North Holland.

Nooteboom, S. G., Brokx, J.P.L., & de Rooij, J. J. (1978). Contributions of prosody to speech perception. In W.J.M. Levelt & G. B. Flores d'Arcais (Eds.), *Studies in the perception of language* (pp. 75–107). New York: John Wiley.

Nooteboom, S. G., & Doodeman, G.J.N. (1980). Production and perception of vowel length in spoken sentences. *Journal of the Acoustical Society of America, 67,* 276–287.

Nusbaum, H. C. (1984). Possible mechanisms of duplex perception: "Chirp" identification versus dichotic fusion. *Perception & Psychophysics, 35,* 94–101.

Nusbaum, H. C., Schwab, E. C., & Sawusch, J. R. (1983). The role of "chirp" identification in duplex perception. *Perception & Psychophysics, 33,* 323–332.

Oden, G. C., & Massaro, D. W. (1978). Integration of featural information in speech perception. *Psychological Review, 85,* 172–191.

Oller, D. K. (1973). The effect of position in utterance on speech segment duration in English. *Journal of the Acoustical Society of America, 54,* 1235–1247.

Parker, F. (1977). Distinctive features and acoustic cues. *Journal of the Acoustical Society of America, 62,* 1051–1054.

Pastore, R. E., Schmeckler, M. A., Rosenblum, L., & Szczesiul, R. (1983). Duplex perception with musical stimuli. *Perception & Psychophysics, 33,* 469–474.

Pisoni, D. B. (1971). On the nature of categorical perception of speech sounds. *Supplement to status report on speech research* (SR-27). New Haven, CT: Haskins Laboratories.

Pisoni, D. B. (1973). Auditory and phonetic memory codes in the discrimination of consonants and vowels. *Perception & Psychophysics, 13,* 253–260.

Pisoni, D. B. (1975). Auditory short-term memory and vowel perception. *Memory & Cognition, 3,* 7–18.

Pisoni, D. B. (1977). Identification and discrimination of the relative onset of two component tones: Implications for voicing perception in stops. *Journal of the Acoustical Society of America, 61*, 1352–1361.

Pisoni, D. B., & Luce, P. A. (1986). Acoustic-phonetic representations in spoken word recognition. *Cognition,* in press.

Pisoni, D. B., Carrell, T. D., & Gans, S. J. (1983). Perception of the duration of rapid spectrum changes in speech and nonspeech signals. *Perception & Psychophysics, 34,* 314–322.

Pisoni, D. B., Nusbaum, H. C., Luce, P. A., & Slowiaczek, L. M. (1985). Speech perception, word recognition and the structure of the lexicon. *Speech Communication, 4,* 75–95.

Pollack, I., & Pickett, J. M. (1964). The intelligibility of excerpts from conversation. *Language and Speech, 6,* 165–171.

Port, R. F. (1977). The influence of speaking tempo on the duration of stressed vowel and medial stop in English trochu words. Bloomington: Indiana University Linguistics Club.

Port, R. F., & Dalby, J. (1982). Consonant/vowel ratio as a cue for voicing in English. *Perception & Psychophysics, 32,* 141–152.

Rand, T. C. (1974). Dichotic release from masking for speech. *Journal of the Acoustical Society of America, 55,* 678–680.

Repp, B. H. (1982). Phonetic trading relations and context effects: New experimental evidence for a speech mode of perception. *Psychological Bulletin, 92,* 81–110.

Repp, B. H. (1983a). Categorical perception: Issues, methods, findings. In N. J. Lass (Ed.), *Speech and language: Advances in basic research and practice* (Vol. 10). New York: Academic Press.

Repp, B. H. (1983b). Trading relations among acoustic cues in speech perception: Speech-specific but not special. *Haskins Laboratories Status Report on Speech Research, SR-76,* 129–132.

Repp, B. H. (1984). Against a role of "chirp" identification in duplex perception. *Perception & Psychophysics, 35,* 89–93.

Roberts, M., & Summerfield, A. (1981). Audio-visual adaptation in speech perception. *Perception & Psychophysics, 30,* 309–314.

Sachs, M. B., & Young, E. D. (1979). Encoding of steady-state vowels in the auditory nerve: Representation in terms of discharge rate. *Journal of the Acoustical Society of America, 66,* 470–479.

Sachs, M. B., & Young, E. D. (1980). Effects of nonlinearities on speech encoding in the auditory nerve. *Journal of the Acoustical Society of America, 68,* 858–875.

Searle, C. L., Jacobson, J. F., & Kimberley, B. P. (1980). Speech as patterns in the 3-space of time and frequency. In R. A. Cole (Ed.), Perception and production of fluent speech (pp. 73–102). Hillsdale, NJ: Erlbaum.

Searle, C. L., Jacobson, J. F., & Rayment, S. G. (1979). Stop consonant discrimination based on human audition. *Journal of the Acoustical Society of America, 65,* 799–809.

Shockey, L., & Reddy, R. (1974, August). *Quantitative analysis of speech perception: Results from transcription of connected speech from unfamiliar languages.* Paper presented at the Speech Communications Seminar, Stockholm.

Stevens, K. N. (1960). Toward a model for speech recognition. *Journal of the Acoustical Society of America, 32,* 47–55.

Stevens, K. N. (1975). The potential role of property detectors in the perception of consonants. In G. Fant & M. A. A. Tatham (Eds.), *Auditory analysis and perception of speech* (pp. 303–330). New York: Academic Press.

Stevens, K. N. (1980). Acoustic correlates of some phonetic categories. *Journal of the Acoustical Society of America, 68*, 836–842.

Stevens, K. N., & Blumstein, S. E. (1978). Invariant cues for place of articulation in stop consonants. *Journal of the Acoustical Society of America, 64*, 1358–1368.

Stevens, K. N., & Blumstein, S. E. (1981). The search for invariant acoustic correlates of phonetic features. In P. D. Eimas & J. Miller (Eds.), *Perspectives on the study of speech* (pp. 1–38). Hillsdale, NJ: Erlbaum.

Stevens, K. N., & Halle, M. (1967). Remarks on analysis by synthesis and distinctive features. In W. Wathen-Dunn (Ed.), *Models for the perception of speech and visual form* (pp. 88–102). Cambridge, MA: MIT Press.

Stevens, K. N., & House, A. S. (1972). Speech perception. In J. Tobias (Ed.), *Foundations of modern auditory theory* (Vol. 2, pp. 1–62). New York: Academic Press.

Studdert-Kennedy, M. (1974). The perception of speech. In T. A. Sebeok (Ed.), *Current trends in linguistics* (Vol. XII, pp. 2349–2385). The Hague: Mouton.

Studdert-Kennedy, M. (1976). Speech perception. In N. J. Lass (Ed.), *Contemporary issues in experimental phonetics* (pp. 243–293). New York: Academic Press.

Studdert-Kennedy, M., & Shankweiler, D. (1970). Hemispheric specialization for speech perception. *Journal of the Acoustical Society of America, 48*, 579–594.

Summerfield, Q. (1979). Use of visual information for phonetic perception. *Phonetica, 36*, 314–331.

Summerfield, Q. (1982). Differences between spectral dependencies in auditory and phonetic temporal processing: Relevance to the perception of voicing in initial stops. *Journal of the Acoustical Society of America, 72*, 51–61.

Summerfield, Q., & Haggard, M. (1977). On the dissociation of spectral and temporal cues to the voicing distinction in initial stop consonants. *Journal of the Acoustical Society of America, 62*, 436–448.

Svensson, S. G. (1974). Prosody and grammar in speech perception. *Monographs from the Institute of Linguistics* (No. 2). Stockholm, Sweden: University of Stockholm, Institute of Linguistics.

Treisman, M. (1978). Space or lexicon? The word frequency effect and the error response frequency effect. *Journal of Verbal Learning and Verbal Behavior, 17*, 37–59.

Tyler, L. K., & Marslen-Wilson, W. D. (1982). Speech comprehension processes. In J. Mehler, E.C.T. Walker, & M. Garrett (Eds.), *Perspectives on mental representation: Experimental and theoretical studies of cognitive processes and capacities* (pp. 169–184). Hillsdale, NJ: Erlbaum.

Walley, A. C., & Carrell, T. D. (1983). Onset spectra and formant transitions in the adult's and child's perception of place of articulation in stop consonants. *Journal of the Acoustical Society of America, 73*, 1011–1022.

Wickelgren, W. A. (1969). Context-sensitive coding, associative memory, and serial order in (speech) behavior. *Psychological Review, 76*, 1–15.

Young, E. D., & Sachs, M. B. (1979). Representation of steady-state vowels in the temporal aspects of the discharge patterns of populations of auditory-nerve fibers. *Journal of the Acoustical Society of America, 66*, 1381–1403.

Zwicker, E., Terhardt, E., & Paulus, E. (1979). Automatic speech recognition using psychoacoustic models. *Journal of the Acoustical Society of America, 65*, 487–498.

CHAPTER 2

Auditory and Phonetic Coding of Speech*

James R. Sawusch

*Department of Psychology, State University of
New York at Buffalo, Amherst, New York 14226*

I. INTRODUCTION

The subjective experience of understanding spoken language includes the organization of the speech signal into a sequence of discrete units: phonemes, syllables, and words. The speech signal, however, is continuous, reflecting the continuity of articulator movement in production. This dichotomy between the continuous speech signal and discrete units in speech perception is the basis for the central question to be addressed here. Specifically, how does the listener recover the sequence of discrete units intended by a speaker from the continuous speech signal? The first step in attempting to answer this question is to specify the problem in somewhat greater detail. The next step is to outline a framework for constructing a model of speech perception, including experimental data supporting this framework and a comparison with alternative frameworks. Finally, a computer simulation of a model of speech perception, based on this framework, is described along with additional human perceptual data.

II. THE PROBLEM OF PERCEPTUAL CONSTANCY

The study of phonetics—the linguistic description of the sounds of language—provided the initial basis on which much of the early work in

* The preparation of this chapter and some of the research reported here was supported by National Institute of Neurological, Communicative Disorders and Stroke Grant 5 R01 NS19653 to the State University of New York at Buffalo.

51

speech perception was built. Linguists have described the sound structure of language in terms of a set of 40 to 50 phonemes. These units form a minimal description of the sounds of speech as they relate to the meaning of an utterance. Early work in speech analysis and synthesis began with this linguistic description and focused on the relationship between attributes of the speech signal and its phonetic representation. This early work involved the analysis of the speech waveform using the sound spectrograph, speech synthesis, and perceptual studies of intelligibility in an attempt to specify the minimal acoustic information necessary to cue a phonetic distinction. From this work, three important issues in speech perception emerged: (1) the lack of invariance in the speech waveform; (2) the segmentation of the waveform into units of analysis; and (3) the role of various units of analysis in perception (see Pisoni, 1976, for a discussion of these issues).

II.A. Invariance

The question of invariance came to light with the advent of the sound spectrograph (Koenig, Dunn, & Lacy, 1946) and the first perceptual studies of speech using the pattern playback (Cooper, Delattre, Liberman, Borst, & Gerstman, 1952). The basic problem was that the same acoustic cue could give rise to different percepts in different contexts, and that different acoustic cues could give rise to the same percept in different contexts (see Liberman, Cooper, Shankweiler, & Studdert-Kennedy, 1967, for a review). One classic example of the first of these two phenomena comes from an experiment on the unvoiced stop consonants /p, t, k/ (Liberman, Delattre, & Cooper, 1952). Bursts varying in frequency were added to the front of a series of English vowels. One particular burst, centered at 1400 Hz, gave rise to the perceived syllable /pi/ when placed in front of the /i/ vowel. However, in front of the vowel /a/, this same burst was perceived as /ka/. Finally, in front of the vowel /u/, the resulting percept was /pu/. Thus one acoustic cue gave rise to different percepts, depending on the vowel context. Schematic spectrograms of these syllables are shown in Figure 2.1.

The converse phenomenon, in which multiple cues give rise to the same percept, has also been observed. Liberman, Delattre, Cooper, & Gerstman (1954) investigated the effects of initial formant transitions on the perception of consonants. In front of the vowel /i/, a rising second formant was perceived as /d/. However, in front of the vowel /u/, a falling second formant transition was necessary to hear /d/. Thus in front of one vowel a rising transition yielded the same percept as a falling transition in front of a different vowel. A similar diversity of sound-to-phoneme relationships

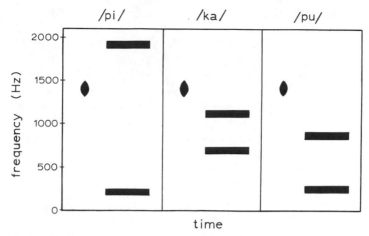

Figure 2.1   Schematic spectrograms of the syllables /pi/, /ka/, and /pu/.

has been found in attempts to read sound spectrograms (Fant, 1962). One reason for focusing on the invariance problem is that the listener hears the /d/ in /di/ and /du/ as the same consonant. This perceptual constancy occurs in spite of the diversity of cues that characterize /d/ in front of different vowels and in different syllable positions.

The search for invariant acoustic properties of stops was given a new impetus by the work of Stevens and Blumstein (1978; Blumstein & Stevens, 1979, 1980). These researchers designed a set of spectral templates based on the shape of the spectrum at stop release. The templates can be used to classify naturally produced stops according to place of articulation by matching the templates against a spectral section of a stop at release. Since stop consonant place of articulation is in a one-to-one correspondence with the set of templates, the templates represent a potential solution to the invariance problem. Two studies have examined whether these spectral templates are an adequate description of human speech perception. Blumstein, Isaacs, and Mertus (1982) and Walley and Carrell (1983) have both compared subjects' identification of synthetic speech syllables with the predictions of the spectral template theory. In both studies, subjects' identification of the stimuli was consistently based on the contextually variable (i.e., noninvariant) formant transitions rather than the invariant shape of the spectrum at onset. Walley and Carrell also tested children with their synthetic speech stimuli and found a close correspondence between the children's identification data and the adult data. Both children and adults seemed to identify the stimuli on the basis of the contextually variable formant transitions.

In addition to these direct studies of the Stevens and Blumstein templates, there is also indirect evidence against their proposal as a model of speech perception. The Stevens and Blumstein templates cannot be used to classify two-formant stops (such as the voiceless stops of Figure 2.1). The reason for this is that the templates are based on the intensity relations among the higher formants (F2 and up). A two-formant stop does not have higher formants, so there is no intensity profile to which the templates can be applied. Blumstein and Stevens (1979, 1980) have responded to this problem by proposing that while their spectral templates are the primary cue to place of articulation, secondary cues such as formant transitions can also be used. To the extent that the formant transitions are secondary cues, they might be useful to adults only because they have been learned by association with the primary, invariant template cues. However, Kuhl and Padden (1983) have shown that monkeys discriminate two-formant stops in a fashion very similar to humans. Walley (1979) tested human infants with two-formant stops and also found a correspondence between the infant's discrimination and adult labeling. Both of these studies would seem to indicate that the two-formant stops carry sufficient information by themselves to allow partitioning into categories without recourse to learning by association (see also Kuhl & Padden, 1983).

As part of a study of two-formant stops, Sawusch (1980) compared subjects' categorization of two-formant and five-formant stops. In the five-formant syllables the third, fourth, and fifth formants were steady-state. Thus the critical place information was contained in the second-formant transitions in both series. Identification data for the two sets were virtually identical, indicating that the two- and five-formant syllables were classified according to the same cues rather than secondary cues for the two-formant stimuli and spectral templates (primary cues) for the five-formant stimuli. Thus the static spectral templates proposed by Blumstein and Stevens (1979, 1980) as a possible model for human speech processing cannot handle human perceptual data from synthetic speech studies (see also Lahiri, Gewirth, & Blumstein, 1984).

Variations of the spectral template approach, along with supporting data, have been proposed by Kewley-Port (1983; Kewley-Port, Pisoni, & Studdert-Kennedy, 1983) and by Lahiri et al. (1984). Kewley-Port employed single, invariant templates for bilabial (/b/) and alveolar (/d/) stops plus a temporal sequence of templates for velars (/g/). The temporal sequence for /g/ corresponds to using voice-onset time information to distinguish /g/ from the other stops. However, this approach suffers from many of the same problems that the original Stevens and Blumstein (1978) proposal contained. In particular, the data of Walley and Carrell (1983)—

which show that subjects use the formant trajectories rather than the static spectrum at onset to categorize the bilabials (/b/) and alveolars (/d/)—plus the various two-formant studies both pose problems for the approach taken by Kewley-Port (1983; Kewley-Port et al., 1983).

Lahiri et al. (1984) proposed that the pattern of change in the spectrum from release to the onset of voicing represents the essential information for stop place categorization. They also showed that this metric could correctly classify stops across different languages, including cases where the Blumstein and Stevens (1979, 1980) templates failed. Since these "invariants" incorporate some of the information conveyed by the formant transitions, they may be able to account for the Walley and Carrell (1983; also Blumstein et al., 1982) results. However, these dynamic templates still appear to be inadequate for dealing with voiced two-formant stops, where release and the onset of voicing are simultaneous. In these cases, the templates would be reduced to being similar to the static templates of Blumstein and Stevens (1979, 1980). Nevertheless, the dynamic template approach is promising and offers the hint of an eventual solution to the invariance and perceptual constancy problem. We return to this and similar dynamic template approaches later.

II.B. Segmentation and Perceptual Units

The problem of segmenting the speech signal into units is intimately tied to the invariance question. For much of the speech signal, sementation according to acoustic criteria is exceedingly difficult. Speech is a continuously varying signal, and any particular stretch of the speech waveform carries information about a number of segments. This phenomenon is generally referred to as contextual variability (see Fant, 1962; Liberman, Cooper, Shankweiler, & Studdert-Kennedy, 1967, for examples). The importance of this variability is in the processing that the perceptual system must go through to decode the message from the speech signal. Since the acoustic elements are not in a one to-one linear mapping with phonemes or phonetic features, a complex restructuring process is involved in production (see MacNeilage, 1970), and consequently a complex decoding process must be involved in perception (Liberman, 1970, 1982).

In various attempts to solve the joint problems of the lack of invariance and segmentation, different-sized perceptual units have been proposed. The phonetic feature, phoneme, and syllable have all been considered at one time or another by various investigators. However, the problems of a lack of invariance and segmenting a continuous signal are common to all of these units of analysis (see Pisoni, 1976; Studdert-Kennedy, 1976). The coarticulation phenomena that carry attributes of one phonetic feature or phoneme onto the surrounding phonemes are also found for syllables (Öhman, 1966). Coarticulation refers to the influence of the muscle movements necessary to produce one sound onto preceding and succeeding muscle movements and their resulting acoustic manifestations. Thus the production of a stop consonant is conditioned or influenced by the production of the adjacent phonemes.

The acoustic consequences of coarticulation are that one sound segment may carry information about a number of phonemes or syllables. Coarticulation effects obscure the boundaries between all potential units of analysis in speech: phonetic features, phonemes, and syllables. As a result, syllabic units are difficult to segment by acoustically defined criteria and show the same context-conditioned variability (i.e., lack of invariance) exhibited by phonemes. Furthermore, experimental results such as those of Martin and Bunnell (1982) show that these coarticulatory effects have perceptual consequences, even when they span a syllable boundary. Using natural speech, Martin and Bunnell edited CV_1CV_2 syllable sequences so that all versions of the second syllable (CV_2) were paired with all versions of the first syllable (CV_1). They found that both the reaction time to identify the vowel in the second syllable (V_2) and the number of false alarms were influenced by the editing. The original CV_1CV_2 sequences produced faster reaction times and a lower false alarm rate than edited sequences, which disrupted the coarticulatory information of CV_1 about CV_2. Thus the information in the speech signal that is useful to a listener clearly spans both phoneme and syllable boundaries. Consequently, it would appear that the relevant question is not that of the basic unit of perception but rather concerns the roles of all of these units in perception and how the processing of each unit is carried out (see Studdert-Kennedy, 1976).

III. A FRAMEWORK FOR A MODEL OF SPEECH PERCEPTION

The framework to be outlined here is an information processing approach similar to the outlines presented by Bondarko, Zagorujko, Kozevnikov, Molcanov, and Cistovic (1970), Pisoni and Sawusch (1975), and Sawusch and Nusbaum (1983). Perceptual constancy results from a sequence of auditory and phonetic coding operations. The auditory coding processes involved in speech perception reflect the operation of the mammalian auditory system, which humans share with other animals (see Kuhl, 1981). This auditory coding of speech provides the basic information on which phonetic and language-specific processes operate to transform an auditory input into a sequence of linguistic units. Different theories have given different weights to the auditory and phonetic coding of speech. Motor theory (Liberman, Cooper, Harris, MacNeilage, & Studdert-Kennedy, 1967; Liberman et al., 1967) and related proposals which specify a relationship between speech perception and articulation (e.g., Liberman, 1982; Liberman & Pisoni, 1977; Repp, 1982; Stevens & Halle, 1967) have emphasized the language-specific phonetic coding of speech.

At the opposite end of the spectrum of possible approaches to theories of speech perception, Schouten (1980) has concluded that there is no speech mode. This conclusion was based on a review of much of the data that was once cited as evidence for a specialized speech mode of processing. Schouten concluded that auditory processing, according to psychoacoustic principles, is sufficient to explain speech perception (see also Fant, 1967). Other investigators, while not necessarily making the same extreme proposal of Scouten, have emphasized the auditory coding of speech (e.g., Cutting, 1978; Pastore, 1981; Zwicker, Terhardt, & Paulus, 1979). Given these different approaches, it is critical to distinguish those aspects of speech perception that reflect general, auditory coding processes from those that reflect language-specific, phonetic processing operations.

III.A. Auditory Coding and Selective Adaptation

In order to investigate the auditory coding of speech, two requirements must be met. The first is that the stimuli used must either be speech (natural or synthetic) or speech-based (in which certain properties of speech are preserved in a nonspeech stimulus). The second requirement is that the experiments must contain some method of assessing whether the subject is using a "speech mode" of coding the stimulus, which relies on the phonetic and language-based knowledge of the listener, or an "auditory mode" of coding, which is not based on phonetic categories (but which may form the foundation for them).

One route to this second requirement is to use converging operations with speech stimuli to demonstrate a dissociation between the auditory and phonetic coding of speech. This approach has been used extensively in selective adaptation research. When the selective adaptation procedure was first applied to speech by Eimas and his co-workers, the adaptation effects were claimed to demonstrate the operation of phonetic feature detectors (Eimas, Cooper, & Corbit, 1973; Eimas & Corbit, 1973). However, further experimental work demonstrated that this interpretation was probably not correct. Bailey (1975) found that adaptation did not transfer

substantially from a /ba/-/da/ series to a /bi/-/di/ series. From the perspective of a phonetic adaptation explanation, the /d/ in /da/ should be equivalent to the /d/ in /di/. Nevertheless, Bailey's results demonstrate that this
is not the case at the level of coding affected by adaptation.

   Ades (1974) and Sawusch (1977b) have explored adaptation with CV
and VC syllables. To the extent that adaptation affects the phonetic coding of speech, we would expect that its effects should be independent of
the position of the critical phoneme within the syllable. In Ades's experiment, a /bae/-/dae/ series was used along with a mirror image /aeb/-/aed/
series. In the work of Sawusch, a /bae/-/dae/ CV series was used along
with an /∧b/-/∧d/ VC series. The second and third formant transitions of
the /∧d/ and /bae/ endpoints were identical. Both Ades and Sawusch
failed to find any evidence of a transfer of selective adaptation across
syllable positions. Again, based on a phonetic process explanation, the
transfer of adaptation across syllable positions would have been expected. On the basis of these and many other results, Ades (1976) proposed that the effects of selective adaptation with speech were entirely
auditory in nature and were governed by the degree of spectral overlap
between the adapter and the test syllable. This explanation of adaptation
effects is also consistent with the effects of isolated formant transitions on
speech series (Tartter & Eimas, 1975) and with various other effects of
nonspeech adapters (Diehl, 1976; Pisoni & Tash, 1975; Samuel & New-
port, 1979).

   In addition to the spectral overlap explanation (Ades, 1976), two additional explanations of selective adaptation phenomena need to be considered. One is a response-bias interpretation. The subjects in adaptation
experiments, having heard the adapting syllable many more times than
the other syllables, used the response category other than (or opposite to)
that of the adapter more frequently. In essence, the repeated presentation
of the adapter induces a bias toward using the other available response
categories more frequently. This is the type of explanation offered by
range–frequency theory (Parducci, 1965, 1975). The second alternative is
an adaptation-level theory approach (Helson, 1964) in which the repeated
presentation of the adapter causes a change in the listener's adaptation
level. This adaptation level represents a weighted average of the stimuli
used in the experiment, and its value determines the boundary between
response categories. After repeated presentation, the adapting syllable
would have the largest weight in the adaptation level and, consequently,
the category boundary in the test series would move toward the adapting
syllable.

   Both range–frequency theory and adaptation-level theory predict that
the effect of selective adaptation should be to move the category bound-

ary of a test series toward the category of the adapter (i.e., to produce contrast effects). However, these theories also predict that the same contrast effects should be found if one of the endpoint stimuli of the test series were simply presented more often than the other test stimuli. This prediction has been tested for stop consonants by Sawusch and Pisoni (1973), Sawusch, Pisoni, and Cutting (1974), and Simon and Studdert-Kennedy (1978). One of the general findings has been that at a ratio of extra occurrences of a stimulus which produces contrast effects for nonspeech stimuli or nonlinguistic dimensions of speech stimuli, no contrast effects were found for stops.

In a direct comparison of adaptation and anchoring, Sawusch and Mullennix (1985) used both adaptation and anchoring procedures with a /bae/-/dae/ speech series. The number of repetitions of the adapter and the number of extra occurrences of the anchoring syllable were identical. In adaptation, the adapting syllable was presented in a short sequence. This produced the usual contrast effect. In anchoring, the extra occurrences of the anchoring syllable were widely scattered throughout the test sequence. No contrast effects were found for the anchoring condition.

Nusbaum (1979) used an anchoring procedure with a /di/-/ti/-/si/ speech series. While /si/ anchoring produced a consistent contrast effect on the /ti/-/si/ category boundary, neither /di/ nor /ti/ anchoring produced any contrast effects. A similar set of stimuli had previously been used by Ainsworth (1977) in a selective adaptation study. Ainsworth found that both /di/ and /ti/ adapters produced consistent contrast effects, while no /si/ adaptation effect was found. For this speech series, at least, the combined results of Ainsworth (1977) and Nusbaum (1979) show that adaptation and anchoring produced complementary results. Thus the effects of adaptation and anchoring are clearly not the same. Since both range–frequency theory and adaptation-level theory predict that anchoring and adaptation should produce similar patterns of results, it would appear that neither of these theories offers an adequate account for selective adaptation results.

Diehl (1981) has offered a modified version of adaptation-level theory that treats auditory and phonetic coding as acting together to determine the adaptation level. In support of this claim, Diehl, Elman, and McCusker (1978) and Diehl, Lang, and Parker (1980) have presented data showing that a single presentation of a good exemplar of a phonetic category is sufficient to produce contrast effects. Diehl and his colleagues presented stimuli in pairs consisting of a good exemplar and an ambiguous test item (a paired-comparison procedure). Subjects consistently identified the ambiguous item as belonging to the category opposite that of the exemplar with which it was paired, regardless of whether the order of presentation was exemplar–ambiguous or ambiguous–exemplar. Diehl (1981) cites this data to argue against a feature-detector fatigue model of adaptation and for a unified adaptation-level account.

The data presented here comparing adaptation and anchoring, especially those of Ainsworth (1977) and Nusbaum (1979), can be used to argue against the unified adaptation-level account. An alternative approach would be to demonstrate directly that selective adaptation and paired-comparison procedures do not always produce the same results. In particular, it is possible that while selective adaptation affects the auditory coding of speech, the paired-comparison procedure affects a later, phonetic coding process.

A rigorous test of this proposal requires an adapting syllable that shares its acoustic structure (and hence its auditory processing) with one end of a test series while sharing its phonetic identity with the opposite end of the test series. A number of experiments have employed this approach. Sawusch and Jusczyk (1981) used stimuli similar to those shown in Figure 2.2. Their test series was a /ba/-/pa/ series varying in voice-onset time (VOT). The middle panel of Figure 2.2 shows a /spa/ syllable. This syllable shares, with the /pa/ end of the test series, the presence of the phoneme /p/.[1] The acoustic structure of /spa/, however, is such that it is composed of /s/, followed by silence, followed by a 10-ms VOT /ba/— identical to one of the stimuli from the /ba/ end of the test series. When used as adapting syllables, /spa/ and /ba/ produced identical results, even though subjects reported that the /spa/ syllable contained the phoneme /p/.

The results of a second experiment reported by Sawusch and Jusczyk shed further light on the nature of selective adaptation with speech. In this experiment, subjects were presented with pairs of stimuli in a manner analogous to that used by Diehl et al. (1978, 1980). One of the stimuli in each pair was an ambiguous syllable drawn from near the /ba/-/pa/ category boundary. The other stimulus was a good phonetic exemplar, such as /ba/, /pa/, or /spa/. The subjects identified both of the syllables in each pair. Both the /ba/ and /pa/ exemplars produced phonetic contrast. The ambiguous test syllable was identified with the category opposite the good exemplar with which it was paired, while the /spa/ syllable produced results that were virtually identical to those of /pa/. These results represent a phonetic contrast in that the influence of the exemplars followed

---

[1] While the syllables /spa/ and /pa/ both share the phoneme /p/, they are by no means identical. The syllable initial /p/ of /pa/ is aspirated and voiceless. The /p/ of /spa/, on the other hand, is not aspirated and is voiced (see Davidsen-Nielsen, 1974; Klatt, 1975). These variations are part of the phonological structure of English.

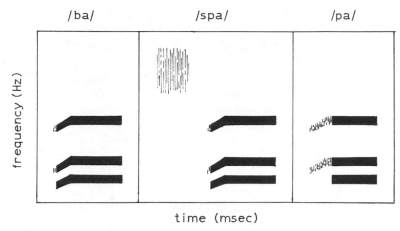

Figure 2.2   Schematic spectrograms of the syllables /ba/, /spa/, and /pa/.

their perceived phonetic identity. At the same time, the opposite results produced by /spa/ in the adaptation and paired-comparison procedures clearly implicate two different perceptual processes in the coding of speech. Selective adaptation seems to tap the auditory coding of speech, while the paired-comparison procedure taps the phonetic coding of speech.

Results essentially similar to these have been reported by Sawusch and Nusbaum (1983) for a place-of-articulation series varying from /da/ to /ga/. In this case, a /ska/ adaptor was constructed from a synthetic /s/ plus a stimulus identified by subjects as /da/. Mann and Repp (1981) had previously demonstrated a trading relation wherein the alveolar (/d/ and /t/) versus velar (/g/ and /k/) category boundary for stops was shown to be dependent on the presence or absence of a preceding /s/. Sawusch and Nusbaum (1983) replicated the Mann and Repp result and then chose, as an adapting stimulus, a syllable that was identified by subjects as /da/ (alveolar) in isolation but as /ka/ (velar) in the environment /sCV/. Their pattern of results mirrored those of Sawusch and Jusczyk (1981). For adaptation, /ska/ and /da/ produced identical results, while the /ga/ adaptor produced an opposite effect. Thus adaptation again followed the spectral overlap between adapter and test series. In a paired-comparison procedure, however, the effects of /ska/ followed its perceived phonetic category.

Garrison and Sawusch (1985) have also found this general pattern of results for /pa/-/ka/ place-of-articulation series. Their test series was constructed by varying the frequency locus of the initial release burst. Two additional stimuli were constructed using the burst from the /ka/ endpoint stimulus. This burst was synthesized with the vowels /i/ and /u/, producing syllables that were identified by subjects as /pi/ and /tu/, respectively (see Liberman et al., 1952; see also Figure 2.1). The syllables /pi/, /ka/, and /tu/ all contained identical spectral information (over the first 60 ms of the syllable) and produced identical adaptation effects. In the paired-comparison procedure, however, /pi/ and /pa/ produced identical effects, while /ka/ produced an opposite effect and /tu/ produced a null effect. Thus the pattern of results that has been found across all three of these studies is that selective adaptation effects follow the spectral overlap (and auditory coding) of the adapter with the test series, while results with the paired-comparison procedure consistently follow the perceived phonetic status of the stimuli.

Using a slightly different approach, Roberts and Summerfield (1981) tested the same hypothesis with audio-visual adaptation. They employed a procedure developed by McGurk and MacDonald (1976), who had demonstrated that the visual presentation of a face producing one syllable could modify subjects' perception of a second, auditory syllable presented in synchrony with the visual syllable. Roberts and Summerfield synchronized the audio presentation of a /bɛ/ syllable with the video presentation of an individual producing a /gɛ/ syllable. The resulting phonetic percept was usually /dɛ/ or /δɛ/. Using this audio-visual stimulus as an adapter, Roberts and Summerfield found effects virtually identical to those of a /bɛ/ adapter on a /bɛ/-/dɛ/ test series. Thus the adaptation effects again followed the spectral similarity between the adapter and test series and were opposite the phonetic overlap between adapter and test series.

The one set of experimental data that could be used to argue against an auditory-level explanation of selective adaptation effects is that of Elman (1979). Elman used a signal detection analysis on subjects' ratings of stimuli both before and after selective adaptation. Elman found that the effects of selective adaptation could be accounted for in terms of a criterion shift on the part of subjects and concluded that adaptation reflected cognitive (as opposed to sensory) processes. While Elman did not specify the nature of the representation involved in adaptation, his interpretation of adaptation as being a "higher-level" effect is clearly opposite the early, auditory level explanation offered here.

There are, however, problems with Elman's conclusion that adaptation results reflect a change in cognitive processes (response bias). One is that in a system with multiple levels of processing, it is impossible to know ahead of time which of these processes contribute to the signal detection parameter of sensitivity and which contribute to the criterion. Signal detection is, in essence, a single-stage model. Consequently, without converging evidence it is impossible to identify signal detection parameters of sensitivity and criteria with particular levels or stages of processing.

A second problem with Elman's interpretation is that in analyzing the adaptation data, the six-point rating scale that subjects used for responding was collapsed into two categories. The two-category data were then analyzed only for the presence of a criterion shift. No attempt was made to analyze the data for systematic changes in sensitivity, which may have been present in the rating data. Furthermore, the effect of adaptation could have been to change the variance of underlying distributions. This effect would have shown up in the rating data as a change in the slope of the receiver operating characteristic functions (on normal–normal coordinates) from the preadaptation to the postadaptation rating data. Elman (1979) did not report such an analysis. Consequently, his data cannot be adequately evaluated with regard to where, in a multilevel (multicode) perceptual system, adaptation effects are occurring. Instead, the nearly identical types of results found by Sawusch and Jusczyk (1981), Sawusch and Nusbaum (1983), Garrison and Sawusch (1985), and Roberts and Summerfield (1981), using different stimuli and approaches, seem to provide compelling evidence that selective adaptation affects only the auditory coding of speech.

III.B. Auditory Pattern Processes

If we accept the contention that selective adaptation with speech has its effects at an auditory level of processing, we can then use the selective adaptation procedure to explore the nature of the auditory coding of speech. While this literature has become too extensive to review in its entirety here (see Ades, 1976, for a partial review or Cooper, 1979), some of these experiments do have particular relevance to the question of auditory coding processes. Sawusch (1977a) employed a /bae/-/dae/ test series in which the phonetic distinction was cued by the direction and extent of the second and third formant transitions. Among the adapters were /bae/ and /dae/ syllables in which all of the formants had been scaled upward in frequency. This shift was designed to eliminate the spectral overlap between the acoustic representation of the adapters and that of the test series. The scaling factor used was one and one-half critical bandwidths. The critical band has previously been described as a filter mechanism that represents the initial transformation of sound into a spectrogram-like auditory code (see Patterson, 1974; Scharf, 1970; Searle, Jacobson, & Rayment, 1979).

The rescaled /bae/ and /dae/ syllables produced significant adaptation effects on the test series, indicating that precise spectral overlap is not required for adaptation to be found. In a second experiment, the interaural transfer of adaptation effects was assessed. The endpoints of the test series produced a transfer of roughly 50% of their monaural effectiveness as adapters. That is, if the adapter was presented to the right ear and the test syllables to the left ear, the size of the resulting adaptation effect was about one-half the size found when adapter and test series were both presented to the same ear. However, the rescaled /bae/ and /dae/ adapters produced a 100% interaural transfer.

These different adaptation results were interpreted by Sawusch (1977a) as reflecting different processing mechanisms. One of the two proposed mechanisms was a spectrally specific process similar to that described by Ades (1976) and Bailey (1975). Sawusch (1977a) characterized this analysis as being mediated by auditory feature detectors (see the auditory work of Whitfield & Evans, 1965, and the visual work of Hubel & Wiesel, 1965, 1968). In support of this interpretation, Sawusch (1976, 1977a) reports data showing that when the adapter and test series shared common spectral components, adaptation produced changes both at the category boundary and within the phonetic category of the adapter. This is precisely the result that a feature detector explanation of selective adaptation would suggest. Fatiguing a detector by repeated presentation of an adapter should lower the detector's sensitivity over its entire range. This effect would appear in a phonetic categorization task as a lowered rating within the adapted category and as a shift in the phonetic category boundary toward the adapted category. These are precisely the results reported by Sawusch (1976, 1977a).

The second mechanism proposed by Sawusch was an integrative pattern processing mechanism reflecting the common formant transition trajectories of the adapting and test syllables. The adaptation effects found with the rescaled stimuli were confined to the category boundary, providing further evidence for adaptation effects arising at two different processing stages. Ganong (1975) has also reported evidence of adaptation that does not depend on a spectral overlap between the adapter and the test series. In this study, an /sae/ adapter was found to produce changes in the identification of a /bae/-/dae/ test series similar to that produced by a /dae/ adapter. The /sae/ contained friction (noise excitation) that was above 3000 Hz in frequency. None of the test stimuli contained a friction component or formant transition above 3000 Hz. However, the /dae/ end of the test series was cued by falling second and third formant transitions at syllable onset. The /dae/ end of the series was cued by a change in the spectrum over time: The locus of the peaks in the spectrum moved from higher to lower frequencies over the initial part of the syllable. The change from /s/ to /ae/ in /sae/ can be characterized in a similar fashion—a movement of the peaks in the spectrum from higher to lower frequencies. Thus, while the initial consonants in /sae/ and /dae/ did not contain the same frequency components, both consonants could be characterized as containing the same pattern of frequency change over time.

Combining the work of Roberts and Summerfield (1981) and Sawusch (Sawusch & Jusczyk, 1981; Garrison & Sawusch, 1985; Sawusch & Nusbaum, 1983) with the results that we have just considered suggests a picture of the auditory coding of speech that involves two distinct types of auditory coding processes. One process is spectrally specific and can be described in terms of feature detectors. The other, however, seems to respond to patterns of change in the spectrum and does not require precise spectral overlap. In addition, because the effects of this pattern-based adaptation are confined to the category boundary, the modeling of auditory pattern coding in terms of feature detectors would seem to be inappropriate.

Several studies on categorical perception have produced results that can be interpreted as reflecting the auditory coding of patterns. Although categorical perception was once claimed as support for a specialized speech processor, later studies have shown that certain nonspeech stimuli are also perceived categorically (see Pastore, Ahroon, Baffuto, Friedman, Puleo, & Fink, 1977).[2] In particular, two studies have used stimuli that preserve some of the properties of the speech dimension of VOT (Miller, Wier, Pastore, Kelly, & Dooling, 1976; Pisoni, 1977). The stimuli of Miller et al. (1976) were noise–buzz combinations that varied in noise-lead time. This is analogous to the lead time of the initial burst and aspiration, relative to voicing, in stop-vowel syllables. In the work of Pisoni (1977), two tones were used in which the higher frequency component could start after, synchronous with, or before the lower frequency component. This arrangement emulates the conditions of prevoiced stops, in which a low-frequency voice bar precedes the rest of the syllable; voiced stops, with their synchronous onsets of formants; and voiceless stops, in which the higher formants, carrying the burst and aspiration, lead the onset of the first formant. The critical factor here is that the stimuli of both Miller et al. and Pisoni preserve the temporal onset pattern present in the voicing distinction in stops.

Categorical perception was found with both of these sets of stimuli. In

---

[2] The term "categorical perception" refers to a situation in which an individual can only discriminate between stimuli to the extent that he or she labels them differentially (see Liberman, Harris, Hoffman, & Griffith, 1957; Pisoni, 1973).

the experiment reported by Pisoni (1977), for example, subjects were first trained to consistently label the endpoints of the series. The subjects were then given both identification and ABX discrimination trials. Discrimination performance was found to reach a peak across the labeling category boundary and was at near-chance levels within the categories. Consequently, it appears that the categorical perception of voiced and voiceless stops has as its basis an auditory coding process that registers whether events are synchronous or asynchronous. This auditory coding of the stimulus described by Miller et al. (1976) and Pisoni (1977) may represent a processing operation similar to the auditory pattern processes that have been implicated in selective adaptation studies.

Sawusch and Nochajski (1982) provide yet another line of evidence concerning auditory pattern coding. They adapted their methodology from studies of visual perception. The object superiority work of Weisstein and her colleagues (Weisstein & Harris, 1974; Wong & Weisstein, 1982) and the configurational superiority effects demonstrated by Pomerantz, Sager, and Stoever (1977) have provided evidence that a visual object or configuration is often identified faster and/or more accurately than its component parts. Sawusch and Nochajski (1982) found similar effects in the perception of tone glides. That is, a combination of tone glides was identified faster than the individual tone glide components.

The tone glide stimuli used by Sawusch and Nochajski were designed to emulate either the isolated second-formant transitions or the combined second- and third-formant transitions of the speech syllables /ba/, /wa/, /ga/, and /ja/. Figure 2.3 shows schematic spectrograms of these syllables. Previous work with synthetic speech has shown that the duration of formant transitions is a sufficient cue for the perception of the stop–semivowel manner distinction (Liberman, Delattre, Gerstman, & Cooper, 1956). In particular, with all other aspects held constant, the duration of the second-formant transition is a sufficient cue to manner (Schwab, Sawusch, & Nusbam, 1981). The place-of-articulation distinction between labials (/b/ and /w/) and palatal/velars (/g/ and /j/) can be cued by the direction of the second formant transition (Cooper et al., 1952).

In the work of Sawusch and Nochajski (1982), these dimensions of duration and direction of a formant transition were used to generate the two sets of tone glides shown in Figure 2.4. The top set of stimuli consisted of single tone glides that emulated the second formant transitions of the speech syllables in Figure 2.3. The bottom set of stimuli was formed from the top set by the addition of a high-frequency, redundant tone glide that always rose in frequency and was of the same duration as the lower-frequency component. This higher-frequency component emulates the third-formant transitions of the speech syllables shown in Figure 2.3.

Synthetic Syllables

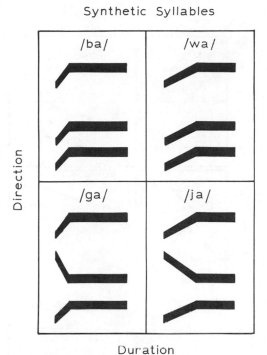

Figure 2.3   Schematic spectrograms of the syllables /ba/, /ga/, /wa/, and /ja/.

Subjects were asked to categorize the stimuli on either the dimension of duration (short versus long) or the direction of pitch change (rising versus falling) in a reaction-time task similar to that used by Garner (1974) to assess integral–separable dimensions.

One of the main findings of Sawusch and Nochajski (1982) was that subjects were able to categorize the more complex stimuli (Figure 2.4, bottom) faster than the simpler, single tone glide stimuli (Figure 2.4, top). On the basis of this and other aspects of their results, Sawusch and Nochajski concluded that auditory pattern processes were operating in the perception of these tone glides. Instead of extracting the individual tone glides, the auditory coding processes treated these stimuli as unitary events representing a pattern of change over time. Since the stimuli in this study, as well as in the studies by Miller et al. (1976) and Pisoni (1977), were based on speech stimuli and mimicked part of the spectral/temporal structure of speech, it seems reasonable to infer that the auditory coding processes uncovered by these studies are also involved in the auditory coding of speech. Consequently, the combination of adaptation, categori-

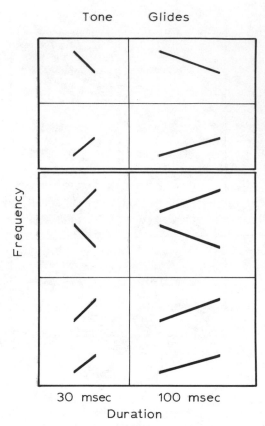

Tone   Glides

Frequency

Duration

30 msec   100 msec

Figure 2.4   Schematic spectrograms of single tone glides (top) and two tone glides (bottom) in which a second, higher frequency glide has been added to the single tone glides.

cal perception, and reaction-time results presented here represents convergent evidence that pattern-like auditory coding processes are involved in the perception of speech. These processes represent part of the solution to the problem posed by the lack of simple invariance in the speech signal. However, as the next section on phonetic coding attempts to show, the auditory coding of speech is only part of a complete solution to the joint problems of invariance and segmentation.

III.C. Phonetic Coding

A number of researchers have made a case for the specialized, phonetic coding of speech (Liberman, 1982; Liberman et al., 1967; Liberman &

Pisoni, 1977; Repp, 1982). Furthermore, a number of experimental studies have demonstrated a distinct, phonetic mode of processing. Repp (1982) has reviewed many of these studies and argues that they represent evidence for a separate, modular, specialized language processor. However, the adaptation data described earlier, which demonstrate the distinct involvement of auditory coding processes in speech perception, place some limits on this concept. Rather than repeat all of the data supporting phonetic processing, we now describe a few critical studies that contrast the auditory and phonetic processing of speech. More complete reviews can be found in Jusczyk (in press b) and Repp (1982).

In order to claim that some aspect of speech perception represents distinct phonetic (language) processing, it must be demonstrated that auditory processing of the same physical stimuli yields different results. This is impossible with natural speech or the usual synthetic speech stimuli, since, as Fant (1973) notes, processing speech into phonetic categories seems to be obligatory. It is possible, however, to generate highly schematized stimuli that can be identified by either their phonetic label or their auditory characteristics. Replacing the formant structure of voiced speech with sinewaves that track the formant center frequencies yields a sinewave analog of a speech stimulus. Since Cutting (1974) first introduced these stimuli, additional work has shown that these sinewave analogs yield results similar to their formant-based counterparts when subjects are instructed to use phonetic categories (Bailey, Dorman, & Summerfield, 1977; Best, Morrongiello, & Robson, 1981). Further, entire sentences can be synthesized in this fashion and still retain their meaning (Remez, Rubin, Pisoni, & Carrell, 1981). Thus this method seems to preserve the essential phonetic information in the stimulus. However, without speech listening instructions, isolated syllables generated in this fashion are usually reported by subjects as chirps, whistles, quacks, and assorted other (nonspeech) acoustic events (see Best et al., 1981; Remez et al., 1981; Schwab, 1982). Consequently, this type of stimulus seems to be ideally suited for comparing phonetic and auditory processing.

Sinewave stimuli were used by Schwab (1982) in studying the auditory and phonetic processing of place-of-articulation information for stops in syllable-initial and syllable-final positions. Among the stimuli in her experiments were sinewave analogs of various formant combinations derived from the speech syllables /bU/, /dU/, /Ub/, and /Ud/. When subjects listened to the sinewave equivalent of an isolated second formant (T2), the group with auditory processing instructions generally yielded higher performance. However, once the first formant sinewave equivalent (T1) was added to the stimuli, subjects given phonetic labels exhibited superior performance.

In a second experiment, Schwab found that the influence of the T1 component was due to the stop-like transition. If this transition was eliminated and a flat T1 component was used, the overall difference between the auditory and phonetic label groups disappeared. Further results of her experiments showed that initial transitions (CV) of all types were badly identified by the auditory label groups relative to final transitions (VC). This effect, which Schwab interpreted as representing backward masking in auditory processing, was not found for the phonetic instructions groups, who labeled CV and VC stimuli equally accurately. Finally, a signal detection analysis showed that all of the effects described here were the result of systematic sensitivity differences and that phonetic labeling does not represent a simple criterion shift relative to auditory labeling.

Another set of data demonstrating differences between auditory and phonetic labeling groups is that of Best et al. (1981). The stimuli in this study were sinewave equivalents of a synthetic speech continuum from /se/ ("say") to /ste/ ("stay"), which varied the silent interval between the noise and the sinewave syllable. Two series, varying in the onset frequency of the T1 sinewave component, were generated. Phonetic labeling groups produced two slightly different labeling functions, indicative of what Repp (1982) has called a "phonetic trading relation." That is, the phonetic category boundary between /se/ and /ste/ occurred at a shorter silence duration for the low T1 onset frequency series than for the high T1 series. No such trading relation was found for the auditory labeling subjects where some subjects consistently categorized according to silence duration while others used the T1 onset frequency.

The results of Schwab (1982) and Best et al. (1981) show consistent differences between the auditory and phonetic processing of identical stimuli (see also Bailey et al., 1977; Summerfield, 1982). These results suggest that the role of phonetic processing in speech is to integrate diverse acoustic cues into a unitary event. In the stimuli of Schwab, this integration resolves the conflict among sinewave transitions with different trajectories (some rising, some falling). Further, phonetic coding is immune to typical auditory processing effects such as backward masking. In the data of Best et al., the phonetic coding integrates diverse acoustic cues (e.g., silence, T1 onset frequency) that occur over a substantial temporal interval (see Repp, 1982).

Repp (1982) has summarized numerous other examples of trading relations and context effects in speech perception. Many of these were interpreted as resulting from a phonetic mode of processing. However, unlike the studies cited earlier, many of these investigations did not and could not explore a possible auditory basis, since synthetic speech or natural speech (rather than sinewave analogs) were used as stimuli.

Repp (1982) has argued that the long integration period (200–300 ms) and diverse nature of the acoustic cues present make it unlikely that auditory processes underlie these results. However, data reported by Carrell, Pisoni, and Gans (1980) demonstrate that speechlike context effects can be found for the auditory processing of sinewave analogs of speech, even when the information is distributed over 200–300 ms of the stimulus. Carrell et al. explored a context effect that had previously been reported by Miller and Liberman (1979), who found that the duration of a syllable influenced the locus of the stop-semivowel boundary in a /b/-/w/ series. For longer syllable durations, the category boundary moved to longer transition durations. Miller and Liberman claimed that this effect reflected a language-specific normalization process in which the listener adjusted his or her phonetic boundary to the speaker's rate of speech. Carrell et al. replicated these results. In addition, they constructed sinewave analogs of the stop-semivowel speech series. Subjects given training in auditory labeling with these nonspeech stimuli showed the same shift in their category boundary as a function of stimulus duration as that found for phonetic labels with synthetic speech. Thus the context effect described by Miller and Liberman (1979) would seem to have an auditory coding basis. Further work in the pattern established by Best et al. (1981), Carrell et al. (1980), and Schwab (1982), which compares auditory and phonetic processing of the same stimuli, seems to be needed to sort out the relative contributions of auditory and phonetic coding processes in speech perception.

IV. A PROCESS MODEL

At this point, with these data on the auditory and phonetic coding of speech as a background, we now outline a process model of speech perception. Alternative proposals to this model will then be considered. Finally, we describe the results of a computer simulation of the process model. The model is shown in outline form in Figure 2.5. The input to this model is the acoustic waveform at the ear. The output from the model is a string of phonemes which could be used for word recognition. Between the input and output, a cascaded succession of processing stages analyze the information in the speech waveform.

The first stage of analysis, labeled Spectral Transformation in Figure 2.5, involves a transformation of the acoustic waveform into its compo-

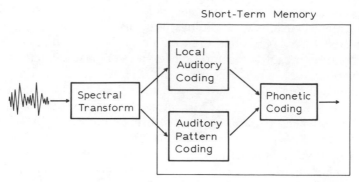

Figure 2.5 Outline of a process model for speech perception.

nent frequencies and their intensities over time. This coding would be very similar to that produced by a sound spectrograph, with the exception that the frequency scale mirrors the critical band data found in audition (see Patterson, 1974; Scharf, 1970). Critical band filter banks have been used previously in speech perception models proposed by Searle et al. (1979; Searle, Jacobson, & Kimberly, 1980) and Zwicker et al. (1979).

The second stage of analysis, local auditory analysis, is similar to the auditory stage proposed by Bondarko et al. (1970). At this stage, a number of spectral and temporal "features" are extracted from the output of the previous stage. Examples of such information include: (1) the presence or absence of noise in the spectrum; (2) the bandwidth of noise; (3) the duration and intensity of noise; (4) the presence and frequency of the fundamental; and (5) the presence and nature of rapid spectral changes. The extraction of these cues at the local auditory level is done in a spectrally specific manner (hence the term local). This is not to say that these detectors track formants. Rather, they respond to a sequence of spectral cross-sections with peaks in particular frequency regions (see Klatt, 1980, or Miller, 1984). Thus a particular detector will be tuned to a specific frequency (or spectral) region. The detector will respond only if a particular cue is present in that region. This can account for some of the dichotic masking results that have been found for CV syllables. When the vowels of the target syllable and the masking syllable are identical, more masking is found than when the vowels are not identical.

For the case of dichotic masking using CV syllables, Pisoni (1975b; Pisoni & McNabb, 1974) used masking syllables with either [a], [ae], or [ε] vowels. The target syllable always had the [a] vowel. As the masker vowel was changed from [a] to [ae] to [ε], the frequency separation between the formants of the target and the masker increased. As this separation increased, the amount of masking on the CV target decreased. These results, together with the spectral specificity that has been found in many selective adaptation studies (see Ades, 1976; Sawusch, 1977a), indicate the operation of a frequency-sensitive stage of processing in speech perception.

The third stage, auditory pattern coding, operates to extract auditory patterns directly from the spectral representation. The auditory property detectors proposed by Stevens (1975), the sequences of spectral templates described by Lahiri et al. (1984), and the cue of synchronous versus asynchronous onsets between formants or bursts and formants (Miller et al., 1976; Pisoni, 1977) are examples of the kinds of mechanisms that may be involved at this level. It should be noted, however, that the abstract patterns extracted here are not completely invariant; they still depend on context and the extraction of other information to determine invariant phonemes. This analysis is distinguished from other processes in that it is driven binaurally rather than monaurally. The adaptation data of Sawusch (1977a) showing 100% interaural transfer of adaptation for an adapter and test series which share a common formant pattern but do not overlap spectrally supports this description. Although this coding process is auditory, it also appears to show a right ear advantage (see Cutting, 1974). The outline in Figure 2.5 shows the local auditory coding and auditory pattern coding processes operating in parallel, although there are no current data that force this choice.

The last stage, phonetic coding, takes the outputs of the various auditory coding processes and integrates them to form phonemes. In certain respects, the syllable is the unit of analysis here since, as noted by Studdert-Kennedy (1976), the acoustic information necessary to obtain an invariant feature matrix is distributed over the entire syllable. One possible conception of the operations that occur at this stage is in terms of a set of phonetic prototypes. The knowledge of the listener about particular articulatory constraints in speech production may enter into these prototypes, as suggested by Liberman (1982; Liberman et al., 1967; Liberman and Pisoni, 1977) and Repp (1982).

One last point to note about the model shown in Figure 2.5 concerns the role of memory in this system. All of stages 2 thru 4 are connected to, and in certain respects considered a part of, short-term memory. The interaction between the processing system and memory is similar to that proposed by Craik (Craik & Lockhart, 1972) and Shiffrin (1975). As one stage of processing produces some form of output, it is maintained in short-term memory for a certain period of time. How long it is maintained depends on the demands on memory for storing other information. While in short-term memory, this information is available for further processing or, if appropriate, for generating a response (see the blackboard in Hearsay, Reddy, 1980). Thus memory is a limiting factor in the performance of this model. Accordingly, when the demands on short-term memory due to a specific task are high (such as in certain discrimination or masking tasks), performance is expected to decrease in a systematic fashion (see Pisoni, 1973, 1975a).

IV.A. Alternative Theories

The alternatives to this outline of a process model can be broadly classed into two groups: auditory theories and motor theories. Auditory theories have been outlined by Cutting (1978), Fant (1967), and Schouten (1980). These proposals were framed with attention to the auditory coding of speech and omit a phonetic mode of processing. As stated previously, Schouten argues against the need for a phonetic mode. The data from sinewave studies involving both auditory and phonetic labeling provide compelling evidence against this position and for a specialized phonetic mode. In contrast, the motor theory proposals take the exact opposite point of view. As exemplified in the recent discussion by Repp (1982), the articulation-based theories play down or deny the involvement of auditory coding processes, especially abstract, patternlike auditory coding processes, in speech perception. However, the auditory coding data summarized earlier, together with the ability of both infants (see Jusczyk, in press-a) and animals (Kuhl, 1981; Kuhl & Miller, 1978; Kuhl & Padden, 1983) to discriminate speech categories in a manner similar to human adults, lead to the conclusion that complex auditory coding processes are intimately involved in speech processing.

At this point, three other process models should be mentioned. In outline, the models of Searle et al. (1979) and Zwicker et al. (1979) are similar to that presented here. However, the implementation details differ, a result, no doubt, of the differential emphasis on background data used to develop the models. The present model draws substantially on the speech perception literature, while that of Zwicker et al., for example, is more psychoacoustically oriented.

The third process model is the Scriber system proposed by Klatt (1980). In this system, the input spectral representation is similar to that described earlier and to the input used by Searle et al. (1979) and Zwicker et al. (1979). Following this spectral structuring, a phonetic decoding network is used to parse the speech waveform. The nodes in this network are static spectral configurations or templates similar to those of Blumstein and Stevens (1980). The network consists of a linked assembly of these spectra which describes sequences that are likely to be found in speech (a finite-state transition network). The parsing process is context-sensitive (unlike that of Blumstein & Stevens, 1980, which is invariant) so that different paths through the network may be followed in recognizing the syllables /di/ and /du/. Thus the phonetic representation is similar to the context-sensitive allophones proposed by Wickelgren (1969). The output of the Scriber system is a phonetic transcription of the speech waveform. Overall, Scriber is similar to the system outlined here.

IV.B. Computer Simulation

The process model outlined in Figure 2.5 has been implemented as a computer simulation of speech perception. This simulation was originally formulated to account for stop consonant place perception and the selective adaptation data for place-of-articulation (see Sawusch, 1977c). In its present version, spectral transformation is accomplished via a discrete Fourier transform using approximately 1/3-octave bandwidths which operate at 5-ms intervals. This type of coding, which resembles the critical band data of auditory masking studies (see Patterson, 1974) has been used previously by Searle et al. (1979). Local auditory coding is implemented as a set of feature detectors which respond to the various parameters listed earlier (e.g., rapid spectral changes). Because these feature detectors are spectrally and temporally specific, they operate only over "local" regions of the spectral representation. The auditory pattern coding operates in parallel with the local auditory coding. The mechanisms employed here are prototypes that code general changes in the shape of the spectrum and temporal relations among events in the spectrum. Thus they are not frequency specific. These two auditory levels are both affected by selective adaptation. The local auditory feature detectors produce a lower, "fatigued" output following adaption, while the auditory pattern prototypes are retuned, narrowing their range around that of the adapting stimulus (see Samuel, 1982; Sawusch, 1977a; Simon & Studdert-Kennedy, 1978, for a further description of fatigue and retuning).

The major changes in this simulation since the original proposal for this model (Sawusch, 1977c) have been at the phonetic coding level. The analysis here is in terms of context-sensitive allophones (see Wickelgren, 1969). While these allophones might be represented in a multidimensional prototype space, the implementation in the simulation is in terms of procedural knowledge (see Winograd, 1975). Each of these phonetic procedures attempts to verify the presence of its particular allophones by matching itself against the auditory information provided by both the local and pattern coding processes. In addition, each procedure contains vowel-sensitive specifications of the auditory information that should be

present for its particular phoneme. The output of the phonetic coding
level is a string of phonemes suitable for entry into a word recognition
process (see, e.g., Cole & Jakimik, 1980; Foss, Harwood, & Blank, 1980;
Marslen-Wilson, 1976).

To illustrate the operation of the model, we examine its coding of the
two-formant stops shown in Figure 2.6 and compare the labeling performance of the model with the human labeling data reported by Sawusch
(1980) for these same stimuli. As an aid to visualizing the operation of the
model, Figure 2.7 contains the onset spectra (at release) for the stimuli
whose spectrograms are shown in Figure 2.6. Figure 2.8 contains the
human labeling data for the synthetic two-formant series. Panel (a) of
Figures 2.6 and 2.7 corresponds to stimulus 1 in the top half of Figure 2.8.
Panel (c) of Figures 2.6 and 2.7 corresponds to stimulus 7, and panel (e)
corresponds to stimulus 13 in Figure 2.8 (top half).

In the case of the voiced two-formant stop shown in panel (a) of Figure
2.6, the local auditory coding of this syllable would register two closely

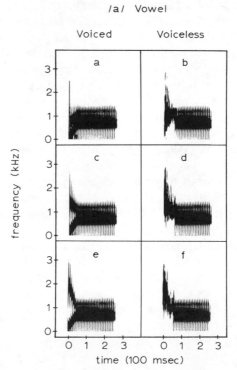

Figure 2.6 Spectrograms of two-formant synthetic speech stimuli: voiced stop-vowel syllables (left) and their voiceless counterparts (right).

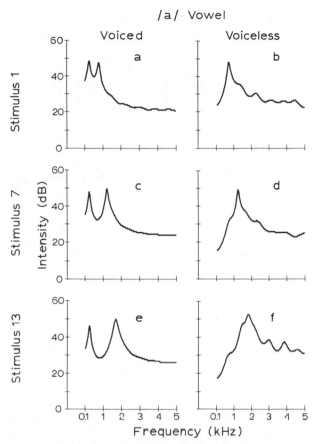

Figure 2.7 Spectral sections of two-formant synthetic stop-vowel syllables: voiced stimuli (left) and voiceless stimuli (right). The spectral sections are centered on the stop release.

spaced peaks in the spectrum whose frequency locus rises over time (see also panel (a) of Figure 2.7). The syllable in panel (c) would register as a convergence in the peaks of the spectrum over time as the higher-frequency peak moves downward to lower frequencies. The panel (e) syllable would also register as a convergence in the spectral peaks but would be coded by a different feature detector than that which responds to the syllable in panel (c). This difference reflects the different frequency loci of the spectral peaks at syllable onset (compare panels (c) and (e) in Figures 2.6 and 2.7).

The auditory pattern coding of the syllable in panel (a) is similar to its local auditory coding, revealing an overall increase in the frequency locus

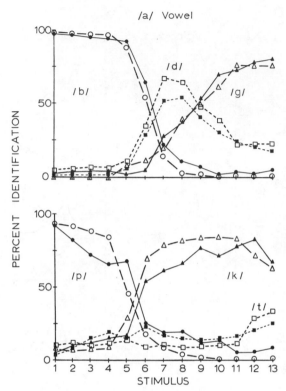

Figure 2.8 Subject identification data and predictions of the computer simulation for two-formant synthetic stop-vowel syllables. Subject data (filled points) and simulation predictions (open points) for voiced stops are shown in the top panel, while the bottom panel shows data (filled points) and predictions (open points) for voiceless stops.

of the spectral peaks over the initial part of the syllable. For the syllable in panel (c), the overall frequency locus of the spectral peaks is constant as the peaks converge. The panel (e) syllable is coded as an overall decrease in frequency and as a change in the spectrum from a large, relatively isolated peak (see panel (e), Figure 2.7) to the more closely spaced spectral peaks of the vowel. Thus the auditory coding processes provide a distinctive coding of these stimuli. Presumably, the discrimination of these types of stimuli by infants (Walley, 1979) and monkeys (Kuhl & Padden, 1983) is based on this same type of coding.

The mapping of this auditory coding onto phonetic categories is accomplished by the phonetic coding procedures. The procedure for /b/ includes the specification of a spectrum whose frequency loci and overall frequency are rising over time in syllable initial position and falling over time in final position. This procedure approximates the auditory coding of the syllable in panel (a), while the other phonetic procedures produce only a minimal match (see the identification data for stimulus 1, Figure 2.8).

The procedure for /d/ includes the specification of a spectrum dominated by high frequencies at stop release and a decrease in the locus of the peaks in the spectrum over time. (Again, this is the syllable intial pattern. The reverse is true for syllable-final /d/.) This pattern of information is not present to a great extent in any of the voiced stops of Figure 2.6. However, the best match to the syllable in panel (c) is provided by the /d/ procedure because of the minimal match by the /b/ procedure (described previously) and the relatively poor match provided by /g/. The /d/ procedure also provides a fair match to the syllable in panel (e). However, the best match is provided by the /g/ procedure, to be described next.

The /g/ procedure specifies a spreading of the peaks in the spectrum over time in which the initial spectrum (at release) is dominated by a single large peak which changes over time into the pattern characteristic of the vowel (see Blumstein & Stevens, 1980; Kewley-Port, 1983; Stevens, 1975). For a syllable-final /g/, this specification is reversed. This procedure provides the best match to the syllable in panel (e), which has a large, well-defined spectral peak at onset that gradually merges into the following vowel (see panel (e) of Figures 2.6 and 2.7). As is apparent in the top half of Figure 2.8, there is substantial agreement between the labeling performance of the simulation and the human subject data of Sawusch (1980) for the entire synthetic speech series.[3]

An equivalent analysis can be made for the voiceless stops shown on the right-hand side of Figures 2.6 and 2.7. In overview, the simulation codes the syllable in panel (b) of Figure 2.6 in much the same way as that of panel (a): as a sequence of spectral peaks that rise in their frequency locus over time. This result leads to a classification by the phonetic procedures of this syllable as /p/ (see stimulus 1, bottom half of Figure 2.8). The syllables in panels (d) and (f) are coded as falling in frequency over time and as being dominated by a single middle-frequency peak that changes into the peaks typical of the vowel /a/. This coding leads to a best fit by the /k/ procedure with only a very weak /t/ response. As can be seen in the bottom half of Figure 2.8, the fit between the predictions of the model and the human subject data is again quite good.

Sawusch (1980) also reports data comparing the perception of two-

---

[3] In all cases, the fit of the simulation predictions to the obtained subject data was evaluated with a chi-square goodness of fit test. None of the chi-square values were significant. This measure of the fit between the model and subject data simply indicates that there are no grounds for rejecting the model's predictions.

formant and five-formant stops (where the higher formants were steady-state). The subject data for the voiced and voiceless five-formant syllables are shown in the top and bottom panels of Figure 2.9. Also shown in the Figure are the predictions of the simulation. The primary difference between the simulation's processing of the two-formant and five-formant stimuli is the larger /d/ category in the voiced series and the emergence of a /t/ category in the voiceless series. Both of these changes are traceable to the same source: The greater high-frequency information in the five-formant stimuli (due to the presence of F3, F4, and F5) increases the closeness of match between the auditory coding processes and the alveolar stop procedures (/d/ and especially /t/).

Figures 2.10, 2.11, and 2.12 compare subject labeling and simulation predictions for several additional CV and VC synthetic speech series. The human subject data are from Sawusch (1977c). Again, the fit of the simula-

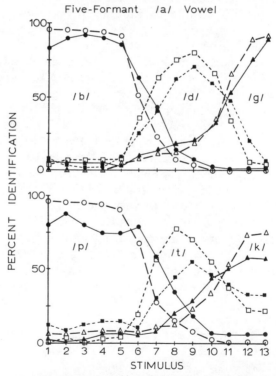

Figure 2.9   Subject identification data and computer simulation predictions for five-formant synthetic stop-vowel syllables. Subject data (filled points) and predictions (open points) for the voiced stimuli are shown in the top panel, while the bottom panel shows the data (filled points) and predictions (open points) for voiceless stops.

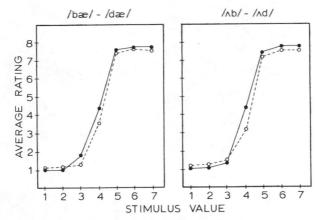

Figure 2.10 Subject identification data (filled points) and computer simulation predictions (open points) for synthetic /bae/-/dae/ and //ʌb/-//ʌd/continua.

tion to the obtained labeling data is uniformly excellent. This simulation can also account for much of the selective adaptation data for stops varying in place of articulation (see Sawusch, 1977c).

In terms of the issues raised at the beginning of this chapter, the lack of invariance in the speech signal is dealt with through multiple codings of the input signal and complex, context-sensitive pattern properties rather than simple, one-to-one invariant cues. The perceptual units of the system are phonemes which integrate diverse sources of information over at least

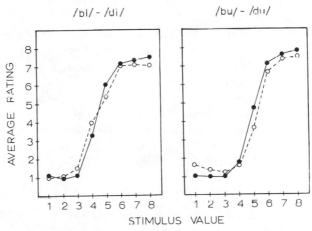

Figure 2.11 Subject identification data (filled points) and computer simulation predictions (open points) for synthetic /bi/-/di/ and /bu/-/du/ continua.

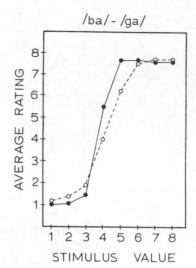

Figure 2.12 Subject identification data (filled points) and computer simulation predictions (open points) for a synthetic /ba/-/ga/ continuum.

a syllable-size temporal window of the speech signal. The segmentation of the speech signal is a by-product of the phonetic analysis. This model is distinct from early information processing theories, such as Pandemonium (Selfridge, 1959), in that auditory patterns are extracted directly from the spectral structure of speech rather than being built out of simpler features. Thus this model has certain gestalt-like characteristics. In addition, phonetic coding is implemented as a set of procedures for imposing units of analysis on the signal.

The simulation of this model demonstrates that it is sufficient in its ability to mimic human phonetic labeling of stop consonants. This feature puts the model on a par with other sufficiency models, such as those of Klatt (1980), Searle et al. (1979), and Zwicker et al. (1979). However, as this chapter has attempted to justify, the details of this model are based on the results of experimental studies designed to explore both the types of coding that humans impose on speech and possible coding mechanisms. Thus the model outlined here is a step toward specifying both a necessary and sufficient theory of the human perception of speech.

REFERENCES

Ades, A. E. (1974). How phonetic is selective adaptation? Experiments on syllable position and vowel environment. *Perception & Psychophysics, 16,* 61–67.

Ades, A. E. (1976). Adapting the property detectors for speech perception. In. R. J. Wales & E. Walker (Eds.), *New approaches to language mechanisms*. Amsterdam: North Holland.

Ainsworth, W. A. (1977). Mechanisms of selective feature adaptation. *Perception & Psychophysics, 21*, 365–370.

Bailey, P. J. (1975). *Perceptual adaptation in speech: Some properties of detectors for acoustical cues to phonetic distinctions*. Unpublished doctoral dissertation, University of Cambridge, Cambridge, England.

Bailey, P., Dorman, M., & Summerfield, Q. (1977). Identification of sine-wave analogues of CV syllables in speech and nonspeech modes. *Journal of the Acoustical Society of America, 61*, S66.

Best, C. T., Morrongiello, B., & Robson, R. (1981). Perceptual equivalence of acoustic cues in speech and nonspeech perception. *Perception & Psychophysics, 29*, 191–211.

Blumstein, S. E., Isaacs, E., & Mertus, J. (1982). The role of the gross spectral shape as a perceptual cue to place of articulation in initial stop consonants. *Journal of the Acoustical Society of America, 72*, 43–50.

Blumstein, S. E., & Stevens, K. N. (1979). Acoustic invariance in speech production: Evidence from measurements of the spectral characteristics of stop consonants. *Journal of the Acoustical Society of America, 66*, 1001–1017.

Blumstein, S. E., & Stevens, K. N. (1980). Perceptual invariance and onset spectra for stop consonants in different vowel environments. *Journal of the Acoustical Society of America, 67*, 648–662.

Bondarko, L. V., Zagorujko, N. G., Kozevnikov, N. A., Molcanov, A. P., & Cistovic, L. A. (1970). A model of speech perception in humans. *Working papers in linguistics* (Tech. Rep. 70-12). Columbus: Ohio State University, Computer & Information Science Research Center.

Carrell, T. D., Pisoni, D. B., & Gans, J. J. (1980, November). *Perception of the duration of rapid spectrum changes: Evidence for context effects with speech and nonspeech signals*. Paper presented at the 100th Annual Meeting of the Acoustical Society of America, Los Angeles.

Cole, R. A., & Jakimik, J. (1980). A model of speech perception. In R. A. Cole (Ed.), *Perception and production of fluent speech*. Hillsdale, NJ: Erlbaum.

Cooper, F. S., Delattre, P. C., Liberman, A. M., Borst, J. M., & Gerstman, L. J. (1952). Some experiments on the perception of synthetic speech sounds. *Journal of the Acoustical Society of America, 24*, 597–606.

Cooper, W. E. (1979). *Speech perception and production: Studies in selective adaptation*. Norwood, NJ: Ablex.

Craik, F. I. M., & Lockhart, R. S. (1972). Levels of processing: A framework for memory research. *Journal of Verbal Learning and Verbal Behavior, 11*, 671–684.

Cutting, J. E. (1974). Two left-hemisphere mechanisms in speech perception. *Perception & Psychophysics, 16*, 601–612.

Cutting, J. E. (1978). There may be nothing peculiar to perceiving in a speech mode. In J. Requin (Ed.), *Attention and performance VII*. Hillsdale, NJ: Erlbaum.

Davidsen-Nielsen, N. (1974). Syllabification in English words with medial sp, st, sk. *Journal of Phonetics, 2*, 15–45.

Diehl, R. L. (1976). Feature analyzers for the phonetic dimension stop vs. continuant. *Perception & Psychophysics, 19*, 267–272.

Diehl, R. L. (1981). Feature detectors for speech: A critical reappraisal. *Psychological Bulletin, 89*, 1–18.

Diehl, R. L., Elman, J. L., & McCusker, S. B. (1978). Contrast effects in stop consonant identification. *Journal of Experimental Psychology: Human Perception and Performance, 4,* 599–609.

Diehl, R. L., Lang, M., & Parker, E. M. (1980). A further parallel between selective adaptation and response contrast. *Journal of Experimental Psychology: Human Perception and Performance, 6,* 24–44.

Eimas, P. D., Cooper, W. E., & Corbit, J. D. (1973). Some properties of linguistic feature detectors. *Perception & Psychophysics, 13,* 247–252.

Eimas, P. D., & Corbit, J. D. (1973). Selective adaptation of linguistic feature detectors. *Cognitive Psychology, 4,* 99–109.

Elman, J. L. (1979). Perceptual origins of the phoneme boundary effect and selective adaptation to speech: A signal detection theory analysis. *Journal of the Acoustical Society of America, 65,* 190–207.

Fant, G. (1962). Descriptive analysis of the acoustic aspects of speech. *Logos, 5,* 3–17.

Fant, G. (1967). Auditory patterns of speech. In W. Wathen-Dunn (Ed.), *Models for the perception of speech and visual form.* Cambridge, MA: MIT Press.

Fant, G. (1973). *Speech sounds and features.* Cambridge, MA: MIT Press.

Foss, D. J., Harwood, D. A., & Blank, M. A. (1980). Deciphering decoding decisions: Data and devices. In R. A. Cole (Ed.), *Perception and production of fluent speech.* Hillsdale, NJ: Erlbaum.

Ganong, W. F. (1975). An experiment on "phonetic adaptation." *RLE Progress Report, 116,* 206–210.

Garner, W. R. (1974). *The processing of information and structure.* Potomac, MD: Erlbaum.

Garrison, L. F., & Sawusch, J. R. (1985). Adaptation of place perception for stops: Manipulation of the spectral match between adaptor and test series. Manuscript submitted for publication.

Helson, H. (1964). *Adaptation level theory.* New York: Harper & Row.

Hubel, D. H., & Wiesel, T. N. (1965). Receptive fields and functional architecture in two nonstriate visual areas (18 and 19) of the cat. *Journal of Neurophysiology, 28,* 229–289.

Hubel, D. H., & Wiesel, T. N. (1968). Receptive fields and functional architecture of monkey striate cortex. *Journal of Physiology, 195,* 215–243.

Jusczyk, P. W. (in press-a). On characterizing the development of speech perception. In J. Mehler & R. Fox (Eds.), *Neonate cognition: Beyond the blooming, buzzing confusion.* Hillsdale, NJ: Erlbaum.

Jusczyk, P. W. (in press-b). A review of speech perception research. In L. Kaufman, J. Thomas, & K. Boff (Eds.), *Handbook of perception & performance.* New York: John Wiley.

Kewley-Port, D. (1983). Time-varying features as correlates of place of articulation in stop consonants. *Journal of the Acoustical Society of America, 7,* 322–335.

Kewley-Port, D., Pisoni, D. B., & Studdert-Kennedy, M. (1983). Perception of static and dynamic acoustic cues to place of articulation in initial stop consonants. *Journal of the Acoustical Society of America, 73,* 1779–1793.

Klatt, D. H., (1975). Voice onset time, frication and aspiration in word-initial consonant clusters. *Journal of Speech and Hearing Research, 18,* 686–706.

Klatt, D. H. (1980). Speech perception: A model of acoustic–phonetic analysis and lexical access. In R. A. Cole (Ed.), *Perception and production of fluent speech.* Hillsdale, NJ: Erlbaum.

Koenig, W., Dunn, H. K., & Lacy, L. Y. (1946). The sound spectrograph. *Journal of the Acoustical Society of America, 17,* 19–49.

Kuhl, P. K. (1981). Discrimination of speech by nonhuman animals: Basic auditory sensitivities conducive to the perception of speech–sound categories. *Journal of the Acoustical Society of America, 70,* 340–349.

Kuhl, P. K., & Miller, J. D. (1978). Speech perception by the chinchilla: Identification functions for synthetic VOT stimuli. *Journal of the Acoustical Society of America, 63,* 905–917.

Kuhl, P. K., & Padden, D. M. (1983). Enhanced discriminability at the phonetic boundaries for the place feature in macaques. *Journal of the Acoustical Society of America, 73,* 1003–1010.

Lahiri, A., Gewirth, L., & Blumstein, S. E. (1984). A reconsideration of acoustic invariance for place of articulation in diffuse stop consonants: Evidence from a cross-language study. *Journal of the Acoustical Society of America, 76,* 391–404.

Liberman, A. M. (1970). Some characteristics of perception in the speech mode. In D. A. Hamburg (Ed.), *Perception and its disorders: Proceedings of the ARNMD.* Baltimore, MD: Williams & Wilkins.

Liberman, A. M. (1982). On finding that speech is special. *American Psychologist, 37,* 148–167.

Liberman, A. M., Cooper, F. S., Harris, K. S., MacNeilage, P. F., & Studdert-Kennedy, M. (1967). Some observations on a model for speech perception. In W. Wathen-Dunn (Ed.), *Models for the perception of speech and visual form.* Cambridge, MA: MIT Press.

Liberman, A. M., Cooper, F. S., Shankweiler, D. P., & Studdert-Kennedy, M. (1967). Perception of the speech code. *Psychological Review, 74,* 431–461.

Liberman, A. M., Delattre, P. C., & Cooper, F. S. (1952). The role of selected stimulus variables in the perception of the unvoiced stop consonants. *American Journal of Psychology, 65,* 497–516.

Liberman, A. M., Delattre, P. C., Cooper, F. S., & Gerstman, L. J. (1954). The role of consonant-vowel transitions in the perception of the stop and nasal consonants. *Psychological Monographs, 68,* 1–13.

Liberman, A. M., Delattre, P. C., Gerstman, L. J., & Cooper, F. S. (1956). Tempo of frequency change as a cue for distinguishing classes of speech sounds. *Journal of Experimental Psychology, 52,* 127–137.

Liberman, A. M., Harris, K. S., Hoffman, H. S., & Griffith, B. C. (1957). The discrimination of speech sounds within and across phoneme boundaries. *Journal of Experimental Psychology, 54,* 358–368.

Liberman, A. M., & Pisoni, D. B. (1977). Evidence for a special speech-perceiving subsystem in the human. In T. H. Bullock (Ed.), *Recognition of complex acoustic signals.* Berlin: Dahlem Konferenzen.

MacNeilage, P. F. (1970). Motor control of serial ordering of speech. *Psychological Review, 77,* 182–196.

Mann, V. A., & Repp, B. H. (1981). Influence of preceding fricative on stop consonant perception. *Journal of the Acoustical Society of America, 69,* 548–558.

Marslen-Wilson, W. (1976). Linguistic descriptions and psychological assumptions in the study of sentence perception. In R. J. Wales and E. Walker (Eds.), *New approaches to language mechanisms.* Amsterdam: North Holland.

Martin, J. G., & Bunnell, H. T. (1982). Perception of anticipatory coarticulation effects in vowel-stop consonant-vowel sequences. *Journal of Experimental Psychology: Human Perception & Performance, 8,* 473–488.

McGurk, H., & MacDonald, J. (1976). Hearing lips and seeing voices. *Nature, 264,* 746–748.

Miller, J. D. (1984). Auditory processing of the acoustic patterns of speech. *Archives of Otolaryngology, 110,* 154–159.

Miller, J. D., Wier, C. C., Pastore, R., Kelly, W. J., & Dooling, R. J. (1976). Discrimination and labeling of noise-buzz sequences with varying noise-lead times: An example of categorical perception. *Journal of the Acoustical Society of America, 60,* 410–417.

Miller, J. L., & Liberman, A. M. (1979). Some effects of later-occurring information on the perception of stop consonant and semivowel. *Perception & Psychophysics, 25,* 457–465.

Nusbaum, H. C. (1979). Anchoring and selective adaptation may affect different processing mechanisms. In J. J. Wolf & D. H. Klatt (Eds.) *Speech communication papers.* New York: Acoustical Society of America.

Öhman, S. E. G. (1966). Coarticulation in VCV utterances: Spectrographic measurements. *Journal of the Acoustical Society of America, 39,* 151–168.

Parducci, A. (1965). Category judgment: A range-frequency model. *Psychological Review, 72,* 407–418.

Parducci, A. (1975). Contextual effects: A range-frequency analysis. In E. C. Carterette & M. P. Friedman (Eds.), *Handbook of perception* (Vol II). New York: Academic Press.

Pastore, R. E. (1981). Possible psychoacoustic factors in speech perception. In P. D. Eimas & J. L. Miller (Eds.), *Perspectives on the study of speech.* Hillsdale, NJ: Erlbaum.

Pastore, R. E., Ahroon, W. A., Baffuto, K. J., Friedman, C., Puleo, J. S., & Fink, E. A. (1977). Common-factor model of categorical perception. *Journal of Experimental Psychology: Human Perception & Performance, 3,* 686–696.

Patterson, R. D. (1974). Auditory filter shape. *Journal of the Acoustical Society of America, 55,* 802–809.

Pisoni, D. B. (1973). Auditory and phonetic memory codes in the discrimination of consonants and vowels. *Perception & Psychophysics, 13,* 253–260.

Pisoni, D. B. (1975a). Auditory short-term memory and vowel perception. *Memory & Cognition, 3,* 7–18.

Pisoni, D. B. (1975b). Dichotic listening and processing phonetic features. In F. Restle, R. M. Shiffrin, N. J. Castellan, H. Lindman, & D. B. Pisoni (Eds.), *Cognitive theory* (Vol. I). Hillsdale, NJ: Erlbaum.

Pisoni, D. B. (1976). Speech perception. In W. K. Estes (Ed.), *Handbook of learning and cognitive processes.* Hillsdale, NJ: Erlbaum.

Pisoni, D. B. (1977). Identification and discrimination of the relative onset time of two component tones: Implications for voicing perception in stops. *Journal of the Acoustical Society of America, 61,* 1352–1361.

Pisoni, D. B., & McNabb, S. D. (1974). Dichotic interactions and phonetic feature processing. *Brain & Language, 1,* 351–362.

Pisoni, D. B., & Sawusch, J. R. (1975). Some stages of processing in speech perception. In A. Cohen & S. G. Nooteboom (Eds.), *Structure and process in speech perception.* New York: Springer-Verlag.

Pisoni, D. B., & Tash, J. B. (1975). Auditory property detectors and processing place features in stop consonants. *Perception & Psychophysics, 18,* 401–408.

Pomerantz, J. R., Sager, L. C., & Stoever, R. J. (1977). Perception of wholes and of their component parts: Some configurational superiority effects. *Journal of Experimental Psychology: Human Perception and Performance, 3,* 422–435.

Reddy, D. R. (1980). Machine models of speech perception. In R. A. Cole (Ed.), *Perception and production of fluent speech.* Hillsdale, NJ: Erlbaum.

Remez, R. E., Rubin, P. E., Pisoni, D. B., & Carrell, T. D. (1981). Speech perception without traditional speech cues. *Science, 212,* 947–950.

Repp, B. H. (1982). Phonetic trading relations and context effects: New experimental evidence for a speech mode of perception. *Psychological Bulletin, 92,* 81–110.

Roberts, M., & Summerfield, Q. (1981). Audiovisual presentation demonstrates that selective adaptation in speech perception is purely auditory. *Perception & Psychophysics, 30*, 309–314.

Samuel, A. G. (1982). Phonetic prototypes. *Perception & Psychophysics, 31*, 307–314.

Samuel, A. G., & Newport, E. L. (1979). Adaptation of speech by nonspeech: Evidence for complex acoustic cue detectors. *Journal of Experimental Psychology: Human Perception & Performance, 5*, 563–578.

Sawusch, J. R. (1976). Selective adaptation effects on end-point stimuli in a speech series. *Perception & Psychophysics, 20*, 61–65.

Sawusch, J. R. (1977a). Peripheral and central processes in selective adaptation of place of articulation in stop consonants. *Journal of the Acoustical Society of America, 62*, 738–750.

Sawusch, J. R. (1977b). Processing of place information in stop consonants. *Perception & Psychophysics, 22*, 417–426.

Sawusch, J. R. (1977c). The structure and flow of information in speech perception: Evidence from selective adaptation of stop consonants. (Doctoral dissertation, Indiana University, 1976). *Dissertation Abstracts International, 37*, 4195B.

Sawusch, J. R. (1980). The perception of initial two formant stops. *Speech Research* (Prog. Rep. No. 1). Buffalo: State University of New York at Buffalo, Department of Psychology.

Sawusch, J. R., & Jusczyk, P. (1981). Adaptation and contrast in the perception of voicing. *Journal of Experimental Psychology: Human Perception & Performance, 7*, 408–421.

Sawusch, J. R., & Mullennix, J. W. (1985). *Anchoring, adaptation and contrast in the perception of stops.* Unpublished manuscript.

Sawusch, J. R., & Nochajski, T. H. (1982, November). *Stimulus integrality in the auditory coding of speech.* Paper presented at the 23rd Annual Meeting of the Psychonomic Society, Minneapolis.

Sawusch, J. R., & Nusbaum, H. C. (1983). Auditory and phonetic processes in place perception for stops. *Perception & Psychophysics, 34*, 560–568.

Sawusch, J. R., & Pisoni, D. B. (1973, November). *Category boundaries for speech and non-speech sounds.* Paper presented at the 86th Annual Meeting of the Acoustical Society of America, Los Angeles.

Sawusch, J. R., Pisoni, D. B., & Cutting, J. E. (1974, April). *Category boundaries for linguistic and nonlinguistic dimensions of the same stimuli.* Paper presented at the 87th Annual Meeting of the Acoustical Society of America, New York.

Scharf, B. (1970). Critical bands. In J. V. Tobias (Ed.), *Foundations of modern auditory theory.* New York: Academic Press.

Schouten, M.E.H. (1980). The case against a speech mode of perception. *Acta Psychologia, 44*, 71–98.

Schwab, E. C. (1982). Auditory and phonetic processing for tone analogs of speech. (Doctoral dissertation, State University of New York at Buffalo, 1981). *Dissertation Abstracts International, 42*, 3853B.

Schwab, E. C., Sawusch, J. R., & Nusbaum, H. C. (1981). The role of second-formant transitions in the stop-semivowel distinction. *Perception & Psychophysics, 29*, 121–128.

Searle, C. L., Jacobson, J. Z., & Kimberley, B. P. (1980). Speech as patterns in the 3-space of time and frequency. In R. A. Cole (Ed.), *Perception and production of fluent speech,* Hillsdale, NJ: Erlbaum.

Searle, C. L., Jacobson, J. Z., & Rayment, S. G. (1979). Stop consonant discrimination based upon human audition. *Journal of the Acoustical Society of America, 65*, 799–809.

Selfridge, O. G. (1959). Pandemonium: A paradigm for learning. In *Symposium on the mechanization of thought processes*. London: Stationery Office.

Shiffrin, R. M. (1975). Short-term store: The basis for a memory system. In F. Restle, R. M. Shiffrin, N. J. Castellan, H. Lindman, & D. B. Pisoni (Eds.), *Cognitive theory* (Vol. I). Hillsdale, NJ: Erlbaum.

Simon, H. J., & Studdert-Kennedy, M. (1978). Selective anchoring and adaptation of phonetic and nonphonetic continua. *Journal of the Acoustical Society of America, 64*, 1338–1357.

Stevens, K. N. (1975). The potential role of property detectors in the perception of consonants. In G. Fant & M. A. A. Tatham (Eds.), *Auditory analysis and perception of speech*. London: Academic Press.

Stevens, K. N., & Blumstein, S. E. (1978). Invariant cues for place of articulation in stop consonants. *Journal of the Acoustical Society of America, 64*, 1358–1368.

Stevens, K. N., & Halle, M. (1967). Remarks on analysis by synthesis and distinctive features. In W. Wathen-Dunn (Eds.), *Models for the perception of speech and visual form*. Cambridge, MA: MIT Press.

Studdert-Kennedy, M. (1976). Speech perception. In N. J. Lass (Ed.), *Contemporary issues in experimental phonetics*. New York: Academic Press.

Summerfield, Q. (1982). Differences between spectral dependencies in auditory and phonetic temporal processing: Relevance to the perception of voicing in initial stops. *Journal of the Acoustical Society of America, 72*, 51–61.

Tartter, V. C., & Eimas, P. D. (1975). The role of auditory and phonetic feature detectors in the perception of speech. *Perception & Psychophysics, 18*, 293–298.

Walley, A. (1979). Infants' discrimination of full and partial cues to place of articulation in stop consonants. *Research on Speech Perception* (Prog. Rep. No. 5). Bloomington: Indiana University.

Walley, A. C., & Carrell, T. D. (1983). Onset spectra and formant transitions in the adult's and child's perception of place of articulation in stop consonants. *Journal of the Acoustical Society of America, 73*, 1011–1022.

Weisstein, N., & Harris, C. S. (1974). Visual detection of line segments: An object–superiority effect. *Science, 186*, 752–755.

Whitfield, I. C., & Evans, E. F. (1965). Responses of auditory cortical neurons to stimuli of changing frequency. *Journal of Neurophysiology, 28*, 655–672.

Wickelgren, W. A. (1969). Context-sensitive coding, associative memory and serial order in (speech) behavior. *Psychological Review, 76*, 1–15.

Winograd, T. (1975). Frame representations and the declarative-procedural controversy. In D. C. Bobrow & A. Collins (Eds.), *Representation and understanding*. New York: Academic Press.

Wong, E., & Weisstein, N. (1982). A new perceptual context-superiority effect: Line segments are more visible against a figure than against a ground. *Science, 218*, 587–589.

Zwicker, E., Terhardt, E., & Paulus, E. (1979). Automatic speech recognition using psychoacoustic models. *Journal of the Acoustical Society of America, 65*, 487–498.

CHAPTER 3

The Role of the Lexicon in Speech Perception*

Arthur G. Samuel

*Department of Psychology, Yale University,
New Haven, Connecticut 06520*

I. THE MUSING

If a psycholinguist were to walk up to you and ask what you knew about the word "bizarre," you could probably provide a surprisingly long response. You would probably note that the word is an adjective meaning roughly the same thing as "strange." You could give examples of its use, such as "Only a bizarre psycholinguist would ask such a question." Moreover, you could probably spell the word, report that it has two syllables (with stress falling on the second one), and that it started with the same sound as the word "buffoon." If you reflected a bit longer, you might even note that you knew another word that sounded just like the one you were asked about—"bazaar." In fact, given the proper motivation, you could probably spend the better (or worse) part of a coffee break discussing what you know about the word "bizarre."

Now consider the number of words a typical adult knows. Estimates vary, depending on the level of knowledge involved, but all are in the tens of thousands; whatever the number is, it is certainly very large. The normal adult thus has access to tens of thousands of words, and for each word, a surprising amount of knowledge. It is remarkable that, despite the enormity of information that is stored, access to a particular piece of information is generally accomplished rapidly and effortlessly. This fact suggests that the information is organized in a useful way and that there is a very efficient retrieval process that is well-matched to the organization.

Over the years, psychologists have come to call the organized body of

---

* Preparation of this chapter was partially supported by Contract N00014-82-C-0160 from the Office of Naval Research.

89

one's knowledge of words the "lexicon" and the process of finding an entry in it "lexical access." The lexicon is usually envisaged as being rather like a dictionary, with words organized in some fashion and the desired information (the meaning, spelling, pronunciation, etc.) available once the right entry has been found. Viewed this way, there are two central questions that must be answered: (1) How are the entries organized? and (2) How does the lexical access process find the desired entry?

Unfortunately, the answers to these questions are not currently known. The impact of our ignorance on these issues is felt when we try to understand processes that may depend on the structure of the lexicon and how it is accessed. For example, consider what a listener does when the sentence, "Only a bizarre psycholinguist would ask such a question," is spoken. In order to understand the sentence, the listener must access some representation of at least most of the words. Thus, at least in this weak sense, the lexicon and lexical access are involved in understanding a spoken utterance. However, there is a much stronger sense in which lexical representations could be involved in understanding a sentence. In this sense, not only are lexical representations accessed but they serve as the "currency of exchange" used by various subprocesses. This notion may be understood in the context of computer recognition of speech, particularly the approach taken in the HEARSAY project (Reddy, Erman, Fennell, & Neely, 1973).

The conceptual heart of the HEARSAY approach to speech recognition was the decision to have several different knowledge sources interactively decide on the identification of an utterance. In this system, syntactic and semantic constraints on what *should* have been said counted at least as much as an acoustic analysis of the speech waveform. At the time of its creation, the HEARSAY approach was rather radical. It was prompted by the realization that the output of HEARSAY's acoustic analysis was terribly unreliable; recognition rates based on it alone were very low. A measure of the importance of HEARSAY is that its once radical idea of interactive knowledge sources has now been generally accepted by psychologists as the way in which human speech understanding works (e.g., Cole & Jakimik, 1980; Marslen-Wilson & Welsh, 1978; Rumelhart & McClelland, 1982; Samuel, 1981a).

There is an interesting and (I believe) little appreciated corollary to the interactive sources hypothesis: Some level (or levels) of representation must be available for the different knowledge sources to use in interacting. Note that this problem does not arise in a simple bottom-up approach to recognition. In such a system, the first level of analysis takes some fairly veridical representation of the acoustic stimulus and produces as output a more abstract representation. Several different levels of abstraction have been proposed, including the phonetic feature (Eimas & Corbit, 1973; Pisoni, 1973), the syllable or demisyllable (Fujimura, Macchi, & Lovins, 1977; Massaro, 1975), and the word (Klatt, 1980). In most such models, the information goes through at least one more transformation, culminating in the perception of the spoken utterance. Note that the kind of information that each level of processing deals with is quite variable. Since each process must conform only to the immediately preceding and following processes, no generally usable type of representation is required.

In contrast, consider a fully interactive model of speech perception, one in which all processes must be able to exchange information. For example, consider a situation in which a listener has heard: "Senator Proxmire awarded the psychologist a Golden . . . ," and the last word is now arriving. There is ample evidence (some of it reviewed here) that the syntactic and semantic constraints of the sentential context reduce the time needed to know that the last word is "Fleece." In fact, if the final /s/ is mispronounced as /d/, listeners will be considerably faster in detecting the mispronunciation in this context than in "The next word you will hear is . . ." (see Cole & Jakimik, 1980). The question is, how can a decision based on a phonetic criterion (/s/ vs /d/) be influenced by syntactic and semantic factors? There must be some common level of representation that both the phonetic process and higher-level processes can make sense of. The level of representation that seems best suited to fill this role is the word, or lexical level (see Foss, Harwood, & Blank, 1980, for a similar argument). Recall that the lexicon has been described as an organized set of information about words and that each entry includes information about a word's phonetic makeup as well as its syntactic and semantic properties. The lexical level thus provides a natural meeting ground for quite different knowledge sources. In fact, as I have argued, postulating an interactive model of speech perception imposes the involvement of some common level for communication as a logical necessity.

Even if one accepts the necessity of lexical representations in speech perception, it remains to be seen whether or not they are *sufficient*. By this I mean that no intermediate level of representation need be postulated between an utterance's initial auditory representation and its recognition as a particular word. It is difficult to know what kinds of arguments would directly support the sufficiency of lexical representations. However, a number of researchers have argued that there are enough problems with any intermediate levels to reject them, making the lexical level the representation of choice by default. Klatt (1980) provides a very nice summary of some of the problems that any model of recognition must deal with and highlights the problems specific to sublexical units.

The most familiar of these problems is that of acoustic–phonetic nonin-variance—there is no simple one-to-one mapping of sound units onto phonetic units. This problem has been known for over a quarter of a century and has been the focus of much research (e.g., Liberman, Cooper, Shankweiler, & Studdert-Kennedy, 1967; but see Cole & Scott, 1974; Stevens & Blumstein, 1981). To the extent that acoustic cues cannot be directly mapped onto a putative perceptual unit, doubt is cast on that unit's role. Three points should be noted, however, First, the researchers who have provided the bulk of the evidence that no simple one-to-one mapping exists have not, in general, abandoned sublexical theories. Rather, they argue for more abstract representations of units of roughly syllabic length (Liberman et al., 1967). Second, more generally, there is no need for a one-to-one mapping as long as some scheme for combining multiple cues is available (see Oden & Massaro, 1978; Samuel & New-port, 1979). Finally, even if the lack of a one-to-one mapping poses seri-ous problems for sublexical units, it remains to be shown that such a mapping can be found at the lexical level.

Klatt (1980) has outlined a number of other problems in addition to the acoustic–phonetic mapping complexity. However, most of these prob-lems apply to whatever units are used. For example, speakers vary widely in how they produce speech sounds that are nominally the same. An adequate model of speech perception will have to account for the rela-tively easy time people appear to have in dealing with such variation. Moreover, such variation is probably equally problematic for lexical and sublexical units.

At first glance, one might think that the problem of segmentation could be similarly described. It has long been noted that in general, neither words nor phones are segmentable on the basis of any simple acoustic analysis of the waveform. Adjacent phones typically are coarticulated sufficiently that there is no single point that can be identified as dividing the two. Similarly, in normal speech adjacent words are run together, preempting any simple segmentation. Despite these similarities, it may be easier to devise a plausible lexical segmentation strategy than a phonetic one. Cole and Jakimik (1980) have suggested one such scheme. They argue that in running speech, the combination of acoustic cues and higher-level constraints is generally sufficient to provide identification of a word before it actually ends acoustically. If this is so, the word segmentation problem can generally be solved, because the end of the word is known. The beginning of the following word can then be identified as the first part of the waveform that is not consistent with the (known) ending. There is at least one difficulty in applying this sort of scheme at a phonetic level. As noted earlier, the use of higher-level constraints at lower levels is relatively easy if lexical units are used as the medium of exchange but rather difficult with smaller (or larger) units.

Based on his review of relatively unsuccessful speech recognition systems, Klatt (1980) makes the point that such systems were often devastated by early (phonetic) errors propagating through the recognition process. From this observation he argues for a general strategy of delaying decisions as long as possible. This strategy, of course, is quite consistent with lexical units in perception rather than smaller ones. Klatt's point is well taken and should be considered seriously. To the extent that the recognition process is dependent on analysis at low levels, any mistakes can be very damaging, since decisions at subsequent levels may be erroneously forced into agreement with the error. Ironically, the most telling response to this argument is based on research that generally agrees with the lexical view. Marslen-Wilson (1973) has shown that if instructed to repeat incoming utterances rapidly, people can recognize words long before they end. At least under some circumstances, then, people do not put off decisions, but instead accomplish rapid (and generally accurate) recognition of speech. People show little of the kind of breakdown that machines exhibit, even when subjects are deprived of the opportunity to delay decisions. This suggests that the general principle of delaying decisions is less important in human speech perception than would be supposed on the basis of machine recognition performance.

The preceding arguments suggest that many current models require the involvement of lexical representations in the perception of speech. Moreover, there is reason to believe that the lexical level may be the smallest one used in perception (but see Sawusch, this volume and Foss & Blank, 1980). At this point, it may be useful to clarify what it might mean for lexical representations to play a role in perception. As a starting point, we may assume that an incoming waveform gets represented at a number of levels of representation, including a lexical one. For the moment, we may further assume that the lexical level is not sufficient, but is instead preceded by other transformations (the exact nature of the smaller units, whether phonetic, demisyllabic, or syllabic, is not important for the present purpose). Given this general framework, it is possible to define three classes of theories.

In the first class of theories (Type I), the lexical level plays no role at all in the perceptual process. For example, consider a model in which the initial auditory representation is first transformed into a phonetic representation and the phonetic strings are then combined to form syllables. The product of the perceptual process—a sequence of syllables—is then matched by a postperceptual decision stage to entries in the lexicon. Such a decision stage could use higher-level knowledge to combine syllables properly in the matching process, so that "let" "her" might be matched to two lexical entries following "She wanted to go out, but her parents wouldn't . . . ," and to one entry following "She mailed the . . . ." The key to theories of Type I is that they assert that the *perceptual* process is essentially nonlinguistic, or at least independent of whether the utterance is meaningful. The fact that people are capable of perceiving utterances like "garfimamy" supports a perceptual mechanism that does not require lexical-level involvement.

The second class of theories (Type II) is similar to the first, except that in this case the lexical level is thought of as the last stage of the perceptual process. Thus, in models of this sort, the same kinds of transformations of the signal might occur through the syllabic level. At this point, the *perceptual* process itself would combine syllables to match lexical entries. Note that the only distinction between Type I and Type II theories is where we draw the line between perception and what follows (cognition?). One purpose of this exercise is to make clear that what we want to call "speech perception" is not very well defined: Do we want to include any inferences that the listener draws while listening? What if the inferences are essential to understanding the next sentence, or the next word? As we note shortly, the distinction between perception and later (or higher-level) processing becomes even less clear-cut in Type III theories. For the moment, we simply define Type II theories as outlined; the lexical level is the last stage of perceptual processing. In its simplest form, Klatt's (1980) Lexical Access from Spectra model may be taken as an example of this Type of theory. Klatt suggests that the lexical level is derived directly from spectral cues; he assigns a minimal role in speech perception to any higher-level information sources.

The final class of theories (Type III) includes models in which the lexical level is just one of several interacting levels of representation. In such interactive models, levels of representation can receive input both from the incoming signal (or its successive transformations) and from higher levels of representation. This is the class of models discussed earlier, for which it was argued that lexical-level representations were essential. Theories of this class have been put forth by Marslen-Wilson and Welsh (1978), Rumelhart (1977), and others. Theorists who favor interactive models usually allow for essentially any level to affect any other level. However, it may be the case that the perceptual system allows an exchange of information only between a subset of levels—for example, between "directly adjacent" levels of processing. Samuel (1981a) argues for such a limited interactive model.

The three classes of models derive from different beliefs about what constitutes perception and the kinds of information flow involved in it.

Type I and II models are basically bottom-up classes of theories—perception is driven by the incoming sensory data. Type III models allow both data-driven and expectation-based information to determine the percept. The model classes also differ in the kinds of perceptual units postulated. In Type I theories, the perceptual units are quite small, of syllabic length or smaller. These theories conform to the view that information can be held in a preperceptual form only for a very short time. Massaro (1975), for example, has suggested an upper bound of about 250 ms, a value sufficient for demisyllables in general, or possibly syllables. The perceptual units in Type II theories are somewhat larger, of word length. Note that if Massaro's estimate of preperceptual storage time is correct, a problem exists for Type II theories: How can the information be available long enough for a word percept to be formed? Either longer preperceptual storage must be available, or some intermediate units (such as phones or syllables) must be used, or perception must occur before much of the word has actually occurred. Marslen-Wilson (1973) and Cole and Jakimik (1980) have both suggested that the last alternative—rapid lexical access from just the beginnings of words—is possible. They have done so, however, in the context of Type III models. In these models, higher-level constraints are used to help in such rapid recognition. Note that in highly interactive models of this sort, it may be difficult to specify what the unit or units of perception might be, since identification occurs at several levels in parallel. Put another way, perception and cognition are inseparable.

II. THE FACTS

The possibility of dividing classes of theories into several categories is indicative of the range of research and theorizing that has been done in recent years. A number of findings and paradigms are particularly important in clarifying the role of the lexicon in speech perception. Some of these findings are reviewed below, with a focus on how they bear on the role of the lexicon.

II.A. Perception of Words in Noise: Word Frequency

It is well established that in many paradigms, subjects are better at reporting common words (high frequency of occurrence) than unusual ones (low frequency). This is true both for visual presentation (e.g., Howes & Solomon, 1951), and for auditory presentation (e.g., Broadbent, 1967). In Broadbent's study, high- (greater than 100 occurrences per million) and moderate- (10–49 per million) frequency English words were recorded on audiotape and played back to listeners in a background of noise. The listeners correctly reported a third of the high-frequency words versus only 12% of the lower-frequency words. The theoretical question is why word frequency should affect how well people perceive spoken words. It turns out that all three Types of theories can account for the frequency effect, each in a somewhat different way. Recall that in Type I theories, the perceptual process produces a set of phones or syllables and that some higher-level cognitive process must put them together to form words. Just as it was suggested that sentential context could bias the assignment of syllables to words, so we might expect a lexical-level bias to be present: The cognitive process that puts words together could be sensitive to a priori probabilities of words and, if possible, match pieces to more likely candidates producing the observed pattern.

In Type II theories, lexical access is the last stage of the perceptual process. To account for the frequency effect, we could assume that the lexicon is ordered in a frequency-sensitive way. Forster (1976), for example, suggests that for recognition of spoken words, words that sound alike are "near" each other in the lexicon's "directory" and that the search through these words is ordered on the basis of frequency: Higher-frequency words are higher on each "sublist" of the lexicon. Note that in this view, the ordering or *structure* of the lexicon is used to explain the frequency effect, whereas in Type I theories the emphasis is on a bias in the matching *process*.

In Type III theories, the word frequency effect could arise in ways that are similar to either Type I's process or Type II's structure. In structural terms, it might be the case that lexical representations of high-frequency words are more easily "found" by lower-level information flowing up the system, for reasons similar to those offered for Type II theories. A more process-oriented explanation would be that less confirmation is needed to cause a high-frequency word's representation to respond than would be the case for a low-frequency word. If we assume that some threshold exists for noticing that a word is activated (as in Morton's, 1969, logogen system), the frequency effect could be realized in two ways: Either the resting level for high-frequency words is higher or the threshold for "firing" is lower. Based on an analysis of correct and incorrect responses, Broadbent (1967) argues for an explanation of the frequency effect similar to the process-oriented models outlined here. Note that this situation poses a problem for our endeavor of understanding the role of the lexicon in speech perception, since both Type I and Type III theories posit process-oriented explanations but they differ in whether the lexicon plays an active role in speech perception.

II.B. Speech Synthesis

One way to take advantage of Broadbent's (1967) analysis in choosing a model class to pursue is to combine it with the results of a study by Ganong (1980). Ganong's study is particularly useful in this regard because his goal was to choose between an interactive model (Type III) and a bottom-up one (Type I or II). By coordinating Broadbent's choice (Type I or III) with Ganong's results, we may be able to converge on a particular class.

Ganong synthesized a number of speech continua that varied in voice onset time (VOT)—a set of acoustic cues that distinguishes voiced and voiceless stops. For half of the continua, the voiced endpoint was a real word (e.g., "dash") and the voiceless endpoint was not (e.g., "tash"). For the other half, the reverse was true (e.g., "dask" and "task"). At issue was whether the phoneme boundary would shift as a function of the lexical status of the endpoints. In fact, such a shift was observed: Labeling was biased toward the real-word end of the continuum. For example, a token with a given VOT would be more likely to be labeled "dash" on the "dash-tash" continuum than a corresponding token with the same VOT in the "dask-task" series. This result suggests that lexical representations can affect the perception of speech.

Ganong points out that there are a number of ways in which this effect might arise. He considers two classes of models. In "categorical" models, the acoustic signal is first transformed into a phonetic code, which is then mapped onto a lexical representation (if one is available). This is clearly either a Type I or II model, depending on whether the last mapping is considered part of the perceptual process or not. Ganong contrasts the "categorical" model with an "interactive" one. In the latter, the presence of a lexical representation can change the criterion for judging the acoustic cues (VOT). This feature puts the model into Type III, since it calls for a top-down flow of information. Ganong argues that the categorical model predicts an equal lexical bias across the VOT range because the lexical effect cannot take place until after a phonetic judgment has been made. In contrast, the interactive model allows for differential effects across the continuum because the effect happens before (or during) the interpretation of the acoustic cues. Since the data indicate that the lexical bias is strongest for tokens near the phoneme boundary, Ganong chose the interactive model over the categorical one.

It is instructive to examine the three instantiations of an interactive model outlined by Ganong. The one that he favored was a model in which the acoustic cues produce a type of phonetic code with "implicit confidence ratings." These phonetic ratings are combined with a value based on a lexical influence to derive the perceived word. With a boundary stimulus, the implicit rating of an initial alveolar sound might be low for both /d/ and /t/, and any lexical input could be decisive. Endpoint stimuli would produce strong phonetic codes that would be difficult for a lexical influence to override. An interesting aspect of this Type III model is that it illustrates the need for a common language for the lexical and phonetic levels. In this case, Ganong phrases things as though the lexical level were offering phonetic codes, but one could just as easily describe it as the phonetic level postulating different syllable- or word-level candidates.

Also of interest is an analysis of the two alternatives considered by Ganong. In one model he suggests that a phonetic analysis may produce a "voiced," "voiceless," or "don't know" output, with lexical bias playing a role only where the phonetic analysis was inconclusive. Since the probability of a "don't know" output must be higher for boundary stimuli than for good exemplars, the observed concentration of the lexical effect at the boundary can be accounted for. This model is of interest because even though Ganong offered it as an interactive model, it is best characterized as falling into the Type I class: Syllabic codes are output by the perceptual process, and a smart cognitive process then does the lexical matching.

Ganong's final instantiation of his interactive class is one in which low-level acoustic information is kept available all the way to the lexical matching stage. The lexical bias can have a direct effect in this case by forcing the lexical interpretation on acoustic patterns that could have two syllabic matches (the boundary stimuli). Note that this model is in fact an example of Type II, since there really is no downward flow of information; the acoustic cues get mapped directly onto a lexical representation (if one is available) or into a syllabic code (if a lexical code is not available). Ganong argues that this type of model requires better memory for acoustic detail than is consistent with the results of studies of echoic memory. Nevertheless, it is instructive to note that just as in the case of the word frequency effect, models of all three Types can be constructed to account for the data. As in that case, a clear advantage is enjoyed by items which have a more established lexical representation. What remains difficult to pin down is when and how the lexical representations exert their influence.

II.C. Phoneme Monitoring

A number of investigators have tried to resolve these questions by using the phoneme-monitoring paradigm. In this task, subjects are told to respond to the occurrence of a prespecified target sound. Rubin, Turvey, and van Gelder (1976) used this technique to investigate whether lexicality affects detection time. For example, if Type II theories are correct, one might expect a word advantage, since words are what the perceptual system is working to derive. In contrast, Type I theories might predict no difference, since Rubin et al.'s monosyllables could be perceived similarly regardless of whether they were words or not. The results of their study revealed a reliable word advantage: Targets (/b/ or /s/) were detected about 50 ms faster if they started a word than if they began a nonword. Once again we see an advantage for stimuli with lexical representations. Rubin et al. correctly point out, however, that this effect does not necessarily imply a lexical role in *perception*. Instead, they suggest that the difference may reflect different accessibility of the word and nonword encodings by the decision process required for the detection task. Note, however, that a Type III theory would predict the observed results for *perceptual* reasons: The lexical information could support the lower-level analyses when a word was present, thus producing more rapid perception.

The phoneme-monitoring technique has been used most extensively by Foss and his colleagues. A virtue of this paradigm is that it can be used as naturally with running speech as with segmented words. This permits investigation of the influence of sentential constraints in perceiving speech. For example, Blank and Foss (1978) found that targets in predictable words were detected faster than those in less predictable words: A similar result has been reported by Morton and Long (1976). For our purposes, the question of interest is whether lexically based manipulations produce similar differences. Foss and Blank (1980) have investigated two such factors: lexicality per se and frequency of critical words. Like Rubin et al., the lexicality test contrasted targets in words with targets in pseudowords. However, Foss and Blank's stimuli were sentences rather than syllable lists. Furthermore, Rubin et al. had asked their subjects to detect the occurrence of either an /s/ or a /b/, whereas Foss and Blank used a single target. The differences in procedure were apparently important, since Foss and Blank found no difference between reaction times to targets in words and nonwords. They argued that the critical procedural difference was Rubin et al.'s use of two targets, and supported their argument by noting that Rubin (1975) obtained data like their own when he required subjects to monitor for only a single target.

As noted earlier, Type I theories can accommodate the equivalence of word and pseudoword targets, since the two kinds of utterances are processed similarly. Interestingly, they can also account for a second result in the Foss and Blank experiment. For half of the sentences, the target sound began the word or nonword *after* the previously described words and nonwords. In contrast to targets *in* those tokens, targets coming after them showed a strong effect of lexicality: The detection of targets after a nonword was 100 ms slower than for those following a word. All three model Types might predict this result, since the recent occurrence of an anomalous nonword could draw processing resources away from the detection task. The previous result—no difference when the target begins a word vs a nonword—seems problematic for both Type II and Type III models. Since the lexical level is involved in the perceptual process for these models, one would expect the occurrence of a nonword to be directly disruptive.

In a second experiment, Foss and Blank compared high- and low-frequency words, using a design analogous to the one just described. The pattern of results was quite similar, with a delay in detection observed for targets after low-frequency words but not in them. The same sort of analysis applied earlier seems appropriate here—Type I models appear most capable of accommodating the results. Rubin et al.'s caveat about the detection paradigm should be repeated, however: The reaction times may be reflecting the relative accessibility of information after perception has occurred rather than differences in rates of perceptual processing. This is a warning that Foss himself provides (Foss & Swinney, 1973). In fact, it is for exactly this reason that Type I theories are well suited to deal with the results. They are just those theories in which much of the interesting processing occurs postperceptually.

II.D. Gating

Like phoneme monitoring, the gating paradigm (Grosjean, 1980) may be tapping postperceptual processes. In this procedure, listeners hear words that have been truncated. On successive trials, more and more of the word is played until the complete word is provided. On each trial, the subject must guess the word being presented. Grosjean used this technique to investigate three factors, two of which depend directly on information in the lexicon—word frequency and word length. The third factor—context—is not directly a lexical factor but, as we have seen, is important in Type III theories. Grosjean used three contextual conditions: no context, short context (moderately predictive of the word), and long context (highly predictive). All three factors produced reliable effects on how soon subjects could identify the truncated test words. High-frequency words were recognized with less acoustic information than low-frequency words, while longer words required longer pieces for recognition than short words. The contextual manipulation also produced a predictable pattern, with less acoustic information required in a more predictive context.

If the gating paradigm results reflect perceptual processing, they can be accounted for only by interactive theories (Type III), since contextual cues were traded off against acoustic information. However, the subjects made their reports at their leisure and were explicitly encouraged to guess (i.e., to use whatever cognitive skills they had to determine a word's identity). Thus the reports undoubtedly contain strong influences of post-perceptual processing. Nevertheless, it may be possible to distinguish perceptual and postperceptual effects in this paradigm by using confidence ratings. For example, Grosjean had his subjects rate their confidence in each guess they made. One result is of particular interest. Grosjean defined the "isolation point" for a word as the duration of acoustic information beyond which the subject made no errors; from the isolation point onward, all of a subject's guesses were the same, and all were correct. Grosjean distinguished this point from "recognition" because subjects could still be quite unsure of their guesses for some time beyond the isolation point. Indeed, the case of interest here concerns the conditions that produce such a lack of confidence.

One can compare subjects' confidence at the isolation point as a function of the experimental conditions. Grosjean found that at the isolation point, subjects were significantly more confident of their guesses in the no-context condition than in either of the context conditions. If we assume that the confidence judgments were based on what subjects were sure they had heard (as opposed to what they inferred or guessed), this result suggests that context works at a postperceptual level. In contrast, Grosjean found no significant difference in confidence at the isolation point as a function of word frequency. Since the high-frequency words reached the isolation point sooner than the low-frequency words, it appears that frequency was producing a true perceptual effect. This pattern of results is inconsistent with Type III models because of the lack of a perceptual effect of sentential context. In addition, the perceptual potency of a lexical-level factor like word frequency favors theories of Type II over Type I models.

II.E. Shadowing and Mispronunciation Detection

Two closely related lines of research have had a particularly strong impact on current models of lexical access and speech perception. One line is based on the mispronunciation task (Cole, 1973; Cole & Jakimik, 1978, 1980; Cole, Jakimik, & Cooper, 1978; Marslen-Wilson & Welsh,

1978), while the other focuses on the shadowing paradigm (Marslen-Wilson, 1973, 1975; Marslen-Wilson & Welsh, 1978). Subjects performing the detection task listen to passages and are told to push a button whenever they detect a mispronunciation. Using this technique, Cole and his colleagues have obtained a number of interesting findings. A recurring result is that mispronunciations are better detected when they occur early in a word rather than late. This effect has resulted in both faster detection for early sounds (Cole, 1973) and more accurate detection (Cole et al., 1978).

A second potent factor in determining detection performance is predictability. Cole and Jakimik (1978) found that mispronunciations were detected significantly faster in contextually predictable words than in less predictable ones. Moreover, the same effect obtained even if the determining context was based on the word immediately before the critical word. This result suggests a very rapid use of contextual constraints. Indeed, Cole and Jakimik (1980) argue that this result and others indicate that words are perceived in "left-to-right" order, with the perceptual process for word N taking advantage of any information obtained about word N−1. Jakimik (1979) has also demonstrated an interesting left-to-right processing effect *within* words. She compared detection times for second-syllable mispronunciations in words that varied in what one might call "lexical uniqueness." Half of her words began with very common first syllables; the other half began with rather unusual syllables found in few other English words. She found that detection times were significantly faster for the words with unique beginnings and argued that this result was due to faster lexical access for those items. Indeed, more rapid access would be expected if the recognition process depends on eliminating all possibilities except the correct one, and if it proceeds from left to right (i.e., starts with the first syllable).

Results analogous to those obtained in the detection paradigm have been reported by Marslen-Wilson and his colleagues using a shadowing paradigm. In this procedure, listeners repeat incoming speech aloud, staying as close in time as possible to the input. Marslen-Wilson (1973) has demonstrated that some listeners can stay remarkably close; seven subjects (of 65 tested) could shadow at average latencies of less than 270 ms. As he points out, this result implies that shadowers are generally not more than a syllable behind the input, suggesting a very rapid recognition process. Such a process would be consistent with Type I theories, since these theories are based on syllable-by-syllable recognition. However, Marslen-Wilson notes that when listeners make errors in shadowing, the errors are virtually always consistent with the current syntactic and semantic constraints. Thus he argues that the perceptual process is of Type III, with higher-level information being used extensively in the perceptual process. In accord with Jakimik (1979), he suggests that the higher-level information is combined with acoustic information from the beginnings of words to accomplish rapid lexical access.

Marslen-Wilson's view of lexical access is laid out most clearly in Marslen-Wilson and Welsh's (1978) study, in which the authors also provide a useful comparison of the shadowing and detection paradigms. Tapes were prepared of passages with mispronunciations and were presented to some listeners for shadowing and to others for detection. Three factors were varied: the predictability of the critical word, the severity of mispronunciation, and the position within the word of the mispronunciation. Marslen-Wilson and Welsh measured the probability of subjects "fluently restoring" mispronunciations to what they should have been, and of subjects failing to detect mispronunciations. Both of these measures may be taken to reflect subjects' perceptions of speech sounds in accordance with their expectations rather than on the basis of the acoustic input.

If one leaves out the detection condition for severe mispronunciations (because performance was near-ceiling in all of its cells), the results may be glossed fairly simply: For both tasks, the highest percentage of "restorations," or misses, occurred for third-syllable (as opposed to first-syllable) mispronunciations in highly constrained contexts. Marslen-Wilson and Welsh took this result as evidence for what they called a "cohort" theory. In this model, the acoustic information at the beginning of a word suggests a group of candidate lexical items (the cohort). As more of the word is heard, fewer and fewer candidates remain viable. In addition, the sentential context rules out many of the contenders, thus speeding up the weeding out process. Eventually (and rapidly), only one candidate remains—the correct word. Note that this is clearly an interactive model (Type III), with higher-level constraints playing a strong role in the perceptual process.

Although the preceding analysis produces a rather tidy summary, the situation is actually somewhat more complicated. One problem concerns the effect of predictability on performance in each task. Recall that "fluent restorations" were used as an index of the extent to which a listener followed higher-level constraints rather than the actual signal. What this effect really means is that in high-constraint situations, the listeners were performing less accurately, since the subjects were told to shadow what was being said, not what should have been said. Marslen-Wilson and Welsh's data indicate that shadowing accuracy *declined* when the mispronounced word was predictable; this was true for both first syllable and third-syllable mispronunciations. The results in the detection paradigm were quite different. Recall that Cole and Jakimik (1978) reported *better* performance for more predictable words rather than the worse performance found with shadowing. In Marslen-Wilson and Welsh's data, the effect of predictablity was mixed: For first-syllable targets, detection was better in more predictable contexts. For third-syllable targets, however, there was a small reversal (78% misses for high constraint versus 73% for low); overall, no reliable effect emerged. In this analysis of the shadowing and detection results, the role of semantic and syntactic predictability is much less clear than it appeared initially. Moreover, it is not even clear what predictions for predictability an interactive model should make for the two measures used, since better performance appears to be indicated in one case, and worse performance in the other.

It should be noted that the situation is much clearer with respect to the effect of target position within words. For both tasks, and at both levels of predictability used, first-syllable mispronunciations were always better reported than third-syllable mispronunciations. The overall pattern of results thus supports a role of lexical influences in perception (Type II or III) but leaves the role of higher-level factors (Type III) in doubt.

II.F. Phonemic Restoration

If part of an utterance is excised and replaced by a noise, listeners generally report that the utterance sounded intact; they appear to perceptually "restore" the missing speech sound (Warren, 1970). Samuel (1981a, 1981b) has reported an extensive set of experiments on this "phonemic restoration" effect. Samuel (1981a) introduced a method for studying the illusion that was specifically designed to separate perceptual effects from any postperceptual biases that might play a role in the illusion. In this paradigm, listeners hear two kinds of stimuli: *Replacement* items are like those described above—noise replaces a phoneme (and parts of its preceding and following phonemes)—while *added* items are made by adding noise to the corresponding part of the utterance, without excising anything. To the extent that listeners are perceptually restoring any missing speech sounds, the added and replaced versions of a word should sound alike. By using signal detection analyses, a measure of their discriminability (d') can be computed. Given the proper controls, low d' scores indicate that the two versions sound alike: People are perceptually restoring the missing sound. Signal detection analyses also provide a measure of bias (beta) toward reporting an utterance as intact. These scores index any effects of postperceptual decision processes in the restoration illusion.

Using this technique, Samuel (1981a) investigated a number of factors that bear on the role of the lexicon in speech perception. For example, if lexical representations play a role in perception, one might expect high-frequency words to produce more restoration of their component speech sounds than low-frequency words. Exactly this result was obtained: Listeners were significantly worse at discriminating the added and replaced versions of high-frequency words than comparable versions of low-frequency words, indicating more restoration in more frequent words. However, the effect was rather small and is apparently not robust; Samuel (1981b) failed to find the effect under similar experimental conditions. A more extreme manipulation of frequency is to use items with frequency zero—pseudowords. Samuel conducted this comparison and found a large effect: Added and replaced versions of pseudowords were significantly *better* discriminated than word items. Since pseudowords have no lexical entries, no lexical influence is possible, thus accounting for the reduction in the restoration effect.

A similar explanation can account for the difference observed between primed and unprimed test words. In the priming condition, an added or replaced item was preceded by the auditory presentation of the original, unmanipulated version of the test word. Discrimination performance was significantly *worse* when the test item was preceded by its prime. Samuel argues that this was due to the prime activating the relevant lexical representation, leading to more input from the lexical level in the perception of the test item and thereby increasing restoration. Interestingly, the priming effect was concentrated on sounds near the end of the test words, an effect reminiscent of the positional effect found in the shadowing and mispronunciation detection paradigms.

Using the restoration methodology, Samuel (in preparation) has replicated Jakimik's (1979) effect of lexical uniqueness. Added and replaced versions of four-syllable words were constructed using the first, second, or third vowels as the critical phonemes. For half of the words, the first syllable was relatively unique (e.g., "tonsilitis," "fluctuating"); for the other half, it was quite common (e.g., "carbohydrate," "complicated"). Syllabic stress, word frequency, and identity of the third vowel were matched in the two classes of words. If lexical representations are involved in the perception of words, and if lexical access can be accomplished rapidly (as suggested by Marslen-Wilson, 1973, and Cole & Jakimik, 1980), different patterns of restoration would be expected for the two word types. The words with unique beginnings should afford faster lexical access, and the accessed lexical representation should produce more restoration of its component sounds. Thus, by the middle or end of these four-syllable words, we should see more restoration in the ones with unique beginnings. In fact, just this result occurred: The two word classes did not differ when the critical phoneme was in the first or second syllable but differed significantly on third-syllable restorations. Unique beginnings apparently produced more restoration, and thus lower d's.

The set of results just described converges nicely with the results outlined for other paradigms. We have seen repeatedly that the lexical status of the test word influences the results obtained on a number of measures. The results obtained by Samuel (1981a) on the effect of sentential context on restoration provide an interesting contrast. The experimental situation was basically the same as in the studies just described, except that the test words were presented in sentences. The sentential context was either predictive of the critical word or it wasn't. In contrast to the priming results, no increase in perceptual restoration was found for predictive context. In fact, there was a small *increase* in the discriminability of added and replaced versions when the word was predictable. Does this mean that listeners were insensitive to the context? No—the predictive context did significantly increase the probability of subjects reporting an utterance as intact. However, the effect was due entirely to a change in beta, the index of postperceptual decision factors.

III. THE ANSWER

What answers do the facts presented here suggest to the questions considered at the outset? The central question being considered is what role the lexicon might play in speech perception. Toward this end, three classes of theories have been considered: Type I theories, in which the lexicon plays no role in perception; Type II, in which the lexicon is the last stage of perception; and Type III, in which lexical representations interact with knowledge sources at higher and lower levels.

All of the studies examined here revealed strong effects of lexical-level factors on performance. For example, word frequency effects were found in perceiving speech in noise, detecting phoneme targets, recognizing gated words and restoring excised speech sounds. The question is whether the observed effects of such lexical factors reflect perceptual processing or not. For some of the tasks, this question is difficult or impossible to answer. For example, the superior report of high-frequency words when presented in noise could reflect either better perception or a stronger tendency to guess more frequent words than less common ones. Although Broadbent (1967) tried to sort these possibilities out, the task is by nature one that could produce such nonperceptual effects. The phoneme-monitoring task, as noted earlier, has similar properties, since the judgment to respond must be based on the availability of the target, not necessarily on its perception.

Ganong's (1980) synthesis technique appears at first glance to have similar limitations, since the basic result is a bias effect. However, Ganong's clever analysis of the data, based on the nonuniformity of bias as a function of VOT, provides some support for a true perceptual role of the lexical representation. Grosjean's (1980) gating technique also initially seems unlikely to reveal anything about perception, since subjects are basically playing a guessing game. However, like Ganong, Grosjean included a useful analysis that may reveal perceptual effects. Recall that more frequent words were recognized with less acoustic information than less frequent words. More importantly, this difference was not undercut by subjects' confidence ratings. If we assume, as before, that the subjects based their ratings on what they actually perceived, rather than what they guessed, we are led to the conclusion that listeners can perceive more frequent words with less acoustic support than is needed for low-frequency words. Thus the lexicon is playing a role in speech perception.

The results from the shadowing, mispronunciation detection, and phonemic restoration paradigms suggest a similar conclusion. In all three tasks, the left-to-right structure of words and its relationship to other words in the lexicon significantly affected performance. In all three, the data suggested that early parts of words are processed more accurately than later parts, and that this difference is dependent on whether other words are "nearby" in the lexicon. The perceptual nature of these effects is easier to pin down in some tasks than in others; however, it is difficult to generate a convincing nonperceptual explanation for the detection data, and the restoration results are based on d', an explicitly perceptual measure. Thus, across a wide range of tasks, the data support a role of the lexicon in speech perception. In terms of the theory classes that have been outlined, either Type II or Type III models are supported.

Can we narrow the choice any further, to either Type II or Type III theories only? One approach is to consider the role of syntactic and semantic knowledge sources, since most Type III theories are fully interactive. A review of the results of contextual predictability reveals surprisingly little support for the role of syntactic and semantic knowledge in speech perception. For example, phoneme-monitoring studies (e.g., Blank & Foss, 1978) have demonstrated faster detection of targets in predictable words. As we have seen, however, it is difficult to draw conclusions about perception from this task. All we can say is that more predictable words become available sooner to the process that detects mispronunciations; no direct inferences about perception can be made.

The story is similar for the gating paradigm. The fact that more predictable words reach the "isolation point" sooner suggests that contextual constraints are traded off with acoustic cues. However, the confidence ratings (the only plausible connection to perception in this task) revealed that this tradeoff is probably postperceptual, since reports based on contextual information were rated significantly lower than ones based on acoustic information. Once again, the perceptual role of semantic and syntactic properties is questionable.

The results of the shadowing and mispronunciation detection tasks show a similar pattern. Here again we see a consistent role for a lexical factor (target position in the word) coupled with inconsistent results for higher-level factors. Recall that both tasks revealed better performance on word-initial targets than on later ones but that the tasks differed with respect to the effect of predictability: Shadowing accuracy was worse in predictable contexts (Marslen-Wilson & Welsh, 1978), while detection performance was unaffected (Marslen-Wilson & Welsh, 1978) or better (Cole & Jakimik, 1978). This inconsistency of results is probably due to the interaction of the predictability manipulation with task demands. For example, in shadowing, subjects may use predictability to guess the upcoming word, as suggested by the consistency of errors with the context. This strategy would produce a speed–accuracy tradeoff, with faster and more erroneous shadowing in a predictive context. Such a tradeoff could account for the faster detection of mispronunciations in predictive contexts reported by Cole and Jakimik (1978). These strategic explanations are consistent with a nonperceptual, rather than a perceptual, role for contextual constraint.

Finally, consider the results of the phonemic restoration studies. As mentioned earlier, these experiments were specifically designed to separate perceptual and decision stage processes. Several different lexical-level factors produced significant perceptual effects. In contrast, sentential predictability influenced subjects to call utterances "intact" but did so at a postperceptual level. Thus, in a direct test, syntactic and semantic influences failed to produce a perceptual effect.

The set of results just presented suggests that we must eliminate Type III theories from consideration. Since we have previously eliminated Type I models, this step seems to provide an answer to our question: The role of the lexicon in speech perception is to be the last stage of the process. One clarification should be added, however. Type II models were initially described as being quite similar to Type I models, differing only in whether the lexical level was included in the perceptual process. Both classes were assumed to include only a bottom-up flow of information. The results that we have seen suggest that this characteristic is incorrect: Samuel's (1981a) restoration results, and possibly Ganong's (1980) synthesis experiment, indicate that lexical-level information can influence the perception of lower-level units. Thus the correct characterization of the role of the lexicon should include the interactive nature of Type III models but with a lower limit on where in the system the perceptual process ends. It might be best to conclude that models of Type II_{II}^{I} are best supported: The lexical level is the last stage of perception, and its role is important, active, and interactive.

ACKNOWLEDGMENT

Some of the ideas expressed in this chapter developed during a seminar taught jointly with Louis Goldstein. I would like to thank him for his role in developing such ideas. Of course, his endorsement of the positions taken here should not be assumed—the responsibility for any foolishness is mine.

REFERENCES

Blank, M. A., & Foss, D. J. (1978). Semantic facilitation and lexical access during sentence processing. *Memory & Cognition, 6,* 644–652.

Broadbent, D. E. (1967). Word-frequency effect and response bias. *Psychological Review, 74,* 1–15.

Cole, R. A. (1973). Listening for mispronunciations: A measure of what we hear during speech. *Perception & Psychophysics, 13,* 153–156.

Cole, R. A., & Jakimik, J. (1978). Understanding speech: How words are heard. In G. Underwood (Ed.), *Strategies of information processing.* London: Academic Press.

Cole, R. A., & Jakimik, J. (1980). A model of speech perception. In R. Cole (Ed.), *Perception and production of fluent speech.* Hillsdale, NJ: Erlbaum.

Cole, R. A., Jakimik, J., & Cooper, W. E. (1978). Perceptibility of phonetic features in fluent speech. *Journal of the Acoustical Society of America, 64,* 44–56.

Cole, R. A., & Scott, B. (1974). Towards a theory of speech perception. *Psychological Review, 81,* 348–374.

Eimas, P., & Corbit, J. (1973). Selective adaptation of linguistic feature detectors. *Cognitive Psychology, 4,* 99–109.

Forster, K. I. (1976). Accessing the mental lexicon. In R. J. Wales & E. Walker (Eds.), *New approaches to language mechanisms.* Amsterdam: North Holland.

Foss, D. J., & Blank, M. A. (1980). Identifying the speech codes. *Cognitive Psychology, 12,* 1–31.

Foss, D. J., Harwood, D. A., & Blank, M. A. (1980). Deciphering decoding decisions: Data and devices. In R. Cole (Ed.), *Perception and production of fluent speech.* Hillsdale, NJ: Erlbaum.

Foss, D. J., & Swinney, D. A. (1973). On the psychological reality of the phoneme: Perception, identification, and consciousness. *Journal of Verbal Learning and Verbal Behavior, 12,* 246–257.

Fujimura, O., Macchi, M., & Lovins, J. (1977). *Demisyllables and affixes for speech synthesis.* Paper presented to the Ninth International Congress on Acoustics, Madrid.

Ganong, W. F. (1980). Phonetic categorization in auditory word perception. *Journal of Experimental Psychology: Human Perception and Performance, 6,* 110–125.

Grosjean, F. (1980). Spoken word recognition processes and the gating paradigm. *Perception & Psychophysics, 28,* 267–283.

Howes, D. H., & Solomon, R. L. (1951). Visual duration threshold as a function of word probability. *Journal of Experimental Psychology, 41,* 401–410.

Jakimik, J. (1979). *The interaction of sound and knowledge in word recognition from fluent speech.* Unpublished doctoral dissertation, Carnegie-Mellon University, Pittsburgh.

Klatt, D. H. (1980). Speech perception: A model of acoustic–phonetic analysis and lexical access. In R. Cole (Ed.), *Perception and production of fluent speech.* Hillsdale, NJ: Erlbaum.

Liberman, A. M., Cooper, F. S., Shankweiler, D. P., & Studdert-Kennedy, M. (1967). Perception of the speech code. *Psychological Review, 74,* 431–461.

Marslen-Wilson, W. D. (1973). Linguistic structure and speech shadowing at very short latencies. *Nature, 244,* 522–523.

Marslen-Wilson, W. D. (1975). Sentence perception as an interactive parallel process. *Science, 189,* 226–228.

Marslen-Wilson, W. D., & Welsh, A. (1978). Processing interactions and lexical access during word recognition in continuous speech. *Cognitive Psychology, 10,* 29–63.

Massaro, D. W. (Ed). (1975). *Understanding language: An information processing analysis of speech perception, reading, and psycholinguistics.* New York: Academic Press.

Morton, J. A. (1969). Interaction of information in word perception. *Psychological Review, 76,* 165–178.

Morton, J., & Long, J. (1976). Effect of word transitional probability on phoneme identification. *Journal of Verbal Learning and Verbal Behavior, 15,* 43–51.

Oden, G., & Massaro, D. W. (1978). Integration of featural information in speech perception. *Psychological Review, 85,* 172–191.

Pisoni, D. B. (1973). Auditory and phonetic memory codes in the discrimination of consonants and vowels. *Perception & Psychophysics, 13,* 253–260.

Reddy, D. R., Erman, L. D., Fennell, R. D., & Neely, R. B. (1973). The Hearsay speech understanding system: An example of the recognition process. *Proceedings of the International Joint Conference on Artificial Intelligence,* Stanford, California.

Rubin, P. E. (1975). *Semantic influences on phonetic identification and lexical decision.* Unpublished doctoral dissertation, University of Connecticut, Storrs.

Rubin, P., Turvey, M. T., & van Gelder, P. (1976). Initial phonemes are detected faster in spoken words than in spoken nonwords. *Perception & Psychophysics, 19,* 394–398.

Rumelhart, D. E. (1977). Toward an interactive model of reading. In S. Dornic (Ed.), *Attention and performance VI.* Hillsdale, NJ: Erlbaum.

Rumelhart, D. E., & McClelland, J. L. (1982). An interactive model of context effects in letter perception: Part 2. The contextual enhancement effect and some tests and extensions of the model. *Psychological Review, 89,* 60–94.

Samuel, A. G. (1981a). Phonemic restoration: Insights from a new methodology. *Journal of Experimental Psychology: General, 110,* 474–494.

Samuel, A. G. (1981b). The role of bottom-up confirmation in the phonemic restoration illusion. *Journal of Experimental Psychology: Human Perception and Performance, 7,* 1124–1131.

Samuel, A. G. (1986). The effect of lexical uniqueness on the phonemic restoration illusion. In preparation.

Samuel, A. G., & Newport, E. L. (1979). Adaptation of speech by nonspeech: Evidence for complex acoustic cue detectors. *Journal of Experimental Psychology: Human Perception and Performance, 5,* 563–578.

Stevens, K., & Blumstein, S. (1981). The search for invariant acoustic correlates of phonetic features. In J. Miller & P. Eimas (Eds.), *Perspectives on the study of speech*. Hillsdale, NJ: Erlbaum.

Warren, R. M. (1970). Perceptual restoration of missing speech sounds. *Science, 167,* 392–393.

CHAPTER 4

The Role of Attention and Active Processing in Speech Perception*

Howard C. Nusbaum† and Eileen C. Schwab‡

† Department of Psychology, Indiana University, Bloomington, Indiana 47405, and ‡ AT&T Information Systems, Indianapolis, Indiana 46206

I. INTRODUCTION

Every day, human listeners understand speech directly, effortlessly, and seemingly automatically. In most cases we seem to comprehend each word as it is spoken, with little or no conscious effort. However, the immediacy with which spoken words enter consciousness belies the complexity of the first stage of perceptuolinguistic operations—the extraction of phonetic information from the speech signal. It has been estimated that the conversion of speech sounds into phonemes reduces the information transfer rate of speech from 40,000 bits per second to 40 bits per second (Liberman, Mattingly, & Turvey, 1972). These figures indicate that the first stage of perceptuolinguistic coding must be considerably more complicated than introspection would imply.

I.A. Perceptual Units in Speech

If phonemes were produced as unique and discrete sounds, speech perception would be similar to reading printed English one letter at a time, from left to right. Unfortunately, it is seldom the case that any single acoustic segment corresponds to a unique phonetic percept (Liberman, Cooper, Shankweiler, & Studdert-Kennedy, 1967). The difficulty in parti-

* Preparation of this chapter was partially supported by NIH Research Grant NS-12179 and NIH Training Grant NS-07134 to Indiana University.

PATTERN RECOGNITION BY HUMANS
AND MACHINES: Speech Perception
Volume 1

tioning an utterance into phonemes ultimately stems from the way in which speech is produced. The process of articulation converts a mental representation of language into speech through the physical movement of various parts of the mouth (e.g., the tongue). One of the inherent characteristics of this process is that one set of articulatory gestures may influence and modify other temporally proximal articulatory movements. It is through this coarticulatory influence that phonemes become "encoded" into sound (Liberman, 1970). The result is context-conditioned variability in the acoustic–phonetic structure of speech—that is, the acoustic information corresponding to one phonetic segment is distributed in time, overlapping and modifying the cues to preceding and succeeding phones. Furthermore, while there is evidence for perceptible acoustic cues to word boundaries in speech (e.g., Nakatani & Dukes, 1977), coarticulatory effects can have consequences that may cross syllable and word boundaries (Kent & Minifie, 1977; Öhman, 1966).

I.B. Perceptual Research on Units in Speech

Although for a number of years there has been some controversy over the nature of the basic unit of speech perception (e.g., Klatt, 1980; Liberman, 1970, 1982; Massaro, 1972; Wickelgren, 1969), to date no direct evidence has been found that specifically rules out one particular unit in favor of another. Instead, it has been generally accepted that different perceptual units may serve different perceptual functions (see Pisoni, 1978; Studdert-Kennedy, 1976). As a result, theories of speech perception must account for the perception of phonemes and words and must specify the perceptual function of acoustic cues, phonetic features, and syllables.

While much of the research on speech perception has focused on the earliest levels of acoustic–phonetic processing, there has also been substantial interest in word perception as well (see Luce & Pisoni, in press, for a review). However, while many studies of speech perception have considered problems such as the relationship between acoustic cues and phonetic percepts, or the role of word-initial information in word recognition, there has been little theoretical attention paid to the types of computational mechanisms that might be necessary for speech perception. By far, most of the perceptual research conducted on phoneme perception has been more concerned with exploring "perceptual phenomena," such as duplex perception or audio-visual speech perception (see Repp, 1982, for a review), than with testing basic theoretical assumptions. And, while work on auditory word perception has been more theoretically motivated (see Pisoni, in press), very little is understood about the different classes of theoretical mechanisms that might account for the perception of spoken words. As a result, we feel that it is important to begin to consider the type of evidence necessary for understanding the basic computational processes that mediate speech perception.

II. CONTROL STRUCTURES IN PERCEPTION

Any information processing system has three basic characteristics: coding schemes for representing information, computations for transforming one representation into another, and control structures that direct the flow of transformations. The organization of the control structures in perceptual information processing systems can be sorted into two broad classes—passive processes and active processes (MacKay, 1951, 1956). Since this distinction between control structures can be used to categorize theories of speech perception (see Licklider, 1952), it can have important implications for understanding and testing those theories.

II.A. Passive Perceptual Mechanisms

The control structure of a passive process is an open-loop system (i.e., no feedback is involved) that consists of an invariant and unconditioned sequence of computations. While it may be possible to modify the nature or sequence of transformations over a long period of time (e.g., through learning), for any particular input the computational sequence is considered to be fixed. Figure 4.1 shows a schematic representation of a passive process. Some input representation (e.g., a stimulus) is ultimately transformed, through an unspecified number of computations, into an output representation (e.g., a response). In this type of system, a stimulus is recognized by the product of the final computation. Computations may be performed in serial or in parallel, cascaded (see McClelland, 1979) or not (Sternberg, 1969), and with any number of intermediate representations.

The critical distinguishing characteristic of a passive process is that the sequence and nature of the computations is invariant for any input. A passive process, then, can be viewed as a direct associative mechanism that takes stimulus energy as input and produces some perceptual categorization or response as output. Therefore, simple cascaded hierarchical feature detector systems without feedback (e.g., Abbs & Sussman, 1971, for speech; Barlow, 1972, for vision) are passive systems, as are some

Figure 4.1   Schematic representation of a passive process. A stimulus (S_i) is successively modified by a sequence of transformations (T_j). Recognition of a stimulus is determined by the outcome of the last computation in the system (R_{ni}).

content-addressable, parallel-access, distributed memory systems (Kohonen, 1978).

Despite the extremely large differences in the types of computations performed by these passive systems, they share one characteristic: The sequence of computations and the association between input and output is invariant for any particular stimulus. This kind of control structure is quite different from the active control process described by MacKay (1951, 1956).

II.B. Active Perceptual Mechanisms

In active control processes, the flow of computation is contingent on the outcome of certain comparisons or computations. In one form of active process, neurally coded sensory input is compared with representations that are generated internally as hypotheses or expectations about the input. If a mismatch occurs, a new hypothesis is generated and the process is reiterated. A stimulus is recognized when an acceptable match between the hypothesis and the input occurs and the iterative process is terminated. In another form, an active process may use recurrent feedback (or perhaps even "feedforward") as a means of inhibiting competing hypotheses or controlling other computations. Thus active processes are characterized by directing subsequent operations or the flow of computation contingent on the outcome of previous processes.

As shown in Figures 4.2 and 4.3, active processes may be distinguished from each other by the source of "hypothesis generation." Hypotheses about stimulus identity may be generated from the top down or from the bottom up. In this context, hypothesis generation is not restricted to describing those systems that make explicit symbolic predictions about the identity of a stimulus. Rather, it is also meant to refer to the activation of a set of nodes or states that implicitly code either a collection of local interpretations or a temporary global interpretation in a parallel, distributed processing system.

Figure 4.2 is a schematic representation of an active process that produces hypotheses either from prior context or from some long-term knowledge base. This portrayal is not intended to represent a flowchart of the computational process. Instead, it is an abstract characterization of the relationships among some of the key computational elements in an active process. No assumptions are made about the nature of the computations or data structures involved.

In this active system, a stimulus (indicated by S_i) is first coded internally by passive processes as an internal representation (R_i). This initial representation of the stimulus (R_i) is compared with a set of hypothesized representations (R_x) generated from a knowledge base (K). If a match

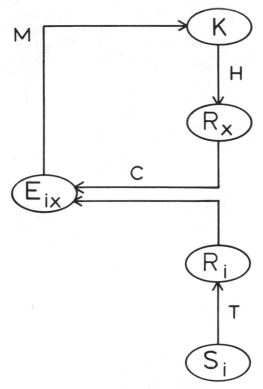

Figure 4.2   Schematic representation of a concept-driven, top-down active process. A stimulus (S_i) is coded by transformations (T) to produce an internal representation of the stimulus (R_i). A knowledge base (K) is used to generate (through H) hypotheses (R_x) about the stimulus. Hypotheses and stimulus code are compared (by C), producing an error signal (E_{ix}) that either indicates correct recognition or is used to modify (by M) the knowledge base.

occurs between R_i and R_x, the stimulus is recognized. If, however, a sufficient discrepancy is obtained between the coded stimulus (R_i) and a particular hypothesis (R_x), an error signal (E_{ix}) is generated to the knowledge base to aid in selecting a new hypothesis. Conceptually driven (i.e., top-down) processing of this sort is generally invoked to account for perception when the clarity or salience of the input signal is in doubt (Newell, 1975). Perhaps the most prototypical example of this type of system was described by Minsky (1975), in which long-term memory structures called "frames" encode schematic representations of perceptual objects providing a knowledge base for directing the recognition process.

While a concept-driven active process is the most common way of

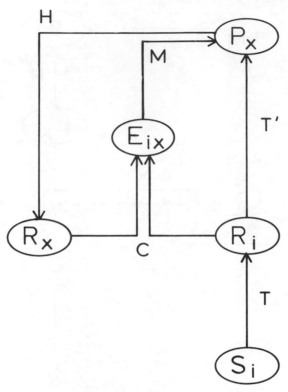

Figure 4.3 Schematic representation of a data-driven, bottom-up active process. A stimulus (S_i) is coded by transformations (T) to produce an internal representation (R_i) of the stimulus. A second transformation sequence (T') produces a new code (R_x) that represents a tentative classification of the stimulus. To confirm this classification, hypotheses (R_x) are proposed (by H) to determine which stimulus evoked P_x. The hypotheses are then compared to the representation of the stimulus (by C), and an error signal (E_{ix}) is generated to signal a correct match or to select a new classification (P_x) or hypothesis (R_x) for further testing. This error signal could be used to learn a new category code or category instance.

conceptualizing active systems, data-driven (or bottom-up) active processes are also possible. In a bottom-up active process, shown in Figure 4.3, an input stimulus (S_i) is transformed by passive processes until some coded representation of the input is achieved (R_x). A second set of transformations produces a new code (P_x) from this representation that might, for instance, represent the hypothesized perceptual category in which the input belongs. It is this new code that is subsequently used to determine the identity of the stimulus, perhaps by choosing instances of the category (R_x). In other words, through appropriate computations, the category code (P_x) tries to "guess" which category member activated the category code. Matching the hypothesis (R_x) with the representation of the input (R_i) would then confirm the categorization of the input. A mismatch generates an error signal (E_{ix}) that is used to generate a new category member (R_x) for testing, or to activate a new category code (P_x). Failing any type of match, this error signal might be used with either subsequent or prior context to form a novel category or to make the input a new member of an old category. Grossberg (1980) has proposed that this sort of data-driven active process may play a critical role in any adaptive recognition system that is capable of perceptual learning.

In summary, then, it is apparent that an active process cannot be distinguished from a passive process simply by the predominant direction of information transmission (i.e., bottom-up versus top-down). The active/ passive distinction is based instead on the different *control structures* employed by these systems. An active mechanism incorporates a control structure that directs the flow of processing based on the outcome of tests or comparisons or on other computations. This closed-loop organization contrasts sharply with the open-loop structure of a passive process in which the computational sequence is, in the short run, obligatory and invariant.

II.C. Active and Passive Models of Speech Perception

The basic theoretical motivation for active models of speech perception derives primarily from the context-conditioned variability in speech. Active models have generally been proposed as the solution to the problem of segmenting and recognizing discrete perceptual units in the continuous speech waveform. In general, the best known active models of speech perception fall into two broad categories based on the knowledge used to direct the recognition process. The motor theory of speech perception (Liberman, Cooper, Harris, & MacNeilage, 1962) and analysis by synthesis (Stevens & Halle, 1967; Stevens & House, 1972) both proposed that knowledge of speech production could be used to decode or recognize phonetic segments. Since it is through articulation that phonemes are encoded into sound, knowledge about the encoding process should be critical to recovering phonetic information from the speech waveform.

In contrast with theories of speech perception that make use of articulatory knowledge, other active theories have invoked linguistic knowledge as a means of overcoming acoustic–phonetic variability. These linguistic-knowledge-based theories do not view speech perception as a process of acoustic–phonetic decoding but instead as a problem of deducing or inferring the intended message from a noisy signal. These active models of speech perception generally contend that the acoustic information in the speech waveform underdetermines the phonetic content of the message (Newell, 1975). What differs among these models is the specific nature of the linguistic knowledge that is used and the way in which the knowledge is applied. Chomsky and Miller (1963; also Chomsky & Halle, 1968) have proposed that acoustic information in the speech signal could be used to construct hypotheses about the syntactic structure of an utterance. The claim here was that expectations and linguistic knowledge are used to generate syntactic structures that are then compared to the acoustically generated hypotheses. Recognition in this theory occurs by matching phonological-form surface structures (see Miller, 1962).

Attempts at modeling speech recognition using the techniques of artificial intelligence have been similar, in spirit, to this approach. For example, the Hearsay system used a heterarchical control structure in which syntactic, semantic, lexical, and phonological "experts" proposed various interpretations of an utterance (Lesser & Erman, 1977). Thus the comprehension of an utterance in Hearsay is the product of a number of different interacting knowledge sources. Elman and McClelland (in press) have proposed an interactive activation account of speech perception in which lexical knowledge interacts with phonetic knowledge to constrain the recognition process. In this model, active processing is instantiated in recurrent feedback loops between different levels of representation, such as between words and phonemes or between phonemes and features.

It is not at all clear that an active control system using articulatory or linguistic knowledge is necessary for recognizing phonetic segments. Research on spectrogram reading (Cole, Rudnicky, Zue, & Reddy, 1980; Greene, Pisoni, & Carrell, 1984) and on the classification of speech sounds by nonhuman animals (e.g., Miller, 1977) and infants (see Jusczyk, 1981) clearly indicates that the acoustic structure of an utterance contains sufficient information to recover phonemes directly without the use of articulatory or linguistic knowledge, thus arguing against a major motivating factor for active processes. Indeed, Fant (1967) asserts that active theories are not necessary to explain phoneme perception, nor are they unequivocally supported by the available data. Instead, he claims that phonetic labeling occurs through the action of bottom-up passive procedures in which the speech waveform undergoes successive transformations that do not require intervention by higher-level processes or active mediation. First, the acoustic signal is transduced by the ear and subjected to a preliminary auditory analysis. The output of this analysis is then directly encoded into distinctive auditory features (Fant, 1962). At successively higher levels, these features are combined into phonemes that are used to construct syllables. Finally, words are perceived.

This outline for a perceptual theory has served as an important starting place for several hierarchically organized information processing theories of speech perception (e.g., Bondarko, Zagorujko, Kozhevnikov, Molchanov, & Chistovich, 1970; Pisoni & Sawusch, 1975). In these models, the speech signal is encoded into a set of auditory features, such as formant frequency and formant bandwidth. These features are then combined to form phonetic segments at a stage of processing later in the system. Since it is acknowledged that there is no simple or direct relationship between acoustic and phonetic segments, each phone may be derived from a number of adjacent acoustic features. Thus the problem of context-conditioned variability is resolved by reference to all the acoustic segments affected by the articulation of a single phoneme. Each successively higher unit of analysis (syllables, morphemes, words, and phrases) is constructed and interpreted using the output of the immediately preceding stage.

Variations on this basic theme may involve the use of an active control structure after phonetic segments are recognized to allow phonological and lexical knowledge to interact with and modify the phonemes that have been recognized (see Foss & Blank, 1980; Pisoni & Sawusch, 1975). In these hybrid models, phonetic labeling occurs automatically by passive, bottom-up processes (Pisoni, 1978). However, phoneme (i.e., phonological) perception is not based solely on the bottom-up processing of phonetic segments but instead results from interactions between the output of phonetic recognition, phonological rules, and the active mediation of higher-order linguistic processes.

An alternative to the information processing approach to modeling passive phonetic perception is feature detector theory (Abbs & Sussman, 1971). This theory derives from the finding that there exist neural units in the auditory cortex of animals that are selectively sensitive to spectrotemporal acoustic patterns (see Evans, 1974) such as the formant transitions in speech. Not only are there detectors tuned to respond to auditory features, such as the direction of frequency change, but there are also higher-order analyzers that fire to signal species-specific calls (see Scheich, 1977). Cooper (1979) has described a feature detector model that could explain phoneme perception and serve to forge a theoretical link between speech perception and production. This theory clearly shows the potential explanatory power of feature detectors.

Unfortunately, feature detector theories of speech perception are substantiated only by research using a single methodological paradigm—selective adaptation. Furthermore, Cooper's theory depends on the use of phoneme detectors, whereas selective adaptation research has indicated that while there is some evidence for the operation of auditory feature detectors (Ades, 1976; Sawusch, 1977), phoneme recognition is probably mediated by more complex decision processes (Sawusch & Jusczyk, 1981; Sawusch & Nusbaum, 1983). However, feature detector models have been proposed that are consistent with these data. In such models, auditory features are extracted from the waveform and a passive phonetic decision is then carried out on those features (Massaro & Oden, 1980; Sawusch, 1976; Searle, Jacobson, & Kimberly, 1980).

Other passive models of speech perception have focused on word perception and have either ignored the problem of phoneme perception or attempted to circumvent it entirely. Morton's (1969) logogen theory proposes that each word is represented by a passive computational device, called a "logogen," that simply increments a count representing the number of features present in a stimulus that are consistent with each logogen. When the count exceeds a logogen's threshold, the word represented by the logogen is recognized. However, logogen theory has little to say about the specific features that are counted or how phonemes are recognized.

Klatt (1980) has proposed a passive model of word recognition called lexical access from spectra (LAFS) that does away with the need for an intermediate stage of phoneme perception prior to word recognition. Instead, words are recognized by matching short-term power spectra extracted from an utterance against a network of diphone power spectra representing word patterns. A word is recognized when a path through the network has been successfully matched against the stimulus word. In this model, knowledge about the acoustic structure of words has been precompiled into the recognition network to allow linguistic knowledge to constrain recognition in a passive system similar to the Harpy system (Lowerre & Reddy, 1979).

While many of these active and passive theories of speech perception have garnered some support from research on speech perception, there is clearly no overwhelming evidence for any particular theory. Furthermore, many of these theories have never been described in sufficient detail to allow researchers to generate and test specific predictions. Moreover, there have been no systematic attempts to test predictions that might rule out entire subsets of these theories. However, by classifying theories according to their control structures, it is possible to formulate testable predictions that could discriminate between these classes.

II.D. Evidence for Active and Passive Control Structures

Although data-driven theories of phoneme perception have received some support from a number of different experimental paradigms (e.g., spectrogram reading, infant speech perception, and classification of speech sounds by nonhuman animals), none of this research can adequately distinguish passive processes from data-driven active systems. Both types of data-driven mechanisms rely on the same source of information (the acoustic structure of speech), and the flow of information within both systems is predominantly from the bottom up. While it is true that the distinction between bottom-up and top-down processes is an important theoretical issue, it does not resolve the question regarding the nature of the control structures used in speech perception. Experiments intended to discriminate the operation of a passive process from the operation of a bottom-up active process must derive their predictions from the differences in control structure between these theories.

The basic differences between active and passive processes can be summarized quite simply. Passive processes represent computationally invariant mappings between an input and its classification. While this sort of process would be most appropriate if there existed direct invariant mappings of acoustic properties onto phonetic features (see Stevens, 1975), the search for such mappings has been inconclusive to date (but see Kewley-Port, 1983; Stevens & Blumstein, 1978). The invariant nature of passive processes does not necessarily require invariant acoustic–phonetic relationships, but it does entail a lack of flexibility in responding to a stimulus. In general, the same physical stimulus should be processed in the same way regardless of the expectations of the listener or the perceptual or linguistic context in which the stimulus occurs. By comparison, an active process should be flexible in its ability to meet the demands of any context or situation. Thus the expectations of a listener should affect active processing, while a passive process should not be influenced by expectations or context.

In addition, by virtue of its control structure, a passive process should operate "automatically" (see Posner & Snyder, 1975; Shiffrin, 1976), directly associating a stimulus with a response without requiring attention or interfering with other cognitive or perceptual processes. By contrast, an active system would be expected to place demands on cognitive resources, thus purchasing perceptual flexibility at the price of cognitive capacity limitations (see Posner, 1978). Thus active and passive processes should differ in the capacity demands they place on the human information processing system.

III. CAPACITY LIMITATIONS IN SPEECH PERCEPTION

Although we have asserted that the relative capacity demands imposed by a perceptual process should indicate the type of control structure used by that process, it is necessary to establish the rationale for this assertion through a linking hypothesis between control structure differences and theories of attention. It is particularly important to show that the capacity limitations that we claim should be imposed by a control structure are not tied directly to any particular theory of selective attention. In fact, we argue that control structure differences can serve as a metatheoretical principle for analyzing theories of selective attention in perception. It should be noted that although our ultimate goal is to derive predictions about capacity limitations in speech perception, the link between control structures and attention is equally valid for the perception of visual form.

While a complete review of the myriad theories of attention is clearly beyond the scope of this discussion, the general trend in theoretical issues is important. Earlier theories described attention as an independent mechanism (e.g., a "filter" or "attenuator") that was interposed between two other stages of processing to avoid overloading central perceptual processes by the vast array of impinging sensory input (e.g., Broadbent, 1958; Treisman, 1964). However, later theories have depicted attention as a consequence of the inherent limitations of other human information processing mechanisms. In this characterization, there is no single process called "selective attention." Instead, selective attention simply results from the operation of a process that can only handle a single input, produce a single output, or that requires a great amount of effort or computational resources. Thus there may be many different loci of attention throughout the human information processing system, each with its own inherent limitations.

III.A. Theories of Attention

Looking over the many diverse ways of characterizing attention, a relatively simple dichotomy appears. Attention may be selective because of resource limitations or process limitations (Norman & Bobrow, 1975). A resource-limited theory attributes the limitation of selective attention to limitations on a pool of resources, such as effort (see Kahneman, 1973) or memory (see Shiffrin, 1976), necessary for cognitive processing. By contrast, a process-limited theory attributes selectivity to the inherent computational structure of the cognitive operations themselves. This dichotomy serves quite nicely to classify theories of attention.

A prototypical example of a resource-limitation theory of attention is that proposed by Shiffrin (1976; Shiffrin & Schneider, 1977). This theory derives from Atkinson and Shiffrin's (1968) view of memory as a collection of nodes that become associated with each other through spatial and temporal contiguity. Atkinson and Shiffrin proposed that a set of "control processes" operate in this memory space to carry out various functions such as recall and recognition.

Shiffrin's (1976) description of "automatized" (or automatic) and controlled processing is a logical extension of this theory of memory. An automatized process is one that becomes activated without the need for conscious direction or the use of "control processes" and that does not require cognitive resources (e.g., short-term memory). Automatized processing is said to occur when a collection of nodes in long-term memory is activated together often enough for associations to "glue" together the nodes. Thus activating part of a collection of nodes automatically (by association) activates the entire collection, much like Hebb's (1949) concept of cell assemblies. By comparison, a controlled process is consciously directed and limited by the capacity of short-term storage. The limitations of short-term memory come into play because it is assumed that independent nodes in memory (not glued together) must be held active there. As a result, the number of "chunks" of long-term memory that can be independently activated is limited by the capacity available in short-term memory.

Process-limitation theories of attention provide an alternative approach to characterizing the selectivity of attention. Perhaps the best known process-limitation theory of attention was described by Neisser (1967), who proposed a theoretical distinction between "preattentive" and "focal-attentive" perceptual processes. Preattentive mechanisms allow subjects to process multiple sensory inputs simultaneously. However, these preattentive processes are restricted to making simple discriminations based on gross physical characteristics such as color or voice (e.g., male versus female). The purpose of these mechanisms is to sort inputs into channels for subsequent analysis and to direct (or orient) focal attention from one channel to another. By comparison, stimulus recognition is carried out, according to Neisser, by focal attention through a "figural analysis-by-synthesis" of the outputs of preattentive channels. The process of synthesizing recognition units (figural analysis by synthesis) is considered to be equivalent to focusing attention on a particular sensory input. The limitations of attention are therefore seen as a consequence of the active perceptual process of figural synthesis.

This description of preattentive and focal-attentive mechanisms is similar to recent theoretical claims made by Treisman and her colleagues (Treisman & Gelade, 1980; Treisman & Schmidt, 1982). They have proposed that early feature encoding mechanisms operate without capacity limitations or interference from other processes. Once the features have been extracted from a stimulus array, they must be integrated to form a perceptual object. In this view, as in Neisser's, it is the process of object perception through feature integration that limits attention, not the coding of the perceptual dimensions of an object.

Our goal in discussing these two classes of attentional theories is to provide the foundation for relating attention to control structure. However, rather than form this relationship between control structure distinctions and any single theory or perspective, it is important to establish it over classes of theories of attention. Thus we must unify resource-limited and process-limited theories at some level of analysis that is more abstract than the specific details of any particular theory. This is by no means a trivial problem. While it is true that there are some surface similarities between process-limited and resource-limited theories of attention, at first glance the differences seem to be far greater. Of course, the first and most obvious difference is in the nature of the limitations on attention—process versus resource. However, an even larger difference is apparent when we consider the type of data accounted for by these theories.

Process-limitation theories of attention such as Treisman and Gelade's (1980) feature integration theory can easily account for both early parallel perceptual processing and selective perceptual attention. However, feature integration theory, while overlapping in some respects with resource-limitation theories, was not proposed to account for the type of data generally used to support the distinction between automatic and controlled processing. The resource-limitation theory proposed by Shiffrin and Schneider (1977) was derived from a theory of memory and was therefore designed to account for learning effects. In other words, part of the motivation for this theory was to account for the way in which a controlled process becomes an automatic process. By contrast, process-limitation theories have focused less on general problems of memory and learning and more on the problems of perceptual recognition. As a result, feature integration theory and other process-limitation theories cannot easily account for the "automatization" of a controlled perceptual process that might occur as a function of learning.

This is a serious problem for some process-limitation theories, because a number of studies have shown that attention-demanding perception can be automatized (i.e., made to appear preattentive) with appropriate training (see LaBerge & Samuels, 1974; Shiffrin & Schneider, 1977). However, in process-limitation theories, the distinction between preattentive and focal-attentive processes is a consequence of the different kinds of perceptual analyses carried out by these systems and not the amount of training given a subject. Simple feature processing is preattentive, while more complex feature integration and pattern analysis procedures require selective attention. In order to automatize focal-attentive processes within the framework of the theories proposed by Neisser (1967) and Treisman and Gelade (1980), the complexity of the analysis performed by these mechanisms must be reduced to the level of the simple feature discriminations conducted preattentively. Of course, this step would defeat the purpose of automatization, since the mechanism would not be capable of carrying out the same sort of perceptual analyses after automatization that it could prior to automatization.

III.B. Control Structures and Attention

We can surmount the apparent differences between process-limited and resource-limited theories by relating these theories directly to the distinction between active and passive processes. This was done, in a preliminary way, by Neisser (1967), who identified the operation of an active process (analysis by synthesis) with selective attention and the operation of passive processes (e.g., feature detectors) with preattentive mechanisms. In other words, according to Neisser, a passive process does not entail or require selective attention, while an active process is, by definition, one that demands (or perhaps results in) selective attention. This distinction provides a relatively simple means for assessing the control structure of a perceptual process: If the performance of a task demands attention, the task is mediated by an active process; if the task does not require attention, a passive process is involved. Of course, this criterion is not quite as simple as it seems. Before this test can be applied for assessing the control structure of speech perception, it is necessary to consider in greater detail what the consequences of active and passive control systems should be for selective attention.

To cope with the problem of the automatization of focal-attentive, active processes, we must make some modifications in Neisser's (1967) definitions of preattentive and focal-attentive processes. Rather than identify selective attention with the operation of a single type of active mechanism (namely, analysis by synthesis), the selectivity of attention might instead indicate the operation of any active system, be it data-driven or concept-driven. For example, Grossberg and Levine (1975) have demonstrated how a data-driven, active neural system would exhibit selective attention. However, the general rationale for the association between selective attention and active processing derives from the differences in active and passive control structures: The use of iterative, feedback-contingent control strategies in active processing maintains protracted computation at one point in the system, thus tying up cognitive processes or resources.

This type of computation-intensive mechanism is canonical with a resource-limited processor (see Norman & Bobrow, 1975). For instance, the controlled search strategy described by Shiffrin and Schneider (1977) is an active process that is subject to the limitations of short-term memory. In fact, active systems might generally be described as performing a controlled search through an abstract space of alternative (hypothesized) interpretations of an input. However, the particular resources needed by an active mechanism depend on the specific instantiation of this process. These resources might be time, memory (Shiffrin, 1976), effort (Kahneman, 1973), sensory analyzers (Treisman, 1969), or other as yet unspecified processes or capacities. Thus we can bring together both process-limited and resource-limited theories of attention under the framework of control structures.

An active process might generate and test hypotheses one at a time (sequentially) or all at once (in parallel). If a system iterates sequentially through the hypothesis space, control cannot be relinquished until the search process is terminated, effectively "locking out" other competing inputs. If multiple computations occur in parallel, a number of processors and/or a great deal of memory or effort would be required, reducing the resources available to other active systems. As a consequence, if performance in each of two single-task conditions is mediated by an active process (when each is performed separately), performance decrements should be found when both tasks are combined (see Sperling & Melchner, 1978).

Regardless of whether two distinct processes must compete for a limited pool of resources (Kinchla, 1980), or whether a single active process is switched between tasks (Wickens, 1980), performance should suffer if the speed of presentation of the inputs is fast enough. Thus the concept of an active process can be invoked both by resource- and process-limited theories of attention as providing the core mechanism that limits attention. For resource-limited theories (e.g., Shiffrin & Schneider, 1977), controlled search is, by definition, an active process that is limited by the capacity of short-term memory. For process-limited theories (e.g., Treisman & Gelade, 1980), the recognition of perceptual objects is carried out by an active mechanism that is responsible for feature integration. By comparison, passive processes are data-limited, not resource-limited, and thus several passive processes could operate simultaneously.

At first glance, this situation suggests that passive processes might be identical to the current concept of automatic processes, which have been characterized as representing an invariant relationship between inputs and outputs (Posner, 1978). An automatic process may be initiated without conscious intention (Posner, 1978) and must be completed once started (Shiffrin & Schneider, 1977). Furthermore, automatic processes operate as "sealed-channel" systems (see Pomerantz, 1978) so that intermediate computations are not open to introspection (Posner, 1978; Shiffrin & Schneider, 1977). Finally, automatic processes do not require attention or resources (Posner, 1978; Shiffrin & Schneider, 1977). All of these statements are also characteristic of passive processes. In short, passive systems should operate automatically to associate an input representation with an output code. Thus, in resource-limited theories (e.g., Shiffrin & Schneider, 1977), passive processes are simply identified as automatized associative responses, while in process-limited theories (e.g., Treisman & Gelade, 1980), passive processes are the early feature-extracting mechanisms that operate prior to the object recognition process.

This relationship between control structure and attention is straightforward enough, but it also seems to present the problem, discussed earlier, that is faced by process-limitation theories. How does a focal-attentive (active) process become automatized? In order to bring both process-limited and resource-limited theories of attention under the same metatheoretical framework of control structure, it is important to be able to account for automatization within this framework. That is, there must be some way, within the control structure framework, to account for the transition from controlled processing to the automatic processing that occurs with practice and learning.

If the distinction between automatic (passive) and controlled (active) processes is fundamentally a difference in control structure, must changes in control structure result from automatization? While this is certainly a possibility (albeit a far-fetched one), a corollary of this account would be the problem discussed earlier, in which feature integration processes would have to be transformed into feature-coding processes. Fortunately, there is a much simpler solution. The answer resides in the hypothesis–test iteration of an active process. If the first (or only) hypothesis proposed by an active process is always "correct" (i.e., it matches the stimulus), the computational demands of the system would be radically reduced. If an input is always recognized on the first (or only) pass through the system, an active process would appear behaviorally to be an automatic (passive) process. In this situation, automaticity is only a behavioral description that separates both automatized–active and passive processes from controlled (active) systems. Thus, while evidence for attentional demands necessarily implicates the operation of an active control structure, the ability to process multiple inputs simultaneously would only indicate that either a passive or automatized–active system is involved.

There is one remaining question. How does an active system "know" which hypothesis is the right one to propose first? The answer is that the system must *learn* which hypothesis is the correct one. The adaptability of an active system (see Grossberg, 1980) is the advantage that offsets the penalty of heavy computational demands. This perceptual plasticity allows an active system to learn extremely fine discriminations among initially similar stimuli. This acquired knowledge enables the system to map each stimulus onto a unique internal representation. It is this internal code that is subsequently generated as the first hypothesis.

In order to achieve automaticity, the system would require a great deal of training with a relatively small and constant set of stimuli. Once training is completed, automaticity would be restricted to the set of stimuli used in training; other novel stimuli would still require controlled processing as a consequence of the fact that automaticity is achieved by over-learning the perceptual distinctions indigenous to the training set. Switching to a new set of stimuli would entail a new set of discriminations and, therefore, a much larger hypothesis space demanding resources and attention. Indeed, Shiffrin and Schneider (1977) found that automatization requires perceptual training, the effects of which are restricted to the training stimuli.

When the effects of masking and response competition are eliminated, an inability to perceive more than one stimulus at a time indicates the limitations of selective attention. Within the theoretical framework presented here, such limitations constitute evidence for the operation of either data-driven or concept-driven active processes. Thus, if the perception of speech requires selective attention, we can conclude that speech perception is mediated by recurrent, feedback-controlled active mechanisms.

In contrast, the ability to perceive several streams of speech simultaneously would seem to constitute evidence that speech perception is accomplished by passive mechanisms (e.g., feature detectors). While it is true that behavioral automaticity could be produced by either passive or automatized–active processes, it is unlikely that automatized–active processing could occur for speech, despite a lifetime of perceptual experience. The highly variable acoustic–phonetic structure of speech should prevent the automatization of an active speech processing mechanism. As a result, the demands of attention during speech perception should constitute strong evidence for determining the control structure of the computational processes underlying speech perception. Automaticity in phoneme perception would strongly suggest that speech perception is mediated by passive processes that directly associate an input waveform onto phonemes. However, if speech perception can only be effectively conducted on one message at a time, we can conclude that it requires selective attention and is carried out by active (feedback-contingent) processes.

III.C. Attention and Speech Perception

On the basis of introspection, we might expect that phoneme perception occurs automatically. After all, we are seldom aware of the phonetic processes that occur during the perception of speech. It is the meaning of a word, not its constituent sounds, to which our conscious attention is drawn. However, introspection alone is hardly a scientific procedure for determining the nature of phonetic perception. Of course, as we have already seen, the notion of attentional limitations can be used to distinguish between passive (automatic) and active (controlled) models of phonetic perception. If speech perception occurs automatically, processing two different channels of speech (dichotic presentation) should be as easy as processing a single message. Since no resources are required by passive processes, there should be no theoretical limit on the number of channels that can be processed simultaneously. Conversely, if speech perception depends on active processing, performance in a dichotic task should be substantially worse than in a single-channel condition.

III.D. Limitations in Auditory Word Recognition

The question of capacity limitations in the recognition of spoken words has been addressed by a plethora of studies, but with no firm conclusion. The early research on selective attention and word perception produced convincing evidence that attention could not be successfully divided between two distinct messages (see Moray, 1969; Treisman, 1969). Later studies tried to demonstrate that some perceptual analysis of the spoken words in an unattended message occurs even when there is no conscious recognition of the words (Corteen & Wood, 1972; Lackner & Garrett, 1972; Lewis, 1970; MacKay, 1973; von Wright, Anderson, & Stenman, 1975).

The validity of each of these studies has been questioned, largely on methodological grounds (Johnston & Wilson, 1980; Newstead & Dennis, 1979; Treisman, Squire, & Green, 1974; Wardlaw & Kroll, 1976). Nevertheless, there is some indication that the perception of speech requires processing capacity. Some evidence has come from studies of selective attention using a shadowing procedure (Treisman & Geffen, 1967; Treisman & Riley, 1969). In these studies, subjects were asked to perform a primary shadowing task that was intended to focus the subjects' attention on one of two dichotic messages. The subjects were also instructed to perform a secondary task in which a response was required whenever a specified target word was detected in either message. The results indicated that perceptual sensitivity to targets was diminished when the targets were not presented on the channel being shadowed. In other words, when attention is directed toward processing one message, there is little surplus perceptual capacity for recognizing words in other channels.

Bookbinder and Osman (1979) have reported similar results using a different paradigm. In their experiment, subjects were instructed to monitor a spoken word list in one of two dichotic channels and to make a button-pressing response whenever a color word (primary target) was heard. The subjects were also asked to make a vocal response whenever a secondary target word (a noncolor word) was recognized in either channel. Each trial consisted of 20 dichotic pairs of words. Six primary target words were presented per trial, always to the same ear to focus the subjects' attention on one channel of the input. When subjects maintained a constant level of performance on the primary task, secondary targets were detected more often on the primary target channel than on the unattended channel. However, some subjects showed a redistribution of processing capacity such that primary task performance suffered but secondary task performance improved on the unattended channel. These results indicate that auditory word perception does require processing resources, as would be predicted by an active model.

Poltrock, Lansman, and Hunt (1982) have reported results from an auditory word recognition study suggesting that the capacity limitations imposed by speech perception may indeed by considerable. The authors examined the effects of memory load on target recognition for spoken letters as a function of practice for consistent mapping (CM) and varied mapping (VM) conditions. Following the arguments of Schneider and Shiffrin (1977), they expected automaticity to develop in the CM condition, in which targets and distractors were always items from mutually exclusive (i.e., complementary) sets of stimuli. That is, the effect of memory load should have disappeared or been significantly decreased with increasing amounts of practice. However, their results indicate that after the first day of training, the effect of memory load was constant and significant in the CM condition.

From this result, we can conclude that although performance was better in the CM condition (clearly an easier condition than the VM condition), automaticity did not develop fully. Instead, there was still a significant capacity limitation affecting performance that did not seem to be reduced with increasing amounts of practice after the first day of the experiment. This result provides strong support for the conclusion, based on earlier studies of auditory word recognition, that speech perception does indeed require attention and that it places significant demands on the cognitive capacity of the listener. In turn, speech perception appears to be mediated by active perceptual processes.

Shadowing and word detection studies require word perception, and auditory word perception is a complex perceptuolinguistic process involving a number of computational mechanisms (see Pisoni, in press; Pisoni, Nusbaum, Luce, & Slowiaczek, in press). Listeners must not only recognize the phonemes in an utterance but also the words, and in some instances they must retrieve the meanings of those words prior to making a response. Since word perception involves a number of processes beyond phonetic labeling, it is not clear precisely where the locus of active mediation exists. Certainly, based on these studies of auditory word perception, there is no evidence that implicates a single stage of processing as an actively controlled mechanism. It is therefore important to determine whether word perception alone is an active process or whether phoneme perception is also actively controlled.

III.E. Limitations in Phoneme Perception

In order to make claims about the nature of phonetic perception, it is necessary to eliminate any higher-order task requirements such as word identification. Shiffrin, Pisoni, and Castaneda-Mendez (1974) attempted to do just this using an experimental procedure in which subjects reported which of four possible phoneme targets (/b/, /d/, /p/, or /g/ combined with the vowel /a/) had been presented on a specific trial. In simultaneous trials, a single target was presented to one ear and a distractor syllable (/wu/), differing in consonant and vowel, was presented to the other ear. Shiffrin et al. assumed that in this type of trial, subjects had to analyze both channels (ears) simultaneously to identify the target. In sequential trials, subjects were presented with two detection intervals, each preceded by a warning tone. In these trials, a target could be presented in the right ear during the first judgment interval or in the left ear during the second interval. Since subjects were informed of the ear order before the experiment, they could selectively attend to the appropriate ear for each judgment interval.

If phonetic perception is actively mediated, performance in the sequential condition should be easier, because attention could be focused on one channel at a time, compared to the simultaneous condition in which attention would be divided. However, the results showed no difference between performance in the simultaneous condition and the sequential condition. These results have been interpreted as demonstrating the automaticity of phonetic perception (Shiffrin, 1976).

The principal problem with this experiment is that there is no indication of the degree to which the nontarget (i.e., the distractor) channel was processed. Shiffrin et al. (1974) assumed that the subjects had to process both channels equally in the simultaneous condition, especially when the distractor competed with the target. Unfortunately, there was no direct measure of the extent to which the distractor was processed. It is possible that subjects focused their attention on the channel containing a stop consonant and ignored the channel with the semivowel distractor. This could have been accomplished through passive selection of the target channel based on gross waveform differences between the target and the distractor. Since the target and the distractor differed in both the rise time of the consonant transitions and in the vowel, differences in the waveform envelope of the targets and the distractor syllables would be large and could be used to passively select the target channel for phoneme recognition. Previous research has demonstrated that target detection is significantly enhanced when the target can be distinguished from distractors by envelope differences such as those between voices (e.g., Treisman & Riley, 1969).

Other attempts to provide behavioral evidence for the capacity demands of phoneme perception have produced somewhat ambiguous results (e.g., Blank, 1979; Isenberg, 1977; Newman & Dell, 1978). Furthermore, the lack of adequate controls or comparisons to test for response bias, response competition, or shifts in processing strategy makes it difficult to unequivocally interpret the results of prior research. There is, however, some research that has managed to circumvent the need for overt responding on the part of subjects. In these studies, the electrical activity evoked in the human brain by an auditory stimulus has been used as a dependent measure of perceptual processing (see Hillyard, 1984; Picton, Campbell, Baribeau-Braun, & Proulx, 1978).

In reponse to an attended stimulus, two significant events appear in the auditory evoked potential of a listener (see Picton et al., 1978). One of these events occurs shortly after stimulus onset, apparently prior to recognition, and is elicited by any stimulus on an attended channel. The second evoked response seems to index recognition of an attended (designated) target stimulus.

In one set of experiments conducted by Hink and Hillyard (1976), the electrical activity evoked by attended and unattended vowel probes was compared. Two different spoken passages of text were recorded by different voices on separate tracks of audio tape. Two tokens of an isolated steady-state vowel probe were then synthesized to match the different voices in pitch. The subjects listened to these vowel probes alone, embedded in the spoken passages, and embedded in reversed speech. Auditory evoked potentials to these probes were recorded in different task conditions. When the probe was heard on an attended channel, evoked responses were significantly enhanced relative to the probe-evoked potentials from an unattended channel (Hink & Hillyard, 1976). These results suggest that a message must be attended to in order to process the vowels in it.

In a second set of experiments, Hink, Hillyard, and Benson (1978) investigated the neuroelectric signs of consonant perception. Subjects were presented with two random sequences of CV syllables, with a different sequence presented to each ear. The syllables were naturally produced tokens differing in both consonant and speaker. Different voices were presented to different ears. One group of subjects counted the number of designated consonant targets heard in one ear. A second group pressed a button when the target was detected. The results were very similar to those obtained in other attention-evoked-potential experiments (e.g., Picton et al., 1978).

All of the syllables in the attended ear evoked an early electrical response not found for unattended stimuli. A second, auditory-evoked response was produced only by target consonants in the attended ear. These differences between attended and unattended brain responses indicate that selectively attending to one channel of speech effectively excludes the processing of the unattended channel. Hink et al. (1978) also found a significant drop in detection performance when subjects were instructed to divide their attention between both ears. This performance decrement was produced by a reduction in perceptual sensitivity (compared with a focused condition) and was not attributable to a criterion shift. From these results it appears that selective attention to a message is a prerequisite for the accurate perception of phonemes. This conclusion in turn suggests that phoneme perception is mediated by active processes.

This interpretation is supported by a series of studies on capacity limitations in phoneme perception reported by Nusbaum (1981). The general experimental procedure used in these studies was based on the method outlined by Bookbinder and Osman (1979) for word perception. On each trial, subjects were presented with a list of spoken syllables over headphones. In each condition, subjects were given two tasks to perform. The primary task was to monitor one ear for occurrences of a primary target phoneme in a list of syllables. The primary target occurred several times within each trial at randomly chosen locations in the stimulus list. The secondary task was to detect the single occurrence of a secondary target phoneme.

Subjects participated in two conditions. In the monaural condition, a single list of primary and secondary targets and distractors was presented to one ear. In the second condition, two lists of syllables were presented dichotically, synchronized with one syllable to each ear. In this dichotic condition, all primary targets were presented to one ear to focus attention (through the primary task) on that ear. The secondary target was presented once per trial to either ear. In the dichotic condition, a synthetic male voice produced syllables for one ear and a synthetic female voice produced syllables for the other ear. The phonetic identity of the segments always differed between ears for any dichotic pair of stimuli, and a primary target was never presented at the same time as a secondary target. Thus subjects had no problem discriminating input channels, and no response conflicts should have occurred; that is, there was never any occasion for simultaneous primary and secondary target recognition responses.

In two experiments investigating the perception of isolated vowels and consonants in CV syllables, the results demonstrated that primary and secondary target phoneme recognition was most accurate and fastest in the monaural condition. Performance was significantly worse (decreased hits and increased response times) in the dichotic condition for primary and secondary target recognition. However, in this condition secondary targets on the primary target (attended) channel were recognized faster and more accurately than secondary targets on the unattended channel. Since response times increased when accuracy decreased, these results cannot be attributed to a speed–accuracy tradeoff. Furthermore, when the false alarm rate changed significantly, the probability of a false alarm increased only when the probability of a hit dropped. Thus these results cannot be attributed to the induction of a response bias but instead reflect changes in subjects' perceptual sensitivity to phonetic information.

These results strongly confirm the predictions of an active model of phoneme perception. Phonetic recognition performance was best for both tasks when only one channel of input was presented; that is, when attention was focused on the input channel that contained all the target information. In addition, the results from a control condition indicate that this finding can be attributed to the focus of attention on one channel and that it was not a function of dichotic masking effects. Furthermore, when subjects were required to monitor two channels of input for secondary targets, they recognized targets on the unattended channel (the one without primary targets) at the expense of performance on the primary task. This pattern of results for consonant and vowel recognition suggests that subjects could not automatically recognize phoneme targets on two input channels simultaneously without a cost to performance. In fact, the results show that even with a significant reduction in primary task performance, subjects did not share attention between channels efficiently enough to equate secondary task performance on the two channels.

Although these results suggest that phoneme perception is mediated by an active control structure, there is an alternative account of these findings. That account, proposed by Deutsch and Deutsch (1963), asserts that the "importance" of an input channel determines the level of performance for tasks on that channel. As described by Deutsch and Deutsch, channel importance is simply determined by the number of targets occurring on a particular input channel. Thus the primary target channel was more important because both primary and secondary targets were presented on that channel, compared to the unattended channel which only received secondary targets. Channel importance therefore predicts that target recognition should be most accurate on the primary target channel, although it does not, by itself, account for the cost in primary task performance of recognizing secondary targets on either channel.

To test whether the apparent attentional limitations in this procedure could be accounted for by channel importance, two experiments were conducted in which subjects monitored for a phoneme target as one of the two tasks and, for the second task, monitored for a 1000-Hz sinewave tone. An active theory of phoneme perception predicts that the tone will not interfere with phoneme recognition, since the nonspeech tone should not invoke the phonetic processor. In contrast, a channel-importance account would predict that, since channel importance was unchanged from the previous experiments (only the identity of some of the targets was changed), the same pattern of performance deficits should be observed. However, the results of these experiments were quite different from the previous two studies. The requirement of detecting a tone and a phoneme did not impair performance for either consonant targets or vowel targets. Compared to the findings of the first two experiments, these results reject the channel-importance account of the phoneme recognition limitations.

One could argue, of course, that the limitations in phoneme recognition were not the result of active control of the recognition process per se but instead were a consequence of the task demands of the experiment. Even though subjects did not ever have to make both a primary response and a secondary response at the same time, they did have to be prepared to make either response at any point within a trial. Thus it could be the cognitive load imposed by response preparation, and not the recognition process, that incurred the observed capacity limitations.

To test this alternative account, an experiment was conducted using a modified version of the dual-target monitoring task. For both the monaural and dichotic conditions, a secondary target vowel was presented on half the trials; no secondary target was presented on the remaining trials. Subjects were instructed simply to note the presence of the secondary target if it occurred within a trial. Then, after each trial was over, the subjects pressed a button to indicate if the secondary target had been heard. The number of occurrences of the primary target vowel within each trial was varied to prevent subjects from using a mental tally of primary targets as a means of allocating attention between the primary and secondary tasks.

By deferring the secondary target recognition response to the end of the trial, subjects did not have to be prepared to make either of two responses at any time. However, in spite of this reduction in the real-time demands of the dual-target monitoring task, the results were virtually identical to the first vowel recognition experiment: Performance was best for both tasks in the monaural task and, in the dichotic condition, secondary target vowels were recognized more accurately on the primary target (attended) channel than on the unattended channel. Moreover, in this experiment the performance deficits were virtually identical to the deficits observed in the first experiment for secondary vowel target recognition. Clearly, these results support the conclusion that vowel recognition is mediated by an active process.

Such a comparison of performance in the first two studies for consonant recognition and vowel recognition provides some insight into the nature of the limitation on phoneme perception. The performance decrement for secondary target recognition from the attended channel to the unattended channel was considerably larger for consonant targets (about 42 percentage points) than for vowel targets (about 18 percentage points). Furthermore, the cost of this secondary task performance on the unattended channel, in terms of primary task performance (comparing monaural and dichotic conditions), was quite similar for vowels and consonants: 11 percentage points for vowel targets and 14 for consonants.

These results suggest that subjects were not dividing attention between input channels in the sense of sharing capacity but instead were switching their attention between ears. For vowels, this strategy could be reasonably successful, since auditory memory for vowels is quite salient and could be sampled between stimulus presentations. For consonants, however, this strategy would be unsuccessful because of the poor persistence of stop consonants in auditory memory (Pisoni, 1973). Thus the relatively high level of performance for vowel recognition (compared to consonant recognition) on the unattended channel may reflect a strategy in which listeners focus attention on the primary target channel and then, following recognition of the most recently presented stimulus, switch their attention to auditory memory for the unattended stimulus. Regardless of the specific interpretation of the strategy used by subjects in the dual-target monitoring task, these results argue for an actively controlled phonetic processor.

An alternative explanation of these results is that the actual memory set size varied between the consonant and vowel studies. The assumption behind this explanation is that in the vowel studies, subjects had to respond only to a single token of a vowel target in a male or female voice. By comparison, in the stop consonant study consonants were paired with each of five different vowels in the male and female voice. Thus the effective memory set could be viewed as five times larger in the consonant study than in the vowel experiments.

From the research of Schneider and Shiffrin (1977), it could be hypothesized that the larger working memory set should lead to poorer performance. The assumption is that subjects maintain in memory all possible syllable targets instead of the consonant targets alone. This account can be ruled out easily, however, because research has indicated that when subjects are instructed to recognize the identity of stop consonants, the number of vowels in the stimulus set has no effect on performance (Saslow, 1958; Sawusch, Mullenix, & Garrison, 1983). By implication, when subjects are recognizing consonant targets in CV syllables, they do not hold in memory all possible CV targets but instead maintain only the target phoneme. Therefore, it is unlikely that the greater attentional limitations found for stop consonant perception can be attributed to memory set size effects. Rather, the results of these experiments strongly suggest that phonetic recognition is carried out by perceptual processes that require selective attention. In other words, phoneme perception is mediated by mechanisms that are limited in their processing capacity. From this we can conclude that phoneme recognition is directed by an active control system.

IV. TOWARD AN ACTIVE THEORY OF SPEECH PERCEPTION

Based on the conclusion that phoneme perception is mediated by an active control structure rather than a passive system, we can immediately rule out models of phoneme recognition that employ passive control. The capacity limitations in phoneme perception argue against simple cascaded, hierarchical feature detector systems in which the ultimate recognition decision is carried out by phoneme detectors at the highest level of abstraction in the recognition network (e.g., Abbs & Sussman, 1971; Cooper, 1979). This conclusion converges on the account of phoneme perception arrived at by Sawusch and Nusbaum (1983) from a comparison of selective adaptation and paired-stimulus contrast in phonetic identification (see also Sawusch & Jusczyk, 1981).

Since selective adaptation appears to be determined by the acoustic structure of a syllable, and paired-stimulus contrast seems to be determined by the perceived identity of the syllable, Sawusch and Nusbaum claim that there must be at least two levels of processing in phoneme perception—an auditory level and a phonetic level. Moreover, they conclude that the earliest auditory level of processing appears to be mediated by feature detectors (i.e., passive recognition), while the later stage of phoneme identification appears to be carried out by decision mechanisms that are more complex than simple feature detectors. Together with the capacity limitations observed in phoneme perception, this conclusion suggests that auditory cues are passively extracted from the speech signal and that the locus of selective attention appears to be at the level of the phonetic decision.

Further support for this view of passive auditory cue extraction and attention-mediated phoneme recognition comes from the finding that "illusory conjunctions" (see Treisman & Gelade, 1980) occur in dichotic listening tasks with speech syllables. Illusory conjuctions occur when at least two stimuli are presented and when features from one stimulus become combined with features from the other(s). A percept is then formed that does not correspond to any stimulus that was physically present but is instead purely a mental construct. When two syllables are presented, one to each ear, illusory conjunctions called "blends" occur such that if [pi] and [di] are presented, the listener might report [bi], using the voicing of [d] and the place of [p] to form an illusory phonetic segment (see Pisoni, 1975, for discussion).[1] Following the logic of Treisman and Gelade (1980), these blends result from the inability to focus attention simultaneously on both syllables, since attention to a stimulus is necessary to correctly integrate all of its component features to form a percept. The authors' claim is that the features of a stimulus are coded automati-

---

[1] Although we described the construction of the blend of voicing and place (e.g., [di] and [pi] yield [bi]) in terms of phonetic features, that description was simply for notational convenience. As Klatt (1980) points out, in this type of experiment it is difficult to distinguish whether the blend occurs from the conjunction of phonetic features or from the conjunction of the auditory correlates of those features.

cally by (passive) detectors but that integration of those features to form a perceptual object requires attention.

IV.A. Phonetic Cue Integration

The conclusion that phoneme recognition is an actively controlled, complex decision process is also supported by research on the coding and integration of acoustic–phonetic cues in phoneme perception. Research on phonetic cue trading has indicated that listeners are flexible enough in perception to compensate for the ambiguity of one acoustic cue by relying more strongly on other cues to identify a phoneme (see Repp, 1982, for review). In essence, listeners can use their knowledge of the natural co-variation of spectral and temporal cues in speech to compensate for tradeoffs between different cues in recognizing phonemes. For example, silence (closure) duration appears to be perceptually equivalent to formant transitions in cuing the presence or absence of a stop consonant in the distinction between "slit" and "split" (Fitch, Halwes, Erickson, & Liberman, 1980) or between "say" and "stay" (Best, Morrongiello, & Robson, 1981). Although it is possible that the observed "phonetic trading relations" between these cues may be due to auditory masking or other auditory interactions, such explanations cannot account for the range of different types of trading relations (see Repp, 1982).

One trading relation that has been studied in some detail is the perceptual equivalence of closure duration and duration of the vocalic segment preceding closure in the perception of voicing (see, e.g., Denes, 1955). Port and Dalby (1982) have reported that the duration of the voiced syllable preceding consonant closure could be traded against the duration of closure to shift the perception of voicing in a stimulus series varying from "digger" to "dicker." Nusbaum (1982) has shown that a similar tradeoff did *not* occur for judgments of silence duration in nonspeech analogs of the digger–dicker series. Nusbaum concluded that for these stimuli, the perceptual equivalence of acoustic cues in phoneme identification was not determined by auditory interactions among the cues but rather at a level of phonetic processing (see also Liberman, 1982; Repp, 1982).

In another study, Nusbaum (1985) used a speeded classification task with speech stimuli based on the stimuli used by Port and Dalby to determine whether the cues of vowel duration and closure duration are perceptually integral (see Garner, 1974). The issue was whether the two duration cues to voicing are perceived directly (automatically) as a unitary phonetic percept. The results suggested that listeners extract the two duration cues separately and then combine them to arrive at a voicing decision (see also Massaro & Cohen, 1983). Furthermore, it appeared that listeners are extremely efficient in detecting and responding to phonetically "appropriate" combinations of acoustic cues and that they are equally able to ignore or filter out phonetically "inappropriate" combinations. That is, listeners respond fastest when both cues "cooperate" to signal the same value of voicing (voiced or voiceless). When both cues vary randomly (sometimes conflicting in the voicing value they would nominally indicate), listeners appear to attend only to closure duration, ignoring vowel duration in the judgment of voicing.

These studies indicate that the phonetic recognition system is sensitive to the way in which acoustic cues covary as a result of speech production. This variability is not treated by the perceptual system as "noise" to be filtered out or overcome but is processed instead as critical information concerning the phonetic structure of an utterance (see Elman & McClelland, in press). The picture that emerges of the earliest stages of speech perception is that low-level auditory feature detectors passively code the acoustic parameters of speech and pass this information on to a more complex, active decision-making system that integrates (over time) information about the sequence of acoustic parameters in the speech signal, together with knowledge of the variability that can occur in acoustic–phonetic representations. At this level of description, this emerging view of the process of phoneme perception is quite similar to that offered by Studdert-Kennedy (1976).

IV.B. Expectations and Phonetic Processing

One of the predictions made by a passive model of phoneme perception is that the expectations of the listener should have no impact on the recognition process. The only possible means of modifying a passive system might be through some long-term learning process. However, active systems can easily account for findings that indicate that perception can be influenced by knowledge, expectations, and context. Context effects in speech perception are well known, even beyond the basic influence of coarticulatory context (see, e.g., Liberman, Cooper, Shankweiler, & Studdert-Kennedy, 1967; Lindblom & Studdert-Kennedy, 1967). For example, Ladefoged and Broadbent (1957) have demonstrated that the formant frequencies of a context sentence shift the perception of a target vowel at the end of the sentence.

Later studies have shown that the expectations of the listener can radically change the way in which a speech stimulus is coded and these effects cannot be accounted for by a passive system. For example, Carden, Levitt, Jusczyk, and Walley (1981) have shown that the location of the identification boundary for the place of articulation of consonants shifts depending on the *manner* of articulation: The place-of-articulation boundary is in different locations for stop consonants and fricatives. What was most surprising about these findings was that for the same set of stimuli, the identification boundary between place-of-articulation categories could be shifted depending on the subjects' expectations about the manner of the stimuli. That is, when subjects were told to identify stop consonants as if they were fricatives, the category boundary shifted to the boundary position that was obtained when the subjects were actually presented with fricatives. Thus the phonetic decision about place of articulation was affected by listeners' expectations in the same way as when acoustic information about fricative manner was present.

An even more dramatic demonstration of the power of listeners' expectations on speech perception has come from studies of the perception of "sinewave speech." Remez, Rubin, Pisoni, and Carrell (1981) presented listeners with nonspeech stimuli constructed from sinewaves matched to the center frequencies of the first three formants of spoken sentences. One group of subjects was simply asked to report what they heard, and these subjects perceived the stimuli as nonspeech sounds. A second group of subjects was instructed to identify the linguistic content of the sinewave speech, and these subjects were able to recognize the nonspeech sounds as sentences. A subsequent study by Grunke and Pisoni (1982) demonstrated that instructions to identify sinewave analogs of CV and VC syllables using phonetic labels or acoustic labels produced very different patterns of results when the complexity of the stimuli was varied from one to three tones. The results indicated that the group that used phonetic labels showed better identification performance as stimulus complexity increased, while the group that used acoustic labels showed poorer performance with more complex stimuli.

In the most detailed study of sinewave speech to date, Schwab (1981) investigated the locus of the effects of speech or nonspeech expectations on the perception of tone analogs. In these studies, the stimuli were tone analogs of CV and VC syllables varying in complexity from one to three tones. Subjects that used acoustic labels to identify the location and direction of the tone transitions showed poorer performance as the number of tones per stimulus increased, replicating the results reported by Grunke and Pisoni (1982). In addition, these subjects showed backward masking effects in the CV analogs compared to the VC analogs, as well as spread-of-frequency masking from the lower tone component to higher components. By comparison, the subjects that used phonetic labels to identify the sinewave syllables showed better performance as the number of tone components per stimulus increased, and there was no evidence of either backward masking or frequency masking effects. Thus phonetic labeling performance improved as the stimuli became more speechlike, while acoustic labeling performance was worse for more speechlike sounds. Furthermore, a signal detection analysis indicated that the expectations (speech versus nonspeech) affected the perceptual sensitivity of the subjects and were not simply inducing a response bias. Two conclusions can be drawn from these findings.

First, it is clear that sinewave analogs of speech do not automatically engage phonetic processing. In other words, speech perception is not an obligatory process that is passively invoked by the stimulus. Rather, phoneme perception appears to depend, to some extent, on the expectations of the listener regarding the nature of the stimuli. Of course, for natural, fluent speech, the rich and redundant prosodic and acoustic–phonetic structural characteristics of the speech signal may give rise to the expectations necessary to initiate phonetic processing. But for impoverished stimuli such as sinewave speech, it appears to be necessary to explicitly tell the listener to process the sounds as speech.

Second, activation of the phonetic processor is not just a matter of the listener using a different system of responses (e.g., phonetic versus acoustic) to identify tone analogs. Instead, the impact of engaging phonetic processing is on the perceptual sensitivity of the listener. Thus the locus of the listener's expectations is on the type of perceptual analysis used to identify the sounds, and not simply on a stage of response selection. When the listener uses a phonetic process to identify sinewave speech, knowledge about the acoustic–phonetic structure of speech can be brought to bear on the problem of recognizing the stimulus. In contrast, a listener using an acoustic labeling strategy has much less knowledge about how to identify the location and direction of a frequency change and which aspects of the stimuli should be processed.

The observation that it is not the stimulus that engages phonetic processing strongly argues against passive control in speech perception. Indeed, it suggests that phoneme perception is accomplished by a mechanism that is considerably more complex and flexible than a process that is instantiated as a static neural network. The processes that underlie speech perception must be responsive to the ever-changing demands on perception that result from variability in speakers, rate of speech, environmental conditions, and of course context and expectations. Even adult listeners can be trained to discriminate novel phonetic contrasts that are not part of their native language (see Pisoni, Aslin, Perey, & Hennessy, 1982). Thus the mechanisms of phoneme perception must be flexible enough to incorporate new information about acoustic–phonetic structures and to acquire new categories for identification.

IV.C. Mechanisms of Phoneme Perception

In the preceding discussion we outlined a description of the earliest stages of speech perception. In our view, the acoustic parameters of speech are first extracted and encoded by passive auditory feature detectors. The task of these detectors is not to solve the recognition problem (i.e., phoneme identification) but instead to provide a preliminary representation of the information in the speech signal that is relevant to phoneme perception. At this level of processing, the auditory features are frequency-specific and are computed over a fairly narrow time window. Thus they are highly redundant and stimulus-specific.

At this first stage of processing relevant to phoneme recognition, the continuously varying acoustic energy in the speech waveform is encoded into symbols that serve to describe those aspects of the acoustic structure of an utterance that are relevant to phoneme perception.[2] This description of the acoustic structure of speech is quite different from the notion of a "neural spectrogram" (see Licklider, 1959) and is more similar to some later approaches to modeling neural representations of speech (e.g., Delgutte, 1982; Goldhor, 1983; Seneff, 1984). These models attempt to emphasize, in the nature of the code, those properties that are relevant to the phoneme recognition process. However, it is our view that these properties alone do not determine recognition; they only serve to characterize an utterance in terms that are most appropriate for recognition.

Once an utterance has been described as a set of auditory features (or perhaps even throughout the computation of that description), a second stage of processing is envisioned that attempts to describe the stimulus as a series of acoustic events that are more abstract than the auditory features computed in the previous stage. These descriptions may be computed over several auditory features and may be thought of (at some level of description) as canonical with articulatory gestures, since there is an intrinsic relationship between the sequence of acoustic events in speech and the generation of those events in speech production.

---

[2] The use of the term "symbol" to describe the early coding of the speech signal is not meant to imply a completely discrete representation. In some respects, this first level of auditory coding can be viewed as similar to the notion of the "primal sketch" proposed by Marr (1982) as the first level of representation in vision. The role of Marr's primal sketch was to translate the continuously varying intensity levels in the visual stimulus into an initial symbolic representation—in this case, a structure akin to a symbolic line drawing of the stimulus. This early level of coding is not just the translation of stimulus energy into a new analog representation in neural firing rates. Instead, the primal sketch represents a visual scene with a limited vocabulary of symbols that describe visual elements at a low level of abstraction (as lines, edges, and blobs).

This process of acoustic event description represents the first level of perceptual recognition in which several auditory features are recognized as arising from a particular acoustic event. This process should not be viewed simply as the integration of these features across frequency and time (in the sense of energy summation or smearing) but as similar to pattern matching with prototypes. The need for this stage of processing derives from the need to represent speech as a speaker-independent sequence of symbols that can be used to identify phonemes. The simpler auditory features, being frequency- and time-dependent, necessarily encode the variability in acoustic–phonetic structure that is due to speech rate and speaker differences, as well as that due to the acoustic–phonetic context.

The acoustic event description is proposed to normalize many speaker and speech rate effects prior to phoneme recognition. For example, Pisoni, Carrell, and Gans (1983) have demonstrated that the perception of nonspeech analogs of syllables (heard as nonspeech) shows the same temporal compensation effects as have been found for the perception of speech syllables (see Miller & Liberman, 1979). Furthermore, these effects are also found for the perception of sinewave analogs by prelinguistic infants (Jusczyk, Pisoni, Reed, Fernald, & Myers, 1983). Thus it is clear that this sort of time normalization is performed at an auditory level of processing and not carried out by the phonetic processor. Moreover, there is some evidence for this intermediate level of description from research on selective adaptation with speech and the rapid classification of nonspeech analogs of speech cues (see Sawusch, this volume). At this point, however, there is no strong evidence to indicate whether this level of acoustic event description is an active or passive process.

At the next level of processing, phonemes are recognized from the sequence of acoustic events. We assume that the process of phoneme recognition continuously transmits or cascades (see McClelland, 1979) partial phonetic information about the identity of a segment until the segment has been identified as completely as possible. Even before a phoneme is identified, the partial phonetic information about a segment can be used by word recognition processes to reduce the number of alternative word candidates (see Huttenlocher & Zue, 1983; Shipman & Zue, 1982). In addition, phoneme perception is actively controlled and may use several acoustic events to identify one or more phonemes (see Cole et al., 1980). Thus phoneme recognition is viewed as a many-to-many mapping in which several acoustic segments may contribute to the identification of several phonemes. It is at this level of processing that we believe attention is first limited.

The need for an active control structure in phoneme recognition is dictated by the complexity of the decision process, which must recognize discrete phonemes in the continuous speech waveform (see Liberman, Cooper, Harris, et al., 1967). Whether this recognition process is a bottom-up active process that relies on sophisticated signal processing strategies or a top-down active process that uses knowledge about the acoustic–phonetic structure of speech is, at this point, unclear. However, it is clear that passive phoneme detector systems can be ruled out as a theoretical account of phoneme perception.

It is unlikely that phoneme recognition can be fully explained by the type of perceptual theory described by McClelland and Elman (1984) in the TRACE model. This interactive activation model does use active control through recurrent feedback, and it can account for some of the findings in phoneme perception (such as phonetic cue trading), but its major explanatory mechanism is also its major drawback.

The success of TRACE and other interactive activation models, such as the model of visual word perception described by McClelland and Rumelhart (1981), can be attributed to the use of competition and cooperation in a structural network that, in its structure, directly reflects the structure of the perceptual objects it must recognize. That is, a word is linked to its constituent phonemes, which are linked to their features, which in turn are connected to some representation of acoustic cues. The problem with this structural account of perception is that there is no simple way to justify the structure of the model, other than by its success. In other words, the model does not learn its structure from the experience of perception, nor can it acquire new structures in any simple fashion. As a consequence, TRACE cannot account for the perceptual flexibility that human listeners show. By comparison, work by Grossberg (this volume) and Anderson, Silverstein, Ritz, and Jones (1977) has demonstrated neural modeling principles that can account for sophisticated cognitive processes such as categorization and learning using active control structures. These approaches may ultimately yield a more powerful model of phoneme recognition.

IV.D. Mechanisms of Auditory Word Recognition

It has often been claimed that word perception is an automatic and unconscious (and therefore passive) process (see, e.g., Marcel, 1983; Seidenberg, Tanenhaus, Leiman, & Bienkowski, 1982; Shiffrin, 1976). There are at least two corollaries of this assertion that are readily apparent. First, the elements (e.g., phonemes) that are used to recognize words must also be recognized automatically. This condition is necessary because a process cannot be automatic if any of its components (i.e., subprocesses) or precursors are controlled processes. Second, the recognition process should be a sealed channel that is not open to psychological inspection (see Pomerantz, 1978).

However, as we have seen, there is strong evidence to suggest that phoneme perception is not automatic—that it is directed by active control. Similarly, letter perception also appears to impose capacity limitations (Paap & Ogden, 1981). Thus there is good reason to believe that the elements that support word recognition are *not* themselves automatically recognized. Furthermore, there is evidence that the elements within words are accessible to perception during word recognition. For example, Nusbaum, Walley, Carrell, and Ressler (1982) found that listeners could focus their attention on the segments of a spoken word and thus improve their perceptual processing of the attended segments. Therefore, there is evidence against the two corollaries of the assertion that auditory word perception is automatic. Taken together with evidence indicating that word perception requires selective attention (e.g., Bookbinder & Osman, 1979), it appears that word perception may be mediated by active control structures.[3]

Much evidence suggests that auditory word perception is actively controlled. As a result, this evidence argues against several theories of word recognition. For example, Morton's (1969) logogen theory and Klatt's (1980) LAFS model both employ passive control structures and therefore can be ruled out. Similarly, any theory of word recognition that uses strictly sequential network processing or the simple accumulation of evidence for or against word condidates can also be ruled out.

There are, however, a number of theories of word recognition that employ active control structures. For example, in the cohort theory of word recognition proposed by Marslen-Wilson and Welsh (1978), a cohort of word candidates is activated based on the structural similarity of word-initial acoustic–phonetic information to the stimulus. Candidates are deactivated as disconfirming acoustic–phonetic information is processed or when the prior linguistic context can eliminate candidates. Thus, in this theory, an active control structure must be used to mediate the interaction between top-down and bottom-up processing. Similarly, the TRACE model of auditory word recognition described by McClelland and Elman (1984; Elman & McClelland, in press) employs an active control structure to direct interactions between top-down and bottom-up processsng. In this

---

[3] Of course, it is difficult to determine whether the attentional limitations found in auditory word perception result from limitations at the phoneme and word level or at the phoneme level alone. However, it seems to be a reasonable working hypothesis that word recognition requires selective attention.

model, however, active control is achieved using recurrent feedback loops between levels of representation in the model.

In contrast, Forster (1979) has proposed a search model of word recognition that does not allow interactions between top-down and bottom-up processes. Instead, this model is autonomous and independent of higher-level processes and context. Words are recognized in the lexicon by a controlled search through "files" or structured collections of lexical information. Thus an active control structure is instantiated in the iterative search process which scans the lexicon for a match with the structural properties of the stimulus.

It is interesting to note that of all these models, only the search model directly addresses the problem of accessing lexical knowledge after a word is recognized. Once a word is recognized in Forster's model, pointers allow access to semantic, syntactic, and phonological knowledge about the recognized word. Thus, although the recognition process is actively controlled, lexical access is mediated by a passive (pointer look-up) process. In general, almost all other theories of word perception have neglected to deal with the issue of lexical access (i.e., of retrieving lexcal knowledge for a recognized word). However, it is clear that more research is needed on the problem of access to semantic, syntactic, pragmatic, morphological, and phonological information about a recognized word before the control structure of lexical access can be specified.

V. CONCLUSIONS

In this chapter we have established a link between theories of attention and the control structure of information processing systems. Our claim is that systems that employ active control should require attention, while systems that are passively controlled should not place demands on attention. This link provides the means for investigating the control structures that direct processing in perception and cognition. Although the control structure of a process is only one part of an information processing system, understanding the way a process is controlled is the first step toward developing a detailed description of the process. In general, however, it is a step that has often been overlooked in efforts to characterize the representations and transformations of cognition.

By examining issues surrounding the capacity limitations and coding strategies in speech perception, we have argued that phoneme perception and word perception are mediated by active control structures. This immediately rules out passive models of speech perception such as those based on hierchical, cascaded feature detector systems. However, it is also clear that the "traditional" active theories of speech perception, such as motor theory (Liberman et al., 1962), are not specified well enough to account for or make detailed predictions about speech perception. Instead, it is necessary to develop new active theories of phoneme and word perception that are both powerful enough to account for the flexibility of the perceptual system and yet defined in sufficient detail to generate hypotheses that are explicit and testable. Research on activation models of parallel, distributed processing has demonstrated that many of the phenomema of speech perception, such as cue trading, can be explained by these models (e.g., Grossberg, this volume; McClelland & Elman, 1984).

Although we have concluded that speech perception is mediated by active processes, it is still necessary to determine more precisely which processes are active and which are passive. While there is some evidence to suggest that auditory feature extraction and acoustic event description stages are passive, and that phoneme recognition is active, it is entirely possible that all of the early stages of speech processing are actively controlled, including auditory feature extraction. Furthermore, the specific nature of the active control mechanisn is unknown, as is the way in which control structures interact across different levels of the perceptual system (e.g., between phoneme recognition and word recognition). However, by classifying the basic control structure of phoneme and word recognition as an active process, we have taken an important first step toward understanding the basic mechanisms of speech perception.

REFERENCES

Abbs, J. H., & Sussman, H. M. (1971). Neurophysiological feature detectors and speech perception: A discussion of theoretical implications. *Journal of Speech and Hearing Research, 14,* 23–36.

Ades, A. E. (1976). Adapting the property detectors for speech perception. In R. J. Wales & E. Walker (Eds.), *New approaches to language mechanisms.* Amsterdam: North Holland.

Anderson, J. A., Silverstein, J. W., Ritz, S. A., & Jones, R. S. (1977). Distinctive features, categorical perception, and probability learning: Some applications of a neural model. *Psychological Review, 84,* 413–451.

Atkinson, R. C., & Shiffrin, R. M. (1968). Human memory: A proposed system and its control processes. In K. Spence & J. Spence (Eds.), *The psychology of learning and motivation* (Vol. 2). New York: Academic Press.

Barlow, H. B. (1972). Single units and sensation: A neuron doctrine for perceptual psychology? *Perception, 1,* 371–394.

Best, C. J., Morrongiello, B., & Robson, R. (1981). Perceptual equivalence of acoustic cues in speech and nonspeech perception. *Perception & Psychophysics, 29,* 191–211.

Blank, M. A. (1979). *Dual-mode processing of phonemes in fluent speech.* Unpublished doctoral dissertation, University of Texas at Austin.

Bondarko, L. V., Zagorujko, N. G., Kozhevnikov, N. A., Molchanov, A. P., & Chistovich, L. A. (1970). A model of speech perception in humans. *Working Papers in Linguistics* (Tech. Rep. 70-12). Columbus: Ohio State University, Computer & Information Science Research Center.

Bookbinder, J., & Osman, E. (1979). Attentional strategies in dichotic listening. *Memory & Cognition, 7,* 511–520.

Broadbent, D. (1958). *Perception and communication.* London: Pergamon Press.

Carden, G., Levitt, A. G., Jusczyk, P. W., & Walley, A. C. (1981). Evidence for phonetic processing of cues to place of articulation: Perceived manner affects perceived place. *Perception & Psychophysics, 29,* 26–36.

Chomsky, N., & Halle, M. (1968). *The sound pattern of English.* New York: Harper & Row.

Chomsky, N., & Miller, G. A. (1963). Introduction to the formal analysis of natural languages. In R. D. Luce, R. Bush, & E. Galanter (Eds.), *Handbook of mathematical psychology* (Vol. 2). New York: John Wiley.

Cole, R. A., Rudnicky, A. I., Zue, V., & Reddy, D. R. (1980). Speech as patterns on paper. In R. A. Cole (Ed.), *Perception and production of fluent speech.* Hillsdale, NJ: Erlbaum.

Cooper, W. E. (1979). *Speech perception and production: Studies in selective adaptation.* Norwood, NJ: Ablex.

Corteen, R. S., & Wood, B. (1972). Autonomic responses to shock-associated words in an unattended channel. *Journal of Experimental Psychology, 94,* 308–313.

Delgutte, B. (1982). Some correlates of phonetic distinctions at the level of the auditory nerve. In R. Carlson & B. Granstrom (Eds.), *The representation of speech in the peripheral auditory system.* Amsterdam: Elsevier.

Denes, P. (1955). Effect of duration on the perception of voicing. *Journal of the Acoustical Society of America, 27,* 761–764.

Deutsch, J. A., & Deutsch, D. (1963). Attention: Some theoretical considerations. *Psychological Review, 70,* 80–90.

Elman, J. L., & McClelland, J. L. (in press). Exploiting lawful variability in the speech wave. In J. S. Perkell & D. H. Klatt (Eds.), *Variability and invariance of speech processes.* Hillsdale, NJ: Erlbaum.

Evans, E. F. (1974). Neural processes for the detection of acoustic patterns and for sound localization. In F. O. Schmidt & F. G. Worden (Eds.), *The neurosciences: Third study program.* Cambridge: MIT Press.

Fant, G. (1962). Descriptive analysis of the acoustic aspects of speech. *Logos, 5,* 3–17.

Fant, G. (1967). Auditory patterns of speech. In W. Walthen-Dunn (Ed.), *Models for the perception of speech and visual form.* Cambridge: MIT Press.

Fitch, H. L., Halwes, T., Erickson, D. M., & Liberman, A. M. (1980). Perceptual equivalence of two acoustic cues for stop-consonant manner. *Perception & Psychophysics, 27,* 343–350.

Forster, K. I. (1979). Levels of processing and the structure of the lexicon. In W. E. Cooper & E. C. T. Walker (Eds.), *Sentence processing: Psycholinguistic studies presented to Merrill Garrett.* Hillsdale, NJ: Erlbaum.

Foss, D. J., & Blank, M. A. (1980). Identifying the speech codes. *Cognitive Psychology, 12,* 1–31.

Garner, W. R. (1974). *The processing of information and structure.* Potomac, MD: Erlbaum.

Goldhor, R. (1983). A speech signal processing system based on a peripheral auditory model. *Proceedings of ICASSP-83,* 1368–1371.

Greene, B. G., Pisoni, D. B., & Carrell, T. D. (1984). Recognition of speech spectrograms. *Journal of the Acoustical Society of America, 76,* 32–43.

Grossberg, S. (1980). How does the brain build a cognitive code? *Psychological Review, 87,* 1–51.

Grossberg, S., & Levine, D. (1975). Some developmental and attentional biases in the contrast enhancement and short term memory of recurrent neural networks. *Journal of Theoretical Biology, 53,* 341–380.

Grunke, M. E., & Pisoni, D. B. (1982). Some experiments on perceptual learning of mirror-image acoustic patterns. *Perception & Psychophysics, 31,* 210–218.

Hebb, D. O. (1949). *The organization of behavior.* New York: John Wiley.

Hillyard, S. A. (1984). Event-related potentials and selective attention. In E. Donchin (Ed.), *Cognitive psychophysiology: Event-related potentials and the study of cognition.* Hillsdale, NJ: Erlbaum.

Hink, R. F., & Hillyard, S. A. (1976). Auditory evoked potentials during selective listening to dichotic speech messages. *Perception & Psychophysics, 20,* 236–242.

Hink, R. F., Hillyard, S. A., & Benson, P. J. (1978). Event-related brain potentials and selective attention to acoustic and phonetic cues. *Biological Psychology, 6,* 1–16.

Huttenlocher, D. P., & Zue, V. W. (1983). Phonotactic and lexical constraints in speech recognition. *Speech Communication Group Working Papers* (Vol. III). Cambridge, MA: MIT, Research Laboratory of Electronics.

Isenberg, D. S. (1977). *Attention demands of processing phonetic information in the perception of dichotic speech.* Unpublished doctoral dissertation, California Institute of Technology, Pasadena.

Johnston, W. A., & Wilson, J. (1980). Perceptual processing of nontargets in an attention task. *Memory & Cognition, 8,* 372–377.

Jusczyk, P. W. (1981). Infant speech perception: A critical appraisal. In P. D. Eimas & J. L. Miller (Eds.), *Perspectives on the study of speech.* Hillsdale, NJ: Erlbaum.

Jusczyk, P. W., Pisoni, D. B., Reed, M. A., Fernald, A., & Myers, M. (1983). Infants' discrimination of the duration of rapid spectrum changes in nonspeech signals. *Science, 222,* 175–177.

Kahneman, D. (1973). *Attention and effort.* Englewood Cliffs, NJ: Prentice-Hall.

Kent, R. D., & Minifie, F. D. (1977). Coarticulation in recent speech production models. *Journal of Phonetics, 5,* 115–133.

Kewley-Port, D. (1983). Time-varying features as correlates of place of articulation in stop consonants. *Journal of the Acoustical Society of America, 73,* 322–335.

Kinchla, R. A. (1980). The measurement of attention. In R. S. Nickerson (Ed.), *Attention and performance VIII.* Hillsdale, NJ: Erlbaum.

Klatt, D. H. (1980). Speech recognition: A model of acoustic–phonetic analysis and lexical access. In R. A. Cole (Ed.), *Perception and production of fluent speech.* Hillsdale, NJ: Erlbaum.

Kohonen, T. (1978). *Associative memory: A system-theoretical approach.* New York: Springer-Verlag.

LaBerge, D., & Samuels, S. J. (1974). Toward a theory of automatic information processing in reading. *Cognitive Psychology, 6,* 293–323.

Lackner, J. R., & Garrett, M. F. (1972). Resolving ambiguity: Effects of biasing context in the unattended ear. *Cognition, 1,* 359–372.

Ladefoged, P., & Broadbent, D. E. (1957). Information conveyed by vowels. *Journal of the Acoustical Society of America, 29,* 98–104.

Lesser, V. R., & Erman, L. D. (1977). A retrospective view of the Hearsay-II architecture.

Proceedings of the 5th International Joint Conference on Artificial Intelligence, Cambridge, Massachusetts.

Lewis, J. L. (1970). Semantic processing of unattended messages using dichotic listening. *Journal of Experimental Psychology, 85,* 225–228.

Liberman, A. M. (1970). The grammars of speech and language. *Cognitive Psychology, 1,* 301–323.

Liberman, A. M. (1982). On finding that speech is special. *American Psychologist, 37,* 148–167.

Liberman, A. M., Cooper, F. S., Harris, K. S., & MacNeilage, P. F. (1962). A motor theory of speech perception. *Proceedings of the Speech Communication Seminar,* Stockholm.

Liberman, A. M., Cooper, F. S., Harris, K. S., MacNeilage, P. F., & Studdert-Kennedy, M. (1967). Some observations on a model for speech perception. In W. Walthen-Dunn (Ed.), *Models for the perception of speech and visual form.* Cambridge, MA: MIT Press.

Liberman, A. M., Cooper, F. S., Shankweiler, D. P., & Studdert-Kennedy, M. (1967). Perception of the speech code. *Psychological Review, 74,* 431–461.

Liberman, A. M., Mattingly, I. G., & Turvey, M. T. (1972). Language codes and memory codes. In A. W. Melton & E. Martin (Eds.), *Coding processes in human memory.* New York: John Wiley.

Licklider, J.C.R. (1952). On the processes of speech perception. *Journal of the Acoustical Society of America, 24,* 590–594.

Licklider, J.C.R. (1959). Three auditory theories. In S. Koch (Ed.), *Psychology: A study of a science.* New York: McGraw-Hill.

Lindblom, B.E.F., & Studdert-Kennedy, M. (1967). On the role of formant transitions in vowel recognition. *Journal of the Acoustical Society of America, 42,* 830–843.

Lowerre, B. T., & Reddy, D. R. (1979). The HARPY speech understanding system. In W. A. Lea (Ed.), *Trends in speech recognition.* Englewood Cliffs, NJ: Prentice-Hall.

Luce, P. A., & Pisoni, D. B. (in press). Speech perception: Recent trends in research, theory, and applications. In H. Winitz (Ed.), *Human communication and its disorders.* Norwood, NJ: Ablex.

MacKay, D. G. (1973). Aspects of the theory of comprehension, memory and attention. *Quarterly Journal of Experimental Psychology, 25,* 22–40.

MacKay, D. M. (1951). Mindlike behaviour in artefacts. *British Journal for the Philosophy of Science, 2,* 105–121.

MacKay, D. M. (1956). The epistemological problem for automata. In C. E. Shannon & J. McCarthy (Eds.), *Automata studies.* Princeton, NJ: Princeton University Press.

Marcel, A. (1983). Conscious and unconscious perception: An approach to the relations between phenomenal experience and perceptual processes. *Cognitive Psychology, 15,* 238–300.

Marr, D. (1982). *Vision: A computational investigation into the human representation and processing of visual information.* San Francisco: Freeman.

Marslen-Wilson, W. D., & Welsh, A. (1978). Processing interactions and lexical access during word recognition in continuous speech. *Cognitive Psychology, 10,* 29–63.

Massaro, D. W. (1972). Preperceptual images, processing time, and perceptual units in auditory perception. *Psychological Review, 79,* 124–145.

Massaro, D. W., & Cohen, M. M. (1983). Consonant/vowel ratio: An improbable cue in speech. *Perception & Psychophysics, 33,* 501–505.

Massaro, D. W., & Oden, G. C. (1980). Speech perception: A framework for research and theory. In N. J. Lass (Ed.), *Speech and language: Advances in basic research and practive* (Vol. 3). New York: Academic Press.

McClelland, J. L. (1979). On the time relations of mental processes: An examination of systems of processes in cascade. *Psychological Review, 86,* 287–330.

McClelland, J. L., & Elman, J. L. (1984). *The TRACE model of speech perception.* Unpublished manuscript.

McClelland, J. L., & Rumelhart, D. E. (1981). An interactive activation model of context effects in letter perception, Part I: An account of basic findings. *Psychological Review, 88,* 375–407.

Miller, G. A. (1962). Decision units in the perception of speech. *IEEE Transactions on Information Theory, 8,* 81–83.

Miller, J. D. (1977). Perception of speech sounds by animals: Evidence for speech processing by mammalian auditory mechanisms. In T. H. Bullock (Ed.), *Recognition of complex acoustic signals.* Berlin: Dahlem Konferenzen.

Miller, J. L., & Liberman, A. M. (1979). Some effects of later-occurring information on the perception of stop consonant and semivowel. *Perception & Psychophysics, 25,* 457–465.

Minsky, M. (1975). A framework for representing knowledge. In P. H. Winston (Ed.), *The psychology of computer vision.* New York: McGraw-Hill.

Moray, N. (1969). *Listening and attention.* Baltimore: Penguin.

Morton, J. (1969). Interaction of information in word recognition. *Psychological Review, 76,* 165–178.

Nakatani, L. H., & Dukes, K. D. (1977). Locus of segmental cues for word juncture. *Journal of the Acoustical Society of America, 62,* 714–719.

Neisser, U. (1967). *Cognitive psychology.* New York: Appleton-Century-Crofts.

Newell, A. (1975). A tutorial on speech understanding systems. In D. R. Reddy (Ed.), *Speech recognition.* New York: Academic Press.

Newman, J. E., & Dell, G. S. (1978). The phonological nature of phoneme monitoring: A critique of some ambiguity studies. *Journal of Verbal Learning and Verbal Behavior, 17,* 359–374.

Newstead, S. E., & Dennis, I. (1979). Lexical and grammatical processing of unshadowed messages: A re-examination of the MacKay effect. *Quarterly Journal of Experimental Psychology, 31,* 477–488.

Norman, D. A., & Bobrow, D. G. (1975). On data-limited and resource-limited processes. *Cognitive Psychology, 7,* 44–64.

Nusbaum, H. C. (1981). *Capacity limitations in phoneme perception.* Unpublished doctoral dissertation, State University of New York at Buffalo.

Nusbaum, H. C. (1982). Perceiving durations of silence in nonspeech contexts. *Research on Speech Perception* (Prog. Rep. No. 8). Bloomington: Indiana University, Speech Research Laboratory.

Nusbaum, H. C. (1985). Classification of durations of silence in speech and nonspeech. Unpublished manuscript.

Nusbaum, H. C., Walley, A. C., Carrell, T. D., & Ressler, W. (1982). Controlled perceptual strategies in phoneme restoration. *Research on Speech Perception* (Prog. Rep. No. 8). Bloomington: Indiana University, Speech Research Laboratory.

Öhman, S.E.C. (1966). Coarticulation in VCV utterances: Spectrographic measurements. *Journal of the Acoustical Society of America, 39,* 151–168.

Paap, K. R., & Ogden, W. C. (1981). Letter encoding is an obligatory but capacity demanding operation. *Journal of Experimental Psychology: Human Perception and Performance, 7,* 518–527.

Picton, T. W., Campbell, K. B., Baribeau-Braun, J., & Proulx, G. B. (1978). The neurophysiology of human attention: A tutorial review. In J. Requin (Ed.), *Attention and performance VIII*. Hillsdale, NJ: Erlbaum.

Pisoni, D. B. (1973). Auditory and phonetic memory codes in the discrimination of consonants and vowels. *Perception & Psychophysics, 13*, 253–260.

Pisoni, D. B. (1975). Dichotic listening and processing phonetic features. In F. Restle, R. M. Shiffrin, N. J. Castellan, H. R. Lindman, & D. B. Pisoni (Eds.), *Cognitive theory* (Vol. 1). Hillsdale, NJ: Erlbaum.

Pisoni, D. B. (1978). Speech perception. In W. K. Estes (Ed.), *Handbook of learning and cognitive processes*. Hillsdale, NJ: Erlbaum.

Pisoni, D. B. (in press). Acoustic–phonetic representations in the mental lexicon. *Cognition*.

Pisoni, D. B., Aslin, R. N., Perey, A. J., & Hennessy, B. L. (1982). Some effects of laboratory training on identification and discrimination of voicing contrasts in stop consonants. *Journal of Experimental Psychology: Human Perception and Performance, 8*, 297–314.

Pisoni, D. B., Carrell, T. D., & Gans, S. J. (1983). Perception of the duration of rapid spectrum changes in speech and nonspeech signals. *Perception & Psychophysics, 34*, 314–322.

Pisoni, D. B., Nusbaum, H. C., Luce, P. A., & Slowiaczek, L. M. (1985). Speech perception: Word recognition and the lexicon. *Speech Communication. 4*, 75–95.

Pisoni, D. B., & Sawusch, J. R. (1975). Some stages of processing in speech perception. In A. Cohen & S. G. Nooteboom (Eds.), *Structure and process in speech perception*. Berlin: Springer-Verlag.

Poltrock, S. E., Lansman, M., & Hunt, E. (1982). Automatic and controlled attention processes in auditory target detection. *Journal of Experimental Psychology: Human Perception and Performance, 8*, 37–45.

Pomerantz, J. R. (1978). Are complex visual features derived from simple ones? In E.L.J. Leeuwenberg & H.F.J.M. Buffart (Eds.), *Formal theories of visual perception*. New York: John Wiley.

Port, R. F., & Dalby, J. (1982). Consonant/vowel ratio as a cue for voicing in English. *Perception & Psychophysics, 32*, 141–152.

Posner, M. I. (1978). *Chronometric explorations of mind*. Hillsdale, NJ: Erlbaum

Posner, M. I., & Snyder, C.R.R. (1975). Attention and cognitive control. In R. L. Solso (Ed.), *Information processing and cognition: The Loyola Symposium*. Hillsdale, NJ: Erlbaum.

Remez, R. F., Rubin, P. E., Pisoni, D. B., & Carrell, T. D. (1981). Speech perception without traditional speech cues. *Science, 212*, 947–950.

Repp, B. H. (1982). Phonetic trading relations and context effects: New experimental evidence for a speech mode of perception. *Psychological Bulletin, 92*, 81–110.

Saslow, M. G. (1958). Reaction time to consonant–vowel syllables in ensembles of various sizes. *Quarterly Progress Report*, MIT, Research Laboratory of Electronics, Cambridge, MA.

Sawusch, J. R. (1976). The structure and flow of information in speech perception. *Research on Speech Perception* (Tech. Rep. No. TR-2). Bloomington: Indiana University.

Sawusch, J. R. (1977). Peripheral and central processes in selective adaptation of place of articulation in stop consonants. *Journal of the Acoustical Society of America, 62*, 738–750.

Sawusch, J. R., & Jusczyk, P. (1981). Adaptation and contrast in the perception of voicing. *Journal of Experimental Psychology, 7*, 408–421.

Sawusch, J. R., Mullenix, J. W., & Garrison, L. F. (1983, Nov.). *Automatic and controlled processing of speech syllables.* Paper presented at the 24th Annual Meeting of the Psychonomic Society, San Diego, CA.

Sawusch, J. R., & Nusbaum, H. C. (1983). Auditory and phonetic processes in place perception for stops. *Perception & Psychophysics, 33,* 560–568.

Scheich, H. (1977). Central processing of complex sounds and feature analysis. In T. H. Bullock (Ed.), *Recognition of complex acoustic signals.* Berlin: Dahlem Konferenzen.

Schneider, W., & Shiffrin, R. M. (1977). Controlled and automatic human information processing, I: Detection, search, and attention. *Psychological Review, 84,* 1–66.

Schwab, E. C. (1981). *Auditory and phonetic processing for tone analogs of speech.* Unpublished doctoral dissertation, State University of New York at Buffalo.

Searle, C. L., Jacobson, J. Z., & Kimberley, B. P. (1980). Speech as patterns in 3-space of time and frequency. In R. A. Cole (Ed.), *Perception and production in fluent speech.,* Hillsdale, NJ: Erlbaum.

Seidenberg, M. S., Tanenhaus, M. K., Leiman, J. M., & Bienkowski, M. (1982). Automatic access of the meanings of ambiguous words in context: Some limitations of knowledge-based processing. *Cognitive Psychology, 14,* 489–537.

Seneff, S. (1984). Pitch and spectral estimation of speech based on auditory synchrony model. *Proceedings of ICASSP-84,* 36.2.1–36.2.4.

Shiffrin, R. M. (1976). Capacity limitation in information processing, attention, and memory. In W. K. Estes (Ed.), *Handbook of learning and cognitive processes.* Hillsdale, NJ: Erlbaum.

Shiffrin, R. M., Pisoni, D. B., & Castaneda-Mendez, K. (1974). Is attention shared between the ears? *Cognitive Psychology, 6,* 190–215.

Shiffrin, R. M., & Schneider, W. (1977). Controlled and automatic information processing, II: Perceptual learning, automatic attending, and a general theory. *Psychological Review, 84,* 127–190.

Shipman, D. W., & Zue, V. W. (1982). Properties of large lexicons: Implications for advanced isolated word recognition systems. *Proceedings of ICASSP-82,* 199–202.

Sperling, G., & Melchner, M. J. (1978). Visual search, visual attention, and the attention operating characteristic. In J. Requin (Ed.), *Attention and performance VIII.* Hillsdale, NJ: Erlbaum.

Sternberg, S. (1969). The discovery of processing stages: Extensions of Donder's method. In W. G. Koster (Ed.), *Attention and performance II.* Amsterdam: North Holland.

Stevens, K. N. (1975). The potential of property detectors in the perception of consonants. In G. Fant & M.A.A. Tatham (Eds.), *Auditory analysis and perception of speech.* New York: Academic Press.

Stevens, K. N., & Blumstein, S. E. (1978). Invariant cues for place of articulation in stop consonants. *Journal of the Acoustical Society of America, 64,* 1358–1368.

Stevens, K. N., & Halle, M. (1967). Remarks on analysis by synthesis and distinctive features. In W. Walthen-Dunn (Ed.), *Models for the perception of speech and visual form.* Cambridge, MA: MIT Press.

Stevens, K. N., & House, A. S. (1972). Speech perception. In J. Tobias (Ed.), *Foundations of modern auditory theory* (Vol. 2). New York: Academic Press.

Studdert-Kennedy, M. (1976). Speech perception. In N. J. Lass (Ed.), *Contemporary issues in experimental phonetics.* New York: Academic Press.

Treisman, A. M. (1964). Selective attention in man. *British Medical Journal, 20,* 12–16.

Treisman, A. M. (1969). Strategies and models of selective attention. *Psychological Review, 76,* 282–299.

Treisman, A. M., & Geffen, G. (1967). Selective attention: Perception or response? *Quarterly Journal of Experimental Psychology, 19*, 1–17.

Treisman, A. M., & Gelade, G. (1980). A feature integration theory of attention. *Cognitive Psychology, 12*, 97–136.

Treisman, A. M., & Riley, J.G.A. (1969). Is selective attention selective perception or selective response? A further test. *Journal of Experimental Psychology, 79*, 27–34.

Treisman, A. M., & Schmidt, H. (1982). Illusory conjunctions in the perception of objects. *Cognitive Psychology, 14*, 107–141.

Treisman, A., Squire, R., & Green, J. (1974). Semantic processing in dichotic listening? A replication. *Memory & Cognition, 2*, 641–646.

von Wright, J. M., Anderson, K., & Stenman, U. (1975). Generalization of conditioned GSRs in dichotic listening. In P.M.A. Rabbitt & S. Dornic (Eds.), *Attention and performance V*. New York: Academic Press.

Wardlaw, K. A., & Knoll, N.E.A. (1976). Autonomic responses to shock-associated words in a nonattended message: A failure to replicate. *Journal of Experimental Psychology: Human Perception and Performance, 2*, 357–360.

Wickelgren, W. A. (1969). Auditory of articulatory coding in verbal short term memory. *Psychological Review, 76*, 1–15.

Wickens, C. D. (1980). The structure of attentional resources. In R. S. Nickerson (Ed.), *Attention and performance VIII*. Hillsdale, NJ: Erlbaum.

CHAPTER 5

Suprasegmentals in Very Large Vocabulary Word Recognition*

Alex Waibel

Department of Computer Science, Carnegie-Mellon University, Pittsburgh, Pennsylvania 15213

I. INTRODUCTION

A typical adult human with average education can recognize words from a vocabulary on the order of 40,000 words quite reliably. By contrast, current speech recognition technology is capable of handling vocabularies of only up to around 500 words when no contextual, semantic, pragmatic, or syntactic information is given (Sugamura, Shikano, & Furui, 1983; Wilpon, Rabiner, & Bergh, 1982) and on the order of 1000 words when syntactic and semantic constraints are successfully incorporated (Lowerre, 1976). Although it is no doubt true that such systems can perform satisfactorily in a number of practical applications, they are nevertheless severely limited in generality, extensibility, and robustness and do not approach human performance.

I.A. The Problem

Unfortunately, very large vocabulary recognition (VLVR) cannot be achieved by a simple extension of computing power and memory to meet

* This research was sponsored in part by National Science Foundation Grant MSC-7825824 and by the Defense Advanced Research Projects Agency (DOD), ARPA Order No. 3597, monitored by the Air Force Avionics Laboratory under Contract F33615-78-C-1551. The views and conclusions contained in this document are those of the authors and should not be interpreted as representing the official policies, either expressed or implied, of the Defense Advanced Research Projects Agency or the U.S. government.

159

the difficulties introduced by large (>500 words) and very large (>10,000 words) vocabularies. Some more fundamental difficulties include:

- *Computational cost*—Blind brute force search becomes increasingly costly in both hardware and speed with increases in vocabulary. Useful VLVR systems should be knowledge-intensive to guide the search intelligently, and it is desirable to precompile all necessary speech knowledge into a suitable representation.
- *Practicality*—The cost of collecting and maintaining a large database of word templates is prohibitive. Practical VLVR systems should be template-independent.
- *The "new word problem"*—Useful VLVR systems must be easily modifiable and expandable to incorporate or eliminate new words or vocabularies gracefully and without major system retraining. They must also be able to recognize an incoming unknown utterance as a new word in order to invoke mechanisms to update the database of known words.
- *Learning and adapting*—Speech recognition systems approaching human performance must be capable of learning new knowledge useful for improved future recognition performance as well as adapting to the particulars of a given task, speaker, environmental noise condition, and so on.
- *Ambiguity*—As we shall see, large vocabularies contain many acoustically ambiguous subsets of words (bat, cat, bad, dad, pat, pet, etc.), resulting in poor recognition performance. To overcome this limitation, detailed featural knowledge must be incorporated so that the multiplicity of available hints in the signal can be exploited more effectively.

As a step in the direction of unrestricted speech recognition, the barriers imposed by vocabulary size must be resolved. A useful goal is the design of recognition systems on the order of 10,000 or 20,000 words. A vocabulary of this size approaches the order of magnitude of a human being's command of language. It also contains the whole spectrum of word recognition problems, since various levels and kinds of confusability will certainly be encountered. Even the most successful recognition strategies still have insurmountable limitations when the vocabulary size rises to the proposed dimensions.

For several reasons, one of the most popular recognition strategies, dynamic programming word template matching, is not easily expandable to very large vocabularies. This strategy (Itakura, 1975; Sakoe & Chiba, 1978) is a search-intensive pattern recognition method that requires an incoming unknown utterance to be matched with one or more templates corresponding to the words in the task domain. As vocabulary size increases, the computation needed on a serial computer to search the vocabulary exhaustively becomes prohibitively expensive. Several methods have been proposed to reduce the amount of computation by means of more efficient search techniques and/or through the use of more compressed representations of the speech signal. For example, the amount of search can be reduced by aborting the matching process as soon as a reference token appears to differ sufficiently from a narrow "beam" of near-miss alternatives (Itakura, 1975; Lowerre, 1976; Waibel, Krishnan, & Reddy, 1981). Alternatively, substantial speed-ups can be achieved by encoding the speech signal into a more compact representation. By using vector-quantized word templates, for example, dynamic programming-based speech recognition systems have been extended in vocabulary size into the 500–1000-word range (Sugamura et al., 1983). In addition, parallel hardware architectures have been developed for very large scale integrated (VLSI) circuit chip implementation to perform dynamic programming search more efficiently (Burr, Ackland, & Weste, 1981; Lincoln Laboratory, 1983).

To achieve real-time large vocabulary recognition, Kaneko and Dixon (1983) have adopted a hierarchical decision approach in which simple spectral and temporal measures are used for an efficient preselection stage to reduce the vocabulary to a small subset, thus immediately discarding obviously inappropriate correspondences between the unknown and a candidate word (for example, the word candidate "antidisestablishmentarianism" should never have to be seriously considered if the incoming unknown utterance is a short word such as "in"). For such a subset, a more detailed analysis such as the dynamic programming algorithm can be used effectively to make the final recognition decision.[1] In spite of these advances, however, the storage requirements for reference templates (at least one) for each word in a large vocabulary become excessively large.

A most serious problem in this context is the usefulness and practicality of a system that has to be trained for (at least one template per vocabulary item in) very large vocabularies. Possible extensions can therefore be obtained only if word templates can be generated synthetically (see Hoehne, Coker, Levinson, & Rabiner, 1983) or if subunits (e.g., syllables, demisyllables, or phonemes) smaller than the word can be extracted from an unknown word and matched to the pertinent templates. This process

---

[1] A hierarchical decision approach has also been adopted by Myers and Rabiner (1982) for a directory listing retrieval system.

has been demonstrated by Rosenberg, Rabiner, Wilpon, and Kahn (1983) as a possible approach to the problem. Demisyllable templates have been generated in a semiautomatic ("bootstrapping") fashion and therefore might render this approach a viable, practical alternative to the word template approach. Unfortunately, a demisyllable-based dynamic programming matching strategy yields significantly lower recognition performance than word template based systems.

Large vocabularies contain phonetically similar-sounding words (buck–duck, two–to). Experimentation by Lee, Silverman, and Dixon (1984) with a measure of acoustic confusability indicates that as vocabulary size increases beyond the 1000-word limit, dramatic increases in confusability are to be expected.[2] Current recognition techniques fall short of meeting those demands. Disambiguation must incorporate intelligently guided fine phonetic and prosodic analysis. This might be done by incorporating more detailed featural knowledge (Cole, Stern, Phillips, Brill, Specker, & Pilant, 1983) and/or by utilizing top-down phonetic (Aikawa, Sugiyama, & Shikano, 1984) or contextual (Erman, Hayes-Roth, Lesser, & Reddy, 1980) constraints. Just like human beings who are able to recognize words they have never heard before and write them down, recognition systems need to bring to bear knowledge from various independent domains in order to arrive at an optimal interpretation of the speech signal.

I.B. The Knowledge-Based Approach

In human information processing, knowledge is a key ingredient to making intelligent inferences efficiently. In speech perception as well as speech recognition by machine, knowledge can reduce a search through a large database of information to only the plausible, useful information. Knowledge is needed to focus attention on the informative parts of an utterance—to make inferences and draw conclusions about what has been said. Furthermore, knowledge provides the generality and flexibility that we expect systems to display in order to perform robustly in processing noisy, incomplete, ungrammatical, or elliptic speech or when new words are presented. At the phonetic level alone, human spectrogram readers (Cole, Rudnicky, Zue, & Reddy, 1980) bring to bear substantial amounts of knowledge in order to decode signals. This knowledge is used to guide and focus the search through the space of all possible candidate words, syllables, or segments. Hence, computationally inexpensive, robust, and powerful mechanisms for search space reduction exploiting

---

[2] This result was presented in the conference talk only; it does not appear in the proceedings.

speech-specific knowledge appear to be necessary ingredients for a successful VLVR system.

Zue and his colleagues (Huttenlocher & Zue, 1984; Shipman & Zue, 1982) have demonstrated that for a 20,000-word dictionary, substantial search space reduction can be achieved by using coarse phonetic analysis as a preliminary robust constraint imposed by an unknown utterance. Such coarse phonetic classes can be detected more reliably than phonemes and allophones. Such coarse classes could consist of a simple two-way distinction between consonants and vowels. Applying this two-way distinction as constraining evidence to a 20,000-word vocabulary, Shipman and Zue (1982) found that the resulting subvocabularies contained, on average, 25 words. Using a six-way coarse phonetic classification scheme (e.g., into vowels, stops, nasals, strong fricatives, weak fricatives, and glides/semivowels), even more dramatic reductions could be obtained. In a later study, Huttenlocher and Zue (1984) report that the expected class size of the remaining subvocabularies would increase only modestly if allowance is made for more likely segment deletions or confusions. Interestingly, the information provided by the stressed syllable of a word appears to provide substantially greater potential for vocabulary reduction than unstressed or destressed syllables (Huttenlocher & Zue, 1984).

Further research is needed to implement and evaluate these coarse classification schemes in an actual large vocabulary speech recognition system. Some work indicates, however, that phonetic classes can indeed be recognized fairly reliably using detailed phonetic knowledge by means of well-designed statistical classifiers exploiting featural information or productionlike rules. Cole et al. (1983) have shown how a systematic knowledge-engineering approach can yield superior performance for very confusable vocabularies (e.g., alpha digits) by using featural knowledge to make fine phonetic distinctions. Productionlike rules (Aikawa et al., 1984; DeMori, Gilloux, Mercier, Simon, Tarridec, Vaissiere, Gillet, & Gerard, 1984) and statistical classifiers (Makino, Kawabata, & Kido, 1983; Makino & Kido, 1984) have also been shown to lead to promising phoneme and word recognition performance.

I.C. Suprasegmentals

Most of the recognition strategies discussed so far are based on the short-time spectral information of speech and therefore address only the segmental properties of speech. A different aspect of human speech is known to have a great impact on intelligibility and naturalness and yet has been largely ignored for speech recognition devices: prosody or, more generally, suprasegmentals. Numerous studies have demonstrated that the presence or absence of prosodic cues dramatically improves or degrades the intelligibility of human speech (Ananthapadmanabha, 1982; Blesser, 1969; Huggins, 1978; Nickerson, 1975). However, only a few recognition systems (e.g., DeMori et al., 1984; Lea, Medress, & Skinner, 1975; Vaissiere, 1981) have actually incorporated prosodic knowledge into the recognition strategy of sentence-level speech understanding systems. The remainder of this chapter is devoted to a study of how suprasegmental cues might be useful for lexical retrieval in knowledge-based speech recognition systems.

We start with an analysis of very large vocabularies, with particular emphasis on their suprasegmental properties. The rhythmic, temporal patterns of English words are found to be especially useful to achieving substantial vocabulary reductions. In the last section these findings are supported by experimental results from an evaluation of a recognition system that uses suprasegmental knowledge sources to achieve vocabulary reduction.

II. ANALYSIS OF LARGE VOCABULARIES

The question we are trying to answer first is whether English words have consistent prosodic patterns that form classes in a large corpus of words. In analogy to the coarse phonetic classes discussed earlier, such classes could provide robust constraints that narrow the search space for lexical retrieval. We start by defining a large vocabulary containing all the necessary information.

II.A. The Database and Method of Evaluation

A database as a research vehicle for the VLVR task has to be designed according to two major criteria. First, it has to comprise a selection of words that are commonly used in natural language/speech, and it must include the whole spectrum of recognition difficulties encountered in VLVR. Second, it has to provide various kinds of information that are needed or useful in the actual recognition process. Several collections of English words were at our disposal for this research (see Waibel, 1982, for detailed discussion). They include a machine-readable version of *Webster's Pocket Dictionary,* the Brown Corpus—Form B (Kucera & Francis, 1967), the Carterette and Freedman Corpus (Carterette & Jones, 1974), and a Pascal version of the MITalk text-to-speech synthesis system (Allen, 1976; Allen, Carlson, Grandstrom, Hunnicutt, Klatt, & Pisoni, 1979) developed at Carnegie-Mellon University.

Based on these collections, an augmented version of the 20,000-word *Webster's Pocket Dictionary* has been created. In addition to the orthographic representation of each word in Webster's, the augmented version contains each word's frequency in written English text as determined from the Brown Corpus and the phonemic, prosodic, and structural descriptions derived by running each word through parts of MITalk's synthesis modules. More specifically, these descriptions include phoneme strings, syllable boundary markers, morph boundary markers, stress markers, phoneme durations, and fundamental frequency (F0) target values. As pointed out earlier, this information has been obtained in part synthetically. For example, segmental durations have not been available so far for corpora of this size, and synthetic data provide the best interim solution. Indeed, the results presented here should be interpreted only as a first-order approximation to the properties of the 20,000 words in Webster's dictionary when spoken by humans. As a motivation to using this corpus, a few supportive comments are in order.

Synthetic information for the VLV database was obtained using a version of MITalk-79 (Allen, 1976; Allen et al., 1979), an ambitious, large-scale effort aimed at unrestricted text-to-speech synthesis. MITalk-79 was developed to a level that is comparable to human speech in intelligibility and naturalness (Allen et al., 1979). Many of the pronunciation rules, as well as prosodic parameters (such as segmental durations), were obtained from measurements of spectrograms taken from a human speaker. Thus, although the particular speech quality might therefore reflect one speaker's pecularities, it also resembles actual human speech. The synthetic segmental durations have been found to differ from measurements on independently collected speech by a standard deviation of 17 ms (Allen *et al.*, 1979). However, these short deviations are less than the just-noticeable difference of temporal variations in actual speech (Allen et al., 1979; Lehiste, 1970). The synthetic durations could thus be considered perceptually accurate.

In the following discussion, all statistics collected involving durations will be limited to the suprasegmental structure of the words. This approach eliminates to some extent the possibility of circular reasoning between synthetic data and the desire to find regularity in the data. More specifically, the segmental durations used in MITalk have been obtained without particular attention to isochrony in English or to the concept of rhythmic beats.[3] Therefore, we believe that it is valid to consider syllable durations obtained in this fashion. The general validity of these assump-

---

[3] Carlson et al., however, report partial isochrony as a result of application of the prosodic component in MITalk (reported in Allen et al., 1979).

tions is also supported by actual speech recognition experiments based on our findings.

We now attempt to define measures of the speech signal that are robust and that reduce the number of likely word candidates in a large vocabulary as much as possible. In other words, we seek to evaluate a measure's power to prune the vocabulary to smaller "cohorts." As a means of evaluation, we use expected cohort size (ECS; Waibel, 1982):

$$\text{ECS}[s] = \Sigma s_0 {}^* p_s(s_0)$$

where $p_s(s_0)$ is the probability of any given word to fall into a cohort of size s_0. The expected cohort size thus takes into consideration the likelihood of any particular cohort size to occur. The result could be interpreted as the size of the cohort into which a given unknown utterance is expected to fall after application of one or more search space reduction mechanisms (filters). In the following, we either report expected cohort size or, whenever useful, maximum cohort size (i.e., worst case assumption).

II.B. Some Properties of a Very Large Vocabulary

Various studies have already examined the statistical properties of phoneme distribution in large vocabularies. For example, Denes (1963) reports phoneme and digram distributions for 72,000 phonemes as well as the frequency distribution of consonantal minimal pairs. He found (phonemes are given in ARPAbet notation) AX (schwa), IH, T, N, S, and D to be the most frequent phonemes, thus making consonants with alveolar place of articulation the most common. These and other results are supported by our data. Denes also reports the most common minimal pairs in such a database—that is, the discriminating phoneme pairs in word pairs that differ only by these phonemes. Most minimal pairs are distinguished by their manner (rather than place) of articulation.

We have found the number of such "similar"[4] word pairs to be surprisingly large. In a previous study using the original phonetic labeling from Webster's dictionary, it was found that a total of 28,335 pairs of words can be found that differ by only one phoneme. A total of 6263 word pairs differ

---

[4] Note that these pairs do not in all cases have to be similar-sounding from a perceptual point of view. "Animation–Annotation" may, for example, cause less confusion to humans than "Meditation–Medication." In some of these cases, prosodic differences or similarities might give rise to better or worse discriminability, since different stress levels might improve discriminability perceptually. Finally, different phonetic categories might differ in their discriminatory power.

by the absence (deletion) of one phoneme in one word with respect to the other. VLVR, however, is complicated not only by the high number of phonetically similar word pairs but also by similarities that cannot be disambiguated on the basis of phonetic identity alone.

- There are 376 word pairs (i.e., the recognition of 752 words is affected) that are indistinguishable by the discrimination of phonemes, stress patterns, or syllable boundary location (e.g., two–too, red–read, etc.) Discrimination can be done only on the basis of contextual cues or the likelihood of occurrence (as primed by cultural bias, experience, context, or simply word frequency).
- An additional 55 word pairs are discriminable on the basis of stress alone (e.g., "*in*crease–incr*ease*). Note that this number is derived from words having identical phonetic spelling, with the exception of stress location. Most word pairs, however, that differ in stress patterns also differ in some aspect of their phonetic realization (*perfect–perfect*). Stressed vowels, when destressed, frequently change to reduced vowels, and therefore their spectral characteristics change. The real number of pairs that are distinguishable mainly by stress is therefore probably much higher.
- 24 word pairs differ in the presence or the location of a syllable boundary only (e.g., unreel–unreal (/ah/ /n/ /r/ /iy/ /lx/), dower–dour (/d/ /aw/ /er/). Again, this number was computed on the basis of words that, other than the syllable boundary, have identical phonetic strings. This number is presumably much greater in reality also, since some word pairs differing in syllable boundary only will nevertheless be represented in our corpus by differing phonetic strings. For example, this might be the case for vowel-vowel sequences that, within one syllable, would be represented by diphthongs. Discrimination between these pairs might be possible based on accurate location of the syllable boundaries or by analysis of the temporal structure of the word in question.

From the points raised here, it seems clear that there is a substantial number of words that are discriminable from others on the basis of prosodic information. But could prosodic or, more generally, suprasegmental information be of use in the form of preliminary filters to eliminate unlikely candidates in general?

II.C. Syllable Counts

One possibility for a crude search space reduction mechanism would be to reject candidates that do not have the same number of syllables as the unknown utterance. It has been shown that the detection of syllable boundaries can be performed with an accuracy of better than 90% on continuous speech (Lea, 1980). Figure 5.1 shows the number of occurrences of words with a specific number of syllables. Assuming that all words are equally probably, the ECS is 5013—an effective pruning down to 25% of the corpus.

The solid line shows the distribution over the 20,000-word vocabulary discussed. The broken line indicates the distribution of the same vocabulary but weighted by the frequency of occurrence in the Brown Corpus (Kucera & Francis, 1967). The implicit assumptions in these two curves are that in the first case all words occur with equal frequency and that in the second case a given word occurs as frequently as indicated by the Brown Corpus frequency. In the latter case, for example, this means that in a recognition task, the word "the" is assumed to have occurred 69,971 times and is counted as such while the word "abnormally" is counted only once. The ECS for the frequency-weighted vocabulary is 12,628, which corresponds to an effective reduction to 63%.

It can be seen that the frequency-weighted distribution has a strong bias toward monosyllabic words: frequent words, particularly function words, tend to be shorter in number of syllables. Indeed, entire paragraphs of monosyllabic words (Crystal & House, 1982) are possible in English without any noticeable distortion in naturalness. Thus syllable counts could be considered as a means for classification in a large vocabulary with relatively limited potential for search space reduction. Note, however, that word frequencies introduce a strong bias toward a set of about 100 most frequent words which occur about 50% of the time in written English text.

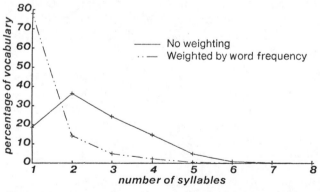

Figure 5.1   Number of occurrences versus number of syllables.

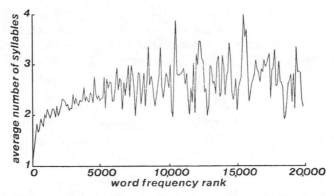

Figure 5.2   Average number of syllables in a lexicon ranked by frequency.

Building a VLVR system optimized for words as they occur most frequently would thus mean building a 100–200 word recognition system
specialized in dealing with the highly (for VLV) atypical class of the 100
most frequent words in English text. This class largely consists of monosyllabic function words which may or may not be useful for VLVR,
depending on the recognition task. These properties of a large vocabulary
are illustrated in Figure 5.2. The average number of syllables per hundred
words is shown for the 20,000 words of Webster's, sorted according to the
word frequencies provided by the Brown Corpus. It can be seen that the
distribution of syllable counts over the frequency-sorted 20,000-word vocabulary stabilizes after the first 300 most frequent words. The words that
rank less frequent than the first 200 or 300 might have different properties
from those very frequent words. To avoid this bias, we consider all words
equally likely in the following analysis.

II.D. Stress Patterns

Stress and rhythmic patterns have been discussed by several authors
(e.g., Classe, 1939; Lehiste, 1970; Liberman, 1978; Martin, 1972). Depending on the specific psycholinguistic model adopted, these two linguistic concepts may not be easily separable. For the present experimental
evaluation, however, we have chosen to explore stress and rhythm as
independent entities.

From our 20,000-word corpus, stress patterns were derived from the
syllables that were either unstressed or that carried primary stress. We
did not consider stress levels other than primary stress, since the prospect

of detecting them robustly appears rather unlikely.[5] A total of only 45 unique stress patterns were identified, some of which occurred very infrequently and may in fact be due to incorrect or questionable stress labels in the input generated by MITalk. The three most frequent stress patterns were (in order of their frequency of occurrence) 1-u, 1, and 1-u-u, where 1 represents the primary stressed syllable and u the unstressed syllable. In all three cases the stressed syllable was in word-initial position. More than half the dictionary (12,252 words) fell into one of these three categories. Following in frequency were u-1 (as in unite) and u-1-u. If we were to use stress patterns as a filter for VLVR, the resulting ECS would be 3055, which corresponds to 15.3% of the corpus.

II.E. Rhythm and Suprasegmental Duration Patterns

Deaf speech (Nickerson, 1975) and foreign accents (Chreist, 1964) cause considerable difficulty in intelligibility to normal native speakers of a language. One major reason is that the temporal structure in both cases is anomalous. The English language is isochronous and stress-timed. In fluent speech, speakers of English place intervals of approximately equal duration between syllables carrying primary stress. If several unstressed syllables are to fill this interval, they are reduced in duration, in theory to 1/2 or 1/4 units (Martin, 1972). A consequence of variable syllable length is the metric feet that make up the rhythmic structure of English speech (Lehiste, 1973). Other languages (e.g., French or Japanese) are syllable-timed—that is, all syllables are of approximately equal length. As a result, in English these differences in rhythmic patterns give rise to some of the difficulties that foreigners encounter when learning a new language. Such patterns also create perceptual problems for those trying to decode foreign accents (Chreist, 1964). When the temporal structure of English speech is corrupted, dramatic degradation in intelligibility results (Huggins, 1978). Indeed, the lack of rhythm is one of the major difficulties in understanding deaf speech (Nickerson, 1975).

If we assume that in normal English speech there is a consistent rhythmic structure, and if native English speakers seem to be making strong use of this structure in the perceptual process, then it is reasonable to examine the duration patterns for VLVR. Two forms of suprasegmental temporal patterns are examined: syllable durations and the ratio of dura-

---

[5] In the psycholinguistic literature, this task has been found to be difficult even for human listeners. Stress may in fact be partially a psychological phenomenon that may or may not be readily available from the signal.

tions of voiced to unvoiced segments in a syllable. In order to render this measure meaningful, we need to define the extent of a syllable. The location of the syllable boundaries given by our synthetic data was found to be rather inconsistent over the whole 20,000-word vocabulary. It should also be our concern here to define a syllable boundary location that is identifiable in the speech signal. Allen (1972) presents a thorough treatment of syllable boundary location and the perception of rhythmic beats by humans. He suggests that the apparent perception of syllable boundaries is in fact the perception of rhythmic beats. Allen measured the location of such beats in a series of click-matching and tapping tasks. Syllable boundaries were located quite reliably (with little variability) at the onset of stressed syllables. Generally, a syllable boundary was placed somewhat before the onset of the nuclear vowel of the syllable in question. The time interval by which the syllable boundary preceded the vowel nucleus was determined by the consonant (cluster) at the boundary. For sonorant syllable junctures, the onset of the return from the maximum formant excursion toward the vowel nucleus determined the boundary.

As a first-order approximation, the onset of the vowel nucleus can be considered to be the syllable boundary. For our database, all syllable boundary markers have been adjusted to reflect this change. One of the disadvantageous side effects of this adjustment is that segments leading a word-initial syllable stand alone and are not included in any syllable. From a practical point of view, however, this is a useful situation, since the duration of leading segments, such as voiceless stops, cannot be measured automatically. If one sets out to measure real speech, one must resort to this solution (Lehiste, 1973).

II.E.1. Syllable Duration

Syllable durations for each syllable defined in this fashion were computed by summing up the segmental durations. Figure 5.3 shows the number of occurrences for syllable durations with the syllable being in non-word-final or word-final position for polysyllabic words. Figure 5.4 shows syllable durations for monosyllabic words. As should be expected, the average syllable length in word-final position was longer than in non-word-final syllables. To provide a unified measure, the word-final and non-word-final distributions of Figure 5.3 were collapsed by "shortening" all word-final syllables by 90 ms (i.e., left-shifting the word-final curve in Figure 5.3 by 90 ms). The resulting distribution in Figure 5.5 shows three major excursions, and we define these peaks as the short, medium, and long syllables assumed in the theory (Martin, 1972). When we place boundaries at the major dips in the histogram (i.e., at 100 and at 160), we

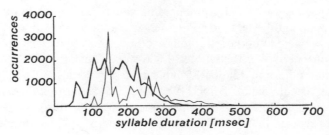

Figure 5.3 Syllable durations in polysyllabic words. ―――――, Non-word-final; ―――――, word-final.

obtain three groups for low, medium, or high syllable duration. In the case of monosyllabic words, only one boundary was chosen at 440 ms, resulting in only two classes, low and high.

Duration and stress were first evaluated together. Of all syllables carrying primary stress, 75% fall under the high category, 10% under the medium category, and 15% under the low category. Of the 15% low duration, primary-stressed syllables, however, 14% were monosyllabic words. Thus it could be said that in the majority of polysyllabic words, stressed syllables carry a high syllable duration. Using this classification scheme, all the words in our corpus were represented by n syllable duration labels (high, medium, or low), where n is the number of syllables in a word.[6] A total of 362 unique patterns were found. The largest group consists of 2965 words with identical patterns. The ECS is 1249; that is, after elimination of the inappropriate prosodic patterns, a subvocabulary of only 6% the size of the original vocabulary remains if we assume that any word of our original corpus is equally likely to be the unknown word.

―――――――――――
[6] Note that syllable count information is used implicitly here.

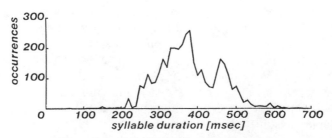

Figure 5.4   Syllables in monosyllabic words.

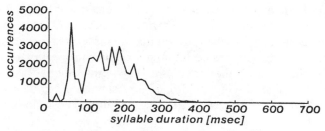

Figure 5.5   Adjusted syllable durations in polysyllabic words.

II.E.2. Voiced/Unvoiced Ratio

An additional measure of duration patterns was motivated by the possibility that the relative share of voiced or unvoiced segments in a syllable could provide some overall early rejection or acceptance of a word candidate. In spectrogram reading experiments, labels such as "mainly voiced," "all voiced," or "mainly unvoiced" have proven to be useful methods for the early rejection of unlikely word candidates (Cole et al., 1980). We have evaluated this measure in a fashion analogous to the syllable durations. For each syllable, the voiced-to-unvoiced ratio was computed. The resulting distribution is shown in Figure 5.6.[7]

Again, three groups can be identified. They will be called low, medium,

---

[7] Separate treatment of word-initial and word-final syllables or monosyllabic words has resulted in similar results. Hence, only the collapsed distribution for all the syllables in the corpus is presented here.

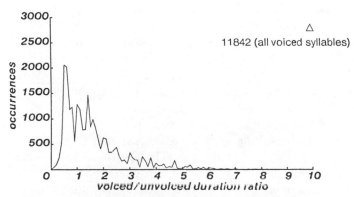

Figure 5.6   Ratio of voiced/unvoiced segment durations in all syllables.

and high, where high represents the "all voiced" syllable case. Low syllables have a voiced-to-unvoiced ratio of less than 1—that is, they contain more unvoiced (frication, silence, aspiration) than voiced (e.g., six) speech. All the syllables containing a smaller proportion of unvoiced to voiced segments are called medium. Finally, all uniquely voiced syllables are called high. In Figure 5.6, high syllables are indicated by the triangle in the upper right corner (the voiced-unvoiced ratio is infinity in this case). It should be noted that we call "unvoiced" or "voiced," respectively, what we believe can be detected in the signal as either an aperiodic or periodic signal. Thus, for example, we call voiced stops (b, d, g) unvoiced, since a pitchtracker might typically label the segment unvoiced in spite of the occasional presence of periodic low-amplitude prevocalization pulses. Alternatively, flaps (e.g., the t in "writing") are labeled as voiced. By grouping all words according to their voiced/unvoiced label patterns, we obtain 352 cohorts, the largest of which contains 2098 words. The ECS is 909 words, or 4.5% of the original corpus.

II.F. Filter Combinations—Results

A number of experiments were performed to examine the effect that a combination of the labeling schemes discussed here could have on pruning the 20,000-word dictionary. Once again, what we are interested in is the application of filters that provide crude, first-pass, robust classifications to eliminate all entries from consideration that do not belong to a set of near-miss alternatives. The thesis is that for a task of this size, prosody might provide a powerful, robust near-miss mechanism that could potentially operate in parallel with segmental classification schemes. In this section we combine some of the suprasegmental classification schemes with each other, as well as with carefully selected sets of segmental classifications. We attempted to use classification criteria that we believe can be derived from the speech signal.

The results of the various experiments are displayed in Figure 5.7. The vertical axis shows the ECS for different filter combinations. In the first and second columns, the ECS is given for the case in which words are classified only by coarse segmental feature patterns or duration patterns, respectively, as discussed in the previous section. The third column shows the case in which primary stress markers were added to the duration patterns. The resulting ECS of 978 corresponds to an expected pruning of the vocabulary down to 4.9%. The fourth column represents the results for the duration ratios of voiced to unvoiced segments in a syllable, as discussed in the previous section. In the fifth column, the duration labels and the voiced/unvoiced ratio labels were jointly used to classify

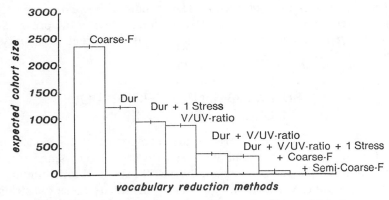

Figure 5.7   Expected cohort sizes using various filter combinations.

the vocabulary into 1891 cohorts, the largest of which identifies 1411 words (no stress markers were used here). The ECS is 381 (1.9% of the original vocabulary). In column 6, as in column 5, the duration labels and V/UV ratios as pattern generators are given along with primary stress markers whenever appropriate.

Columns 7 and 8 illustrate the usage of suprasegmental filters (as in column 6), with the addition of segmental filters. For segmental filters, two levels of detail were chosen. The first attempts only to capture very coarse phonetic features such as the fricatives s, sh, z, zh and the stops p, t, k, ch (as in church) and j (as in just). It is believed (Cole, personal communication, 1982) that these labels can be easily detected in most cases. The resulting ECS is only 62 words, which corresponds to a reduction to 0.3% of the vocabulary. When allowing for a slightly more detailed featural analysis, an even more remarkable search space reduction was achieved. Included were subsets of the closed or open vowels. (Again, the major criterion in the selection was identifiability. Here the guideline was whether a particular sound could be robustly classified by a low or high F1. Ambiguous sounds were left unlabeled and hence do not appear in the patterns.) Voiceless stops were included as well as weak and strong fricatives and the liquids w and wh (Waibel, 1982). When all these classifiers were combined, 14,080 unique patterns were identified. The largest cohort contained 94 words. The ECS was found to be six words, corresponding to a reduction to 0.03% of the search space.

The drop in ECS when combining segmental and suprasegmental features is surprisingly large. This result might be accounted for (at least in part) by the complimentary nature of the two domains. Clearly, suprasegmental information can provide a powerful new perspective from which to analyze a given unknown utterance. These findings, however, need to be put to the test in an actual speech recognition system in the presence of erroneous detection algorithms, noise, and the inherent variability of speech.

III. SUPRASEGMENTAL KNOWLEDGE SOURCES IN RECOGNITION

The general philosophy underlying the development of the system presented in the remainder of this chapter is to create knowledge sources which, based on the acoustic signal, derive robust constraints limiting the number of possible word candidates that might satisfy these constraints. These knowledge sources therefore act as vocabulary "filters" providing an ordering of word candidates based on each source's domain of expertise. The specific constraints obtained from each expert are compared with domain-specific knowledge that was automatically derived and precompiled from the original orthographic spelling (text) for each vocabulary item. The proposed system therefore functions in a template-independent way, and new vocabulary items can be entered simply in their orthographic form.

We discuss in particular several suprasegmental vocabulary filters, briefly outline their operation, and present data evaluating their current performance. It can be seen that suprasegmental cues (i.e., information that most systems largely ignore or warp away) can provide a complementary perspective on the speech signal that leads to considerable constraining of the list of possible word candidates. These suprasegmental cues consist of the rhythmic structure of the utterance, the temporal contribution of voiced and unvoiced regions in a syllable, and the temporal contribution of some sonorant classes (e.g., nasal, l, r, and front and back vowels) to the duration of the syllable nucleus. Because of its importance to the suprasegmental filters, we start with an outline of the syllabification algorithm used. Second, we describe the linear machine that serves as a sonorant feature detector. Next, the knowledge compiler that automatically generates the appropriate prosodic information from text is presented. Finally, we outline current filters and give results of performance evaluation.

III.A. Syllabification

Syllable boundary detection is performed in three stages. The first two use algorithms to perform general contour analysis and are applicable to any contour. They are based on techniques commonly employed in the vision and pattern recognition literature (Duda & Hart, 1973; Fu, 1982; Prazdny, 1983). The third consists of a set of rules that locate the syllable boundary.

In the first stage, an input contour is approximated by line segments describing only the significant events in the contour. This process uses a recursive convex deficiency algorithm. It starts by assuming a straight line between the beginning and end points of an utterance. It finds the point P of maximum deviation of the contour from the straight line, and if this deviation exceeds some stop criterion, it breaks the large line segment into two smaller segments from the beginning point to P and from P to the endpoint and then recurses. This process continues until the deviations of the original contour from the line segment approximation can be considered insignificant. Thus the algorithm attends to increasing levels of detail from one level of recursion to the next, and line segment descriptions can be extracted at varying degrees of coarseness. The algorithm is also edge-preserving such that significant events in a waveform are not smeared out but are preserved with their original amplitude and at their original point in time.

Following the approximation of the original contour by line segments, collections of segments are parsed syntactically into several primitive shapes labeled *hat, plateau, b-skirt* (before a hat), *a-skirt* (after a hat), and *silence*. These shapes provide a symbolic description of the characteristic events in a particular contour.

Following the contour analysis, a set of rules is applied to determine whether a boundary between subsequent events is a syllable boundary or not. At present, the contours used are the smoothed peak-to-peak amplitude, the zero-crossing contour of the input signal, and a sonorant energy contour. The rules take into account the basic shapes and magnitudes of the events in these contours and the possible sequences of events for a syllable to determine voiced or unvoiced portions, to find genuine syllable nuclei, and to place the syllable boundary at a linguistically consistent point in time. The syllable boundaries are placed at the onset of syllable nuclei. In informal experiments with several speakers, the syllable boundary detector in its current form has been found to yield an error rate of approximately 4–10%. Possible improvements might be achieved through adding rules, as well as by incorporating contours of alternate featural measures.

III.B. Sonorant Feature Detectors

The sonorant feature detectors described here are based on the theory of linear machines (Duda & Hart, 1973; Nilsson, 1965). A linear machine is attractive both because nonparametric learning can be achieved easily using error-correcting procedures (e.g., relaxation or perceptron learning) and because recognition can be performed efficiently.

For each of the categories of interest (nasal, l, r, front, and back), relaxation (Duda & Hart, 1973) was used to determine a set of weights for a two-category linear discriminant function. The input features used were dependent on their relevance to the classification of a particular sound. They included 54 spectral coefficients spanning an 8000-Hz spectral range, the peak-to-peak amplitude, formant frequencies as given by a formant tracker (Cole & Brennan, 1983), and, for the special case of r, the 25 spectral coefficients above F2.[8] The algorithm learns the appropriate weights that best combine the given evidence (the features) on a frame-by-frame basis. Learning was performed using a set of 57 randomly selected hand-labeled words uttered by one speaker.

In a second layer, a perceptron-based, multicategory linear classifier was used to select a unique category for each frame. The input to this classifier consisted of the binary decisions derived from the two-category response units, as described earlier, within a 24-ms time window centered on the current frame (see Duda & Hart, 1973; Nilsson, 1965). Finally, the output of this layered piecewise linear machine is smoothed.

III.C. The Knowledge Compiler

The purpose of the knowledge compiler is to generate domain-specific knowledge about a particular word in a template-independent way such that new vocabulary items can be added by simply running the compiler. An important design criterion for the compiler is to perform in the compilation phase (rather than the recognition phase) most of the necessary computation needed to match the properties of an unknown speech utterance with the expected properties of a vocabulary item. Convenient representations have therefore been selected to be generated by the compiler.

The compiler consists of two major elements. The first consists of parts of the MIT text-to-speech synthesis system (Allen et al., 1979). These include reformatting input text, decomposing input words into constituent morphs, phrase-level parsing, letter-to-sound rules or lexicon look-up, phonological rules, and the generation of a phonemic representation and corresponding prosodic information (e.g., F0 target values, segmental

---

[8] These coefficients were found to be very useful, since r's are most easily characterized by a low F3 "riding" on F2.

durations, lexical stress-markers, and syllable boundaries) of the input word. Parts of this system had to be changed to generate alternate pronunciations, such as for the word "letter," in which tt could be pronounced as the voiceless stop t or as a flap dx.

The second part of the knowledge compiler generates additional prosodic information, improves the given information, and compiles the synthetic information needed for a given vocabulary filter into a compact, useful, and consistent representation. For example, syllable boundary markers are placed in the phoneme string, consistent with the syllable boundaries generated by the syllabification unit on incoming natural speech. Syllable durations, as well as durations of voiced and unvoiced segments and of various sonorant portions of the syllable nucleus, can be computed for each lexical item from the segmental durations derived in the first part. The compiler also generates primary stress markers, expected amplitudes, and formant target values. A set of rules generates additional lexical entries for alternate syllabifications (missed boundaries, schwa deletions, etc.) and alternate pronunciations. The resulting compiled dictionary approximately doubles the number of entries. Further rules make adjustments to the prosodic information based on segmental context, position in the word, and the number of syllables in a word. In this way, speech knowledge is incorporated in the compiler in the form of productionlike rules. It is our hope that the addition of further speech-relevant knowledge will continue to improve recognition results.

III.D. The Speech Database

For evaluation, a speech database of approximately 1500 words was created. As the word list for this speech database, the union of the 900 most frequently written words (Kucera & Francis, 1967) and the 900 most frequently spoken words (Carterette & Jones, 1974) was selected. This union contains equal shares of about 450 words that are either unique to the first 900 spoken words, unique to the first 900 written words, or common to both sets. All exclamations, acronyms, titles, and names were preserved. The special punctuation symbols, formulas, and the like contained in the written corpus were eliminated, as was the somewhat arbitrary selection of numbers and isolated letters. Instead, a list of all the numbers from 1 through 20; the numbers 30, 40, 90; 100 and 1000; and a list of all the letters in the alphabet were added to the corpus. Also, to provide instances of long words, a set of 115 words was added that have four or more syllables. The resulting collection of words thus contains 1478 words (approximately 1500 tokens). The word list was randomized and annotated to disambiguate homographs (e.g., *sub*ject, sub*ject,* read (present), read (past). Recording sessions were held under moderate noise conditions in a laboratory environment using a close speaking microphone. Each utterance was sampled at 16 kHz and stored digitally on disk. Evaluation of the algorithms described below was performed using these 1500 speech tokens produced by one male American speaker.

III.E. Suprasegmental Vocabulary Filters—Results

Information derived from the speech signal was matched with the synthetic information given by the knowledge compiler. The following vocabulary filters have been implemented and evaluated:

- *Rhythm*—Various words in a large vocabulary differ in their rhythmic structure. Rhythm is therefore measured and compared with the synthetic rhythm in the database. To do so, syllable durations are measured between the boundaries given by the syllable detector. The syllable durations of the natural utterance are then compared with the synthetic syllable durations by normalizing for overall utterance lengths and computing a Euclidean distance.
- *Voiced/syllable ratios*—The contributions of unvoiced section to overall syllable durations are measured in percentages and compared with the synthetic information. For computational purposes, this is a more convenient formulation of the voiced-to-unvoiced ratios and provides equivalent information.
- *Nasal contribution to syllable duration*—This filter and the following operate in an analogous way to the previous filter. The temporal contribution of nasal portions to the syllable nucleus are compared with the synthetic data.
- *R contributions to syllable duration*—Uses sonorant feature r.
- *L contributions to syllable duration*—Uses sonorant feature l.
- *Front contributions to syllable duration*—Measures the contributions of front vowels to the syllable nucleus.
- *Back contributions to syllable duration*—Measures the contributions of back vowels to the syllable nucleus.
- *Stressed syllable formant measurement*—As an attempt to characterize the vowel nucleus of the stressed syllable in the utterance, formant frequencies were measured (Cole & Brennan, 1983) and compared with synthetic formant target values. This is therefore a very rudimentary segmental vocabulary filter. Stressed syllables were assumed to be the syllable with maximum peak-to-peak amplitude. No major difficulties arose due to stress detection errors, since in such cases a potentially less reliable syllable was considered. In order to

avoid search, this filter attempts to find the steady-state portions of the formant tracks and compares the measurements with the synthetic data. The major difficulty encountered with this method was to determine reliable portions of a syllable in a simple and efficient way. Nonetheless, it does provide discriminatory information and was included in the evaluation.

Note that the temporal contributions of various sonorant features depend heavily on context. For example, l followed by a front vowel will commonly transition through a region classified as "back." These and other properties were included in the compiler rules used to generate the expected information for a word.

Based on the corpus described previously, the knowledge compiler generated prosodic information for 1478 English words. After application of the rules for alternate pronunciations and syllabification, a total of 3207 vocabulary items was obtained. Of the 1478 words, the first 500 utterances were set aside for the development of algorithms. Of these, 57 were used for training the sonorant classifiers. The remaining 978 utterances were set aside as test data to evaluate the performance of our system. They constitute new words whose expected characteristic information was generated automatically from text. No training data had been collected for these words. 116 of these test words were found to be improperly recorded or processed inaccurately during the signal processing, endpoint detection, or syllabification stages. Hence they were not included in the results given here. The effective corpus of words tested therefore consists of 862 utterances from a 1478-word vocabulary.

Results are given in Figure 5.8 for monosyllabic words and in Figure 5.9 for polysyllabic words. For each filter we show the frequency at which the correct word was ranked among the top N candidates. The bold curves labeled "Combi" display the ranking of the correct word candidate after combining the results from all eight filters. Combination was performed for this data by simply computing the geometric means of the individual filter rankings and reranking. Better performance was obtained for polysyllabic words, as seen in Figure 5.9. This result was expected, since polysyllabic words are richer in prosodic information. Also, the rhythm vocabulary filter was not applied to monosyllabic words. In fact, 27% of all the polysyllabic words were uniquely identified (rank 1) by these suprasegmental filters. In contrast, this was the case for only 4% of the monosyllabic words. Note also the sharp discontinuities in both figures for some of the filters. If several utterances matched equally well, they all received the same rank—their median rank. Hence, for some filters, large pools of perfectly and equally matching word candidates yielded lower

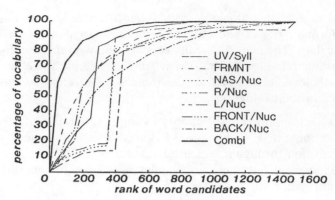

Figure 5.8   Rank of correct monosyllabic word candidates (adapted from Waibel, 1984).

ranks (for example, all 769 monosyllabic dictionary entries without an r-contribution were ranked 384 if the unknown was an utterance containing no r contribution).

In agreement with our theoretical findings, the most constraining information was obtained from the unvoiced/syllable ratio. The least successful vocabulary filter was the l/nuc ratio, presumably due to the difficulty of detecting l's reliably in context (confusions with the back category are very common). In summary, by applying all the constraints given by the eight filters on the list of 3207 candidates, the correct word ranks on average 91st for monosyllabic words, 37th for polysyllabic, and 64th for both. For all words, this ranking corresponds to the top 4.4% of the original vocabulary of 1478 words. Errors (i.e., inappropriate ranking for

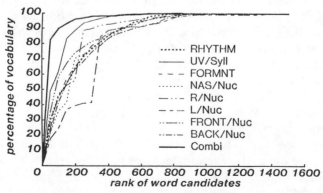

Figure 5.9   Rank of correct polysyllabic word candidates (adapted from Waibel, 1984).

the correct word candidate) were due to alternate pronunciations not yet generated by the knowledge compiler (e.g., British pronunciation of "classes"), sonorant classifier inaccuracies, erroneous voiced/unvoiced decisions, and endpoint detection errors. Some of these problems can be improved by simply adding more speech knowledge to the compiler, while the addition of more filters will further constrain acceptable word candidates and reduce the effective subvocabulary.

IV. CONCLUSIONS

In this chapter we have examined the problems and some potential solutions to very large vocabulary recognition. We have presented a large vocabulary database. Based on synthetic data generated for this vocabulary, we have shown that prosodic features as well as a set of phonetic features can provide powerful cues for narrowing down the large search space that accompanies a very large vocabulary recognition task. The prosodic features of rhythm and the ratio of unvoiced to voiced segments have been found to be largely complementary to phonetic features (i.e., they are not redundant). Stress patterns might yield some additional reduction of the search space, given the rhythmic (durational) patterns.

These encouraging results were further supported by the implementation of suprasegmental knowledge sources. Their power to successfully preselect a small subvocabulary in a large vocabulary speech recognition system was demonstrated. Using a 1500-word speech database, a set of mostly suprasegmental, temporal vocabulary filters was shown to constrain the possible word candidates in such a way that the correct candidate was ranked, on average, 64th in a 1500-word vocabulary. The filters operate in a knowledge-intensive rather than a search-intensive fashion in order to allow for fast candidate preselection. Finally, all information used to describe a vocabulary entry can be generated automatically by rule, so that no training is necessary when new vocabularies or new words are used.

These results indicate that the study of prosody can provide substantial additional information for very large vocabulary (~20,000 words) recognition systems. Moreover, when expanding toward connected speech (e.g., a dictation machine), recognition of the prosodic information in speech appears indispensable. Additional potentially useful prosodic features such as amplitude patterns, pitch contours, stress patterns, and spectral dynamics have not been exploited in most speech recognition systems to date and thus remain to be explored. In our view, a knowledge-intensive approach combining constraints from a collection of multiple complementary knowledge sources is capable of providing the robustness and flexibility required for very large vocabulary speech recognition systems.

REFERENCES

Aikawa, K., Sugiyama, M., & Shikano, K. (1984). Phoneme recognition based on top-down approach. *Review of the Electrical Communication Laboratories, 32,* 200–211.

Allen, G. D. (1972). The location of rhythmic stress beats in English: An experimental study I and II. *Language and Speech, 15, 16,* 72–100; 179–195.

Allen, J. (1976). Synthesis of speech from unrestricted text. *Proceedings of the IEEE, 64,* 433–442.

Allen, J., Carlson, R., Grandstrom, B., Hunnicutt, S., Klatt, D., & Pisoni, D. (1979). *Conversion of unrestricted English text to speech.* Cambridge, MA: MIT Press.

Ananthapadmanabha, T. V. (1982). *Intelligibility in the rhythm and melody of speech: Implications to speech perception* (Tech. Rep.). Stockholm: Royal Institute of Technology.

Blesser, B. A. (1969). *Perception of spectrally rotated speech.* Unpublished doctoral dissertation, MIT, Cambridge, MA.

Burr, D. J., Ackland, B., & Weste, N. (1981). A high speed array computer for dynamic time warping. *ICASSP 1981 Proceedings, 2,* 471–474.

Carterette, E. C., & Jones, M. H. (1974). *Informal speech.* Berkeley: University of California Press.

Chreist, F. M. (1964). *Foreign accent.* Englewood Cliffs, NJ: Prentice-Hall.

Classe, A. (1939). *Rhythm of English prose.* Oxford, England: Basil Blackwell.

Cole, R. A., & Brennan, R. A. (1983). A pretty good formant tracker. *The Journal of the Acoustical Society of America, 74,* S15.

Cole, R. A., Rudnicky, A. I., Zue, V. W., & Reddy, D. R. (1980). Speech as patterns on paper. In *Perception and production of fluent speech.* Hillsdale, NJ: Erlbaum.

Cole, R. A., Stern, R. M., Phillips, M. S., Brill, S. M., Specker, P., & Pilant, A. P. (1983). Feature-based speaker-independent recognition of English letters. *ICASSP 1983 Proceedings, 2,* 731–743.

Crystal, T. H., & House, A. S. (1982). Segmental durations in connected speech signals: Preliminary results. *Journal of the Acoustical Society of America, 72,* 705–716.

DeMori, R., Gilloux, M., Mercier, G., Simon, M. A., Tarridec, C., Vaissiere, J., Gillet, D., & Gerard, M. (1984). Integration of acoustic, phonetic, prosodic and lexical knowledge in an expert system for speech understanding. *ICASSP 1984 Proceedings, 3,* 42.9.1–42.9.4.

Denes, P. B. (1963). On the statistics of spoken English. *Journal of the Acoustical Society of America, 35,* 892–904.

Duda, R. O., & Hart, P. E. (1973). *Pattern classification and scene analysis.* New York: John Wiley.

Erman, L. D., Hayes-Roth, F., Lesser, V. R., & Reddy, D. R. (1980). The Hearsay-II speech-understanding system: Integrating knowledge to resolve uncertainty. *ACM Computing Surveys, 12,* 213–253.

Fu, K. S. (1982). *Syntactic pattern recognition and applications.* Englewood Cliffs, NJ: Prentice-Hall.

Hoehne, H. D., Coker, C., Levinson, S. E., & Rabiner, L. R. (1983). On temporal alignment of sentences of natural and synthetic speech. *IEEE Transactions on Acoustics, Speech, & Signal Processing, 31,* 807–813.

Huggins, A.W.F. (1978). Speech timing and intelligibility. In J. Requin (Ed.), *Attention and performance VII.*Hillsdale, NJ: Erlbaum.

Huttenlocher, D. P., & Zue, V. W. (1984). A model of lexical access based on partial phonetic information. *ICASSP 1984 Proceedings, 2,* 26.4.1–26.4.4.

Itakura, F. (1975). Minimum prediction residual principle applied to speech recognition. *IEEE Transactions on Acoustics, Speech, & Signal Processing, 23,* 67–72.

Kaneko, T., & Dixon, N. R. (1983). A hierarchical decision approach to large-vocabulary discrete utterance recognition. *IEEE Transactions on Acoustics, Speech, & Signal Processing, 31,* 1061–1066.

Kucera, H., & Francis, W. N. (1967). *Computational analysis of present-day American English.* Providence, RI: Brown University Press.

Lea, W. A. (1980). *Trends in speech recognition.* Englewood Cliffs, NJ: Prentice-Hall.

Lea, W. A., Medress, M. F., & Skinner, T. E. (1975). A prosodically guided speech understanding strategy. *IEEE Transactions on Acoustics, Speech, & Signal Processing, 23,* 30–38.

Lee, Y., Silverman, H. F., & Dixon, N. R. (1984). Preliminary results for an operational definition and methodology for predicting large vocabulary DUR confusability from phonetic transcriptions. *ICASSP 1984 Proceedings, 2,* 26.2.1–26.2.4.

Lehiste, I. (1970). *Suprasegmentals,* Cambridge, MA: MIT Press.

Lehiste, I. (1973). Rhythmic units and syntactic units in production and perception. *Journal of the Acoustical Society of America, 54,* 1228–1234.

Liberman, M. Y. (1978). *The intonational system of English.* Bloomington: Indiana University Linguistics Club.

Lincoln Laboratory (1983). *Restructurable VLSI program* (Tech. Rep.). Cambridge, MA: MIT.

Lowerre, B. T. (1976). *The Harpy speech recognition system.* Unpublished doctoral dissertation, Carnegie-Mellon University, Pittsburgh.

Makino, S., Kawabata, T., & Kido, K. (1983). Recognition of consonant based on the perceptron model. *ICASSP 1983 Proceedings, 2,* 738–741.

Makino, S., & Kido, K. (1984). A speaker independent word recognition system based on phoneme recognition for a large size (212 words) vocabulary. *ICASSP 1984 Proceedings, 2,* 17.8.1–17.8.4.

Martin, J. G. (1972). Rhythmic (hierarchical) versus serial structure in speech and other behavior. *Psychological Review, 79,* 487–509.

Myers, C. S., & Rabiner, L. R. (1982). An automated directory listing retrieval system based on recognition of connected letter strings. *Journal of the Acoustical Society of America, 71,* 716–727.

Nickerson, R. S. (1975). Characteristics of the speech of deaf persons. *Volta Review, 77,* 342–362.

Nilsson, N. J. (1965). *Learning machines.* New York: McGraw-Hill.

Prazdny, K. (1983). Waveform segmentation and description using edge preserving smoothing. *Computer Vision, Graphics, and Image Processing, 23,* 327–333.

Rosenberg, A. E., Rabiner, L. R., Wilpon, J. G., & Kahn, D. (1983). Demisyllable-based isolated word recognition systems. *IEEE Transactions on Acoustics, Speech, & Signal Processing, 31,* 713–726.

Sakoe, H., & Chiba, S. (1978). Dynamic programming optimization for spoken word recognition. *IEEE Transactions on Acoustics, Speech, & Signal Processing, 26,* 43–49.

Sugamura, N., Shikano, K., & Furui, S. (1983). Isolated word recognition using phoneme-like templates. *ICASSP 1983 Proceedings, 2,* 723–726.

Shipman, D. W., & Zue, V. W. (1982). Properties of large lexicons: Implications for advanced isolated word recognition systems. *ICASSP 1982 Proceedings, 1,* 546–549.

Vaissiere, J. (1981). Speech recognition programs as models of speech perception. In T. Myers, J. Laver, & J. Anderson (Eds.). *The cognitive representation of speech.* Amsterdam: North Holland.

Waibel, A. (1982). *Towards very large vocabulary word recognition* (Tech. Rep. No. 144). Carnegie-Mellon University, Computer Science Department.

Waibel, A. (1984). Suprasegmentals in very large vocabulary isolated word recognition. *ICASSP 1984 Proceedings, 2,* 26.3.1–26.3.4.

Waibel, A., Krishnan, N., & Reddy, R. (1981). *Minimizing computational cost for dynamic programming algorithms* (Tech. Rep. 124). Carnegie-Mellon University, Computer Science Department.

Wilpon, J. G., Rabiner, L. R., & Bergh, A. (1982). Speaker-independent isolated word recognition using a 129-word airline vocabulary. *Journal of the Acoustical Society of America, 72,* 390–396.

CHAPTER **6**

The Adaptive Self-organization of Serial Order in Behavior: Speech, Language, and Motor Control*

Stephen Grossberg

*Department of Mathematics, Boston University,
Boston, Massachusetts 02215*

I. INTRODUCTION: PRINCIPLES OF SELF-ORGANIZATION IN MODELS OF SERIAL ORDER: PERFORMANCE MODELS VERSUS SELF-ORGANIZING MODELS

The problem of serial order in behavior is one of the most difficult and far-reaching problems in psychology (Lashley, 1951). Speech and language, skilled motor control, and goal-oriented behavior generally are all instances of this profound issue. This chapter describes principles and mechanisms that have been used to unify a variety of data and models, as well as to generate new predictions concerning the problem of serial order.

The present approach differs from many alternative contemporary approaches by deriving its conclusions from concepts concerning the adaptive self-organization (e.g., the development, chunking, and learning) of serial behavior in response to environmental pressures. Most other approaches to the problem, notably the familiar information processing and artificial intelligence approaches, use performance models for which questions of self-organization are raised peripherally, if at all. Some models discuss adaptive issues but do not consider them in a real-time context. A homunculus is often used, either implicitly or explicitly, to make the model work. Where a homunculus is not employed, models are often tested numerically in such an impoverished learning environment

* Supported in part by National Science Foundation Grants NSF IST-80-00257 and NSF-IST-8417756 and Office of Naval Research Contract ONT-N00014-83-K0337.

187

that their instability in a more realistic environment is not noticed. These limitations in modeling approaches have given rise to unnecessary internal paradoxes and predictive limitations within the modeling literature. I suggest that such difficulties are due to the facts that principles and laws of self-organization are rate-limiting in determining the design of neural processes, and that problems of self-organization are the core issues that distinguish psychology from other natural sciences, such as traditional physics.

In light of these assertions, it is perhaps more understandable why a change of terminology or usage of the same concepts and mechanisms to discuss a new experiment can be hailed as a new model. The shared self-organizing principles that bind the ideas in one model to the ideas in other models are frequently not recognized. This style of model building tends to perpetuate the fragmentation of the psychological community into non-interacting specialties rather than foster the unifying impact whereby modeling has transformed other fields.

The burgeoning literature on network and activation models in psychology has, for example, routinely introduced as new ideas concepts that were previously developed to explain psychological phenomena in the neural modeling literature. Such concepts as unitized nodes, the priming of short-term memory, probes of long-term memory, automatic processing, spreading activation, distinctiveness, lateral inhibition, hierarchical cascades, and feedback were all quantitatively used in the neural modeling literature before being used by experimental psychologists. Moreover, the later users have often ignored the hard-won lessons to be found in the neural modeling literature.

The next section illustrates some characteristic difficulties of models and how they can be overcome by the present approach (this discussion can be skipped on a first reading).

II. MODELS OF LATERAL INHIBITION, TEMPORAL ORDER, LETTER RECOGNITION, SPREADING ACTIVATION, ASSOCIATIVE LEARNING, CATEGORICAL PERCEPTION, AND MEMORY SEARCH: SOME PROBLEM AREAS

II.A. Lateral Inhibition and the Suffix Effect

From a mathematical perspective, a model that uses lateral inhibition is a competitive dynamical system (Grossberg, 1980a). Smale (1976) has proven that the class of competitive dynamical systems contains systems capable of exhibiting arbitrary dynamical behavior. Thus to merely say that lateral inhibition is at work is, in a literal mathematical sense, a vacuous statement. One needs to define precisely the dynamics that one has in mind before anything of scientific value can be gleaned. Even going so far as to say that the inhibitory feedback between nearby populations is linear says nothing of interest, because linear feedback can cause such varied phenomena as oscillations that never die out or the persistent storage of short-term memory patterns, depending on the anatomy of the network as a whole (Cohen & Grossberg, 1983; Grossberg, 1978c, 1980a).

An imprecise definition of inhibitory dynamics will therefore inevitably produce unnecessary controversies, as has already occurred. For example, Crowder's (1978) explanation of the suffix effect (Dallett, 1965) and Watkins and Watkins's (1982) critique of the Crowder theory both focus on the purported property of recurrent lateral inhibition that an extra suffix should weaken the suffix effect due to disinhibition. However, this claim does not necessarily hold in certain shunting models of recurrent lateral inhibition that are compatible with the suffix effect (Grossberg, 1978a, 1978e). This controversy concerning the relevance of lateral inhibition to the suffix effect cannot be decided until the models of lateral inhibition used to analyze that effect are determined with complete mathematical precision. A type of lateral inhibition that avoids the controversy is derived from a rule of self-organization that guarantees the stable transfer of temporal order information from short-term memory to long-term memory as new items continually perturb a network (Section XXXIII).

II.B. Temporal Order Information in Long-Term Memory

A more subtle problem arises in Estes's (1972) influential model of temporal order information in long-term memory. Estes (1972, p. 183) writes: "The inhibitory tendencies which are required to properly shape the response output become established in memory and account for the long term preservation of order information." Estes goes on to say that inhibitory connections form from the representations of earlier items in the list to the representations of later items. Consequently, earlier items will be less inhibited than later items on recall trials and will therefore be performed earlier. Despite the apparent plausibility of this idea, a serious problem emerges when one writes down dynamical equations for how these inhibitory interactions might be learned in real time. One then discovers that learning by this mechanism is unstable because, as Estes realized, the joint activation of two successive network nodes is needed for the network to know which inhibitory pathway should be strengthened. As such an inhibitory pathway is strengthened, it can more strongly inhibit its receptive node, which is the main idea of the Estes model.

However, when this inhibitory action inhibits the receptive node, it un-
dermines the joint excitation that is needed to learn and remember the
strong inhibitory connection. The inhibitory connection then weakens,
the receptive node is disinhibited, and the learning process is initiated
anew. An unstable cycle of learning and forgetting order information is
thus elicited through time. Notwithstanding the heuristic appeal of
Estes's mechanism, it cannot be correct in its present form. All conclusions that use this mechanism therefore need revision, such as Rumelhart
and Norman's (1982) discussion of typing and MacKay's (1982) discussion of syntax.

One might try to escape the instability problem that arises in Estes's
(1972) theory of temporal order information by claiming that inhibitory
connections are prewired into a sequential buffer and that many different
lists can be performed from this buffer. Unfortunately, traditional buffer
concepts (e.g., Atkinson & Shiffrin, 1968; Raaijmakers & Shiffrin, 1981)
face design problems that are as serious as the instability criticism (Grossberg, 1978a). In this way, the important design problem of how to represent temporal order information in short-term and long-term memory
without using either a traditional buffer or conditioned inhibitory connections is vividly raised. Solutions of these problems are suggested in Sections XII–XIX and XXXIV.

II.C. Letter and Word Recognition

A similar instability problem occurs in the work of letter perception of
Rumelhart and McClelland (1982). They write: "Each letter node is assumed to activate all of those word nodes consistent with it and inhibit all
other word nodes. Each active word node competes with all other word
nodes . . . " (Rumelhart & McClelland, 1982, p. 61). Obviously, the
selective connections between letter nodes and word nodes are not prewired into such a network at birth. Otherwise, all possible letter-word
connections for all languages would exist in every mind, which is absurd.
Some of these connections are therefore learned. If the inhibitory connections are learned, then the model faces the same instability criticism that
was applied to Estes's (1972) model. Grossberg (1984b) shows, in addition, that if the excitatory connections are learned, then learning cannot
get started.

The connections hypothesized by Rumelhart and McClelland also face
another type of challenge from a self-organization critique. How does the
network learn the difference between a letter and a word? Indeed, some
letters are words, and both letters and words are pronounced using a
temporal series of motor commands. Thus many properties of letters and

words are functionally equivalent. Why, then, should each word compete with all other words, whereas no letter competes with all other words? An alternative approach is suggested in Section XXXVII, where it is suggested that the levels used in the Rumelhart and McClelland model are insufficient.

The McClelland and Rumelhart model faces such difficulties because it considers only performance issues concerning the processing of four-letter words. In contrast, the present approach considers learning and performance issues concerning the processing of words of any length. Its analysis of how a letter stream of arbitrary length is organized during real-time presentation leads to a process that predicts, among other properties, a word-length effect in word superiority studies (Grossberg, 1978e, Sect. 41; reprinted in Grossberg, 1982d, p. 595). Subsequent data have supported this prediction (e.g., Matthei, 1983; Samuel, van Santen, & Johnston, 1982, 1983). No such prediction could be made using Rumelhart and McClelland's (1982) model, since it is defined only for four-letter words. Moreover, the theoretical ideas leading to predictions such as the word-length effect are derived from an analysis of how letter and word representations are learned. An analysis of performance issues per se provides insufficient constraints on processing design.

II.D. Spreading Activation

Similar difficulties arise from some usages of ideas like spreading activation in network memory models. In Anderson (1976) and Collins and Loftus (1975), the amount of activation arriving at a network node is a decreasing function of the number of links the activation has traversed, and the time for activation to spread is significant (about 50–100 ms per link). By contrast, there is overwhelming neural evidence of activations that do not pass passively through nerve cells and that are not carried slowly and decrementally across nerve pathways (Eccles, 1952; Kuffler & Nicholls, 1976; Stevens, 1966). Rather, activation often cannot be triggered at nerve cells unless proper combinations of input signals are received, and when a signal is elicited it is carried rapidly and nondecrementally along nerve pathways. Although these ideas have been used in many neural network analyses of psychological data, their unfamiliarity to many psychologists is still a source of unnecessary controversy (Ratcliff & McKoon, 1981). Most spreading activation models are weakened by their insufficient concern for which nodes have a physical existence and which dynamical transactions occur within and between nodes. Both of these issues are special cases of the general question of how a node can be self-organized through experience.

Anderson's (1983) concept of a "fan effect" in spreading activation illustrates these difficulties. Anderson proposes that if more pathways lead away from a concept node, each pathway can carry less activation. In this view, activation behaves like a conserved fluid that flows through pipelike pathways. Hence, the activation of more pathways will slow reaction time, other things being equal. The number of pathways to which a concept node leads, however, is a learned property of a self-organizing network. The pathways that are strengthened by learning are a subset of all the pathways that lead away from the concept node. At the concept node itself, no evidence is available to label which of these pathways was strengthened by learning (Section III). The knowledge of which pathways are learned is only available by testing how effectively the learned signals can activate their recipient nodes. It is not possible, in principle, to make this decision at the activating node itself.

Since many nodes may be activated by signals from a single node, the network decides which nodes will control observable behavior by restricting the number of activated nodes. Inhibitory interactions among the nodes help to accomplish this task. Inhibitory interactions are not used in Anderson's (1983) theory, although it is known that purely excitatory feedback networks are unstable unless artificially narrow choices of parameters are made. Without postulating that activation behaves like a conserved fluid, a combination of thresholds and inhibitory interactions can generate a slowing of reaction time as the number of activated pathways is increased. In fact, the transition from a fan concept (associative normalization) to inhibitory interactions and thresholds was explicitly carried out and applied to the study of reaction time (Grossberg, 1968b, 1969c). This theoretical step gradually led to the realization that inhibitory interactions cause limited capacity properties as a manifestation of a fundamental principle of network design (Section XIX). Anderson (1983) intuitively justifies his fan concept in terms of a limited capacity for spreading activation, but he does not relate the limited capacity property to inhibitory processes.

II.E. Associative Learning and Categorical Perception

In the literature on associative learning, confusion has arisen due to an insufficient comparative analysis of the adaptive models that are available. For example, some authors erroneously claim that all modern associative models use "Hebbian synapses" (Anderson, Silverstein, Ritz, & Jones, 1977) and thus go on to equate important differences in processing capabilities that exist among different associative models. For example, in their discussion of long-term memory, Anderson et al. (1977) claim that the change in synaptic weight z_{ij} from a node v_i to a node v_j equals the product of the activity f_i of v_i with the activity g_j of v_j, where f_i and g_j may be positive or negative. If both f_i and g_j are negative, two inhibited nodes can generate a positive increment in memory, which is neurally unprecedented. Also, if f_i is positive and g_j is negative, a negative memory trace z_{ij} can occur. Later, if f_i is negative, its interaction with negative memory z_{ij} causes a positive activation of g_j. Thus an inhibited node v_i can, via a negative memory trace z_{ij}, excite a node v_j. This property is also neurally unprecedented. Both of these properties follow from the desire of Anderson et al. (1977) to apply ideas from linear system theory to neural networks. These problems do not arise in suitably designed nonlinear associative networks (Section III).

The desire to preserve the framework of linear system theory also led Anderson et al. (1977) to employ a homunculus in their model of categorical perception, which cannot adequately be explained by a linear model. To start their discussion of categorical perception, they allowed some of their short-term memory activities to become amplified by positive linear feedback. Left unchecked in a linear model, the positive feedback would force the activities to become infinite, which is physically impossible. To avoid this property, the authors imposed a rule that stops the growth of each activity when it reaches a predetermined maximal or minimal size and thereafter stores this extremal value in memory. The tendency of all variables to reach a maximal or minimal value is then used to discuss data about categorical perception. No physical process is defined to justify the discontinuous change in the slope of each variable when it reaches an extreme of activity or to explain the subsequent storage of these activities. The model thus invokes a homunculus to explain both categorical perception and short-term memory storage.

If the discontinuous saturation rule is replaced by a continuous saturation rule, and if the dynamics of short-term memory storage are explicitly defined, then positive linear feedback can compress the stored activity pattern, rather than contrast enhance it, as one desires to explain categorical perception (Grossberg, 1973, 1978d). This example illustrates how perilous it is to substitute formal algebraic rules, such as those of linear system theory, for dynamical rules in the explication of a psychological process. Even in cases where the algebraic rule seems to express an intuitive property of the psychological process—such as the tendency to saturate—the algebraic rule may also suggest the use of other rules—such as linear positive feedback—that produce diametrically opposed results when they are used in a dynamical description of the process. No homunculus is needed to explain categorical perception in suitably designed nonlinear neural networks (Sections XVIII and XXII). Indeed, nonlinear network mechanisms are designed to avoid the types of instabilities and interpretive anomalies that a linear feedback system approach often generates in a neural network context.

II.F. Classical Conditioning and Attentional Processing

Much as Anderson et al. (1977) improperly lumped all associative models into a Hebbian category, so Sutton and Barto (1981) have incorrectly claimed that associative models other than their own use Hebbian synapses. They go on to reject all Hebbian models in favor of their own non-Hebbian associative model. Given the apparent importance of the Hebbian distinction, it is necessary to define a Hebbian synapse and to analyze why it is being embraced or rejected.

Sutton and Barto (1981, p. 135) follow Hebb to define a Hebbian synapse as follows: "When a cell A repeatedly and persistently takes part in firing another cell B, then A's efficiency in firing B is increased." However, in my associative theory, which Sutton and Barto classify as a Hebbian theory, repeated and persistent associative pairing between A and B can yield conditioned decreases, as well as increases, in synaptic strength (Grossberg, 1969b, 1970b, 1972c). This is not a minor property, since it is needed to assert that the unit of long-term memory is a spatial pattern of synaptic strengths (Section IV). Hebb's law by contrast, is consistent with the assumption that the unit of long term memory is a single synaptic strength. This property does not satisfy the definition of a Hebbian synapse; hence, my associative laws are not Hebbian, contrary to Sutton and Barto's claim. Moreover, the associative component of these laws is only one of several interesting factors that control their mathematical and behavioral properties. None of these factors was considered by Hebb.

Notwithstanding these important details, we still need to ask why Sutton and Barto attack "Hebbian" models. The reason is that Hebbian theories are purported to be unable (1) to recall a conditioned response with a shorter time lag after the presentation of a conditioned stimulus (CS) than was required for efficient learning to occur between the CS and the unconditioned stimulus (UCS), or (2) to explain the inverted U in learning efficacy that occurs as a function of the time lag between a CS and UCS on learning trials. Indeed, Sutton and Barto (1981, p. 142) confidently assert: "Not one of the adaptive element models currently in the literature is capable of producing behavior whose temporal structure is in agreement with that observed in animal learning as described above." Unfortunately, this assertion is false. In fact, Sutton and Barto refer to the article by Grossberg (1974) which reviews a conditioning theory that can explain these phenomena (Grossberg, 1971, 1972a, 1972b, 1975), as well as a variety of other phenomena that Sutton and Barto cannot explain due to their model's formal kinship with the Rescorla-Wagner model (Grossberg, 1982b; Rescorla & Wagner, 1972). Moreover, my explanation does not depend on the non-Hebbian nature of my associative laws but rather on the global anatomy of the networks that I derive to explain conditioning data.

This anatomy includes network regions, called "drive representations," at which the reinforcing properties of external cues join together with internal drive inputs to compute motivational decisions that modulate the attentional processing of external cues. No such concept is postulated in Sutton and Barto's (1981) model. Thus the fact that a pair of simultaneous CSs can be processed, yet a CS that is simultaneous with a UCS is not processed, does not depend on the elaboration of the UCS's motivational and attentional properties in the Sutton and Barto model, despite the fact that the UCS might have been a CS just hours before. Sutton and Barto's model of classical conditioning excludes motivational and attentional factors, instead seeking all explanations of classical conditioning data in the properties of a single synapse. Such an approach cannot explain the large database concerning network interactions between neocortex, hypothalamus, septum, hippocampus, and reticular formation in the control of stimulus–reinforcer properties (Berger & Thompson, 1978; Deadwyler, West, & Robinson, 1981; DeFrance, 1976; Gabriel, Foster, Orona, Saltwick, & Stanton, 1980; Haymaker, Anderson, & Nauta, 1969; MacLean, 1970; O'Keefe & Nadel, 1978; Olds, 1977; Stein, 1958; West, Christian, Robinson, & Deadwyler, 1981) and leads its authors to overlook the fact that such interactions are interpreted and predicted by alternative models (Grossberg, 1975). The present chapter also focuses on behavioral properties that are emergent properties of network interactions, rather than of single cells, and illustrates that single cell and network laws must both be carefully chosen to generate desirable emergent properties.

II.G. Search of Associative Memory

The Anderson et al. (1977) model provides one example of a psychological model whose intuitive basis is not adequately instantiated by its formal operations. Such a disparity between intuition and formalism causes internal weaknesses that limit the explanatory and predictive power of many psychological models. These weaknesses can coexist with a model's ability to achieve good data fits on a limited number of experiments. Unfortunately, good curve fits have tended to inhibit serious analysis of the internal structure of psychological models.

Another example of this type of model is Raaijmakers and Shiffrin's (1981) model of associative memory search. The data fits of this model are remarkably good. One reason for its internal difficulties is viewed by the authors as one of its strengths: "Because our main interest lies in the development of a retrieval theory, very few assumptions will be stated concerning the interimage structure" (Raaijmakers & Shiffrin, 1981, p. 123). To characterize this retrieval theory, the model defines learning rules that are analogous to laws of associative learning. However, in information processing models of this kind, terminology like short-term memory (STM) and long-term memory (LTM) is often used instead of terminology like CS, UCS, and conditioning. These differences of terminology seem to have sustained the separate development of models that describe mechanistically related processes.

Although Raaijmakers and Shiffrin's (1981) model intuitively discusses STM and LTM, no STM variables are formally defined; only LTM strengths are defined. This omission forces compensatory assumptions to be made through the remaining theoretical structure. In particular, the LTM strength $S(W_{iT}, W_{jS})$ between the ith word at test (T) and the jth stored (S) word is made a linear function

$$S(W_{iT}, W_{jS}) = bt_{ij} \tag{1}$$

of the time t_{ij} during which both words are in the STM buffer. Thus there is no forgetting, the LTM strength grows linearly to infinity on successive trials, and although both words are supposedly in the buffer when LTM strength is growing, strength is assumed to grow between W_{iT} and W_{iS} rather than between W_{iS} and W_{jS}. A more subtle difficulty is that time per se should not explicitly determine a dynamical process, as it does in Equation 1, unless it parameterizes an external input. All of these problems arise because the theory does not define STM activities which can mediate the formation of long-term memories.

Instead of using STM activities as the variables that control performance, the theory defines sampling and recovery probabilities directly in terms of LTM traces. The sampling probabilities are built up out of products of LTM traces, as in the formula

$$P_S(W_{iS} \mid C_T, W_{kT}) = \frac{S(C_T, W_{iS})S(W_{kT}, W_{iS})}{\sum_{j=1}^{n} S(C_T, W_{jS})S(W_{kT}, W_{jS})} \tag{2}$$

for the probability of sampling the ith word W_{iS} given a probe consisting of a context cue C_T and the kth word W_{kT} at test (T). This formula formally compensates for the problem of steadily increasing strengths by balancing numerator strengths against denominator strengths. It also formally achieves selectivity in sampling by multiplying strengths together. The theory does not, however, explain how or why these operations might occur in vivo.

The context cue C_T is of particular importance because the relative strength of context-to-word associations is used to explain the theory's proudest achievement—the part-list cuing effect. However, the context cue is just an extra parameter in the theory because no explanation is given of how a context representation arises or is modified due to experimental manipulations. In other words, because recall theory says nothing about chunking or recognition, the context cue plays a role akin to that played by the "fixed stars" in classical explanations of centrifugal force.

In addition to the continuous rule for strength increase (Equation 1), the theory defines a discrete rule for strength increase

$$S'(W_{iT}, W_{jS}) = S(W_{iT}, W_{jS}) + g \qquad (3)$$

which also leads to unbounded strengths as trials proceed. The incrementing rule (Equation 3) is applied only after a successful recall. Although this rule helps to fit some data, it is not yet explained why two such different strengthening rules should coexist.

The authors represent the limited capacity of STM by appending a normalization constraint onto their sampling probability rule. They generalize Equation 2 with the sampling rule

$$P_S(I_i \mid Q_1, Q_2, \ldots, Q_n) = \frac{\Pi_{j=1}^n S(Q_j, I_i)^{w_j}}{\Sigma_k \Pi_{j=1}^n S(Q_j, I_k)^{w_j}} \qquad (4)$$

where the weights w_j satisfy

$$\sum_{j=1}^m w_j \leq W. \qquad (5)$$

Equation 4 defines the probability of sampling the ith image I_i, given the set of probe cues $Q_1, Q_2, \ldots, Q_n$. Why these normalization weights, which intend to represent the limited capacity of STM, should appear in a sampling rule defined by LTM traces is unexplained in the theory.

The properties that the formalism of Raaijmakers and Shiffrin (1981) attempts to capture have also arisen within my own work on human memory (Grossberg, 1978a, 1978b). Because this theory describes the self-organization of both recognition and recall using real-time operations on STM and LTM traces, it exhibits these properties in a different light. Its analog of the product rule (Equation 2) is due to properties of temporal order information in STM derived from a principle that guarantees the stable transfer of temporal order information from STM to LTM (Section XXXIV). Its analog of the continuous strengthening rule (Equation 1) is found in the chunking process whereby recognition chunks are formed (Section XXI). Its analog of the discrete strengthening rule (3) is due to the process whereby associations from recognition chunks to recall commands are learned (Section VI). Its analog of the normalization rule (Equation 5) is a normalization property of competitive STM networks that are capable of retuning their sensitivity in response to variable operating loads (Section XVII). Not surprisingly, the part-list cuing effect poses no problem for this theory, which also suggests how contextual representations are learned. In light of these remarks, I suggest that Raaijmakers and Shiffrin (1981) have not realized how much the data they wish to explain depends on the "interimage structure" that their theory does not consider.

A few principles and mechanisms based on ideas about self-organization have, in fact, been the vantage point for recognizing and avoiding internal difficulties within psychological models of cognition, perception, conditioning, attention, and information processing (Grossberg, 1978a, 1978e, 1980b, 1980d, 1981b, 1982b, 1982d, 1983, 1984a, 1984b). Some of these principles and mechanisms of self-organization are defined below and used to discuss issues and data concerning the functional units of speech, language, and motor control. This foundation was originally built up for this purpose in Grossberg (1978e). That article, as well as others that derive the concepts on which it is based, are reprinted in Grossberg (1982d).

III. ASSOCIATIVE LEARNING BY NEURAL NETWORKS: INTERACTIONS BETWEEN STM AND LTM

The foundation of the theory rests on laws for associative learning in a neural network, which I call the "embedding field" equations (Grossberg, 1964). These laws are derived from psychological principles and have been physiologically interpreted in many places (e.g., Grossberg, 1964, 1967, 1968b, 1969b, 1970b, 1972c, 1974). They are reviewed herein insofar as their properties shed light on the problem of serial order.

The associative equations describe interactions among unitized nodes v_i that are connected by directed pathways, or *axons* e_{ij}. These interactions are defined in terms of STM traces $x_i(t)$ computed at the nodes v_i and LTM traces z_{ij} computed at the endpoints, or *synaptic knobs, S_{ij}* of the

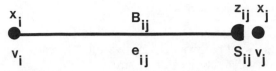

Figure 6.1. An STM trace x_i fluctuates at each node v_i, and an LTM trace z_{ij} fluctuates at the end (synaptic knob) S_{ij} of each conditionable pathway e_{ij}. The performance signal B_{ij} is generated in e_{ij} by x_i and travels at a finite velocity until it reaches S_{ij}. The LTM trace z_{ij} computes a time average of the contiguous STM trace x_j multiplied by a sampling signal E_{ij} that is derived from B_{ij}. The performance signal B_{ij} is gated by z_{ij} before the gated signal $B_{ij}z_{ij}$ perturbs x_j.

directed pathways e_{ij} (Figure 6.1). The simplest realization of these interactions among n nodes $v_1, v_2, \ldots, v_n$ is given by the system of differential equations

$$\frac{d}{dt} x_i = -A_i x_i + \sum_{k=1}^{n} B_{ki} z_{ki} - \sum_{k=1}^{n} C_{ki} + I_i(t) \tag{6}$$

and

$$\frac{d}{dt} z_{ij} = -D_{ij} z_{ij} + E_{ij}[x_j]^+, \tag{7}$$

where $i, j = 1, 2, \ldots, n$; d/dt denotes the rate of change of the contiguous variable, x_i or z_{ij}, as the case might be; and the notation $[\xi]^+ = \max(\xi, 0)$ defines a threshold. The terms in Equations 6 and 7 have the following interpretations.

III.A. STM Decay

Function A_i in Equation 6 is the decay rate of the STM trace x_i. This rate can, in principle, depend on all the unknowns of the system, as in the competitive interaction

$$A_i = A - (B - x_i)g(x_i) + \sum_{k=1}^{n} c_{ik} h(x_k), \tag{8}$$

which I describe more fully in Section XVIII). Equation 8 illustrates that STM decay need not be a passive process. Active processes of competitive signaling, as in this equation or other feedback interactions, can be absorbed into the seemingly innocuous term $A_i x_i$ in Equation 6.

III.B. Spreading Activation

Function B_{ki} in Equation 6 is a performance signal from node v_k to the synaptic knob(s) S_{ki} of pathway e_{ki}. Activation "spreads" along e_{ki} via the signal B_{ki}. Two typical choices of B_{ki} are

$$B_{ki}(t) = b_{ki}[x_k(t - \tau_{ki}) - \Gamma_{ki}]^+ \tag{9}$$

or

$$B_{ki}(t) = f(x_k(t - \tau_{ki}))b_{ki}, \tag{10}$$

where $f(\xi)$ is a sigmoid, or S-shaped, function of ξ with $f(0) = 0$. In Equation 9, a signal leaves v_k only if x_k exceeds the signal threshold Γ_{ki} (Figure 6.2a). The signal moves along e_{ki} at a finite velocity ("activation spreads") and reaches S_{ki} after τ_{ki} time units. Typically, τ_{ki} is a short time compared to the time it takes v_k to exceed threshold Γ_{ki} in response to signals. Parameter b_{ki} measures the strength of the pathway e_{ki} from v_k to v_i. If $b_{ki} = 0$, no pathway exists.

In Equation 10, the signal threshold Γ_{ki} is replaced by attenuation of the signal at small x_k values and by saturation of the signal at large x_k values (Figure 6.2b). The S-shaped signal function is the simplest physical signal function that can prevent noise amplification from occurring due to reverberatory signaling in a feedback network (Section XVIII).

III.C. Probed Read-Out of LTM: Gating of Performance Signals

Term $B_{ki}z_{ki}$ in Equation 6 says that the signal B_{ki} from v_k to S_{ki} interacts with the LTM trace z_{ki} at S_{ki}. This interaction can be intuitively described in several ways. For one, B_{ki} is a probe signal, activated by STM at v_k, that reads out the LTM trace z_{ki} into the STM trace x_i of v_i. For another, z_{ki} "gates" signal B_{ki} before it reaches v_i from v_k so that the signal strength that perturbs x_i at v_i is $B_{ki}z_{ki}$ rather than B_{ki}. Thus even if an input to v_k excited equal signals B_{ki} in all the pathways e_{ki}, only those v_i abutted by large LTM traces z_{ki} will be appreciably activated by v_k. Activation does not merely "spread" from v_k to other nodes; it can be transformed into propagated signals (x_k into B_{ki}) and gated by LTM traces (B_{ki} into $B_{ki}z_{ki}$) before it reaches these nodes.

III.D. Adaptive Filtering

The gated signals from all the nodes v_k combine additively at v_i to form the total signal $T_i = \sum_{k=1}^n B_{ki}z_{ki}$ of Equation 6. Speaking mathematically, T_i is the "dot product," or inner product, of the vectors $B_i = (B_{1i}, B_{2i},$

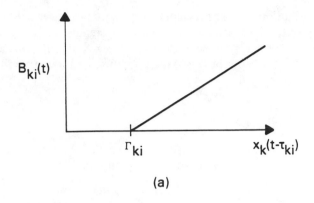

(a)

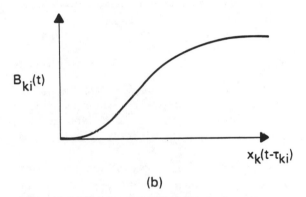

(b)

Figure 6.2   (a) A threshold signal: $B_{ij}(t)$ is positive only if $x_i(t - \tau_{ij})$ exceeds the signal threshold Γ_{ij}. $B_{ij}(t)$ is a linear function of $x_j(t - \tau_{ij})$ above this threshold. (b) A sigmoid signal: $B_{ij}(t)$ is attenuated at small values of $x_i(t - \tau_{ij})$, much as in the threshold case, and levels off at large values of $x_i(t - \tau_{ij})$ after all signaling sites are turned on.

. . . , B_{ni}) and $z_i = (z_{1i}, z_{2i}, . . . , z_{ni})$ of probe signals and LTM traces, respectively. Such a dot product is often written as

$$T_i = B_i \cdot z_i. \qquad (11)$$

The transformation of the vector $x^* = (x_1, x_2, . . . , x_n)$ of all STM traces into the vector $T^* = (T_1, T_2, . . . , T_n)$ of all dot products, specifically

$$x^* \rightarrow T^*, \qquad (12)$$

completely describes how STM traces generate feedback signals within the network.

A transformation by dot products as in Equation 12 is said to define a *filter*. Because the LTM traces z_i that gate the signals B_i can be changed by experience, the transformation (Equation 12) is said to define an *adaptive filter*. Thus the concepts of feedback signaling and adaptive filtering are identical in Equation 6.

III.E. Lateral Inhibition

Term $\sum_{k=1}^{n} C_{ki}$ in Equation 6 describes the total inhibitory signal from all nodes v_k to v_i. An illustrative choice of the inhibitory signal from v_k to v_i is

$$C_{ki}(t) = g(x_k(t - \sigma_{ki}))c_{ki}, \tag{13}$$

where $g(\xi)$ is a sigmoid signal function, σ_{ki} is the time lag for a signal to be transmitted ("spread") between v_k and v_i, and c_{ki} describes the strength of the inhibitory path from v_k to v_i.

III.F. Automatic Activation of Content-Addressable Nodes

Function $I_i(t)$ in Equation 6 is an input corresponding to presentation of the ith event through time. The input $I_i(t)$ can be large during and shortly after the event and otherwise equals zero. The input automatically excites v_i in the sense that the input has a direct effect on the STM activity of its target node.

In all, each STM trace can decay, can be activated by external stimuli, and can interact with other nodes via sums of gated excitatory signals and inhibitory signals. These equations can be generalized in several ways (Grossberg, 1974, 1982d). For example, LTM traces for inhibitory pathways can also be defined (Grossberg, 1969b) and in a way that avoids the difficulties of Estes's (1972) theory in Section I. The appendix describes a more general version of the equations that includes stable, conditionable inhibitory pathways.

III.G. LTM Decay

Function D_{ij} in Equation 7 is the decay rate of the LTM trace z_{ij}. The LTM decay rate, like the STM decay rate, can depend on the state of the system as a whole. For example, in principle it can be changed by attentional signals, probe signals, slow threshold fluctuations, and the like without destroying the invariants of associative learning that I need to carry out my argument (Grossberg, 1972c, 1974, 1982d).

III.H. Read-In of STM into LTM: Stimulus Sampling

Function E_{ij} in Equation 7 describes a learning signal from v_i to S_{ij} that drives the LTM changes in z_{ij} at S_{ij}. In other words, v_i "samples" v_j by turning on E_{ij}. Otherwise expressed, the STM trace x_j is read into the LTM trace z_{ij} by turning on the sampling signal E_{ij}. In the simplest cases, E_{ij} is proportional to B_{ij}. By setting both D_{ij} and E_{ij} equal to zero in Equation 7, a pathway e_{ij} can be converted from a conditionable pathway to a prewired pathway that is incapable of learning.

An important technical issue concerns the most general relationship that can exist between B_{ij} and E_{ij}. It has been proven that, in a precise mathematical sense, unbiased learning occurs if "B_{ij} is large only if E_{ij} is large" (Grossberg, 1972c, 1982d). This condition, called a "local flow" condition, is interpreted physically as follows. After the sampling signal E_{ij} reaches S_{ij}, it influences learning by z_{ij} within S_{ij}. The sampling signal E_{ij} is also averaged, delayed, or otherwise transformed within S_{ij} to give rise to the performance signal B_{ij}. This signal acts at a "later stage" within S_{ij} than E_{ij} because B_{ij} energizes the net effect $B_{ij}z_{ij}$ of v_i on v_j. The mathematical local flow condition shows that this physical interpretation of the relationship between E_{ij} and B_{ij} is sufficient to guarantee unbiased learning.

III.I. Mutual Interaction of STM and LTM

By joining together terms $D_{ij}z_{ij}$ and $E_{ij}x_j$, it follows from Equation 7 that the LTM trace z_{ij} is a time average of the product of learning signals E_{ij} from v_i to S_{ij}, with STM traces at v_j. When z_{ij} changes in size, it alters the gated signals from v_i to v_j via term $B_{ij}z_{ij}$, and thus the value of the STM trace x_j. In this way the STM and LTM traces mutually influence each other, albeit on different spatial and temporal scales.

IV. LTM UNIT IS A SPATIAL PATTERN: SAMPLING AND FACTORIZATION

To understand the functional units of goal-oriented behavior, it is necessary to characterize the functional unit of long-term memory in an associative network. This problem was approached by first analyzing what the minimal anatomy capable of associative learning can actually learn (Grossberg, 1967, 1968a, 1969g, 1970b) and then proving that the same functional unit of memory is computed in much more general anatomies (Grossberg, 1969b, 1972c, 1974). Three properties that were discovered by these investigations will be needed here:

1. The functional unit of LTM is a *spatial pattern* of activity.
2. A spatial pattern is encoded in LTM by a process of *stimulus sampling*.
3. The learning process *factorizes* the input properties which energize learning and performance from the spatial patterns to be learned and performed.

Each of these abstract properties is a computational universal that appears under different names in ostensibly unrelated concrete applications. Henceforth in the chapter, an abstract property will be described before it is applied to concrete examples.

V. OUTSTAR LEARNING: FACTORIZING COHERENT PATTERN FROM CHAOTIC ACTIVITY

The minimal anatomy capable of associative learning is depicted in Figure 6.3a. A single node, or population, v_0 is activated by an external event via an input function $I_0(t)$. This event is called the *sampling event*. For example, in studies of classical conditioning, the sampling event is the conditioned stimulus (CS).

If the sampling event causes the signal thresholds of node v_0 to be exceeded by its STM trace x_0, then learning signals E_{0i} propagate along the pathways e_{0i} toward a certain number of nodes v_i, $i = 1, 2, \ldots, n$. The same analysis of learning applies no matter how many nodes v_i exist, provided that at least two nodes exist ($n \geq 2$) to permit some learning to occur. The learning signals E_{0i} are also called *sampling signals* because their size influences the learning rate, with no learning occurring when all signals E_{0i} are equal to zero.

The sampling signals E_{0i} from v_0 do not activate the nodes v_i directly. In contrast, the LTM-gated performance signals $B_{0i}z_{0i}$ directly influence the nodes v_i by activating their STM traces x_i. The nodes v_i can also be activated directly by the events to be learned. These events are represented by the inputs $I_i(t)$ which activate the STM traces x_i of the nodes v_i, $i = 1, 2, \ldots, n$. Because the signals E_{0i} enable the z_{0i} to sample STM traces, the inputs $I_1(t), I_2(t), \ldots, I_n(t)$ are called the *sampled event*. In studies of classical conditioning, the sampled event is the unconditioned stimulus (UCS). The output signals from the nodes v_i that are caused by the UCS control the network's unconditioned response (UCR).

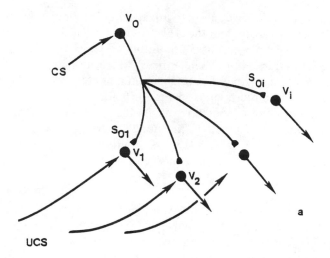

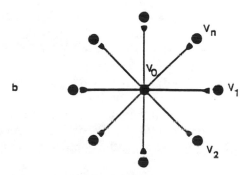

Figure 6.3   The minimal network capable of associative pattern learning: (a) A conditioned stimulus (CS) activates a single node or cell population v_0, which sends sampling signals to a set of nodes $v_1, v_2, \ldots, v_n$. An input pattern representing an unconditioned stimulus (UCS) activates the nodes $v_1, v_2, \ldots, v_n$, which elicit output signals that contribute to the unconditioned response (UCR). The sampling signals from v_0 activate the LTM traces z_{0i} that are computed at the synaptic knobs S_{0i}, $i = 1, 2, \ldots, n$. The activated LTM traces can learn the activity pattern across $v_1, v_2, \ldots, v_n$ that represents the UCS. (b) When the sampling network in (a) is drawn to emphasize its symmetry, the result is an *outstar* wherein v_0 is the sampling source and the set $\{v_1, v_2, \ldots, v_n\}$ is the sampled border.

The sampling signals E_{0i} directly activate the performance signals B_{0i} and the LTM traces z_{0i} rather than the STM traces x_i. These LTM traces are computed at the synaptic knobs S_{0i} that abut the nodes v_i. This location permits the LTM traces z_{0i} to sample the STM traces x_i when they are activated by the sampling signals E_{0i}. Such a minimal network is called an *outstar* because it can be redrawn as in Figure 6.3b.

Mathematical analysis of an outstar reveals that it can learn a *spatial pattern,* which is a sampled event to the nodes $v_1, v_2, \ldots, v_n$ whose inputs I_i have a fixed relative size while v_0's sampling signals are active. If the inputs I_i have a fixed relative size, they can be rewritten in the form

$$I_i(t) = \theta_i I(t) \tag{14}$$

where θ_i is the constant relative input size, or "reflectance," and the function $I(t)$ is the fluctuating total activity, or "background" input, of the sampled event. The convention that $\Sigma_{i=1}^n \theta_i = 1$ guarantees that $I(t)$ represents the total sampled input to the outstar—specifically, $I(t) = \Sigma_{i=1}^n I_i(t)$. The pattern weights of the sampled event is the vector

$$\theta = (\theta_1, \theta_2, \ldots, \theta_n) \tag{15}$$

of constant relative input sizes. The outstar learns this vector.

The assertion that an outstar can learn a vector θ means the following. During learning trials, the sampling event is followed a number of times by the sampled event. Thus the inputs $I_0(t)$ and $I(t)$ can oscillate wildly through time. Despite these wild oscillations, however, learning in an outstar does not oscillate. Rather, the outstar can progressively, or monotonically, learn the invariant spatial pattern θ across trials, corresponding to the intuitive notion that "practice makes perfect" (Figure 6.4). The outstar does this by using the fluctuating inputs $I_0(t)$ and $I(t)$ as energy to

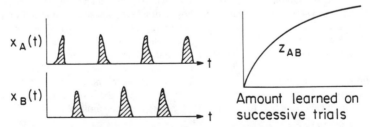

Figure 6.4   Oscillatory inputs due to repetitive A-then-B presentations are translated into a monotonic learned reaction of the corresponding stimulus sampling probabilities. In the text, fluctuations in the sampling input $I_0(t)$ and total sampled input $I(t)$, as well as the monotonic reactions of the relative LTM traces $Z_{0i}(t)$, generalize the A-then-B interpretation.

drive its encoding of the pattern θ. The fluctuating inputs $I_0(t)$ and $I(t)$ determine the rate of learning but not the pattern θ that is learned. This is the property of *factorization*: fluctuating input energy determines learning rate, while the invariant input pattern determines what is learned. The factorization property shows that the outstar can detect and encode temporally coherent relationships among the inputs that represent the sampled event.

In mathematical terms, factorization implies that the relative LTM traces

$$Z_i = z_{0i} \left(\sum_{k=1}^{n} z_{0k} \right)^{-1} \tag{16}$$

are drawn monotonically toward the target ratios θ_i. Stimulus sampling means that the LTM ratios Z_i change only when the sampling signals from v_0 to the synaptic knobs S_{0i} are positive. Because the LTM ratios form a probability distribution (each $Z_i \geq 0$ and $\sum_{i=1}^{n} Z_i = 1$) and change only when sampling signals are emitted, I call them the *stimulus sampling probabilities* of an outstar. The behavior of these quantities explicates the probabilistic intuitions underlying stimulus sampling theory (Neimark & Estes, 1967) in terms of the deterministic learning dynamics of a neural network. In particular, the factorization property dynamically explains various properties that are assumed in a stimulus sampling model—for example, why learning curves should be monotonic in response to wildly oscillating inputs (Figure 6.4).

The property of factorization also has an important meaning during performance trials. Both sampling signals and performance signals are released during performance trials (Grossberg, 1972c). The property of factorization means that the performance signal may be chosen to be any nonnegative and continuous function of time without destroying the outstar's memory of the spatial pattern that was encoded in LTM on learning trials. The main constraint is that the pattern weights θ_i be read out synchronously from all the nodes v_i.

What happens if the sampled event to an outstar is not a spatial pattern, as in the case when a series of sampled events occur, rather than a single event? Such an event series can be represented by a vector input

$$J(t) = (I_1(t), I_2(t), \ldots, I_n(t)), \tag{17}$$

$t \geq 0$, where each input $I_i(t)$ is a nonnegative and continuous function of time. Because each input $I_i(t)$ is continuous, the relative pattern weights

$$\theta_i(t) = I_i(t) \left[\sum_{k=1}^{n} I_k(t) \right]^{-1} \tag{18}$$

are also continuous functions of time, as is the vector function

$$\theta(t) = (\theta_1(t), \theta_2(t), \ldots, \theta_n(t)) \tag{19}$$

of pattern weights.

Mathematical analysis of the outstar reveals that its LTM traces learn a spatial pattern even if the weights $\theta(t)$ vary through time. The spatial pattern that is encoded in LTM is a weighted average of all the spatial patterns $\theta(t)$ that are registered at the nodes v_i while sampling signals from v_0 are active.

This result raises the question, How can each of the patterns $\theta(t)$ be encoded in LTM rather than an average of them all? The properties of outstar learning (Section IV) readily suggest an answer to this question. This answer propelled the theory on one of its roads toward a heightened understanding of the serial order problem. Before following this road, some applications of outstar learning are now summarized.

VI. SENSORY EXPECTANCIES, MOTOR SYNERGIES, AND TEMPORAL ORDER INFORMATION

The fact that associative networks encode spatial patterns in LTM suggests that the brain's sensory, motor, and cognitive computations are all pattern transformations. This expectation arises from the fact that computations which cannot in principle be encoded in LTM can have no adaptive value and thus would presumably atrophy during evolution. Examples of spatial patterns as functional units of sensory processing include the reflectance patterns of visual processing (Cornsweet, 1970), the sound spectrograms of speech processing (Cole, Rudnicky, Zue, & Reddy, 1980; Klatt, 1980), the smell-induced patterns of olfactory bulb processing (Freeman, 1975), and the taste-induced patterns of thalamic processing (Erickson, 1963). More central types of pattern processing are also needed to understand the self-organization of serial order.

VI.A. Sensory Expectancies

Suppose that the cells $v_1, v_2, \ldots, v_n$ are sensory feature detectors in a network's sensory cortex. A spatial pattern across these feature detectors may encode a visual or auditory event. The relative activation of each v_i then determines the relative importance of each feature in the global STM representation of the event across the cortex. Such a spatial pattern code can effectively represent an event even if the individual feature detectors v_i are broadly tuned. Using outstar dynamics, even a single command node v_0 can learn and perform an arbitrary sensory representation of this sort. The pattern read out by v_0 is often interpreted as the representation that v_0 "expects" to find across the field $v_1, v_2, \ldots, v_n$ due to prior experience. In this context, outstar pattern learning illustrates top-down expectancy learning (Section XXV). The expectancy controlled by a given node v_0 is a time average of all the spatial patterns that it ever sampled. Thus it need not equal any one of these patterns.

VI.B. Motor Synergies

Suppose that the cells $v_1, v_2, \ldots, v_n$ are motor control cells such that each v_i can excite a particular group of muscles. A larger signal from each v_i then causes a faster contraction of its target muscles. Spatial pattern learning in this context means that an outstar command node v_0 can learn and perform fixed relative rates of contraction across all the motor control cells $v_1, v_2, \ldots, v_n$. Such a spatial pattern can control a motor synergy, such as playing a chord on the piano with prescribed fingers; making a synchronous motion of the wrist, arm, and shoulder; or activating a pre-scribed target configuration of lips and tongue while uttering a speech sound (Section XXXII).

Because outstar memory is not disturbed when the performance signal from v_0 is increased or decreased, such a motor synergy, once learned, can be performed at a variety of synchronous rates without requiring the motor pattern to be relearned at each new rate. (Kelso, Southard, & Goodman, 1979; Soechting & Laquaniti, 1981). In other words, the factor-ization of pattern and energy provides a basis for independently process-ing the command needed to reach a terminal motor target and the velocity with which the target will be approached.

This property may be better understood through the following example. When I look at a nearby object, I can choose to touch it with my left hand, my right hand, my nose, and so on. Several *terminal motor maps* are simultaneously available to move their corresponding motor organs to-wards the object. "Willing" one of these acts releases the corresponding terminal motor map but not the others. The chosen motor organ can, moreover, be moved toward the invariant goals at a wide range of veloci-ties. The distinction between the invariant terminal motor map and the flexibility programmable performance signal illustrates how factorization prominently enters problems of learned motor control.

VI.C. Temporal Order Information over Item Representations

Suppose that a sequence of item representations is activated in a pre-scribed order during perception of a list. At any given moment, a spatial pattern of STM activity exists across the excited populations. Were the same items excited in a different order by a different list, a different spatial pattern of STM activity would be elicited. Thus the spatial pattern reflects temporal order information as well as item information. An outstar sampling source can encode this spatial pattern as easily as any other spatial pattern. Thus, although an outstar can encode only a spatial pattern, this pattern can represent temporal properties of external events. Such a spatial encoding of temporal order information is perhaps the example par excellence of a network's parallel processing capabilities. How a network can encode temporal order information in STM without falling into the difficulties mentioned in Section II will be described in Section XXXIV.

VII. RITUALISTIC LEARNING OF SERIAL BEHAVIOR: AVALANCHES

The following sections approach the problem of serial order in stages. These stages mark different levels of sophistication in a network's ability to react adaptively to environmental feedback. The stages represent a form of conceptual evolution in the theory reflecting the different levels of behavioral evolution that exist across phylogeny.

The first stage shows how outstar learning capabilities can be used to design a minimal network capable of associatively learning and/or performing an arbitrary sequence of events, such as a piano sonata or a dance. This construction is called an *avalanche* (Grossberg, 1969g, 1970a, 1970b) because its sampling signal traverses a long axon that activates regularly spaced cells (Figure 6.5) in a manner reminiscent of how avalanche conduction along the parallel fibers in the cerebellum activates regularly spaced Purkinje cells (Eccles, Ito, & Szentagothai, 1967; Grossberg, 1969d). The simplest avalanche requires only one node to encode the memory of the entire sequence of events. Thus the construction shows that complex performance per se is easily achieved by a small and simple neural network.

The simplest avalanche also exhibits several disadvantages stemming from the fact that its performance is ritualistic in several senses. Each of these disadvantages has a remedy that propels the theory forward. Performance is temporally ritualistic because once performance has been initiated, it cannot be rhythmically modified by the performer or by conflicting environmental demands. Performance is spatially ritualistic in the sense that the motor patterns to be performed do not have learned sensory referents.

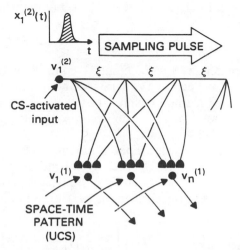

Figure 6.5 An avalanche is the minimal network that can associatively learn and ritualistically perform any space–time pattern. The sampling node $v_1^{(2)}$ emits a brief sampling pulse that serially excites the outstar sampling bouquets that converge on the sampled field $\mathcal{F}^{(1)} = \{v_1^{(1)}, v_2^{(1)}, \ldots, v_n^{(1)}\}$. On performance trials, a sampling pulse resynthesizes the space–time pattern as a series of smoothly interpolated spatial patterns.

The first modification of the avalanche enables performance speed to be continuously modulated, or even terminated, in response to performer or environmental signals. This flexibility can be achieved on performance trials without any further learning of the ordered patterns themselves. The construction thus provides a starting point for analyzing how order information and rhythm can be decoupled in more complex learning situations. The construction is not of merely formal interest, however, since it shares many properties with the command cell anatomies of invertebrates (Dethier, 1968; Hoyle, 1977; Kennedy, 1968; Stein, 1971; Willows, 1968).

With the modified avalanche construction before us, some design issues become evident concerning how to overcome the network's spatially ritualistic properties. The pursuit of these issues leads to a study of serial learning and chunking that in turn provides concepts for building a theory of recognition and recall. The needed serial learning and chunking properties are also properties of the embedding field equations, albeit in a different processing context than that of outstar learning.

Because the avalanche constructions require a hierarchy of network stages, superscripts are used on the following variables. Suppose that the act to be learned is controlled by a set of nodes $v_1^{(1)}, v_2^{(1)}, \ldots, v_n^{(1)}$, henceforth called the field of cells $\mathcal{F}^{(1)}$. This field replaces the nodes $v_1, v_2, \ldots, v_n$ of an outstar. Let each node receive a nonnegative and continuous input $I_i(t)$, $t \geq 0$, $i = 1, 2, \ldots , n$. The set of inputs $I_i(t)$ collectively form a vector input

$$J(t) = (I_1(t), I_2(t), \ldots , I_n(t)), \qquad (17)$$

$t \geq 0$, that characterizes the commands controlling the sequence of events. At the end of Section IV, I raised the question of how such a vector input could be learned despite the outstar's ability to learn only one spatial pattern. An avalanche can accomplish this task using a single encoding cell in the following way.

Speaking intuitively, $J(t)$ describes a moving picture playing through time on the "screen" of nodes $\mathscr{F}^{(1)}$. An avalanche can learn and perform such a "movie" as a sequence of still pictures that are smoothly interpolated through time. Because each input $I_i(t)$ is continuous, the pattern weights

$$\theta_i(t) = I_i(t) \left[\sum_{k=1}^{n} I_k(t) \right]^{-1} \qquad (18)$$

are also continuous and can therefore be arbitrarily closely approximated by a sequence of values

$$\theta_i(0), \ \theta_i(\xi), \ \theta_i(2\xi), \ \theta_i(3\xi), \ \ldots \qquad (20)$$

sampled every ξ time units, if ξ is chosen so small that $\theta_i(t)$ does not change too much in a time interval of length ξ. For every fixed k, the vector of weights

$$\theta^{(k)} = (\theta_1(k\xi), \theta_2(k\xi), \ldots , \theta_n(k\xi)) \qquad (21)$$

sampled across all the cells in $\mathscr{F}^{(1)}$ at a time $t = k\xi$ is a spatial pattern. To learn and perform the movie $J(t)$, $t \geq 0$, it suffices to learn and perform the sequence $\theta^{(1)}$, $\theta^{(2)}$, $\theta^{(3)}$, $\ldots$ of spatial patterns in the correct order. This can be done if a sequence of outstars $\mathcal{O}_1, \mathcal{O}_2, \mathcal{O}_3, \ldots$ is arranged so that the kth outstar $\mathcal{O}_k$ samples only the kth spatial pattern $\theta^{(k)}$ on successive learning trials and is then briefly activated in the order $\mathcal{O}_1, \mathcal{O}_2, \mathcal{O}_3, \ldots$ on performance trials. Using the outstar properties of stimulus sampling and learning in spatial pattern units, an avalanche-type anatomy, such as that in Figure 6.5, instantiates these properties using a single sampling node and a minimum number of pathways.

In Figure 6.5, a brief sampling signal travels along the long pathway (axon) leading from node $v_1^{(2)}$. This node replaces the outstar sampling source v_0 of the previous discussion. This sampling signal moves from left to right, traveling down the serially arranged bouquets of pathways that converge on $\mathscr{F}^{(1)}$. Each bouquet is an outstar and can therefore learn a spatial pattern. This pattern is a weighted average of all the spatial patterns that are active in STM across $\mathscr{F}^{(1)}$ while the outstar samples $\mathscr{F}^{(1)}$. Because each outstar $\mathcal{O}_k$ samples $\mathscr{F}^{(1)}$ briefly, its LTM traces encode essentially only the pattern $\theta^{(k)}$. By the property of stimulus sampling, none of the other patterns $\theta^{(j)}$, $j \neq k$, playing across $\mathscr{F}^{(1)}$ through time will influence the LTM traces of $\mathcal{O}_k$. On performance trials, a performance signal runs along the axon, serially reading out the spatial patterns encoded by the bouquets in the correct order. The STM traces across $\mathscr{F}^{(1)}$ smoothly interpolate these spatial patterns through time to generate a continuously varying output from $\mathscr{F}^{(1)}$.

VIII. DECOUPLING ORDER AND RHYTHM: NONSPECIFIC AROUSAL AS A VELOCITY COMMAND

Performance by an avalanche is temporally ritualistic, because once a performance signal is emitted by node $v_1^{(2)}$, there is no way to temporally modulate or stop its inexorable transit down the sampling pathway. In order to modify performance at any time during the activation of an avalanche, there must exist a locus at each outstar's sampling source where auxiliary inputs can modify the performance signal. These loci are denoted by nodes $v_1^{(2)}$, $v_2^{(2)}$, $v_3^{(2)}$, . . . such that node $v_k^{(2)}$ is the sampling source of outstar $\mathcal{O}_k$, as in Figure 6.6a. These nodes form a field of nodes $\mathscr{F}^{(2)}$ in their own right.

Merely defining the nodes $\mathscr{F}^{(2)}$ does not make avalanche performance less ritualistic as long as a signal from the ith node $v_i^{(2)}$ can trigger a signal from the $(i + 1)$st node $v_{i+1}^{(2)}$. An auxiliary input source (or sources) needs to be defined whose activity is required to maintain avalanche performance. The minimal solution is to define a single node $v_1^{(3)}$ that can activate all the populations in $\mathscr{F}^{(2)}$ (approximately) simultaneously (Figure 6.6b) and to require that node $v_{i+1}^{(2)}$ can elicit a signal only if it receives simultaneous signals from $v_i^{(2)}$ and $v_1^{(3)}$. Shutting off $v_1^{(3)}$ at any time can then abruptly terminate performance, because even if node $v_{i+1}^{(2)}$ receives a signal from $v_i^{(2)}$ at such a time, $v_{i+1}^{(2)}$ cannot emit a signal without convergent input from $v_1^{(3)}$.

Since the signals from $v_1^{(3)}$ energize the avalanche as a whole, I call them *nonspecific arousal* signals. Node $v_1^{(3)}$ may also be called a *command node* because it subliminally prepares the entire avalanche for activation. This node may just as well be thought of as a context node, or contextual bias, in situations wherein the avalanche is interpreted as a subnetwork within a larger network. For example, the same cue can often trigger different behavior depending on the context or plan according to which it is interpreted (e.g., turning left at the end of a hall to enter the

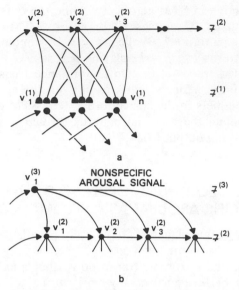

a

b

Figure 6.6 A nonspecific arousal signal can act as a command that decouples order information from the velocity or rhythm of a particular performance. (a) Outstar sampling sources $v_j^{(2)}$ serially excite each other to determine the order with which $\mathscr{F}^{(1)}$ is sampled. (b) Simultaneous input from the nonspecific arousal source $v_1^{(3)}$ and $v_i^{(2)}$ is needed to elicit an output signal from $v_{i+1}^{(2)}$. Continuous variations in the size of the $v_1^{(3)}$ signal are translated into continuous variations in the velocity of performance.

bedroom or right to enter the dining room). A nonspecific arousal source can achieve this result by subliminally sensitizing certain subnetworks more than others for supraliminal activation by a given set of cues. Due to the fact that the arousal source often encodes a contextual cue, I henceforth call the network in Figure 6.6 a *context-modulated avalanche*.

IX. REACTION TIME AND PERFORMANCE SPEED-UP

The requirement that the command node $v_{i+1}^{(2)}$ can fire only if it receives simultaneous signals from $v_i^{(2)}$ and $v_1^{(3)}$ can be implemented in several related ways, all of which depend on the existence of a threshold Γ that each STM trace $x_{i+1}^{(2)}$ must exceed before a signal from $v_{i+1}^{(2)}$ can be emitted. Increasing the arousal signal from $v_1^{(3)}$ to $v_{i+1}^{(2)}$ makes it easier for $x_{i+1}^{(2)}$ to exceed this threshold. Moreover, the threshold of $v_{i+1}^{(2)}$ is exceeded faster in response to a large signal from $v_1^{(3)}$ than to a small signal from $v_1^{(3)}$. The reaction time (RT) for activating any node $v_{i+1}^{(2)}$ can thus be decreased by increasing the nonspecific arousal level at the time when this node is excited by $v_i^{(2)}$. Since this is true for every node $v_{i+1}^{(2)}$, a continuous variation of arousal level through time can continuously modulate performance speed. Indeed, such a feedforward modulation of performance velocity can be achieved at a very rapid rate (Lashley, 1951).

Both additive and multiplicative (shunting) rules can, in principle, be used to restrict avalanche performance except when the nonspecific arousal source is active. A shunting rule enjoys an important formal advantage. It works even without an exquisitely precise choice of the relative sizes of all the avalanche's signals and thresholds. A shunting rule has this advantage because a zero arousal level will gate to zero even a large signal from $v_i^{(2)}$ to $v_{i+1}^{(2)}$. Consequently, $v_{i+1}^{(2)}$ will not be activated at all by $v_i^{(2)}$. Its zero STM trace $x_{i+1}^{(2)}$ will therefore remain smaller than any choce of a positive threshold.

The concept of a shunting arousal signal is illustrated by the following equation for the activation of $v_{i+1}^{(2)}$ by $v_i^{(2)}$ and $v_1^{(3)}$:

$$\frac{d}{dt} x_{i+1}^{(2)} = -Ax_{i+1}^{(2)} + B_i S \tag{22}$$

where B_i is the performance signal from $v_i^{(2)}$ and S is the shunting signal from $v_1^{(3)}$. Often B_i has the form $B_i(t) = f(x_i^{(2)}(t - \xi))$ and S has the form $S(t) = g(x_1^{(3)}(t - \tau))$ where both $f(w)$ and $g(w)$ are sigmoid functions of w. For simplicity, let B_i and S equal zero at times $t < 0$ and equal constant positive values U and V, respectively, at times $t \geq 0$. Define the RT of $x_{i+1}^{(2)}(t)$ as the first time $t = T$ when $x_{i+1}^{(2)}(T) = \Gamma$ and $(d/dt)x_{i+1}^{(2)}(T) > 0$. By Equation 22, if $V = 0$, then the RT is infinite since $x_{i+1}^{(2)} = 0$. Only if $UV > A\Gamma$ does a signal ever leave $v_{i+1}^{(2)}$, and it does so with an RT of

$$\frac{1}{A} \ln \left(\frac{UV}{UV - A\Gamma}\right), \tag{23}$$

which is a decreasing function of U and V. Equation 23 shows that determination of performance rate depends on the threshold of each node, the arousal level when the node exceeds threshold, the size of the signal generated by the previous node, and the delays ξ and τ due to propagating signals between nodes.

In more complex examples, the signals to the nodes $v_i^{(2)}$ can also be altered by LTM traces that gate these signals (Section XIII). Equation 23 illustrates how an increase in such an LTM trace due to learning can cause a progressive speed-up of performance (Fitts & Posner, 1967; Welford, 1968), because an increase in an LTM trace that gates either signal B_i or S in the equation is equivalent to an increase in S.

An interaction between learning, forgetting, and reaction time was used to explain such phenomena as performance speed-up due to learning as well as some backward-masking properties in Grossberg (1969c). Later articles on speed-up have used the same ideas to explain the power law relationship that often obtains between the time it takes to perform a task and the number of practice trials (Anderson, 1982; MacKay, 1982). Although both Anderson and MacKay suggest that their explanation of speed-up lends special support to their other concepts, it is historically more correct to say that both explanations lend support to well-known neural modeling ideas.

There exist many variations on the avalanche theme. Indeed, it may be more appropriate to talk about a theory of avalanches than of assorted avalanche examples (Grossberg, 1969g, 1970b, 1974, 1978e). For present purposes, we can summarize some avalanche ideas in a way that generalizes to more complex situations:

1. A source of nonspecific arousal signals can modulate the performance rhythm.
2. Specific activations encode temporal order information in a way that enables a nonspecific arousal signal to generate temporally ordered performance.
3. The sequential events to be learned and performed are decomposed into spatial patterns.

X. HIERARCHICAL CHUNKING AND THE LEARNING OF SERIAL ORDER

Given the concept of a context-modulated avalanche, the following question generates a powerful teleological pressure for extending the theory. Suppose that the links $v_i^{(2)} \to v_{i+1}^{(2)}$ in the chain of nodes are not prewired into the network. How can a network with the processing capabilities of a context-modulated avalanche be self-organized? For example, if the spatial patterns across the sampled nodes $\mathcal{F}^{(1)}$ control successive chords in a piano sonata, then the individual chords need to be learned as well as the ordering of the chords. This process is typically carried out by reading piano music and transforming these visual cues into motor commands which elicit auditory feedback. Nowhere in a context-modulated avalanche are visual cues encoded before being mapped into motor commands. No sequence of auditory feedback patterns is encoded before being correlated with its generative sequence of motor commands, and no mechanism is included whereby the serial order of the motor commands can be learned.

It is clear from this and many analogous examples that the set of sampling nodes in $\mathcal{F}^{(2)}$ corresponding to a particular behavioral sequence cannot be determined a priori, any more than each mind could contain a priori representations of all the sonatas that ever were or will be composed. For a similar reason, neither the serial ordering of these nodes nor the selective attachment of an arousal source to this set of sampling nodes is determined a priori. All of these structures need to be self-organized by developmental and learning mechanisms, and we need to understand how this happens.

XI. SELF-ORGANIZATION OF PLANS: THE GOAL PARADOX

These formal problems concerning the self-organization of avalanches also arise in many types of goal-oriented behavior. Consider maze learning (Figure 6.7) as an idealization of the many situations in which one learns a succession of choice points leading to a goal, such as going from home to the store or from one's office to the cafeteria. In Figure 6.7, one leaves the filled-in start box and is rewarded with food in the vertically hatched goal box. After learning has occurred, every errorless transit from start box to goal box requires the same sequence of turns at choice points in the maze. In some sense, therefore, our memory traces can encode the correct order at the choice points. Moreover, the goal box always occurs *last* on every learning trial, whether or not errors occur. During goal-directed performance, by contrast, the *first* thing that we think of is the goal, which somehow activates a plan that generates a correct series of actions. How is it possible for the goal event to always occur last on learning trials and for memory to encode the correct perfor-

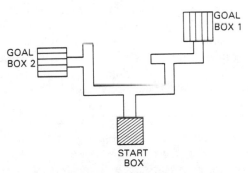

Figure 6.7 The Goal Paradox: Correct performance from start box to a goal box is always order-preserving. On every learning trial, the goal always occurs last. How can the correct order be learned despite the fact that an internal representation of the goal is activated first on performance trials and organizes the correct ordering of acts that preceded the goal on every learning trial?

mance order, and yet for an internal representation of the goal to activate commands corresponding to events that preceded the goal on every learning trial? This is the *goal paradox* (Grossberg, 1978e). Actually, the goal paradox seems paradoxical only if one takes seriously the manner in which a learning subject's information unfolds in real time and vigorously resists the temptation to beg the question by appealing to a homunculus.

To overcome the goal paradox, we need to understand how the individual sensory–motor coordinations leading to a correct turn at each choice point can be self-organized. This problem is formally analogous to the problem of self-organizing the individual nodes $\mathcal{F}^{(2)}$ of a context-modulated avalanche and of associating each of these nodes with a motor command across $\mathcal{F}^{(1)}$. We also need to understand how a plan can serially organize individual choices into a correctly ordered sequence of choices. This latter problem needs to be broken into at least two successive stages.

First, the internal representation corresponding to the plan is determined by the internal representations of the individual choices themselves, since during a correct transit of the maze on a learning trial, these are the relevant data that are experienced. The dependence of the plan on its defining sequence of events is schematized by the upward directed arrow in Figure 6.7a. The process whereby a planning node is selected is a form of code development, or chunking. After the plan is self-organized by its defining sequence of events, the plan in turn learns which internal representations have activated it, so that it can selectively activate only these representations on performance trials (Figure 6.8b). A feedforward, or bottom-up, process of coding (chunking) thus sets the stage for a feedback, or top-down, process of pattern learning (expectancy learning). In its role as a source of contextual feedback signals, the plan is analogous to the nonspecific arousal node $v_1^{(3)}$ in the context-modulated avalanche.

This discussion of the goal paradox emphasizes an issue that was implicit in my discussion of how an arousal-modulated avalanche can be self-organized. Both the nodes in $\mathcal{F}^{(2)}$ and the context-sensitive node in $\mathcal{F}^{(3)}$ are self-organized by a chunking process. Given this conclusion, some specialized processing issues now come into view. What mechanism maintains the activities of the $\mathcal{F}^{(2)}$ nodes long enough for the simultaneously active $\mathcal{F}^{(2)}$ nodes to determine and be determined by the $\mathcal{F}^{(3)}$ planning node? What mechanism enables the planning node to elicit the correct performance order from the $\mathcal{F}^{(2)}$ nodes? Are learned associations between the $\mathcal{F}^{(2)}$ nodes necessary, as is suggested by the links $v_i^{(2)} \rightarrow v_{i+1}^{(2)}$ of a context-modulated avalanche, or can the learned signals from $\mathcal{F}^{(3)}$ to $\mathcal{F}^{(2)}$ encode order information by themselves?

Once we explicitly recognize that the sequence of active $\mathcal{F}^{(2)}$ nodes determines its own $\mathcal{F}^{(3)}$ node, we must also face the following problem.

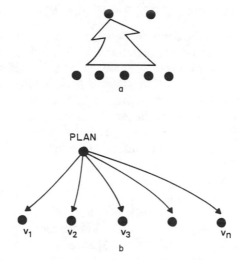

Figure 6.8 The feedback loop between chunking and planned temporal ordering: (a) Activity patterns across the item representations choose their planning nodes via a process of feedforward (bottom-up) code learning (chunking). (b) The chosen planning nodes can learn to activate the item representations which chose them, and the order with which items are activated, by a process of feedback (top-down) associative pattern learning (expectancy learning).

Every subsequence of an event sequence is a perfectly good event sequence in its own right. By the principle of sufficient reason, each subsequence may therefore encode its own node. Not every subsequence may be able to encode a planning node with equal ease. Nonetheless, the single nonspecific arousal source $v_1^{(3)}$ needs to be replaced by a field $\mathcal{F}^{(3)}$ of command nodes which are activated by prescribed subsequences across $\mathcal{F}^{(2)}$. Every node in $\mathcal{F}^{(3)}$ can in turn sample the activity pattern across $\mathcal{F}^{(2)}$ while it is active. As performance proceeds, the event sequences represented across $\mathcal{F}^{(2)}$ and the planning nodes activated across the field $\mathcal{F}^{(3)}$ continually change and mutually influence one another. A more advanced version of the same problem arises when, in addition to feedback exchanges within sensory and motor modalities, intermodality reciprocal exchanges control the unfolding of recognition and recall through time (Grossberg, 1978e).

The deepest issues relating to these feedback exchanges concern their stability and self-consistency. What prevents every new event in $\mathcal{F}^{(2)}$ from destroying the encoding of past event sequences in $\mathcal{F}^{(3)}$? What enables the total output from $\mathcal{F}^{(3)}$ to define a more global and predictive context than could any individual planning node?

XII. TEMPORAL ORDER INFORMATION IN LTM

The design issues raised by the goal paradox will be approached in stages. First I consider how a command node can learn to read out item representations in their correct order without using learned associations between the item representations themselves. I also consider how ordered associations among item representations can be learned. Both of these examples are applications of serial learning properties that were first analyzed in Grossberg (1969f) and generalized in Grossberg and Pepe (1970, 1971). The temporal order information in both examples is learned using the associative learning Equations 6 and 7. Both types of temporal order information can be learned simultaneously in examples wherein pathways within $\mathscr{F}^{(2)}$ and between $\mathscr{F}^{(2)}$ and $\mathscr{F}^{(3)}$ are conditionable. Both examples overcome the instability problem of Estes's (1972) model of temporal order in LTM, and neither example requires a serial buffer to learn its temporal order information. Murdock (1979) has studied serial learning properties using a related approach but one that is weakened by the conceptual difficulties of linear system theory models (Section II). In particular, the Murdock approach has not yet been able to explain the bowed and skewed cumulative error curve in serial verbal learning.

The problem of how a command node learns to read out an STM pattern that encodes temporal order information across item representations has two different versions, depending on whether the command node is excited before the first list item is presented or after the last list item is presented. The former problem will be considered now, but the latter problem cannot be considered until Section XXXIV, since it requires a prior analysis of competitive STM interactions for its solution (Section XVII).

XIII. READ-OUT AND SELF-INHIBITION OF ORDERED STM TRACES

Figure 6.9a depicts the desired outcome of learning. The LTM traces z_{1i} from the command node $v_1^{(3)}$ to the item representations $v_i^{(2)}$ satisfy the chain of inequalities

$$z_{11} > z_{12} > z_{13} > \cdots > z_{1m} \tag{24}$$

due to the fact that the list of items $r_1, r_2, \ldots, r_m$ was previously presented to $\mathscr{F}^{(2)}$. Consequently, when a performance signal from $v_1^{(3)}$ is gated by these LTM traces, an STM pattern across $\mathscr{F}^{(2)}$ is generated such that

$$x_1^{(2)} > x_2^{(2)} > x_3^{(2)} > \cdots > x_m^{(2)}. \tag{25}$$

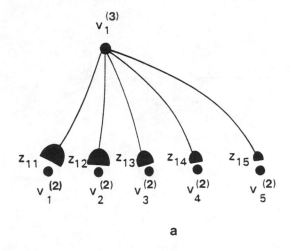

a

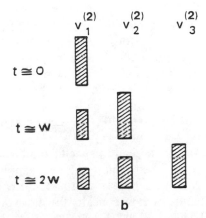

b

Figure 6.9 Simultaneous encoding of context and temporal order by top-down STM–LTM order reversal: (a) The context node $v_1^{(3)}$ reads out a primacy gradient across the item representations of $\mathcal{F}^{(2)}$. (b) The context node $v_1^{(3)}$ can learn a primacy gradient in LTM by multiplicatively sampling and additively storing a temporal series of STM recency gradients across $\mathcal{F}^{(2)}$.

STM PATTERN

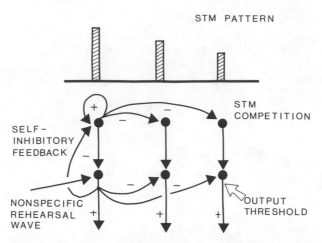

Figure 6.10 A reaction time rule translates larger STM activities into faster output onsets. Output-contingent STM self-inhibition prevents item perseveration.

A reaction time rule such as Equation 23 initiates an output signal faster from a node with a large STM activity than from a node with a small STM activity. The chain of STM inequalities (Equation 25) can thus be translated into the correct order or performance using such a reaction time rule if the following problem of perseveration can be prevented. After the first item r_1 is performed, the output signal from $v_1^{(2)}$ must shut off to prevent a sustained output signal from interfering with the performance of later items. A specific inhibitory feedback pathway thus inhibits $x_1^{(2)}$ after a signal is emitted from $v_1^{(2)}$ (Figure 6.10). The same perseveration problem then faces the remaining active nodes $v_2^{(2)}, v_3^{(2)}, \ldots , v_m^{(2)}$. Hence every output pathway from $\mathscr{F}^{(2)}$ can activate a specific inhibitory feedback pathway whose activation can self-inhibit the corresponding STM trace (Grossberg, 1978a, 1978e; Rumelhart & Norman, 1982). With this performance mechanism in hand, we now consider the more difficult problem of how the chain of LTM inequalities (Equation 24) can be learned during presentation of a list of items $r_1, r_2, r_3, \ldots , r_m$.

XIV. THE PROBLEM OF STM–LTM ORDER REVERSAL

The following example illustrates the problem in its most severe form. The STM properties that I now consider will, however, have to be generalized in Section XXXIV. Suppose that each node $v_i^{(2)}$ is excited by a fixed amount when the ith list item r_i is presented. Suppose also that as time goes on, the STM trace $x_i^{(2)}$ gets smaller due either to internodal competition or passive trace decay. Which of the two decay mechanisms is used does not affect the basic result, although different mechanisms will cause testable secondary differences in the order information to be encoded in LTM. Whichever decay mechanism is used, in response to serially presented lists, the last item to have occurred always has the largest STM trace. In other words, a recency effect exists at each time in STM (Figure 6.9b). Given this property, how is the chain of LTM inequalities learned? In other words, how does a sequence of recency gradients in STM get translated into a primacy gradient in LTM? I call this issue the "STM–LTM order reversal problem" (Grossberg, 1978e).

The same problem arises during serial verbal learning but in a manner that disguises its relevance to planned serial behavior. In this task, the generalization gradients of errors at each list position have the qualitative form depicted in Figure 6.11. A gradient of anticipatory (forward) errors occurs at the beginning of the list, a two-sided gradient of anticipatory and perseverative (backward) errors near the middle of the list, and a gradient of perseverative errors at the end of the list (Osgood, 1953). I suggest that the gradient of anticipatory errors at the beginning of the list is learned in the same way as a primacy gradient in LTM. I have shown (Grossberg, 1969f) that the same associative laws also generate the other position-sensitive error gradients. Thus a command node that is activated after the entire list is presented encodes a recency gradient in LTM rather than the primacy gradient that is encoded by a command node activated before (or when) the first list item is presented. The same laws also provide an explanation of why the curve of cumulative errors versus list position is bowed and skewed toward the end of the list, and of why associations at

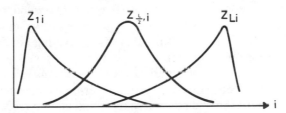

Figure 6.11 Each sampling node v_j learns a different LTM pattern $z_j = (z_{j1}, z_{j2}, \ldots, z_{jn})$ if it samples at different times. In a list of length $n = L$ whose intertrial interval is sufficiently long, a node that starts sampling at the list beginning ($j \cong 1$) learns a primacy gradient in LTM. At the list end ($j \cong L$), a recency gradient in LTM is learned. Near the list middle ($j \cong L/2$), a two-sided LTM gradient is learned. When STM probes read different LTM patterns z_j into STM, the different patterns generate different error gradients due to the action of internal noise, the simultaneous read-out by other probes, and the STM competition that acts after LTM read-out.

the beginning of the list are often, but not always, learned faster than associations at the end of the list (Grossberg & Pepe, 1970, 1971).

From the perspective of planned serial behavior, these results show how the activation of a command node at different times during list presentation causes the node to encode totally different patterns of order information in LTM. Thus the learning of order information is highly context-sensitive. If a command node is activated by a prescribed list subsequence via $\mathcal{F}^{(2)} \rightarrow \mathcal{F}^{(3)}$ signals that subserve chunking and recognition, then this subsequence constrains the order information that its command node will encode by determining the time at which the command node is activated. Moreover, this context sensitivity is not just a matter of determining which item representations will be sampled, as the issue of STM–LTM order reversal clearly shows.

An important conclusion of this analysis is that the same sort of context-sensitive LTM gradients are learned on a single trial regardless of whether command nodes sample item representations at different times or if the item representations sample each other through time. Although the order information that is encoded by the sampling nodes is the same, the two situations are otherwise wholly distinct. In the former case, list subsequences are the functional units that control learned performance, and many lists can be learned and performed over the same set of item representations. In the latter case, individual list items are the functional units that control learned performance, and once a given chain of associations is learned among the item representations, it will interfere with the learning of any other list ordering that is built up from the same item representations (Dixon & Horton, 1968; Lenneberg, 1967; Murdock, 1974).

A third option is also available. It arises by considering a context-modulated avalanche whose serial ordering and context nodes are both self-organized by associative processes (Figure 6.12). In such a network, each of the item nodes can be associated with any of several other item nodes. In the absence of contextual support, activating any one of these item nodes causes only subliminal activation of its set of target item nodes, while activating a particular context node sensitizes a subset of associatively linked item nodes. A serial ordering of supraliminally activated item nodes can thus be generated. Such an adaptive context-modulated avalanche possesses many useful properties. For example, item nodes are no longer bound to each other via rigid associative chains. Hence, a given item can activate different items in different contexts. The inhibition of a given context node can rapidly prevent the continued performance of the item ordering that it controls, while the activation of different context nodes can rapidly instate a new performance ordering among the same items or different items.

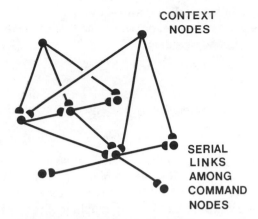

Figure 6.12 In an adaptive context-modulated avalanche, each command node can be associated with a set of command nodes that it subliminally activates. Learned top-down signals from a context node can also sensitize a set of command nodes. The convergent effects of top-down and internodal signals causes the supraliminal activation of command nodes in a prescribed serial order. Different context nodes can generate different serial orders.

In Figure 6.12, the item nodes are called command nodes. This change of terminology is intended to emphasize the fact that in order for this design to be useful, the items must represent chunks on a rather high level of network processing. The number of transitions from each command node to its successors must be reasonably small in order to achieve the type of unambiguous serial ordering that the context chunk is supposed to guarantee. The sequence chunks within the masking field discussed in Section XXXVIII are prime candidates for command nodes in an adaptive context-mediated avalanche. The ability of top-down and serial associative signals to activate ordered STM traces supraliminally without also unselectively activating a broad field of STM traces is facilitated by balancing these excitatory associative signals against inhibitory signals, notably inhibitory masking signals (see Section XXXVIII; Grossberg, 1978e, Sections 41–46).

XV. SERIAL LEARNING

This section indicates how the context-sensitive LTM gradients in Figure 6.11 are learned. Why the same rules imply that the cumulative error curve of serial learning is bowed and skewed is reviewed from a recent perspective in Grossberg 1982a. First, I consider how a primacy gradient

(Equation 24) is encoded by the LTM traces $(z_{11}, z_{12}, \ldots, z_{1m})$ of a node $v_1^{(3)}$ that is first activated before, or when, the first list item is presented. I then show how a recency gradient

$$z_{n1} < z_{n2} < \cdots < z_{nm} \tag{26}$$

is encoded by the LTM traces $(z_{n1}, z_{n2}, \ldots, z_{nm})$ of a node $v_n^{(3)}$ that is first activated after the whole list is presented. A two-sided gradient

$$z_{k1} < z_{k2} < \cdots < z_{kr} > z_{k,r+1} > \cdots > z_{km} \tag{27}$$

encoded by a node $v_k^{(2)}$ that is activated during the midst of the list presentation can then be understood as a combination of these effects.

Let node $v_1^{(3)}$ start sending out a sampling signal E_1 at about the time that r_1 is being presented. After rapidly reaching peak size, the signal E_1 gradually decays through time with its STM trace $x_1^{(3)}$ as future list items $r_2, r_3, \ldots$ are presented. Thus E_1 is largest when STM trace $x_1^{(2)}$ is maximal, smaller when both traces $x_1^{(2)}$ and $x_2^{(2)}$ are active, smaller still when traces $x_1^{(2)}$, $x_2^{(2)}$, and $x_3^{(2)}$ are active, and so on. Consequently, the product $E_1 x_1^{(2)}$ in row 1 of Figure 6.9b exceeds the product $E_1 x_2^{(2)}$ in row 2 of the figure, which in turn exceeds the product $E_1 x_3^{(2)}$ in row 3, and so on. Due to the slow decay of each LTM trace z_{1i} on each learning trial, z_{11} adds up the products $E_1 x_1^{(2)}$ in successive rows of column 1, z_{12} adds up the products $E_1 x_2^{(2)}$ in successive rows of column 2, and so on. An LTM primacy gradient (Equation 24) is thus generated due to the way in which E_1 samples the successive STM recency gradients, and to the fact that the LTM traces z_{1i} add up the sampled STM gradients $E_1 x_i^{(2)}$.

By contrast, the sampling signal E_n emitted by node $v_n^{(3)}$ samples a different set of STM gradients because $v_n^{(3)}$ starts to sample only after all the item representations $v_1^{(2)}, v_2^{(2)}, \ldots, v_m^{(2)}$ have already been activated on a given learning trial. Consequently, when the sampling signal E_n does turn on, it sees the already active STM recency gradient

$$x_1^{(2)} < x_2^{(2)} < \cdots < x_m^{(2)} \tag{28}$$

of the entire list. Moreover, the ordering (Equation 28) persists for a while because no new items are presented until the next learning trial. Thus signal E_n samples an STM recency gradient at every time. When all sampled recency gradients are added up through time, they generate a recency gradient (Equation 26) in the LTM traces of $v_n^{(3)}$. In summary, command nodes that are activated at the beginning, middle, or end of a list encode different LTM gradients because they multiplicatively sample STM patterns at different times and summate these products through time.

XVI. RHYTHM GENERATORS AND REHEARSAL WAVES

The previous discussion forces two refinements in our ideas about how nonspecific arousal is regulated. In a context-modulated avalanche, the nonspecific arousal node $v_1^{(3)}$ both selects the set of nodes $v_i^{(2)}$ that it will control and continuously modulates performance velocity across these nodes. A command node that reads out temporal order information as in Figure 6.9a can no longer fulfill both roles. Increasing or decreasing the command node's activity while it reads out its LTM pattern proportionally amplifies the STM of all its item representations. Arbitrary performance rhythms are no longer attainable, because the relative reaction times of individual item representations are constrained by the pattern of STM order information. Nor is a sustained but continuously modulated supraliminal read-out from the command node permissible, because item representations that were already performed could then be reexcited, leading to a serious perseveration problem.

Thus, if a nonspecific arousal source dedicated to rhythmic control is desired, it must be distinguished from the planning nodes. Only then can order information and rhythm information remain decoupled. The reader should not confuse this idea of rhythm with the performance timing that occurs when item representations are read out as fast as possible (Sternberg, Monsell, Knoll, & Wright, 1978; Sternberg, Wright, Knoll, & Monsell, 1980). Properties of such a performance can, in fact, be inferred from the mechanism for read-out of temporal order information per se (Section XLVII).

Another type of nonspecific arousal is also needed. If read-out of LTM order information is achieved by activating the item representations across $\mathscr{F}^{(2)}$, what prevents these item representations from being uncontrollably rehearsed, and thereby self-inhibited, while the list is being presented? To prevent this from happening, it is necessary to distinguish between STM activation of an item representation and output signal generation by an active item representation. This distinction is mechanized by assuming the existence of a nonspecific rehearsal wave capable of shunting the output pathways of the item representations. When the rehearsal wave is off, the item representations can blithely reverberate their order information in STM without generating self-destructive inhibitory feedback. Only when the rehearsal wave turns on does the read-out of order information begin.

The distinction between STM storage and rehearsal has major implications for which planning nodes in $\mathscr{F}^{(3)}$ will be activated and what they will learn. This is due to two facts working together: The rehearsal wave can determine which item subsequences will be active at any moment by rehearsing, and thereby inhibiting, one group of item representations before the next group of items is presented. Each active subsequence of item representations can in turn chunk its own planning node. The rehearsal wave thus mediates a subtle interaction between the item sequences that occur and the chunks that form to control future performance (Section XXXVII).

XVII. SHUNTING COMPETITIVE DYNAMICS IN PATTERN PROCESSING AND STM: AUTOMATIC SELF-TUNING BY PARALLEL INTERACTIONS

This analysis of associative mechanisms suggests that the unit of LTM is a spatial pattern. This result raises the question of how cellular tissues can accurately register input patterns in STM so that LTM mechanisms may encode them. This is a critical issue in cells because the range over which cell potentials, or STM traces, can fluctuate is finite and often narrow compared to the range over which cellular inputs can fluctuate. What prevents cells from routinely turning on all their excitable sites in response to intense input patterns, thereby becoming desensitized by saturation before they can even register the patterns to be learned? Furthermore, if small input patterns are chosen to avoid saturation, what prevents the internal noise of the cells from distorting pattern registration? This *noise–saturation dilemma* shows that cells are caught between two potentially devastating extremes. How do they achieve a "golden mean" of sensitivity that balances between these extremes?

I have shown (Grossberg, 1973) that mass action competitive networks can automatically retune their sensitivity as inputs fluctuate to register input differences without being desensitized by either noise or saturation. In a neural context, these systems are called shunting on-center off-surround networks. The shunting, or mass action, dynamics are obeyed by the familiar membrane equations of neurophysiology; the automatic retuning is due to automatic gain control by the inhibitory signals.

The fixed operating range of cells should not be viewed as an unmitigated disadvantage. By fixing their operating range once and for all, cells can also define fixed output thresholds and other decision criteria with respect to this operating range. By maintaining sensitivity within this operating range despite fluctuations in total input load, cells can achieve an impressive parallel processing capability. Even if parallel input sources to the cells switch on or off unpredictably through time, thereby changing the total input to each cell, the automatic gain control mechanism can recalibrate the operating level of total STM activity to bring it into the range of the cells' fixed decision criteria. Additive models, by contrast, do not have this capability. These properties are mathematically described in Grossberg (1983, Sections 21–23).

Because the need to accurately register input patterns by cells is ubiqutous in the nervous system, competitive interactions are found at all levels of neural interaction and of my models thereof. A great deal of what is called "information processing" in other approaches to intelligence reduces in the present approach to a study of how to design a competitive, or close-to-competitive, network to carry out a particular class of computations. Several types of specialized competitive networks will be needed. As I mentioned in Section I, the class of competitive systems includes examples which exhibit arbitrary dynamical behavior. Computer simulations that yield an interesting phenomenon without attempting to characterize which competitive parameters control the phenomenon teach us very little, because a small adjustment of parameters could, in principle, generate the opposite phenomenon. To quantitatively classify the parameters that control biologically important competitive networks is therefore a major problem for theorists of mind. Grossberg (1981a, Sections 10–27) and Cohen and Grossberg (1983) review some results of this ongoing classification.

XVIII. CHOICE, CONTRAST ENHANCEMENT, LIMITED STM CAPACITY, AND QUENCHING THRESHOLD

Some of the properties that I use can be illustrated by the simplest type of competitive feedback network:

$$\frac{d}{dt} x_i = -Ax_i + (B - x_i)[I_i + f(x_i)] - x_i \left[J_i + \sum_{k \neq i} f(x_k) \right] \quad (29)$$

where $i = 1, 2, \ldots, n$. In Equation 29, term $-Ax_i$ describes the passive decay of the STM trace x_i at rate A. The excitatory term $(B - x_i)[I_i + f(x_i)]$ describes how an excitatory input I_i and an excitatory feedback signal $f(x_i)$ from v_i to itself excites by mass action the unexcited sites $(B - x_i)$ of the total number of sites B at each node v_i. The inhibitory term $-x_i[J_i + \sum_{k \neq i} f(x_k)]$ describes how the inhibitory input J_i and the inhibitory, or competitive, feedback signals $f(x_k)$ from all v_k, $k \neq i$, turn off the x_i excited sites of v_i by mass action.

Equation 29 strips away all extraneous factors to focus on the following issue. How does the choice of the feedback signal function $f(w)$ influence the transformation and storage of input patterns in STM? To discuss this question, I assume that inputs $(I_1, I_2, \ldots, I_n, J_1, J_2, \ldots, J_n)$ are delivered before time $t = 0$ and switch off at time $t = 0$ after having instated an initial pattern $x(0) = (x_1(0), x_2(0), \ldots, x_n(0))$ in the network's STM traces. Our task is to understand how the choice of f(w) influences the transformation of $x(0)$ into the stored pattern $x(\infty) = (x_1(\infty), x_2(\infty), \ldots, x_n(\infty))$ as time increases.

Figure 6.13 shows that different choices of f(w) generate markedly different storage modes. The function $g(w) = x^{-1}f(w)$ is also graphed in Figure 6.13 because the property that determines the type of storage is whether $g(w)$ is an increasing, constant, or decreasing function at prescribed values of the activity w. For example, as in the four rows of Figure 6.13, a linear f(w) = aw generates a constant $g(w) = a$; a slower-than-linear f(w) = $aw(b + w)^{-1}$ generates a decreasing $g(w) = a(b + w)^{-1}$; a faster-than-linear f(w) = aw^n, $n > 1$, generates an increasing $g(w) = aw^{n-1}$; and a sigmoid f(w) = $aw^2(b + w^2)^{-1}$ generates a concave $g(w) = aw(b + w^2)^{-1}$. Both linear and slower-than-linear signal functions amplify noise. Even tiny activities are bootstrapped into large activities by the

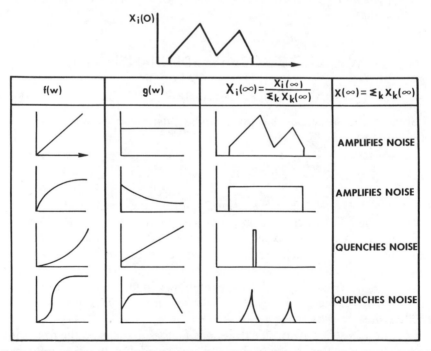

Figure 6.13   Influence of signal function f(w) on input pattern transformation and STM storage.

network's positive feedback loops. This fact represents a serious challenge to linear feedback models (Grossberg, 1978d).

A faster-than-linear signal function can tell the difference between small and large inputs by amplifying and storing only sufficiently large activities. Such a signal function amplifies the larger activities so much more than the smaller activities that it makes a choice: Only the largest initial activity is stored in STM. A sigmoid signal function can also suppress noise, although it does so less vigorously than a faster-than-linear signal function. Consequently, activities less than a criterion level, or quenching threshold (QT), are suppressed, whereas the pattern of activities that exceeds the QT is contrast-enhanced before being stored in STM.

Any network that possesses a QT can be *tuned*. By increasing or decreasing the QT, the criteria of which activities represent functional signals—and hence should be processed and stored in STM—and of which activities represent functional noise—and hence should be suppressed—can be flexibly modified through time. An increase in the QT can cause all but the largest activities to be quenched. Thus the network can behave like a choice machine if its storage criteria are made sufficiently strict. A sudden decrease in the QT can cause all recently presented patterns to be stored. If a novel or unexpected event suddenly decreases the QT, all relevant data can be stored in STM until the cause of the unexpected event is learned (Grossberg, 1975, 1982b). It cannot be overemphasized that the existence of the QT and its desirable tuning properties all follow from the use of a nonlinear signal function.

To illustrate the QT concept concretely, consider a sigmoid signal function $f(w)$ that is faster than linear for $0 \leq w \leq x^{(1)}$ and linear for $x^{(1)} \leq w \leq B$. The slower-than-linear part of $f(w)$ does not affect network dynamics because each $x_i \leq B$ by Equation 29. More precisely, let $f(w) = Cwg(w)$, where $C \geq 0$, $g(w)$ is increasing for $0 \leq w \leq x^{(1)}$, and $g(w) = 1$ for $x^{(1)} \leq w \leq B$. Grossberg (1973, pp. 355–359) has demonstrated that the QT of this network is

$$\frac{x^{(1)}}{B - AC^{-1}}. \tag{30}$$

By this equation, the QT is not the "manifest" threshold of $f(w)$, which occurs in the range where $g(w)$ is increasing. Instead, the QT depends on the transition activity $x^{(1)}$ at which the signal function becomes linear, the slope C of the signal function, the number of excitable sites B, and the STM decay rate A. Thus all the parameters of the network influence the size of the QT. By Equation 30, an increase in C causes a decrease in the QT. In other words, increasing a shunting signal C that nonspecifically gates all the network's feedback pathways facilitates STM storage.

Another property of STM in a competitive network is its limited capacity. This property follows from the network's tendency to conserve, or normalize, the total suprathreshold activity that it can store in STM. Consequently, an increase in one STM trace forces a decrease in other STM traces. As soon as one of these diminished traces becomes smaller than the QT, it is suppressed.

A full understanding of the normalization concept, no less than the QT concept, requires a mathematical study of relevant examples. The case wherein $f(w)$ is faster-than-linear illustrates normalization in its simplest form. Let $x = \sum_{i=1}^{n} x_i$ be the total STM activity, and let $F = \sum_{i=1}^{n} f(x_i)$ be the total feedback signal. Summing over the index i in Equation 29 yields the equation

$$\frac{d}{dt} x = -Ax + (B - x)F. \tag{31}$$

To solve for possible equilibrium activities $x(\infty)$ of $x(t)$, let $(d/dt)x = 0$ in Equation 31. Then

$$\frac{Ax}{B - x} = F. \tag{32}$$

Since a network with a faster-than-linear feedback signal makes a choice, only one STM trace $x_i(t)$ remains positive at $t \rightarrow \infty$. Hence only one summand in F remains positive as $t \rightarrow \infty$, and its $x_i(t)$ value approaches $x(t)$. Consequently, Equation 32 can be rewritten as

$$\frac{Ax}{B - x} = f(x). \tag{33}$$

Equation 33 is independent of the number of active nodes. Hence the total STM activity is independent of the number of active nodes.

XIX. LIMITED CAPACITY WITHOUT A BUFFER: AUTOMATICITY VERSUS COMPETITION

The formal properties of the previous section are reflected in many types of data. A fixed capacity buffer is often posited to explain the limited capacity of STM (Atkinson & Shiffrin, 1968; Raaijmakers & Shiffrin, 1981). Such a buffer is often implicitly or explicitly endowed with a serial ordering of buffer positions to explain free recall data. Buffer models do not, however, explain how items can be read in to one buffer position and still move their representations along buffer positions in such a way that *every* item can be performed from each buffer position, as is required for the buffer idea to meet free recall data. The buffer concept also tacitly implies that the entire hierarchy of codes that is derivable from item representations can also be shifted around as individual item codes move in the buffer.

The normalization property provides a dynamical explanation of why STM has a limited capacity without using a serial buffer. In the special case that new item representations get successively excited by a list of inputs, the normalization property implies that other item representations must lose activity. As soon as one of the activities falls below the QT, it drops out of STM. No motion of item representations through a buffer is required. Hence, no grueling problems of shift-invariant read-in and read-out need to be solved.

In this view of the limited capacity of STM, it is important to know which item representations are mutually inhibitory. Equation 29 represents the atypical situation in which each item representation can inhibit all other item representations with equal ease via the inhibitory terms $\Sigma k \neq i\ f(x_k)$. More generally, an equation of the form

$$\frac{d}{dt} x_i = -A_i x_i + (B_i - x_i)[I_i + \sum_{k=1}^{n} f_k(x_k)C_{ki}]$$

$$- (x_i + D_i)[J_i + \sum_{k=1}^{n} g_k(x_k)E_{ki}] \qquad (34)$$

holds, $i = 1, 2, \ldots, n$, in which the excitatory signal $f_k(x_k)$ from v_k excites v_i with a strength $f_k(x_k)C_{ki}$, whereas the inhibitory signal $g_k(x_k)$ from v_k inhibits v_i with a strength $g_k(x_k)E_{ki}$. If the inhibitory coefficients E_{ki} decrease with the network distance between v_k and v_i, then total STM activity can progressively build up as more items are presented until the density of active nodes causes every new input to be partly inhibited by a previously excited node. Thus sparsely distributed items may, at least at a single network level, sometimes be instated "automatically" in STM by their inputs without incurring competitive "capacity limitations" (Norman & Bobrow, 1975; Schneider & Shiffrin, 1976, 1977). The possibility that total STM activity can build up to an asymptote plays an important part in characterizing stable rules for laying down temporal order information in STM (Section XXXIV).

"Automatic" processing can also occur in the present theory due to the influence of learned top-down expectancies, or feedback templates, on competitive matching processes (Section XXIV). The tendency to sharply differentiate automatic versus controlled types of processing has been popularized by the work of Schneider and Shiffrin (1976, 1977), who ascribe automatic properties to a parallel process and controlled properties to a serial process. This distinction creates conceptual paradoxes when it is joined to concepts about learning (e.g., Grossberg, 1978e, Section 61). Consider the serial learning of any new list of familiar items. Each familiar item is processed by a parallel process, while each unfamiliar inter-item contingency is processed by a serial process. Schneider and Shiffrin's theory thus implies that the brain somehow rapidly alternates between parallel and serial processing when the list is first presented but switches to sustained parallel processing as the list is unitized. Consider the perception of a picture whose left half contains a familiar face and whose right half contains a collection of unfamiliar features. Schneider and Shiffrin's theory implies that the brain somehow splits the visual field into a serial half and a parallel half, and that the visual field gets reintegrated into a parallel whole as the unfamiliar features are unitized.

These paradoxes arise from the confusion of serial properties with serial processes and of parallel properties with parallel processes. All the processes of the present theory are parallel processes, albeit of a hierarchically organized network. The present theory shows how both serial properties and parallel properties can be generated by these parallel processes in response to different experimental paradigms. In particular, "the auditory-to-visual *codes* and *templates* that are activated in VM [varied mapping] and CM [consistent mapping] conditions are different, but the two conditions otherwise share common mechanisms" (Grossberg, 1978e, p. 364). Some evoked potential tests of this viewpoint and explanations of other data outside the scope of the Schneider and Shiffrin theory are described elsewhere (Banquet and Grossberg, 1986; Carpenter and Grossberg, 1986b, 1986c; Grossberg, 1982d, 1984a; Grossberg and Stone, 1986a). A growing number of recent experiments also support this viewpoint (e.g., Kahneman & Chajczyk, 1983).

XX. HILL CLIMBING AND THE RICH GET RICHER

The contrast enhancement property of competitive networks manifests itself in a large body of data. A central role for both contrast enhancement and normalization has, for example, been suggested in order to search associative memory and to self-organize new perceptual and cognitive codes (Carpenter and Grossberg, 1986b; Grossberg, 1978e, 1980c, 1982b). A more direct appearance of contrast enhancement has also been suggested to exist in letter and word recognition (Grossberg, 1978e; McClelland & Rumelhart, 1981). McClelland and Rumelhart introduce a number of evocative phrases to enliven their discussion of letter recognition, such as the "rich-get-richer" effect and the "gang" effect. The former is simply a contrast enhancement effect whereby small differences in the initial activation levels of word nodes get amplified through time into larger differences. The numerical studies and intuitive arguments presented by McClelland and Rumelhart (1981) do not, however, disclose why this can sometimes happen. Figure 6.13 illustrates that a correct choice of signal function is needed for it to happen, but a correct choice of signal function is not enough to guarantee even that the network will not oscillate uncontrollably through time (Grossberg, 1978c, 1980a). The gang effect uses a reciprocal exchange of prewired feedforward filters and feedback templates between letter nodes and word nodes to complete a word representation in response to an incomplete list of letters. This type of positive feedback exchange is also susceptible to uncontrollable instabilities whose prevention has been analyzed previously (Grossberg, 1976a, 1976b, 1980c).

I prefer the use of functional words rather than shibboleths for both an important reason and frivolous reason. The important reason is that an adherence to functional words emphasizes that a single functional property is generating data in seemingly disparate paradigms. Functional words thus tend to unify the literature rather than to fragment it. The frivolous reason is that another rich-get-richer effect had already been so christened in the literature before the usage of McClelland and Rumelhart (1981), and I was the person to blame. In Grossberg (1977), I called the normative drift whereby activity can be sucked from some populations into others due to the amplified network parameters of the latter populations a rich-get-richer effect. At the time, I found this sociological interpretation both amusing and instructive. Later (Grossberg, 1978b), however, I realized that the same mechanism could elicit automatic hill climbing along a developmental gradient, and I suggested (Grossberg, 1978e) how the same hill-climbing mechanism could respond to an ambiguous stimulus by causing a spontaneous STM drift from a representation that was directly excited by the stimulus to a more complete, or normative, nearby representation which could then quickly read out its feedback template to complete the ambiguous database.

This normative mechanism was, in fact, first presented in Levine and Grossberg (1976) as a possible explanation of Gibson's (1937) line neutralization effect. Thus the same functional idea has now been used to discuss visual illusions, pattern completion and expectancy matching, developmental gradients, and even sociology. It thus needs a functional name that is neutral enough to cover all of these cases. It needs a name other than contrast enhancement because it uses a mechanism of lateral masking that is distinct from simple contrast enhancement. This type of masking will be discussed in more detail to show how item sequences can be automatically parsed in a context-sensitive fashion through time (Section XXXVIII).

XXI. INSTAR LEARNING: ADAPTIVE FILTERING AND CHUNKING

With these introductory remarks about competition in hand, I now discuss the issue of how new recognition chunks can be self-organized within the fields $\mathscr{F}^{(2)}$ and $\mathscr{F}^{(3)}$ of a context-modulated avalanche, or more generally within the command hierarchy of a goal-oriented sequence of behaviors. I first consider the minimal anatomy that is capable of chunking or code development; namely, the *instar* (Figure 6.14). As its name suggests, the instar is the network dual of an outstar. An instar is constructed from an outstar by reversing the direction of its sampling pathways. Whereas in an outstar, conditionable pathways radiate from a sampling cell to sampled cells, in an instar conditionable pathways point from sampled cells to a sampling cell. Consequently, the sampling cell of an instar is activated by a sum of LTM-gated signals from sampled cells. These signals may be large enough to activate the sampling cell and thus cause the sampled cells to be sampled. If a spatial pattern of inputs persistently excites the sampled cells, it can cause alterations in the pattern

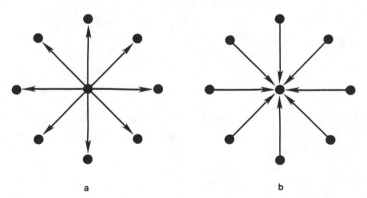

a   b

Figure 6.14 The duality between expectancy learning and chunking: (a) An *outstar* is the minimal network capable of associative pattern learning, notably expectancy learning. (b) An *instar* is the minimal network capable of code development, notably chunking. The source of an outstar excites the outstar border. The border of an instar excites the instar source. In both outstars and instars, source activation is necessary to drive LTM sampling. Since the signals from the instar border are gated by LTM traces before activating the instar source, code learning both changes the efficacy of source activation and is changed by it in an STM–LTM feedback exchange.

of LTM traces across the conditionable pathways that gate the sampled signals. These LTM changes can enable a practiced input pattern to excite the instar's sampling node with greater efficacy. The heightened activation of the sampling node measures how well the sampling source has come to represent, or chunk, the input pattern.

Although this version of chunking is too simplistic, two aspects of the problem as studied in this form have far-reaching consequences (Grossberg, 1976a, 1980c). To fix ideas, denote the sampling node by v_0 and the sampled nodes by $v_1, v_2, \ldots, v_n$. For simplicity, let the cells $v_1, v_2, \ldots, v_n$ rapidly normalize any input pattern $I_i = \theta_i I$ that they receive into STM activities $x_i = \theta_i$. Denote the signal emitted from v_i into pathway e_{i0} by $f(\theta_i)$. This signal is gated by the LTM trace z_{i0} before the gated signal $f(\theta_i)z_{i0}$ reaches v_0 from v_i. All of these signals are added at v_0 to get a total signal $T_0 = \sum_{i=1}^{n} f(\theta_i)z_{i0}$. As in Equation 11, T_0 is the dot product

$$T_0 = f_\theta \cdot z_0 \tag{35}$$

of the two vectors $f_\theta = (f(\theta_1, f(\theta_2), \ldots, f(\theta_n))$ *and* $z_0 = (z_{10}, z_{20}, \ldots, z_{n0})$.

To characterize the STM response at v_0 to signal T_0, suppose for simplicity that the total activity of v_0 is normalized to 1 and that v_0 possesses a QT equal to ε. Then

$$x_0 = \begin{cases} 1, & \text{if } T_0 \geq \varepsilon, \\ 0, & \text{if } T_0 < \varepsilon. \end{cases} \tag{36}$$

Moreover, suppose that the LTM traces z_{i0} satisfy the equation

$$\frac{d}{dt} z_{i0} = [-z_{i0} + f(\theta_i)]x_0. \tag{37}$$

Equation 37 is a special case of Equation 7 in which no learning occurs unless T_0 succeeds in exciting x_0. When learning does occur, z_{i0} is attracted towards $f(\theta_i)$, $i = 1, 2, \ldots, n$.

Under these conditions, it is easily shown that as input trials proceed, the vector $z_0(t)$ of LTM traces is monotonically attracted to the vector f_θ of signal pattern weights. In other words, $z_0(t)$ becomes parallel to f_θ as practice proceeds. This trend tends to maximize the signal $T_0(t) = f_\theta \cdot z_0(t)$ as trials proceed because the dot product is maximized when vectors of fixed length are made parallel to each order. As $T_0(t)$ grows, its ability to activate v_0 by exceeding its QT also increases. Speaking intuitively, v_0 "codes" θ due to learning trials, or the adaptive filter T_0 is "tuned" by experience.

Unfortunately, this example is deficient in several ways. For one, there is no nontrivial coding: v_0 can become more sensitive to a single pattern θ, but no one node can differentially encode a large number of patterns into more than two categories. Clearly, more sampling nodes are needed. This can be accomplished as follows.

XXII. SPATIAL GRADIENTS, STIMULUS GENERALIZATION, AND CATEGORICAL PERCEPTION

Let the nodes $v_1, v_2, \ldots, v_n$ be replaced by a field $\mathcal{F}^{(1)}$ of nodes, and let v_0 be replaced by a field $\mathcal{F}^{(2)}$ of nodes. Each pattern across $\mathcal{F}^{(1)}$ can now send a positive signal to many nodes of $\mathcal{F}^{(2)}$. How is an increasingly selective response across $\mathcal{F}^{(2)}$ to be achieved as sequences of input patterns perturb $\mathcal{F}^{(1)}$?

Both networks $\mathcal{F}^{(1)}$ and $\mathcal{F}^{(2)}$ include competitive interactions to solve the noise–saturation dilemma. The easiest way to achieve learned selectivity is thus to design $\mathcal{F}^{(2)}$ as a sharply tuned competitive feedback network that chooses its maximal input for STM storage, quenches all other inputs, and normalizes its total STM activity. By analogy with the previous example, let the total input to $v_j^{(2)}$ in $\mathcal{F}^{(2)}$ equal

$$T_j = f_\theta \cdot z_j, \tag{38}$$

let

$$x_j^{(2)} = \begin{cases} 1, & \text{if} \quad T_j \geq \max[\varepsilon, T_k : k \neq j] \\ 0, & \text{if} \quad T_j < \max[\varepsilon, T_k : k \neq j], \end{cases} \tag{39}$$

and let

$$\frac{d}{dt} z_{ij} = (-z_{ij} + f(\theta_i))x_j^{(2)}. \tag{40}$$

Now let a sequence of spatial patterns perturb $\mathcal{F}^{(1)}$ in some order. What happens?

This is a situation where the good news is good and the bad news is better. If the spatial patterns are not too densely distributed in pattern space, in a sense that can be made precise (Grossberg, 1976a), then learning partitions the patterns into mutually exclusive and exhaustive subsets $P_1, P_2, \ldots, P_m$ such that every input pattern θ in P_j excites its recognition chunk $v_j^{(2)}$ with the maximal possible input, given the constraint that the LTM vector z_j is attracted to all the vectors f_θ of patterns θ in P_j.

Node $v_j^{(2)}$ is also activated by patterns θ that are weighted averages of patterns in P_j, even if these patterns θ are novel patterns that have never been experienced. Hence a generalization gradient exists across $\mathcal{F}^{(2)}$. The adaptive filter *projects* novel patterns into the classification set spanned by the patterns in P_j.

If a pattern θ is deformed so much that it crosses from one set P_j to another set P_k, then a rapid switch from choosing $v_j^{(2)}$ to choosing $v_k^{(2)}$ occurs. The boundaries between the sets P_j are categorical. Categorical perception can thus be anticipated whenever adaptive filtering interacts with sharply competitive tuning, not just in speech recognition experiments (Hary & Massaro, 1982; Pastore, 1981; Studdert-Kennedy, 1980).

The categorical boundaries are determined by how each input pattern is filtered by all the LTM vectors z_j, and by how all the dot product signals T_j fare in the global competition for STM activity. Consequently, practicing one pattern θ can recode the network's STM response to a novel pattern θ^* by changing the global balance between filtering and competition. This conclusion can be understood most easily by substituting Equations 38 and 39 into Equation 40. One then observes that the rate of change (d/dt) z_{ij} of each LTM trace depends on the global balance of all signals and all LTM traces, and thus on the entire history of the system as a whole.

Factors that promote adherence to or deviations from categorical perception are more subtle than these equations indicate. Section XXIII notes that an interplay of attentional factors with feature coding factors can cause the same network to react categorically or continuously to different experimental conditions. Such a result is not possible in the categorical perception model of Anderson et al. (1977), because the activities in that model must always reach a maximal or a minimal value (Section II).

XXIII. THE PROGRESSIVE SHARPENING OF MEMORY: TUNING PREWIRED PERCEPTUAL CATEGORIES

The requirement that $\mathcal{F}^{(2)}$ make an STM choice is clearly too strong. More generally, $\mathcal{F}^{(2)}$ possesses a tunable QT due to the fact that its competitive feedback signals are sigmoidal. Then only those signals T_j whose LTM vectors z_j are sufficiently parallel to an input pattern, within some range of tolerance determined by the QT, will cause suprathreshold STM reactions $x_i^{(2)}$. In this case, the competitive dynamics of $\mathcal{F}^{(2)}$ can be approximated by a rule of the form

$$x_j^{(2)} = \begin{cases} \dfrac{h(T_j)}{\displaystyle\sum_{T_k \geq \varepsilon} h(T_k)} & \text{if} \quad T_j \geq \varepsilon \\[3mm] 0, & \text{if} \quad T_j < \varepsilon \end{cases} \tag{41}$$

instead of Equation 39. In Equation 41, the inequality $T_j \geq \varepsilon$ says that the dot product input to $v_j^{(2)}$ exceeds the QT of $\mathcal{F}^{(2)}$. The function $h(T_j)$ approximates the contrast-enhancing action of sigmoid signaling within $\mathcal{F}^{(2)}$. The ratio of $h(T_j)$ to $\sum_{T_k \geq \varepsilon} h(T_k)$ approximates the normalization property of $\mathcal{F}^{(2)}$.

Due to Equation 41, a larger input T_j than T_k causes a larger STM reaction $x_j^{(2)}$ than $x_k^{(2)}$. By Equation 40, a larger value of $x_j^{(2)}$ than $x_k^{(2)}$ causes faster conditioning of the LTM vector z_j than of z_k. Faster conditioning of z_j causes $h(T_j)$ to be relatively larger than $h(T_k)$ on later learning trials than on earlier learning trials. Due to the normalization property, relatively more of the total activity of $\mathscr{F}^{(2)}$ will be concentrated at $x_j^{(2)}$ than was true on earlier learning trials. The relative advantage of $x_j^{(2)}$ is then translated into relatively faster conditioning of the LTM vector z_j. This feedback exchange between STM and LTM continues until the process equilibrates, if indeed it does. As a result of this exchange, the critical features within the filter $T = (T_1, T_2, \ldots, T_m)$ eventually overwhelm less salient features within the STM representation across $\mathscr{F}^{(2)}$ of input patterns to $\mathscr{F}^{(1)}$. Representations can thus be sharpened, or progressively tuned, due to a feedback exchange between "slow" adaptive coding and "fast" competition.

The tendency to sharpen representations due to training leads to learned codes with context-sensitive properties. This is because the critical features that code a given input pattern are determined by all of the input patterns that the network ever experiences. The ultimate representation of a single "word" in the network's input vocabulary thus depends on the entire "language" being learned, despite the fact that prewired connections in the signaling pathways from $\mathscr{F}^{(1)}$ to $\mathscr{F}^{(2)}$, and within $\mathscr{F}^{(1)}$ and $\mathscr{F}^{(2)}$, constrain the features that will go into these representations.

Other sources of complexity are due to the fact that Equations 38, 40, and 41 approximate only the most elementary aspects of the learning process. The filter in Equation 38 often contains parameters P_{ij}, as in

$$T_j = \sum_{i=1}^{n} f(x_i^{(1)}) P_{ij} z_{ij}, \tag{42}$$

which determine prewired *positional gradients* from $\mathscr{F}^{(1)}$ to $\mathscr{F}^{(2)}$. These positional gradients break up the filtering of an input pattern into sets of partially overlapping channels. *Some* choice of prewired connections P_{ij} is needed to even define a filter such as that in Equation 38 or 42. Thus "tuning an adaptive filter" always means "tuning the prewired positional gradients of an adaptive filter." Infants may thus be "able to perceive a wide variety of phonetic contrasts long before they actually produce these contrasts in their own babbling" (Jusczyk, 1981, p. 156). The fact that developmental tuning may alter the LTM traces z_{ij} in Equation 42 in no way invalidates the ability of the prewired gradients P_{ij} in the equation to constrain the perceptual categories that tuning refines, both before and after tuning takes place.

The special choice $P_{ij} = 1$ for all i and j in Equation 38 describes the simplest (but an unrealistic) case in which all filters T_j receive equal pre-wired connections, but possibly different initial LTM traces, from all nodes v_i. In subsequent formulas, all P_{ij} will be set equal to 1 for notational simplicity. However, the need to choose nonuniform P_{ij} in general should not be forgotten.

Other simplifying assumptions must also be generalized in order to deal with realistic cases. The rule in Equation 41 for competition ignores many subtleties of how one competitive design can determine a different STM transformation than another. This rule also ignores the fact that the input pattern T to $\mathscr{F}^{(2)}$ is transformed into a pattern of STM traces across $\mathscr{F}^{(2)}$ before this STM pattern, not the input pattern itself, is further transformed by competitive feedback interactions within $\mathscr{F}^{(2)}$. Despite these shortcomings, the robust tendency for memory to sharpen progressively due to experience is clarified by these examples (Cermak & Craik, 1979; Squire, Cohen, & Nadel, 1982).

The degree of representational sharpening can be manipulated at will by varying the QT of $\mathscr{F}^{(2)}$. A high QT will cause sharply tuned codes to evolve from $\mathscr{F}^{(1)}$ to $\mathscr{F}^{(2)}$, as in Equation 39. A lower QT will enable a more diffusely distributed map to be learned from $\mathscr{F}^{(1)}$ to $\mathscr{F}^{(2)}$. Such a diffuse map may be protected from noise amplification by the use of sigmoidal competitive signaling at every processing stage that is capable of STM storage. If, however, the QT is chosen so small that fluctuations in internal cellular noise or in nonspecific arousal can exceed the QT, then the network STM and LTM can both be pathologically destabilized. A network in which two successive stages of filtering $\mathscr{F}^{(1)} \rightarrow \mathscr{F}^{(2)} \rightarrow \mathscr{F}^{(3)}$ occur—where the first stage $\mathscr{F}^{(1)} \rightarrow \mathscr{F}^{(2)}$ generates a diffuse map and the second stage $\mathscr{F}^{(2)} \rightarrow \mathscr{F}^{(3)}$ generates a sharply tuned map—is capable of computing significant global invariants of the input patterns to $\mathscr{F}^{(1)}$ (Fukushima, 1980; Grossberg, 1978e).

XXIV. STABILIZING THE CODING OF LARGE VOCABULARIES: TOP-DOWN EXPECTANCIES AND STM RESET BY UNEXPECTED EVENTS

Now for the bad news. If the number of input patterns to be coded is large relative to the number of nodes in $\mathscr{F}^{(2)}$, and if these input patterns are densely distributed in pattern space, then no temporally stable code may develop across $\mathscr{F}^{(2)}$ using only the interactions of the previous section (Grossberg, 1976a). In other words, the STM pattern across $\mathscr{F}^{(2)}$ that is caused by a fixed input pattern can persistently change through time due to the network's adaptive reaction to the other input patterns. The effort to overcome this catastrophe led to the introduction of the *adaptive resonance theory* (Grossberg, 1976b). I refer the reader to previous articles (Grossberg, 1982b, 1982d, 1984a) for a more thorough analysis of these results.

The main observation needed here is that a developing code can always be temporally stabilized by the action of conditionable top-down templates or feedback expectancies. This fact sheds new light on results which have suggested a role for feedback templates in a diverse body of data, including data about phonemic restoration, word superiority effects, visual pattern completion effects, and olfactory coding, to name a few (Dodwell, 1975; Foss & Blank, 1980; Freeman, 1979; Johnston & McClelland, 1974; Lanze, Weisstein, & Harris, 1982; Marslen-Wilson, 1975; Marslen-Wilson & Welsh, 1978; Rumelhart & McClelland, 1982; Warren, 1970; Warren & Obusek, 1971). My theory suggests that top-down templates are a universal computational design in all neural subsystems capable of achieving temporally stable adaptation in response to a complex input environment. The theory also identifies the mechanisms needed to achieve temporally stable adaptation. Because many articles that use top-down mechanisms consider only performance issues rather than a composite of learning and performance issues, they do not provide a sufficient indication of why top-down expectancies exist or how they work.

My theory consider the basic issue of how a network can buffer the internal representations that it has already self-organized against the destabilizing effects of behaviorally irrelevant environmental fluctuations and yet adapt rapidly in response to novel environmental events which are crucial to its survival. To do this, the network must know the difference between and be able to differentially process both expected and unexpected events. I trace this ability to the properties of two complementary subsystems: an orienting subsystem and an attentional subsystem. Figures 6.15 and 6.16 summarize how these two types of subsystems operate.

In both figures, I assume that an active STM pattern is reverberating across certain nodes in the $(i + 1)$st field $\mathcal{F}^{(i+1)}$ of a coding hierarchy. These active nodes are emitting conditioned feedback signals to the previous stage $\mathcal{F}^{(i)}$ in this hierarchy. The total pattern E of these feedback signals represents the pattern that the active nodes in $\mathcal{F}^{(i+1)}$ collectively "expect" to find across $\mathcal{F}^{(i)}$ due to prior learning trials on which these nodes sampled the STM patterns across $\mathcal{F}^{(i)}$ via an associative process akin to outstar learning. More precisely, an expectancy E is a vector $E = (E_1, E_2, \ldots, E_n)$ such that $E_k = \Sigma_{j=1}^{m} S_j z_{jk}^{(i)}$ where S_j is the sampling

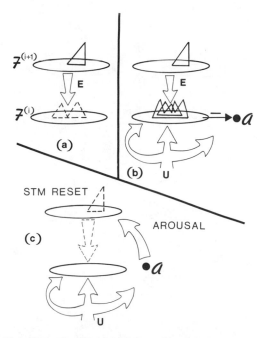

Figure 6.15   Reaction of attentional and orienting subsystems to an unexpected event: (a) A subliminal top-down expectancy E at $\mathscr{F}^{(1)}$ is maintained by a supraliminal STM pattern across $\mathscr{F}^{(2)}$. (b) The input pattern U nonspecifically sensitizes $\mathscr{F}^{(1)}$ as it instates itself across $\mathscr{F}^{(1)}$. The input also sends an activating signal to the nonspecific arousal source α. (c) The event U is unexpected because it mismatches E across $\mathscr{F}^{(1)}$. The mismatch inhibits STM activity across $\mathscr{F}^{(1)}$ and disinhibits α. This in turn releases a nonspecific arousal pulse that rapidly resets STM across $\mathscr{F}^{(2)}$ before adventitious recoding of the LTM can occur and drives a search of associative memory until a better match can be achieved.

signal emitted from $v_j^{(i+1)}$ and $z_{jk}^{(i)}$ is the LTM trace in the synaptic knobs of the pathway e_{jk} from $v_j^{(i+1)}$ to $v_k^{(i)}$.

I assume that the feedback signals E bias $\mathscr{F}^{(i)}$ by subliminally activating the STM traces across $\mathscr{F}^{(i)}$. Only a subliminal reaction is generated by the expectancy because the QT of $\mathscr{F}^{(i)}$ is assumed to be controlled by a nonspecific shunting signal, as in Equation 30. Although the expectancy E is active, the QT of $\mathscr{F}^{(i)}$ is too high for E to cause a supraliminal STM reaction.

A feedforward input pattern U from $\mathscr{F}^{(i-1)}$ to $\mathscr{F}^{(i)}$ has two effects on $\mathscr{F}^{(i)}$. It delivers the specific input pattern U and activates the nonspecific shunting signal that lowers the QT of $\mathscr{F}^{(i)}$. The conjoint action of U and E then determines the STM pattern elicited by U across $\mathscr{F}^{(i)}$.

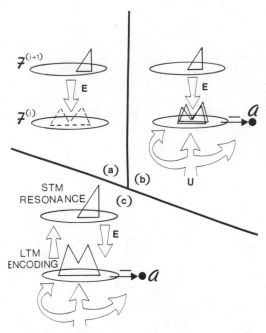

Figure 6.16 Reaction of attentional and orienting subsystems to an expected event: (a) A subliminal top-down expectancy E at $\mathcal{F}^{(1)}$ is maintained by a supraliminal STM pattern across $\mathcal{F}^{(2)}$. (b) The input pattern U nonspecifically sensitizes $\mathcal{F}^{(1)}$ as it instates itself across $\mathcal{F}^{(1)}$. The input also sends an activating signal to the nonspecific arousal source a. (c) The event U is expected because it approximately matches E across $\mathcal{F}^{(1)}$; that is, it falls within the hysteresis boundary defined by E. This match amplifies patterned STM activity across $\mathcal{F}^{(1)}$ and $\mathcal{F}^{(2)}$ into a resonant STM code capable of being encoded in LTM.

It is worth noting at this point that any other input source capable of turning on the nonspecific shunting signal to $\mathcal{F}^{(i)}$ could lower its QT and thereby bootstrap the expectancy signals into a supraliminal STM pattern even in the absence of a feedforward input pattern. I believe that fantasy activities such as internal thinking and the recall of music can be maintained in this fashion.

We now consider how unexpected versus expected input patterns are differentially processed by this network. In Figure 6.15b, an unexpected input pattern U is delivered to $\mathcal{F}^{(i)}$ from $\mathcal{F}^{(i-1)}$. The pattern U is unexpected in the sense that the feedback template E and the unexpected input U are mismatched across $\mathcal{F}^{(i)}$. The concept of mismatch is a technical concept whose instantiation is a property of the interactions within $\mathcal{F}^{(i)}$ (Grossberg, 1980c, Appendix C; Carpenter and Grossberg, 1986a, 1986b).

For present purposes, we need to know only that a mismatch between two input patterns at $\mathcal{F}^{(i)}$ quickly attenuates STM activity across $\mathcal{F}^{(i)}$ (see Figure 6.15c).

Just as the input pattern U activates a nonspecific gain control mechanism within $\mathcal{F}^{(i)}$, it also delivers an input to the orienting subsystem α. Because each node in $\mathcal{F}^{(i)}$ sends an inhibitory pathway to α (Figure 6.15b), suprathreshold STM activity anywhere across $\mathcal{F}^{(i)}$ can inhibit the input due to U at α. If mismatch across $\mathcal{F}^{(i)}$ occurs, however, inhibitory signals from $\mathcal{F}^{(i)}$ to α are attenuated. Consequently, U's input to α is capable of unleashing a nonspecific signal to $\mathcal{F}^{(i+1)}$, which acts quickly to reset STM activity across $\mathcal{F}^{(i+1)}$.

One of the properties of STM reset is to selectively inhibit the active nodes across $\mathcal{F}^{(i+1)}$ that read out the incorrect expectancy of which event was about to happen. STM reset thus initiates a search for a more appropriate code with which to handle the unexpected situation. An equally important effect of inhibiting the active nodes in $\mathcal{F}^{(i+1)}$ is to prevent these nodes from being recoded by the incorrect pattern U at $\mathcal{F}^{(i)}$. STM reset shuts off the active STM traces $x_j^{(i+1)}$ across $\mathcal{F}^{(i+1)}$ so quickly that the slowly varying LTM traces $z_{kj}^{(i)}$ from $\mathcal{F}^{(i)}$ to $\mathcal{F}^{(i+1)}$ cannot be recoded via the LTM law

$$\frac{\mathrm{d}}{\mathrm{d}t} z_{kj}^{(i)} = [-z_{kj}^{(i)} + U_k]x_j^{(i+1)}. \tag{43}$$

The top-down expectancy thus buffers its activating chunks from adventitious recoding.

XXV. EXPECTANCY MATCHING AND ADAPTIVE RESONANCE

In Figure 6.16, the pattern U to $\mathcal{F}^{(i)}$ is expected. This means that the top-down expectancy E and the bottom-up pattern U match across $\mathcal{F}^{(i)}$. This notion of matching is also a technical concept that is instantiated by interactions within $\mathcal{F}^{(i)}$. When a pair of patterns match in this sense, the network can energetically amplify the matched pattern across $\mathcal{F}^{(i)}$ (see Figure 6.16b). These amplified activities cause amplified signals to pass from $\mathcal{F}^{(i)}$ to $\mathcal{F}^{(i+1)}$ (Figure 6.16c). The STM pattern across $\mathcal{F}^{(i+1)}$ is then amplified and thereupon amplifies the feedback signals from $\mathcal{F}^{(i+1)}$ to $\mathcal{F}^{(i)}$. This process of mutual amplification causes the STM patterns across $\mathcal{F}^{(i)}$ and $\mathcal{F}^{(i+1)}$ to be locked into a sustained STM resonance that represents a context-sensitive encoding of the expected pattern U. The resonant STM patterns can be encoded by the LTM traces in the pathways between $\mathcal{F}^{(i)}$

and $\mathcal{F}^{(i+1)}$ because these STM patterns are not rapidly inhibited by an STM reset event. Because STM resonance leads to LTM encoding, I call this dynamical event an *adaptive resonance*.

XXVI. THE PROCESSING OF NOVEL EVENTS: PATTERN COMPLETION VERSUS SEARCH OF ASSOCIATIVE MEMORY

A novel input pattern U can elicit two different types of network reaction, depending on whether U triggers STM resonance or STM reset. When a novel event U is filtered via feedforward $\mathcal{F}^{(i)} \to \mathcal{F}^{(i+1)}$ signaling, it may activate a feedback expectancy E via feedback $\mathcal{F}^{(i+1)} \to \mathcal{F}^{(i)}$ signaling which, although not the same pattern as U, is sufficiently like U to generate an approximate match across $\mathcal{F}^{(i)}$. This can happen because the QT of $\mathcal{F}^{(i)}$ determines a flexible criterion of how similar two patterns must be to prevent the inhibition of all STM activity across $\mathcal{F}^{(i)}$. A large QT implies a strict criterion, whereas a low QT implies a weak criterion. If two patterns are matched well enough for some populations in $\mathcal{F}^{(i)}$ to exceed the QT, then STM resonance will occur and the orienting reaction will be inhibited.

Because U is filtered by feedforward signaling, and because E reads out the optimal pattern that the active chunks across $\mathcal{F}^{(i+1)}$ have previously learned, E will deform the STM reaction across $\mathcal{F}^{(i)}$ that would have occurred to U alone toward a resonant encoding that completes U using the optimal data E. This consequence of buffering LTM codes against adventitious recoding is, I believe, a major source of Gestaltlike pattern completion effects, such as phonemic restoration, word superiority effects, and the like. Grossberg and Stone (1986a) develop such concepts to analyze data about word recognition and recall.

By contrast, if U is so different from E that the QT causes STM suppression across $\mathcal{F}^{(i)}$, then the orienting subsystem will be activated and a rapid parallel search of associative memory will ensue. To understand how such a search is regulated, one needs to analyze how a nonspecific arousal pulse to $\mathcal{F}^{(i+1)}$ can selectively inhibit only the active nodes across $\mathcal{F}^{(i+1)}$ and spare inactive nodes for subsequent encoding of the unexpected event.

This property is instantiated by expanding the design of $\mathcal{F}^{(i+1)}$, as well as all other network levels that are capable of STM reset, in the following fashion. All nodes that have heretofore been posited in the competitive networks are *on-cells;* they are turned on by inputs. Now I supplement the on-cell competitive networks with apposing off-cell competitive networks such that offset of an input to an on-cell triggers a transient activation of its corresponding off-cell. Such an activation is called an *antagonistic rebound*.

Antagonistic rebound at an off-cell in response to offset of an on-cell input can be achieved due to three mechanisms acting together: (1) All the inputs to both the on-cell channel and the off-cell channel are gated by slowly accumulating transmitter substances that generate output signals by being released at a rate proportional to input strength times the amount of available transmitter. (2) The inputs to on-cells and off-cells are of two types: specific inputs that selectively activate an on-cell channel or an off-cell channel, but not both, and nonspecific inputs that activate both on-cell and off-cell channels equally. (3) The gated signals in both the on-channel and off-channel compete before the net gated inputs activate the on-cell or the off-cell, but not both. The network module that carries out these computations is called a *gated dipole* (Figure 6.17). One proves that if a sufficiently large increment in nonspecific arousal occurs while an on-cell is active, this increment can cause an antagonistic rebound that rapidly shuts off the on-cell's STM trace by exciting the corresponding off-cell. This rebound is part of the STM reset event.

The antagonistic rebounds in gated dipoles are due to the fact that unequal inputs to the on-cell and off-cell cause their respective transmitter gates to be depleted, or *habituated,* at unequal rates. When a rapid change in input patterning occurs, it is gated by the more slowly varying transmitter levels. A mathematical analysis shows that either a rapid offset of the specific on-cell input or a rapid increase of nonspecific arousal can cause an antagonistic rebound due to the imbalance in transmitter habituation across the on-cell and off cell channels (Grossberg, 1972b, 1975, 1980c, 1981b, 1984a).

Once a subfield of on-cells is inhibited by dipole rebounds, they remain inhibited for a while due to the slow recovery rate of the transmitter gates. Only a subset of nodes in $\mathcal{F}^{(i+1)}$ can therefore respond to the filtered signals from $\mathcal{F}^{(i)}$ in the next time interval. If another mismatch occurs, more nodes in $\mathcal{F}^{(i+1)}$ are inhibited. As the search continues, the normalized STM patterns across $\mathcal{F}^{(i+1)}$ contract rapidly onto a final subset of $\mathcal{F}^{(i+1)}$ nodes. The STM pattern across this final subset of nodes is used to condition the filter of its corresponding pathways or to stabilize the already conditioned pathways via an adaptive resonance.

One of the intriguing facts about searching associative memory in this way is that transmitter habituation is one of the important mechanisms. Habituation acts in my theory to regulate active memory buffering and adaptive encoding processes; it is not just a passive result of "use," "fatigue," or other classical notions.

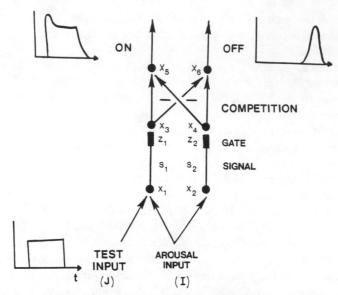

Figure 6.17   Reaction of a feedforward gated dipole to phasic onset and offset of a cue: The
phasic test input J and the arousal input I add in the on-channel, thereby activating the STM
trace x_1. The arousal input I activates the STM trace x_2 in the off-channel. Since $I + J > I$,
$x_1 > x_2$. Traces x_1 and x_2 elicit signals $f(x_1)$ and $f(x_2)$. Because $x_1 > x_2$, $f(x_1) > f(x_2)$. Each
signal is gated by a transmitter z_1 or z_2 (in the square synapses). Transmitters z_1 and z_2 are
released at rates proportional to $f(x_1)z_1$ and $f(x_2)z_2$, respectively. The gated signals $f(x_1)z_1$
and $f(x_2)z_2$ in turn activate x_3 and x_4, respectively, and $x_3 > x_4$. Both x_3 and x_4 excite their
own channel and inhibit the other channel. After competition acts, an output from the on-
channel is elicited that habituates through time. A rapid offset of J causes $x_1 = x_2$ and $f(x_1) =$
$f(x_2)$. However, $z_1 < z_2$ due to greater prior depletion, or habituation, of the on-channel by J,
and to the slow reaction rate of z_1 and z_2 relative to x_1 and x_2. Thus $f(x_1)z_1 < f(x_2)z_2$ and $x_3 <$
x_4. After competition acts, the off-channel wins. Gradually, $z_1 = z_2$ in response to the equal
values of x_1 and x_2. Then $f(x_1)z_1 = f(x_2)z_2$, so the competition shuts off all dipole output. The
same mechanism causes on off-rebound in response to a rapid increment in I while J is
active. In a feedback gated dipole, output from x_5 reexcites x_1, and output from x_6 reexcites
x_2. In a dipole field, the positive feedback loops $x_1 \leftrightarrow x_5$ and $x_2 \leftrightarrow x_6$ form the on-centers of
competitive shunting networks that join on-cells to on-cells and off-cells to off-cells. Such
networks exhibit STM properties such an contrast enhancement and normalization modulated by the slow habituation of activated transmitter gates.

XXVII. RECOGNITION, AUTOMATICITY, PRIMES, AND CAPACITY

These processes are reflected in many types of data. Analyses and
predictions about some of these data are found in Grossberg (1980c,
1982b, 1982c). Carpenter and Grossberg (1986a, 1986b) describe extensive
computer simulations of how adaptive resonance theory mechanisms can
self-organize a self-stabilizing recognition code in response to an arbitrary

list of input patterns. The following remarks summarize some of the other types of data that may be clarified by such processes.

Recent studies of recognition memory point out: "Complex elaborate encoding . . . can be utilized to enhance recognition only when the test conditions permit a reinstatement of the original encoding context" (Fisher & Craik, 1980, p. 400). In a similar vein, other studies support the idea that "the direction of priming effects . . . depend[s] upon the validity of the prime as a predictor of the probe stimulus" (Myers & Lorch, 1980, p. 405). This type of effect holds at every level of reciprocal signaling in the encoding hierarchy, because a particular pattern of feedforward chunking is wed to a characteristic pattern of template feedback. An active pattern of template feedback leads to rapid resonant matching only when it meets with compatible feedforward input patterns. The resonant process is interpreted to be the attentive moment, or recognition event, that groups individual nodal activities into a unitary percept. The "priming" feedback template leads to enhanced recognition only if the "probe" input pattern is sufficiently similar to trigger a resonant match.

This view of template matching and associative memory search suggests a different way to think about automatic versus capacity-limited processing than that of researchers like Norman and Bobrow (1975) or Posner and Snyder (1975). Capacity limitations alone do not determine whether very fast inhibition will slow down reaction times in a search situation. Mismatch can trigger rapid STM reset and associative search, leading to an increase in reaction time, under the same capacity limitations that would speed reaction time if a match were to occur. An increased reaction time is not due merely to a capacity limitation that excites two mutually inhibitory nodes, because mutual inhibition can subserve either a match or a mismatch.

At bottom, the traditional discussion of increased reaction time due to capacity-limited inhibitory effects follows from an inadequate choice of the functional unit of network processing. The functional unit is not the activation of a single node, nor a "spreading activation" among individual nodes. Rather, it is a coherent pattern across a field of nodes. This viewpoint is compatible with the results of Myers and Lorch (1980, p. 405), who showed, among other things: "Reaction time to decide that a sentence was true or false was longer if the preceding prime was a word that was unrelated to the probe than if the prime was the word 'blank' " at prime-to-probe intervals as short as 250 ms.

How can a more direct test of behaviorally unobservable reset and search routines be made? One possible way may be to adapt techniques for measuring the N200 and P300 evoked potentials to letter, word, and sentence recognition and verification tasks. The theory suggests that every mismatch event will elicit the mismatch negativity component of the N200 at α and that every subsequent nonspecific arousal burst will elicit a P300 at $\mathcal{F}^{(2)}$ (Grossberg, 1984a; Karrer, Cohen, & Tueting, 1984).

XXVIII. ANCHORS, AUDITORY CONTRAST, AND SELECTIVE ADAPTATION

Numerous studies of contextual effects in vowel perception have attempted to distinguish between "feature detector fatigue" and "auditory contrast" explanations of how a categorical boundary can shift during a selective adaptation or anchoring experiment. Sawusch and Nusbaum (1979) have interpreted their results as favoring an auditory contrast explanation, because even widely spaced repetitions of an anchor vowel elicit a significant shift in the boundary. The mechanisms of template feedback, STM resonance, STM reset, and transmitter habituation may shed some further light on this discussion by suggesting some new experimental tests of these ideas.

Sawusch and Nusbaum (1979, p. 301) discuss auditory contrast in terms of "incorporating the influence of both information from immediately preceding stimuli (auditory memory) and prototypes in long-term memory into one unified auditory ground against which new stimuli are compared." I represent the "auditory memory" by a pattern reverberating in STM across a field $\mathcal{F}^{(i+1)}$ of nodes, the "prototypes in long-term memory" by LTM traces in the active feedback template pathways from $\mathcal{F}^{(i+1)}$ to $\mathcal{F}^{(i)}$, and the "unified auditory ground" by a subliminal feedback expectancy E across $\mathcal{F}^{(i)}$. This interpretation immediately raises several questions.

Why does an input U that mismatches E cause a boundary shift *away* from the event represented by E? In the framework presented earlier, the answer is: The mismatch event actively inhibits the active nodes across $\mathcal{F}^{(i+1)}$ which represent E. In the time interval after this STM reset event, the pattern U will be encoded by a renormalized field $\mathcal{F}^{(i+1)}$ in which the nodes that encoded E remain inhibited. A similar combination of mismatch-then-reset has been used to discuss bistable visual illusions such as those that occur during the viewing of Necker's cube (Grossberg, 1980c). I suggest that a P300-evoked potential will occur at the moment of switching.

As in the discussion of matching probes to primes, a stronger anchoring effect may cause a faster reaction time when U equals E and a slower reaction time when U mismatches E. Another type of test would start with an event U that equals E and would gradually cause U to mismatch E using a temporally dense series of successive presentations of slightly changing Us. The hysteresis boundary that causes perseveration of the anchor percept may get broader as the anchoring effect is made stronger, even though a stronger anchoring effect causes a larger shift when a discrete event U mismatches E. A P300 may also occur when the hysteresis boundary is exceeded by U. Thereafter, the percept may again be shifted away from E.

The latter test may be confounded by the fact that a dense series of Us may cause persistent STM reverberation of the anchor representation across $\mathcal{F}^{(i+1)}$. Such a reverberation may progressively habituate the transmitter gates in the reverberating pathways. In this way, "fatigue" may enter even an auditory contrast explanation, albeit fatigue of a nonclassical kind. If significant habituation does occur, then the shift due to STM reset may become smaller as a function of longer storage in auditory memory, but this effect would be compensated for by a direct renormalization of the STM response of $\mathcal{F}^{(i+1)}$ to U as a result of habituation. Such habituation effects may occur on a surprisingly long time scale, because a slow transmitter accumulation rate is needed to regulate the search of associative memory.

Sawusch and Nusbaum (1979) suggest that adaptation-level theory (Helson, 1964; Restle, 1978) may be used as a mathematical framework to explain selective adaptation and anchoring effects. I believe that this is a correct intuition. Shunting competitive networks possess an adaptation level that is the basis for their matching properties (Grossberg, 1980c, Appendix C; 1983, Section 22). A feedback template E has the effect of biasing the adaptation level and thereby producing a different reaction to a feedforward input pattern U than would otherwise occur. However, this property of shunting networks controls only one step in the network's total reaction to a shifted input.

In this regard, Sawusch, Nusbaum, and Schwab (1980) show that anchoring by the vowel [i] (as in *beet*) or by [I] (as in *bit*) produce contrast effects in tests involving [i]–[I] vowel series by affecting different mechanisms. "Contrast effects for an [i] anchor were found to be largely the result of changes in sensitivity between various vowel pairs . . . the [i] anchoring effect occurs prior to phonetic labeling. This is clearly the case, since [i] anchoring was found to increase discriminability within the [i] category . . . The [i] anchor seems to alter or retune the prototype space." By contrast, "the [I]-anchor effects were largely the result of criterion shifts . . . The auditory ground would reflect two sources of information: prototype information from long-term memory and certain information from the stimulus being presented . . . some form of auditory memory which contains information about the quality of the stimulus may underlie the changes in criterion for [I] anchoring" (Sawusch et al., 1980, p. 431).

Within the present theory, the changes in discriminability whereby the [i] anchor "retunes the prototype space" may be interpreted as an [i]-induced shift in some of the LTM vectors that form part of the auditory adaptive filter (Sections XXII–XXIII). This LTM tuning process occurs prior to the stage of "phonetic labeling," or STM competition in auditory memory, and changes the outcome of the phonetic competition by altering the pattern of filtered inputs on which the competition feeds.

Both the [i] vowel and the [I] vowel can bias the adaptation level by reading their subliminal feedback templates out of auditory memory. This type of top-down bias can create criterion shifts without redistributing the bottom-up LTM vectors in the adaptive filter that control relative sensitivity. If no change in the adaptive filter takes place, interference with auditory memory will reduce contrast effects due to anchoring. However, if an adaptive filter shift has occurred prior to interference with auditory memory, a large anchoring effect can still occur due to the direct effect on each trial of the shifted bottom-up filtering on top-down template readout. Sawusch et al. (1980) demonstrate an analogous effect. They partially interfere with auditory memory by embedding [i] and [I] in CVC syllables, such as [sis] and [sIs]. In this case, the anchoring effect of [sis] was significantly greater than that of [sIs].

XXIX. TRAINING OF ATTENTIONAL SET AND PERCEPTUAL CATEGORIES

Studdert-Kennedy (1980) has reviewed data that are compatible with this interpretation of the auditory ground. Spanish–English bilinguals can shift their boundaries by a change in language set within a single test (Elman, Diehl, & Buchwald, 1977). This shift can be formally accomplished in a network by activating nodes across $\mathscr{F}^{(i+1)}$ that read out different feedback templates.

Training enables subjects to shift categorical boundaries at will, thereby suggesting that "utilization of acoustic differences between speech stimuli may be determined primarily by attentional factors" (Carney, Widen, & Viemeister, 1977, p. 969). Such training may tune both the adaptive filters and the feedback templates of the subjects, much as American English speakers perceive an [r] to [l] continuum categorically, whereas Japanese speakers do not (Miyawaki, Strange, Verbrugge, Liberman, Jenkins, & Fujimura, 1975).

XXX. CIRCULAR REACTIONS, BABBLING, AND THE DEVELOPMENT OF AUDITORY–ARTICULATORY SPACE

Using the operations that have been sketched above, one can quantitatively discuss how neural networks initiate the process whereby their sensory and motor potentialities are integrated into a unitary system. The main concepts are that endogenously activated motor commands generate patterns of sensory feedback; that internal representations of the activated sensory and motor patterns are synthesized (learned, chunked) by adaptive tuning of coarsely prewired filters (feature detectors, positional gradients); and that the sensory internal representations are joined to their motor counterparts via a learned associative map. The sensory internal representations can also be tuned by sensory inputs other than sensory feedback as soon as external sensory inputs can command the attention—for example, lower the QT (Section XVIII)—of the sensory modality.

These concepts were first used in real-time network models to discuss how motivated and attentive behavior can be self-organized in a freely moving animal (Grossberg, 1971, 1972a, 1972b, 1975). Later, they were used to show how cognitive, attentive, and motivational mechanisms can interact to generate a consistent, goal-oriented sensory-motor plan (Grossberg, 1978e; reprinted in Grossberg, 1982d).

An earlier version of this approach is embodied in Piaget's concept of a *circular reaction* (Piaget, 1963). Then Fry (1966) emphasized the importance of the infant's babbling stage for the later development of normal speech (Marvilya, 1972), notably for the tuning of prewired adaptive sensory filters. The work of Marler and his colleagues (Marler, 1970; Marler & Peters, 1981) on the development of birdsong in sparrows has recognized the relevance of self-generated auditory feedback to the development of normal adult song. Similarly, the motor theory of speech perception recognized the intimate relationship between acoustic encoding and articulatory requirements (Cooper, 1979; Liberman, Cooper, Shankweiler, & Studdert-Kennedy, 1967; Liberman & Studdert-Kennedy, 1978; Mann & Repp, 1981; Repp & Mann, 1981; Studdert-Kennedy, Liberman, Harris, & Cooper, 1970). Studdert-Kennedy (1975, 1980) has written about this approach with particular eloquence: "Only by carefully tracking the infant through its first two years of life shall we come to understand adult speech perception and, in particular, how speaking and listening establish their links at the base of the language system" (Studdert-Kennedy, 1980, p. 45). "The system follows the moment-to-moment acoustic flow, apprehending an auditory 'motion picture,' as it were, of the articulation" (p. 55).

This and the next section sketch a framework for analyzing how individual sensory and motor patterns are integrated. After that, I consider the deeper question of how temporal sequences of patterns are processed. To carry out this discussion, I use the notation $\mathcal{F}_M^{(i)}$ for the ith motor field in a coding hierarchy, and $\mathcal{F}_S^{(i)}$ for the ith sensory field in a coding hierarchy. The example of babbling in an infant can be used to intuitively fix ideas.

Suppose that an activity pattern across $\mathcal{F}_M^{(1)}$ represents a terminal motor map (TMM) of a motor act. Such a map specifies the terminal lengths of target muscles. It is often organized in a way that reflects the agonist–antagonistic organization of these muscles. Suppose that during a specified time interval, a series of TMMs are endogenously activated across $\mathcal{F}_M^{(1)}$, analogous to the babbling of simple sounds. The execution of such a TMM elicits sensory feedback, analogous to a sound, which is registered as an input pattern across $\mathcal{F}_S^{(1)}$ (Figure 6.18a).

As these unconditional events are taking place, they are accompanied by the following adaptive reactions. The active TMM is chunked by adaptive filtering from $\mathcal{F}_M^{(1)}$ to $\mathcal{F}_M^{(2)}$. This motor code in turn learns its corresponding TMM via the conditioning of its feedback template from $\mathcal{F}_M^{(2)}$ to $\mathcal{F}_M^{(1)}$. As this learning is taking place, the corresponding sensory feedback pattern across $\mathcal{F}_S^{(1)}$ is chunked by adaptive filtering from $\mathcal{F}_S^{(1)}$ to $\mathcal{F}_S^{(2)}$. Its sensory code learns the corresponding pattern of sensory features across $\mathcal{F}_S^{(1)}$ by the conditioning of its template feedback from $\mathcal{F}_S^{(2)}$ to $\mathcal{F}_S^{(1)}$ (Figure 6.18b).

Due to the simultaneous activity of the sensory and motor representations in $\mathcal{F}_S^{(2)}$ and $\mathcal{F}_M^{(2)}$, a map from $\mathcal{F}_S^{(2)}$ to $\mathcal{F}_M^{(2)}$ can be self-organized by associative pattern learning (Figure 6.18c). One of the quantitative issues of the theory concerns how diffuse or sharply tuned this map should be (Grossberg, 1978e, Sections 55–58).

The above network matches auditory to articulatory requirements in several ways. It preferentially tunes the sensory "feature detectors" that are activated most often by spoken sounds (Section XXII). It also maps the tuned internal representations of these sounds onto the motor commands that are capable of eliciting the sounds. The construction accomplishes this by associatively sampling the motor commands in the form that succeeded in executing the sounds through endogenous activation. Although the internal representations of sounds and motor commands may differ in many significant ways, they can be joined together by the common coin of pattern learning in associative networks. These patterns are the still pictures in the "motion picture" described by Studdert-Kennedy (1980).

The flow of activity in such a network is circular. It proceeds from $\mathcal{F}_M^{(1)}$

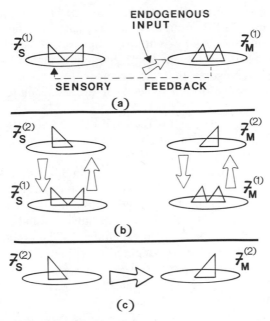

Figure 6.18   A circular reaction that matches acoustic encoding to articulatory requirements: (a) Endogenous motor commands across $\mathcal{F}_M^{(1)}$ elicit babbled sounds that are received
as auditory feedback patterns across $\mathcal{F}_S^{(1)}$. (b) The motor commands and the auditory feed-
back patterns are chunked at $\mathcal{F}_M^{(2)}$ and $\mathcal{F}_S^{(2)}$ via bottom-up adaptive filtering in pathways $\mathcal{F}_M^{(1)} \rightarrow$
$\mathcal{F}_M^{(2)}$ and $\mathcal{F}_S^{(1)} \rightarrow \mathcal{F}_S^{(2)}$, respectively. These chunks learn their generative motor commands and
auditory patterns via top-down expectancy learning in pathways $\mathcal{F}_M^{(2)} \rightarrow \mathcal{F}_M^{(1)}$ and $\mathcal{F}_S^{(2)} \rightarrow \mathcal{F}_S^{(1)}$,
respectively. (c) The sensory and motor chunks are joined together by an associative map
$\mathcal{F}_S^{(2)} \rightarrow \mathcal{F}_M^{(2)}$. The learned map $\mathcal{F}_S^{(1)} \rightarrow \mathcal{F}_S^{(2)} \rightarrow \mathcal{F}_M^{(2)} \rightarrow \mathcal{F}_M^{(1)}$ completes the circular reaction and
enables novel sounds to be imitated and then chunked by the same mechanisms.

to $\mathcal{F}_S^{(1)}$ via external sensory feedback, and in the reverse direction by a
combination of adaptive filtering, associative mapping, and conditionable
template feedback. This is a circular reaction, network-style. The completion of the circle by the internal network flow enables simple imitation to
be accomplished via the learned map

$$\mathcal{F}_S^{(1)} \rightarrow \mathcal{F}_S^{(2)} \rightarrow \mathcal{F}_M^{(2)} \rightarrow \mathcal{F}_M^{(1)}. \tag{44}$$

XXXI. ANALYSIS-BY-SYNTHESIS AND THE IMITATION OF NOVEL EVENTS

After babbling stops, how does language continue to develop? In particular, how does a network learn to recognize and recall novel sounds other

than those learned during the babbling phase? Part of this capability is built into the map in Equation 44 in a way that sheds light on the many successes of the analysis-by-synthesis approach to speech recognition (Halle & Stevens, 1962; Stevens, 1972; Stevens & Halle, 1964). The structure of the map suggests that motor theory and analysis-by-synthesis theory have probed different aspects of the same underlying physical process.

Suppose that a novel sound is received by $\mathcal{F}_S^{(1)}$. This sound is decomposed, or analyzed, into familiar sound components in the following way. The adaptive filter from $\mathcal{F}_S^{(1)}$ to $\mathcal{F}_S^{(2)}$ has been tuned by experience in such a way that the dot products corresponding to familiar sound patterns elicit larger inputs across $\mathcal{F}_S^{(2)}$ than do unfamiliar sound patterns, as in Section XXIII. This conclusion must be tempered by the fact that filter tuning of LTM traces z_{ij} is driven by the initial filtering of sound patterns by pre-wired positional gradients P_{ij}, as in Equation 42. The tuned adaptive filter analyzes the novel sound in a weighted combination of familiar sounds wherein the weights correspond to the relative activations of representational nodes across $\mathcal{F}_S^{(2)}$. Suppose that the associative map from $\mathcal{F}_S^{(2)}$ to $\mathcal{F}_M^{(2)}$ is diffuse. In this case the spatial pattern of weights that represent the novel sound is relayed as signal strengths from $\mathcal{F}_S^{(2)}$ to $\mathcal{F}_M^{(2)}$. Each familiar motor command at $\mathcal{F}_M^{(2)}$ is activated with an intensity corresponding to the size of the signal that it receives. All of the excited motor commands read out their TMMs to $\mathcal{F}_M^{(1)}$ with relative intensities corresponding to the relayed weights. The total read-out of familiar motor commands is then synthesized into a novel TMM across $\mathcal{F}_M^{(1)}$. The net effect of this analysis-by-synthesis process is to construct a novel TMM across $\mathcal{F}_M^{(1)}$ in response to a novel sound at $\mathcal{F}_S^{(1)}$.

The novel TMM needs to process the following *continuous mapping property:* It should elicit a sound that is more similar to the novel sound than to any of the familiar sounds in the network's repertoire. To achieve this property, continuous changes in the TMMs across $\mathcal{F}_M^{(1)}$ need to correspond to continuous changes in the auditory feedback patterns across $\mathcal{F}_S^{(1)}$. The continuous mapping property is most easily achieved by organizing auditory representations and motor representations in a topographic fashion.

If a novel TMM possessing the continuous mapping property is activated at $\mathcal{F}_M^{(1)}$ while the novel sound is still represented at $\mathcal{F}_S^{(1)}$, the network can build internal representations for both the sound and the TMM, as well as an associative map between these representations, just as it did for babbled sounds. As more internal representations and maps are built up, the network's ability to imitate and initiate novel sounds will become progressively refined. The metrical distances between a novel sound pattern or TMM pattern and the familiar sound or TMM patterns into which it is decomposed can be used as an intrinsic measure of the phenomenal complexity, or nonautomaticity, of a new behavior relative to a network code of familiar behaviors.

XXXII. A MOVING PICTURE OF CONTINUOUSLY INTERPOLATED TERMINAL MOTOR MAPS: COARTICULATION AND ARTICULATORY UNDERSHOOT

A topographic structuring of motor representations can be achieved by organizing these representations into agonist–antagonist pairs. The relative activations of such pairs can be signaled independently as part of a larger spatial pattern, much as individual articulators in the vocal tract, such as the lips, tongue, and vocal chords, can move with a large degree of independence (Darwin, 1976). A temporal sequence of TMMs from such a motor field is expressed as a sequence of spatial pattern outputs (Section V). Each spatial pattern controls a motor synergy of articulatory motions to intended positional targets (Section VI). The intrinsic organization of the articulatory system continuously interpolates the motion of the articulators between these targets.

The timing of component subpatterns within a sequence of spatial pattern TMMs can cause coarticulation to occur (Fowler, 1977). A high rate of emitting TMMs, due, say, to an increase in the gain of the read-out system by a nonspecific arousal increment (Section VII), can cause the next TMM to be instated before the last target has been attained. Rapid speech can thus be associated with articulatory undershoot and a corresponding acoustic undershoot (Lindblom, 1963; Miller, 1981).

XXXIII. A CONTEXT-SENSITIVE STM CODE FOR EVENT SEQUENCES

I now sketch some results about how sequences of events can be performed out of STM after a single presentation, and of how sequences of events can generate context-sensitive representations in LTM that are capable of accurately controlling planned, or predictive, behavior. These properties can be achieved by parallel mechanisms. No serial buffer is necessary.

Several classes of phenomena have been analyzed using these concepts, notably phenomena concerning free recall, letter and word recognition, and skilled motor behavior (Grossberg, 1978a, 1978e). A number of other authors have also discussed these phenomena using a network approach (e.g., MacKay, 1982; McClelland & Rumelhart, 1981; Norman, 1982; Rumelhart & McClelland, 1982; Rumelhart & Norman, 1982). Although I am in complete sympathy with these contributions, I believe that they have overlooked available principles and mechanisms that are essential for achieving better understanding of their targeted data. In the next few sections, I focus my discussion on how the functional unit of speech perception is self-organized by "an active continuous process" (Studdert-Kennedy, 1980), notably how backward effects, time-intensity tradeoff effects, and temporal integration processes can alter a speech percept (Miller & Liberman, 1979; Repp, 1979; Repp, Liberman, Eccardt, & Pesetsky, 1978; Schwab, Sawusch, & Nusbaum, 1981) in a manner that is difficult to explain using a computer model of speech perception (Levinson & Liberman, 1981). These ideas are supplemented by some mechanisms helpful in the analysis of rhythmic substrates of speech, skilled motor control, and musical performance (Fowler, 1977; Rumelhart & Norman, 1982; Shaffer, 1982; Studdert-Kennedy, 1980).

XXXIV. STABLE UNITIZATION AND TEMPORAL ORDER INFORMATION IN STM: THE LTM INVARIANCE PRINCIPLE

For simplicity, I begin by supposing that unitized item representations $v_1^{(3)}$, $v_2^{(3)}$, . . . , $v_n^{(3)}$ in a field $\mathcal{F}^{(3)}$ are sequentially activated by a list of events r_1, r_2, . . . , r_n. To fix ideas, the reader may suppose that the unitized representations are generated by adaptive filtering from either $\mathcal{F}_S^{(2)}$ or $\mathcal{F}_M^{(2)}$, since similar temporal order mechanisms are used in both sensory and motor modalities (Kimura, 1976; Kinsbourne & Hicks, 1978; Semmes, 1968; Studdert-Kennedy, 1980).

Suppose that a certain number of nodes $v_1^{(3)}$, $v_2^{(3)}$, . . . , $v_i^{(3)}$ have been activated by the sublist r_1, r_2, . . . , r_i and therefore have active STM traces at a given time t_i. At this moment, the set of active STM traces defines a spatial pattern. Had the same sublist been presented in a different order, a different STM pattern would exist across the same set of nodes. Thus the active STM pattern encodes temporal order information across the item representations.

To achieve a correct read-out of temporal order information directly from STM, a primacy effect in STM,

$$x_1^{(3)} > x_2^{(3)} > \cdots > x_i^{(3)}, \tag{45}$$

is desired, as in Equation 25. Section XII shows how a temporal series of recency effects in STM can elicit a learned read-out from LTM of a primacy effect in STM. We now consider how a primacy effect in STM can sometimes be caused *directly* by experimental inputs, yet also how a recency effect in STM can sometimes be caused by experimental inputs, thereby leading to order errors in the read-out of items from STM.

To understand this issue, I abandon all homunculi and consider how the evolving STM pattern can be encoded in LTM in a temporally stable fashion by the adaptive filter from $\mathscr{F}^{(3)}$ to $\mathscr{F}^{(4)}$. This adaptive filter groups together, or unitizes, sublists of the items that are simultaneously stored in STM at $\mathscr{F}^{(3)}$. The STM pattern at $\mathscr{F}^{(4)}$ codes as unitized sublist chunks those item groupings that are salient to the network when a prescribed list of items is stored at $\mathscr{F}^{(3)}$ (Figure 6.19). Thus I now consider laws for storing individual items in STM at $\mathscr{F}^{(3)}$ which enable the LTM unitization process to proceed in a stable fashion within the adaptive filter from $\mathscr{F}^{(3)}$ to $\mathscr{F}^{(4)}$. In short, I constrain STM to be compatible with LTM. This is a

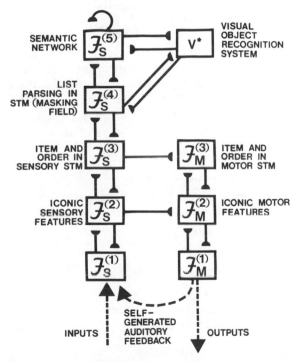

Figure 6.19   A macrocircuit governing self-organization of recognition and recall processes: Auditorily mediated language processes ($\mathscr{F}_S^{(i)}$), visual recognition processes (V*), and motor control processes ($\mathscr{F}_M^{(i)}$) interact internally via conditionable pathways (black lines) and externally via environmental feedback (dotted lines) to self-organize the various processes which occur at the different network stages.

self-organization approach to the unitization and temporal order problems that is invisible to a performance theoretic approach. It turns out that a shunting competitive network of a specialized design for $\mathcal{F}^{(3)}$ does the job.

Two considerations motivate this design. Once a sequence r_1, r_2, . . . , r_i has already been presented, its STM pattern represents "past" order information. Presenting a new item r_{i+1} can alter the total pattern of STM across $\mathcal{F}^{(3)}$, but I assume that this new STM pattern does not cause LTM recoding of that part of the pattern which represents past order information. New events are allowed to weaken the influence of codes that represent past order information but not to deny the fact that the past events occurred. This hypothesis prevents the LTM record of past order information from being obliterated by every future event that happens to occur.

This idea can be stated in a related way that emphasizes the possible destabilizing effects of new events when there are no homunculi present to beg the question. Every subsequence of the sequence $r_1, r_2, . . . , r_i$ is a perfectly good sequence in its own right. In principle, all possible subsequences can be adaptively coded by $\mathcal{F}^{(3)} \rightarrow \mathcal{F}^{(4)}$ pathways. How can the STM activities across $\mathcal{F}^{(3)}$ be chosen so that the relative activities of all possible filterings of a past event sequence are left invariant by future events? These constraints lead to the *LTM invariance principle:* The spatial patterns of STM across $\mathcal{F}^{(3)}$ are generated by a sequentially presented list in such a way as to leave the $\mathcal{F}^{(3)} \rightarrow \mathcal{F}^{(4)}$ LTM codes of past event groupings invariant, even though the STM activations caused across $\mathcal{F}^{(3)}$ and $\mathcal{F}^{(4)}$ by these past groupings may change through time as new items activate $\mathcal{F}^{(3)}$.

This principle is instantiated as follows. To simplify the discussion, let the feedforward signals from $\mathcal{F}^{(3)}$ to $\mathcal{F}^{(4)}$ (but not the internal feedback signals within $\mathcal{F}^{(3)}$ that control contrast enhancement and normalization) be linear functions of the STM activities across $\mathcal{F}^{(3)}$. At time t_i, the STM pattern

$$P_i = (x_1^{(3)}, x_2^{(3)}, . . . , x_i^{(3)}) \qquad (46)$$

is adaptively filtered by the LTM vectors z_j of all nodes $v_j^{(4)}$ in $\mathcal{F}^{(4)}$. By the LTM invariance principle, the relative sizes of *all* the dot products $S_j(t_i) = P_i(t_i) \cdot z_j \cdot (t_i)$ should not change when r_{i+1} occurs. In other words,

$$P_i(t_{i+1}) \cdot z_j(t_i) = \omega_{i+1} P_i(t_i) \cdot z_j(t_i) \qquad (47)$$

for all i and j, where ω_{i+1} is a proportionality constant that is independent of j. The LTM invariance principle thus implies that, after the STM traces $x_1^{(3)}, x_2^{(3)}, . . . , x_i^{(3)}$ are excited by the items $r_1, r_2, . . . , r_i$, they thereafter undergo proportional changes. The STM traces are shunted by multi-plicative factors ω_{i+1}, ω_{i+2}, . . . that are independent of j.

Table 6.1 describes rules for generating these changes. In the table, the ith item r_i is instated in STM at $v_i^{(3)}$ with activity μ_i. At every successive item representation, all past STM traces are simultaneously shunted by the amounts ω_{i+1}, then ω_{i+2}, and so on. The STM activity of the ith item r_i after r_j occurs ($i < j$) is thus

$$x_i^{(3)}(t_j) = \mu_i \prod_{k=i+1}^{j} \omega_k . \tag{48}$$

It remains to be shown how the shunting parameters ω_k can be ex-pressed in terms of the initial STM activities μ_i, where μ_i measures the amount of attention that is paid to r_i when it is first stored in STM. I accomplish this by using the fact that every shunting competitive network exhibits a normalization property to impose the following normalization rule.

The total STM activity across $\mathcal{F}^{(3)}$ after i items have been presented is

$$S_i = \mu_1 \phi_i + M(1 - \phi_i). \tag{49}$$

In Equation 49, ϕ_i is a positive decreasing function of i with $\phi_0 = 1$ and $\lim_{i \to \infty} \phi_i = 0$. By Equation 49, S_i grows from μ_1 to its asymptote $M(\geq \mu_1)$ as more items are stored. The *load parameters* ϕ_i estimate how close $\mathcal{F}^{(3)}$ is to saturating its total capacity. The load parameter ϕ_i estimate how close $\mathcal{F}^{(3)}$ is to saturating its total capacity. The load parameter ϕ_i also estimates how close $v_i^{(3)}$ is to the active item representations $v_1^{(3)}$, $v_2^{(3)}$, . . . , $v_{i-1}^{(3)}$ of previous events. A relatively large decrease of ϕ_i below ϕ_{i-1} means that $v_i^{(3)}$ gets activated with relatively little competition from previous items, due to the fact that r_i is represented in a different region of $\mathcal{F}^{(3)}$ than previous events. As more events are represented within $\mathcal{F}^{(3)}$, all regions of $\mathcal{F}^{(3)}$ become densely activated; hence $\lim_{i \to \infty} \phi_i = 0$. The special case $\phi_i = \theta^i$, where $0 < \theta < 1$, represents a field $\mathcal{F}^{(3)}$ whose activated item

Table 6.1
LTM Invariance Principle Constrains STM Activities of
Sequentially Activated Item Representations

	$x_1^{(3)}$	$x_2^{(3)}$	$x_3^{(3)}$	$x_4^{(3)}$
$t \simeq t_1$	μ_1	0	0	0
$t \simeq t_2$	$\mu_1\omega_2$	μ_2	0	0
$t \simeq t_3$	$\mu_1\omega_2\omega_3$	$\mu_2\omega_3$	μ_3	0

representations are uniformly spaced with respect to each other. In such a "homogeneous" field, $\phi_i/\phi_{i-1} = \theta$, which is independent of i.

By Equation 48, the total STM activity also equals

$$S_i = \sum_{j=1}^{i} \mu_j \prod_{k=j+1}^{i} \omega_k. \tag{50}$$

Equations 49 and 50 for S_i can be recursively identified to prove that the shunting weights satisfy the equation

$$\omega_k = \frac{S_k - \mu_k}{S_{k-1}} = \frac{\mu_1\phi_k + M(1 - \phi_k) - \mu_k}{\mu_1\phi_{k-1} + M(1 - \phi_{k-1})}, \tag{51}$$

$k = 1, 2, \ldots$. By Equations 48 and 51,

$$x_i^{(3)}(t_j) = \mu_i \prod_{k=i+1}^{j} \left[\frac{\mu_1\phi_k + M(1 - \phi_k) - \mu_k}{\mu_1\phi_{k-1} + M(1 - \phi_{k-1})} \right]. \tag{52}$$

Equation 52 characterizes STM across $\mathcal{F}^{(3)}$ for all time in terms of the attention paid to the items when they are stored (μ_i), the STM capacity of the network (M), and the load parameters (ϕ_i). Equation 52 can be rewritten in a way that suggests the relevance of probabilistic ideas to the STM temporal order problem. In terms of the notation $P_i(t_j) = x_i^{(3)}(t_j)S_j^{-1}$ and $p_i = \mu_i S_i^{-1}$, Equation 52 becomes

$$P_i(t_j) = p_i \prod_{k=i+1}^{j} (1 - p_k). \tag{53}$$

The STM patterns that evolve under the law in Equation 52 have been worked out in a number of cases (see Grossberg, 1978a, 1978e, Section 26). It is readily shown that a primacy effect often occurs in STM when a short subsequence of the list activates $\mathcal{F}^{(3)}$ but that this primacy effect is converted into an STM bow (primacy and recency effect) as more items are presented. For sufficiently long lists, the recency effect dominates the STM pattern. Multimodal bows, as in von Restorff STM effects, can also be generated under special circumstances.

All of the equations in this section have obvious generalizations to the case in which each item representation is distributed over many nodes. This is true because the shunting operations on the past field and the STM capacity of the network do not depend on how many nodes subserve each item representation. The same is true of the equations in the next section.

XXXV. TRANSIENT MEMORY SPAN, GROUPING, AND INTENSITY–TIME TRADEOFFS

Some remarks may help the reader to think about these STM results before I consider their implications for what is encoded in LTM. Given a fixed choice of the attentional sequence $\mu_1, \mu_2, \ldots$; the capacity M; and the inhibitory design $\phi_1, \phi_2, \ldots$, it follows that if $r_1, r_2, \ldots, r_K$ is the longest sublist that causes a primacy effect in STM, then every longer sublist $r_1, r_2, \ldots, r_K, r_{K+1}, \ldots, r_i$ will cause an STM bow at item r_K. I call K the *transient memory span* (TMS) of the list. The TMS is the longest sublist that can be directly read out of STM in the correct order. In Grossberg (1978e), I proved under weak conditions that the TMS is always shorter than the more familiar immediate memory span (IMS), which also benefits from LTM read-out. A typical choice of these parameters is TMS $\cong$ 4 and IMS $\cong$ 7 (Miller, 1956). One way to guarantee a correct read-out from STM without requiring template feedback from LTM is to rehearse the list items in subsequences, or groups, of a length no greater than the TMS.

In assigning the values μ_i and ω_k to the STM traces $x_i^{(3)}$, I have tacitly assumed that the times t_i at which items r_i are presented are sufficiently separated to enable these values to reach asymptote. If presentation rates are rapid, then only partial activations may occur, leading to weights of the form

$$\mu_i^* = \mu_i(1 - e^{-\lambda_i T_i}), \tag{54}$$

where λ_i is the rate of activation and $T_i = t_i - t_{i-1}$. Then the STM traces become

$$x_i^{(3)}(t_j) = \mu_i^* \prod_{k=i+1}^{j} \omega_k^*, \tag{55}$$

where by Equation 51,

$$\omega_k^* = \frac{\mu_1^* \phi_k + M(1 - \phi_k) - \mu_k^*}{\mu_1^* \phi_{k-1} + M(1 - \phi_{k-1})}. \tag{56}$$

Due to Equation 54, an intensity–time tradeoff, or Bloch's law (Repp, 1979), holds that may alter the STM pattern across $\mathcal{F}^{(3)}$ under conditions of rapid presentation. Such a tradeoff can limit the accuracy with which temporal order information is encoded in STM, most obviously by preventing some items from being stored in STM at all because they receive inadequate activation to exceed the network QT.

XXXVI. BACKWARD EFFECTS AND EFFECTS OF RATE ON RECALL ORDER

Two more subtle interactions of intensity and rate are worth noting. If items are rapidly presented but some are more drawn out than others, then the relative sizes of the STM activities can be changed. By changing the STM patterns across $\mathcal{F}^{(3)}$, the STM pattern across $\mathcal{F}^{(4)}$ that is caused by the adaptive filter $\mathcal{F}^{(3)} \rightarrow \mathcal{F}^{(4)}$ can also be changed. This STM pattern determines item recognition. Thus a change in rates can cause a contextually induced change in perception. In examples wherein items are built up from consonant and vowel sequences, a relative change in the duration of a later vowel may thus alter the perception of a prior consonant (Miller & Liberman, 1979; Schwab et al., 1981). Such examples support the hypothesis that STM patterns of temporal order information over item representation control network perception, not activations of individual nodes.

A uniform but rapid activation rate can alter both the items that are recalled and the order in which they are recalled. Suppose that the network is instructed to pay attention to a list during an attentional window of fixed duration. Whereas a slower presentation rate may allow a smaller number of items to be processed during this duration, a faster presentation rate may allow a larger number of items to be processed. In the former case, a primacy effect in STM may be encoded; hence correct read-out of order information from STM is anticipated. In the latter case, a bow in STM may be encoded. A fast rate may increase the number of items processed and thereby cause an STM bow in which items near the list middle are recalled worst (Grossberg, 1978a). A fast rate may also cause an STM bow in processing a fixed number of items if attention must be switched to the items as they are presented. Then the items near the list beginning and end may be recalled worst (Grossberg and Stone, 1986b; Reeves and Sperling, 1986; Sperling and Reeves, 1980).

XXXVII. SEEKING THE MOST PREDICTIVE REPRESENTATION: ALL LETTERS AND WORDS ARE LISTS

The LTM invariance principle indicates how a competitive shunting network can instate temporal order information in STM without destabilizing the LTM filters that learn from the STM patterns. We now ask how the outputs from all of these filters are interpreted at the next processing stage $\mathcal{F}^{(4)}$. How does $\mathcal{F}^{(4)}$ know which of its filtered inputs represent reliable data on which to base its output decisions? How does $\mathcal{F}^{(4)}$ select the codes for those sublists across $\mathcal{F}^{(3)}$ that are most predictive of the future? How does $\mathcal{F}^{(4)}$ know how to automatically group, or parse, the total event list represented across $\mathcal{F}^{(3)}$ into sublists that have the best a priori chance of predicting the future within the context defined by the unique past represented by that list?

The next few sections indicate how to design $\mathcal{F}^{(4)}$ so that its best predictive sublist chunks are assigned the greatest STM activity; how these most predictive chunks are differentially tuned by adaptive filtering and differentially gain control of predictive commands; how less predictive chunks are rapidly masked by more predictive chunks, therefore preventing the less predictive chunks from interfering with performance and enabling them to remain uncommitted by learning until they are unmasked in a different context where they are better predictors; how the masking due to predictive sublist chunks compresses the LTM code, computes a "magic number 7" (Miller, 1956), and changes the time scale of STM reset—and thus of LTM prediction—within the subfield of unmasked chunks; how the predictive recognition chunks remain uninhibited by rehearsal, since otherwise they could not sample the sequences to be learned and recalled; and how the predictive chunks can be directly inhibited only by other predictive chunks—say, those activated by new sensory feedback, or by nonspecific gain changes due to attention shifts.

The design of this field thus addresses the fundamental question of how "our conscious awareness . . . is driven to the highest level present in the stimulus" (Darwin, 1976). In contrast to the distinction made by McClelland and Rumelhart (1981) between a separate letter level and a word level (Section II), I suggest that "all letters and words are lists," indeed that all unitized events capable of being represented in $\mathcal{F}^{(4)}$ exist on an equal dynamical footing. This conclusion clarifies how changes in the context of a verbal item can significantly alter the processing of that item, and why the problem of identifying functional units has proved to be so perplexing (Studdert-Kennedy, 1980). In $\mathcal{F}^{(4)}$, no common verbal descriptor of the functional unit, such as phoneme or syllable or letter or word, has a privileged existence. Only the STM patterns of unitized chunks that survive the context-sensitive interaction between associative and competitive rules have a concrete existence. These rules instantiate principles of predictive stability that transcend the distinctions of lay language.

Before describing these rules, I should state what they do not imply. Despite the fact that "all letters and words are lists," a subject can be differentially set to respond to letters rather than words, numbers rather than letters, and so on. Such a capability involves the activation of learned top-down expectancies that selectively sensitize some internal representations more than others. Thus the phrase "all letters and words are lists" is a conclusion about the laws of unitization that letters and words share, not about the top-down attentional and expectational processes that can flexibly modulate the STM and LTM traces that these laws define.

XXXVIII. SPATIAL FREQUENCY ANALYSIS OF TEMPORAL PATTERNS BY A MASKING FIELD: WORD LENGTH AND SUPERIORITY

The main idea is to join together results about positional gradients, lateral masking, and multiple spatial frequency scales to synthesize an $\mathcal{F}^{(4)}$ network—called a *masking field*—that selectively amplifies the STM of $\mathcal{F}^{(4)}$ chunks representing longer sublists at the expense of chunks representing shorter sublists, other things being equal, up to some optimal sequence length (Grossberg, 1978e). Each of these three types of concepts can also be used to analyze aspects of spatial visual processing (Ganz, 1975; Robson, 1975). The network $\mathcal{F}^{(4)}$ thus illustrates that the same mechanisms can be specialized to do either spatial processing or temporal processing.

The results of Samuel et al. (1982, 1983) on a word length effect in word superiority studies were published after the first draft of this chapter was completed. That is, a letter is better recognized as it is embedded in longer words of lengths from 1 to 4. These authors write: "One could posit that the activation of a word is a function of the evidence present for it; more letters could provide more evidence for a word. Very short words would be at an inherent disadvantage, since they only receive a limited amount of support" (Samuel et al., 1983, p. 322). Both their data and their intuitive interpretation support the properties of word processing by a masking field developed in Grossberg (1978e). To clarify the critical issue of how "evidence" is defined to imply a word length effect, I have expanded my review of this issue in the subsequent sections, notably of how $\mathcal{F}^{(4)}$ chunks that represent longer item lists may mask $\mathcal{F}^{(4)}$ chunks that represent shorter item $\mathcal{F}^{(4)}$ lists. Several other predictions in Grossberg (1978e) have not yet been experimentally tested. Some of these predictions concern the rules of neuronal development whereby a masking field is self-organized. My expanded review forms a bridge between these and related levels of description.

XXXIX. THE TEMPORAL CHUNKING PROBLEM

The need for masking rules that are sensitive to the length of a list of items can be understood by considering the *temporal chunking problem:*

Suppose that an unfamiliar list of familiar items is sequentially presented (e.g., a novel word composed of familiar letters). In terms of frequency and familiarity, the most familiar units in the list are the items themselves. The first item starts to be processed before the whole list is even presented. What prevents processing of the first familiar item from blocking the chunking of the unfamiliar list? Another way to state this problem is as follows: In order to completely process a novel list, all of its individual items must first be presented. All of the items are more familiar than the list itself. What prevents item familiarity from forcing the list to always be processed as a sequence of individual items, rather than eventually as a unitized whole?

The temporal chunking problem is only recognized as a serious constraint on processing design when one analyzes frontally how wordlike representations are learned in response to serially scanned sound streams or visual letter arrays. To overcome this problem, somehow the sequence as a whole uses prewired processing biases to overcome, or mask, the learned salience of its constituent items.

The type of masking that I need goes beyond the usual masking models. To emphasize what is new, I briefly review some earlier masking models. The seminal model of Weisstein (1968, 1972) is a model of contrast enhancement. Ganz (1975) modified Weisstein's model to avoid its assumption that inhibition acts faster than excitation. Ganz's (1975) trace-decay-and-lateral-inhibition model is a special case of Equation 6. This model does not, however, discuss how the signal thresholds or LTM traces in Equation 6 interact with STM trace decay and lateral inhibition to alter a network's reaction time in response to target-then-mask. These factors were used by Grossberg (1969c) to provide a unified account of masking and performance speed-up due to learning. In this model, performance speed-up due to learning is a variant of the fan effect (Section II): An increase in a pathway's LTM trace amplifies signals in the pathway; these amplified signals more vigorously activate their receptive node; node activity therefore grows more rapidly and exceeds the output threshold of the node more quickly. The existence of more competing nodes can cause a larger total inhibitory signal to be received by each node; the net rate of growth of activity at each node is thereby decreased; node activity therefore exceeds the output threshold of the node less quickly. These properties also hold in the masking model that I now discuss.

This masking model is not just a model of contrast enhancement. It was introduced to analyze how developmental and attentional biases can alter competitive decision making before STM storage occurs (Grossberg & Levine, 1975). The model was extended to explain certain normative visual illusions, such as neutralization (Gibson, 1937; Levine & Grossberg, 1976). Both investigations analyzed how the STM decision process is altered by giving subsets of nodes different numbers of excitable sites, differentially amplified interaction strengths, and/or broader spatial interactions in shunting networks of the form

$$
\frac{\mathrm{d}}{\mathrm{dt}} x_i = -Ax_i + (B_i - x_i) \left[I_i + \sum_{k=1}^{n} f_k(x_k)C_{ki} \right]
$$
$$
- (x_i + D) \left[J_i + \sum_{k=1}^{n} f_k(x_k)E_{ki} \right],
\tag{57}
$$

$i = 1, 2, \ldots, n$, which are a special case of Equation 34. In these networks, a larger choice of coding sites B_i, or of shunting signals F_i in $f_i(x_i) = f(F_i x_i)$, or of spatial frequencies C_{ik} and E_{ik} endows a node v_i with the ability to mask the STM activities of nodes v_k with smaller parameters. The control of masking by parameters such as B_i, F_i, or E_{ik} is not the same process as contrast enhancement, since the latter is controlled by the choice of the signal function $f(w)$ (Grossberg, 1973).

We discovered that a subtle interaction exists between the choice of parameters and signal functions. A linear signal function $f(w)$ can cause the STM activities of all nodes with smaller parameters to be inhibited to zero no matter how big their STM activities start out relative to the STM activities of nodes with larger parameters. In such a network, structural or attentional biases (larger parameters) win out over the intensities or learned salience of individual cues (larger initial activities). This unsatisfactory state of affairs is overcome by using a sigmoid signal function $f(w)$, in which case nodes with sufficiently large initial activities can mask nodes with larger parameters but smaller initial activities. Thus a flexible tug-of-war between stimulus factors, like intensity or learned salience, and structural factors, like the number of coding sites or spatial frequencies, exists if a nonlinear signal is used but not if a linear signal function is used. This fact poses yet another challenge to linear models.

Masking, as opposed to mere contrast enhancement, thus occurs in networks whose nodes are partitioned into subfields. Within each subfield, each node possesses (approximately) the same parameters. The interactions between nodes in different subfields are biased by the differences between subfield parameters.

XL. THE MASKING FIELD: JOINING TEMPORAL ORDER TO DIFFERENTIAL MASKING VIA AN ADAPTIVE FILTER

Although these masking insights were originally derived to study spatial processing in vision, I soon realized that they are useful, indeed crucial,

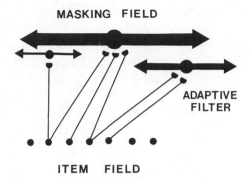

Figure 6.20 Selective activation of a masking field. The nodes in a masking field are organized so that longer item sequences, up to some optimal length, activate nodes with more potent masking properties. Individual items, as well as item sequences, are represented in the masking field. The text describes how the desired relationship between item field, masking field, and the intervening adaptive filter can be self-organized using surprisingly simple developmental rules.

for the study of temporal processing in language and motor control (Grossberg, 1978e). This realization came in stages. First I showed how the LTM invariance principle can be used to generate STM temporal order information over item representations (Section XXXIV). A spatial pattern of STM activity over a set of item representations in $\mathcal{F}^{(3)}$ encodes this information. As more items are presented, a new spatial pattern is registered that includes a larger region of the item field $\mathcal{F}^{(3)}$. The main insight is thus to translate the *temporal* processing of a list of items into a problem about a succession of expanding *spatial* patterns.

Given this insight, the temporal chunking problem can be translated as follows. How do chunks in $\mathcal{F}^{(4)}$ that encode broader regions of the item field $\mathcal{F}^{(3)}$ mask $\mathcal{F}^{(4)}$ chunks that encode narrower regions of $\mathcal{F}^{(3)}$? Phrased in this way, the relevance of the masking field results becomes obvious, because these results show how subfields with larger parameters can mask subfields with smaller parameters. Putting together these ideas about item coding and masking, the temporal chunking problem leads to the following design constraint: *Sequence masking principle:* Broader regions of the item field $\mathcal{F}^{(3)}$ are filtered in such a way that they selectively excite $\mathcal{F}^{(4)}$ nodes with larger parameters (Figure 6.20).

XLI. THE PRINCIPLE OF SELF-SIMILARITY AND THE MAGIC NUMBER 7

In order to realize this functional property in a computationally effective way, some specialized design problems must be solved. First, the masking parameters must be chosen self-consistently. It is inadmissible to allow a node v_i's larger number of sites B_i cancel the masking effect of its smaller spatial frequency E_{ik}. Nodes with more sites need to have broader interactions, other things being equal. This numerical constraint is a special case of a design principle that reappears in several guises throughout my work—the so-called *principle of self-similarity* (Grossberg, 1969e, 1982d). Every use of the principle suggests a different example wherein a local rule for designing individual cells achieves a global property that enhances the operating power of the entire network.

In the present usage, self-similarity means that nodes with larger parameters are excited only by longer sublists. Due to their self-consistent parameters, these nodes can be efectively inhibited only by other nodes that are also excited by longer sublists. Self-similarity thus introduces a pre-wired partial ordering among subfields such that the nodes activated by longer sublists can inhibit the nodes activated by shorter (and related) sublists, but not conversely, unless this partial ordering is modified through learning.

More list items need to be presented to activate a long-list node than a short-list node. Thus many more list items need to be presented to activate the same number of long-list nodes as short-list nodes. Since long-list nodes can be masked only by other long-list nodes, such nodes can remain active long enough to sample many more future events than can short-list nodes.

This last property shows how self-similarity enhances the network's predictive power. The network takes a risk by allowing any node to remain active for a long time. If the node samples inappropriate information on a given trial, on its next activation it can read out errors far into the future. This risk is minimized by letting the long-list nodes stay active the longest, because these nodes are better characterized by the temporal context (list length) into which they are embedded. Self-similarity is thus a structural constraint on individual nodes that enables the network as a whole to resolve uncertain input data without taking untoward predictive risks.

The abstract property of self-similarity also helps to explain a classic experimental property of human information processing, namely Miller's (1956) "magic number seven, plus or minus two." This is because the total length of the lists that can simultaneously be coded by a prescribed subfield increases with the total length of the sublists that can be chunked by the nodes of the subfield. Grossberg (1978e) discusses these properties in greater detail, notably their effects on word recognition, code compression, recall clustering effects, and the synthesis of predictive motor commands leading to rapid planned performance.

XLII. DEVELOPMENTAL EQUILIBRATION OF THE ADAPTIVE FILTER AND ITS TARGET MASKING FIELD

It remains for me to explain how the conditionable pathways that form the adaptive filter from the item field $\mathscr{F}^{(3)}$ to the masking field $\mathscr{F}^{(4)}$ generate the desired sublist masking properties. This explanation cannot merely offer formal rules for connecting the two fields. To be convincing, it must show how the connections can be established by growth rules that are simple enough to hold in vivo. The rules stated here thus amount to predictions about brain development in language-related anatomies.

The main properties to be achieved are all tacitly stated in the sequence masking principle. They may be broken down as follows:

1. *List representation*—The unordered sets of items in all realizable item lists, up to a maximal list length, are initially represented in the masking field.
2. *Masking parameters increase with list length*—The masking parameters of masking field nodes increase with the length of the item lists that activate them. This rule holds until an optimal list length is reached.
3. *Masking hierarchy*—A node that is activated by a given item list can mask nodes that are activated by sublists of this list.
4. *List selectivity*—If a node's trigger list has length n, it cannot be supraliminally activated by lists of length significantly less than n.

Properties 1 and 2 suggest that the adaptive filter contains a profusion of pathways that are scattered broadly over the masking field. Property 3 suggests that closely related lists activate nearby nodes in the masking field. Postulate 4 says that, despite the profusion of connections, long list nodes are tuned not to respond to short sublists.

The main problem is to resolve the design tension between profuse connections and list selectivity. This tension must be resolved both for short-list (e.g., letter) and long-list (e.g., word) nodes: If connections are profuse, why aren't short-list nodes unselective? In other words, what prevents many different item nodes from converging on every short-list node and thus being able to activate it? And if many item nodes do converge on long-list nodes, why aren't these long-list nodes activated by sublists of the items? Somehow the number of item nodes that contact a list node is calibrated to match the output threshold of the list node. A combination of random growth rules for pathways and self-similar growth rules for list nodes can be shown to achieve all of these properties (Cohen and Grossberg, 1986a; Grossberg, 1978c).

Suppose that each item node of $\mathscr{F}^{(3)}$ sends out a large number of randomly distributed pathways toward the list nodes of $\mathscr{F}^{(4)}$. Suppose further that an item node contacts a list node with a prescribed small probability p. This probability is small because there are many more list nodes than item nodes. Let λ be the mean number of such contacts across all of the list nodes. The probability that exactly k pathways contact a given list node is given by the Poisson distribution

$$P_k = \frac{\lambda^k e^{-\lambda}}{k!}. \tag{58}$$

If K is chosen so that $K < \lambda < K + 1$, then P_k is an increasing function of k if $1 \le k \le K$ and a decreasing function of k if $k \ge K$. Thus lists of length k no greater than the optimal length K are represented within the masking field, thereby satisfying properties 1 and 2. Other random growth rules, such as the hypergeometric distribution, also have similar properties. Due to the broad and random distribution of pathways, list nodes will tend to be clustered near nodes corresponding to their sublists, thereby tending to satisfy property 3.

XLIII. THE SELF-SIMILAR GROWTH RULE AND THE OPPOSITES ATTRACT RULE

To discuss property 4, I interpret each list node as a population of cell sites. This population may consist of many neurons, each of which possesses many sites. For simplicity, I consider only a single neuron in such a population.

A list node that receives k pathways somehow dilutes the input due to each pathway so that (almost) all k pathways must be active to generate a suprathreshold response. As k increases, the amount of dilution also increases. This property suggests that long-list cells have larger cellular volumes, since a larger volume can more effectively dilute a signal due to a single output pathway. Larger volumes also permit more pathways to reach the cell's surface, other things being equal. The formal constraint that long-list nodes are associated with larger parameters, such as number of sites and spatial frequencies, is thus extended to a physical instantiation wherein more sites exist partly because the cells have larger surface areas. This conclusion reaffirms the importance of the self-similarity principle in designing a masking field: A cell has longer interactions (e.g., axons) because it has a larger cell body to support them.

How do larger cell surfaces attract more pathways, whereas smaller cell surfaces attract fewer pathways? This property is not as obvious as it may seem. Without further argument, a cell surface that is densely encrusted with axon terminals might easily be fired by a small subset of these axons. To avoid this possibility, the number of allowable pathways must be tuned so that the cell is never overloaded by excitation.

There exist two main ways to guarantee this condition. I favor the second way, but a combination of the two is also conceivable:

1. At an early stage of development, a spectrum of cell sizes is endogenously generated across the masking field by a developmental program. Each cell of a given size contains a proportional number of membrane organelles that can migrate and differentiate into mature membrane receptors in response to developing input pathways (Patterson & Purves, 1982). The number of membrane organelles is regulated to prevent the internal level of cell excitation (as measured, say, by the maximum ratio of free internal Na^+ to K^+ ions) from becoming too large.

2. Pathways from the item field grow to the list nodes via random growth rules. Due to random growth, some cells are contacted by more pathways than others. Before these pathways reach their target cells, these cells are of approximately the same size. As longer item lists begin to be processed by the item field, these lists activate their respective list nodes. The target cells experience an abnormal internal cellular milieu (e.g., abnormally high internal Na^+/K^+ concentration ratios) due to the convergence of many active pathways on the small cell volumes. These large internal signals gradually trigger self-similar cell growth that continues until the cell and its processes grow large enough to reduce the maximal internal signal to normal levels.

The tuning of cell volumes in $\mathcal{F}^{(4)}$ to the number of converging afferent pathways from $\mathcal{F}^{(3)}$ is thus mediated by a self-similar use-and-disuse growth rule. Grossberg (1969e) proposed such a rule for cell growth to satisfy general properties of cellular homeostasis. In the present application, the fact that internal cellular indices of membrane excitation can trigger cell growth until these indices equilibrate to normal levels suggests why the mature cell needs simultaneous activation from most of its pathways before it can fire.

A self-similar growth rule has many appealing properties. Most notably, only item lists that occur in a speaker's language during the critical growth period will be well represented by the chunks of the speaker's masking field. This fact may be relevant to properties of second language learning. If input excitation continues to maintain cell volume throughout the life of the cell, partial transaction of the cell's input pathways should induce a partial reduction in cell volume. Moreover, if the transient memory span of the item field equals K (Section XXXV), the optimal chunk length in the masking field should also approximate K. In other words, the chunk lengths (in the masking field $\mathscr{F}^{(4)}$) to which the speaker is sensitive are tuned by the lengths of item sequences (in the item field $\mathscr{F}^{(3)}$) that the speaker can recall directly out of STM.

A second issue concerning the developmental self-organization of the masking field is the following: How does each masking subfield know how to choose inhibitory pathways that are strong enough to carry out efficient masking but not so strong as to prevent any list from activating the masking field? I have predicted (Grossberg, 1978e, Section 45) that this type of property is developmentally controlled by an "opposites attract" rule, whereby excitatory sites attract inhibitory pathways and inhibitory sites attract excitatory pathways. The prediction suggests how intracellular parameters can regulate the attracting morphogens in such a way that balanced on-center, off-surround pathways result.

It remains to illustrate how constraints on list length, masking hierarchy, and list selectivity can be computationally realized in a network such as that in Equation 57. Cohen and Grossberg (1986a, 1986b) describe computer simulations that demonstrate all the desired properties of a masking field. This masking field obeys equations of the form

$$
\frac{d}{dt} x_i^{(J)} = -A x_i^{(J)} + (B - x_i^{(J)}) \left[\sum_{j \in J} I_j p_{ji}^{(J)} + D_{|J|} f(x_i^{(J)}) \right]
$$
$$
- (x_i^{(J)} + C) \sum_{m,K} g(x_m^{(K)}) F_{|J|} G_{|K|} H_{|K \cap J|}.
$$
(59)

In Equation 59, $x_i^{(J)}$ is the STM activity of the ith cell in $\mathscr{F}^{(4)}$ which receives input pathways from only the item representations of items r_i, $i \in J$, where J is an unordered set of indices. Notation $|J|$ denotes the size of set J. Thus interaction coefficients such as $D_{|J|}$ and $F_{|J|}$ depend only upon the size of the set J of items, not upon the items themselves. These coefficients are chosen to satisfy the growth constraints

$$
\sum_{j \in J} p_{ji}^{(J)} = \text{constant} \quad \text{and} \quad \sum_{m,K} F_{|J|} G_{|K|} H_{|K \cap J|} = \text{constant}. \quad (60)
$$

XLIV. AUTOMATIC PARSING, LEARNED SUPERIORITY EFFECTS, AND SERIAL POSITION EFFECTS DURING PATTERN COMPLETION

I now summarize some of the psychological implications of masking field dynamics. As a list of items is presented to the item field $\mathscr{F}^{(3)}$, the encoding of the list will be updated continuously. At every time, the most predictive chunks of the list that is active at that moment will rapidly mask the activities of less predictive chunks, even though these less predictive chunks may have been dominant in an earlier temporal context. As the total list length exceeds the maximal length of any sublist encoded within the masking field $\mathcal{F}^{(4)}$, the network will automatically parse the total list into that grouping of sublists that can best survive mutual masking across $\mathcal{F}^{(4)}$.

Both of these properties are influenced by learning in important ways. For example, suppose that a given list is familiar to the network (e.g., a familiar word) but that none of its sublists has ever been individually presented to the network. In the $\mathcal{F}^{(3)} \rightarrow \mathcal{F}^{(4)}$ adaptive filter, the pattern of LTM traces corresponding to the chunk of the whole list will be much better tuned than the LTM patterns corresponding to any sublist chunk. This is because rapid masking of all sublist chunks by the whole list has occurred on all learning trials (Section XXIII). Consequently, on recall trials a sufficiently large sublist of the list may activate the chunk corresponding to the whole list rather than its own sublist chunk. This property is due to the differential amplification of the $\mathcal{F}^{(3)} \rightarrow \mathcal{F}^{(4)}$ signals that correspond to the tuned LTM traces of the list chunk. This whole-list pattern completion effect should be weaker in situations wherein the sublists are also familiar lists (e.g., familiar word embedded in familiar word) due to three factors working together: the stronger relative amplification of the sublist chunks by their tuned LTM patterns, the greater innate ease with which a sublist can activate a sublist chunk than a list chunk, and the possibility that nodes with smaller parameters can mask nodes with larger parameters if they receive larger inputs (Section XXXIX). These properties also indicate how a familiar word in a nonword may be recognized.

Which sublist of a list can best activate the full list code? Often the answer is the sublists concentrated at the beginning and end of a list. This is because the pattern of STM temporal order information across $\mathcal{F}^{(3)}$ often exhibits a primacy effect, a recency effect, or an STM bow (Section XXXIV). Thus the strongest STM activities are often at either end of a list. As the LTM pattern of a list chunk becomes parallel through learning to its STM pattern at $\mathcal{F}^{(3)}$, the largest LTM traces correspond to items at the list beginning and end. These large LTM traces are the ones capable of selectively amplifying sublist items. Rumelhart and McClelland (1982) report serial bowing effects in their data on word recognition. However, their model does not explain these data without the benefit of auxiliary hypotheses (see Lawry & LaBerge, 1981, for related data). If certain sublists are practiced often, their LTM patterns will preferentially activate the corresponding sublist chunks in the STM struggle across $\mathcal{F}^{(4)}$.

Different parsings of the same list can thus be determined by changing the alphabet of practiced sublists.

Once a given parsing of sublist codes across $\mathscr{F}^{(4)}$ starts to be activated, it delivers template feedback to $\mathscr{F}^{(3)}$. Word superiority effects (Johnston & McClelland, 1974) are abetted by the larger parameters of long lists, although there exists a tradeoff in reaction time measures of superiority between how long it takes to supraliminally activate a list code and the strength of its top-down feedback. The list length prediction has received experimental support from Samuel et al. (1982, 1983). A template explanation of word superiority is also suggested by Rumelhart and McClelland (1982). There are at least two important differences between our theories. As I noted in Section I, Rumelhart and McClelland (1982) postulate the existence of distinct letter and word levels, and connect letters and words to each other in different ways. My theory replaces letter and word levels by item and list levels, and connects these levels in a different way than would be appropriate if letter and word levels existed. These theories are fundamentally different both in their levels and in their interactions. For example, in a model using letter and word levels, letters such as A and I which are also words are represented on both levels, but letters such as K and L are represented only on the letter level. It remains unclear how such a distinction can be learned without using a homunculus. In contrast, in a model using item and list levels, all familiar letters are represented on both levels, because "all letters and words are lists." Although both letters and words can activate list chunks, they do so with varying degrees of ease due to differences in the spatial and temporal contexts into which they have been embedded.

This fact leads to a second major difference between our theories. Rumelhart and McClelland (1982) consider only four-letter words and do not discuss the role of learning. Therefore, they cannot easily explain how a familiar three-letter word in a four-letter nonword is processed. Instead of being able to use the *parametric biases* due to sublist length, learning, and so on in the coding of individual subsequences, they must derive all of the processing differences between words, pseudowords, and nonwords from differences in the number of activated words in their network hierarchy. This type of explanation does not seem capable of explaining the word length effect. Grossberg (1984b) and Grossberg and Stone (1986a) describe other differences between the theories and their ability to explain word recognition data.

The present theory suggests some of the operations that may prevent a word superiority effect from occurring (Chastain, 1982). Of particular interest is the manner in which attentional factors can modulate this effect. For example, suppose that a subject gives differential attention to the first item in a string, thus amplifying the corresponding item representation in STM. When the adaptive filter responds to the whole list of items, the input to the sublist code that corresponds to the first item is differentially amplified. The additional salience of this sublist code enables it to compete more effectively with the sublist codes of longer list chunks. This competition weakens the activation of the longer chunks in $\mathcal{F}^{(4)}$ and enables the item chunk to generate relatively more the template feedback to $\mathcal{F}^{(3)}$. Item chunk feedback is also the primary source of template feedback when a string of unrelated letters is presented. Attentional processes enter this explanation in two mechanistically distinct but interdependent ways. Attentional mechanisms amplify the item representation in $\mathcal{F}^{(3)}$. Template feedback is also an attentional mechanism but one that is capable of acting on a more global scale of processing. The two attentional mechanisms are linked via the adaptive filter and the masking field.

XLV. GRAY CHIPS OR GREAT SHIPS?

The resonant feedback dynamics between $\mathcal{F}^{(3)}$ and $\mathcal{F}^{(4)}$ also help to explain the interesting findings of Repp et al. (1978). By varying the fricative noise and silence durations in *gray ship*, they found that "given sufficient silence, listeners report GRAY CHIP when the noise is short but GREAT SHIP when it is long" (Repp et al., 1978, p. 621). There exists "a trading relation between silence and noise durations. As noise increases more silence is needed . . . For equivalent noise durations, more silence was needed in the fast sentence frame than in the slow sentence frame to convert the fricative into an affricative" (Repp et al., 1978, p. 625).

Part of an explanation for this phenomenon depends on the fact that articulatory acts influence which "feature detectors" are tuned by auditory feedback (Section XXX). Auditory experience of articulatory acts thus determines not only what item representations of $\mathcal{F}^{(3)}$ will be activated, but also what sequence representations of $\mathcal{F}^{(4)}$ will be activated. Another part of the explanation uses the fact that the list codes in $\mathcal{F}^{(4)}$ group together and perceptually complete auditory signals into familiar articulatory configurations via learned template feedback to $\mathcal{F}^{(3)}$. A subtle issue here is that a particular completion by template feedback is often contingent on the receipt of at least partially confirmatory auditory cues. Yet another part of the explanation uses the fact that a speed-up of speaking rate may alter commensurately all STM activities across $\mathcal{F}^{(3)}$ by changing all the item integration times, as in Equation 54. Due to the LTM invariance principle, a sufficiently uniform speed-up may not significantly alter the list codes selected across $\mathcal{F}^{(4)}$ (Section XXXV) after constrast enhancement has acted to generate tuned categories (Section XXII). Thus "judgments of phonetic structure and tempo are not independent, but are made simultaneously and interactively" (Miller, 1981, p. 69).

Finally, we come to the role of silence, which I consider the most challenging aspect of these data. Silence is not a passive state of "nothingness"; it is an active state that reflects the temporal context in which it is placed. Apart from the featural properties of silence as a temporal boundary to activity pattern onsets and offsets, I believe that the trading relationship reflects the fact that the nonspecific gain of $\mathcal{F}^{(4)}$ is higher during rapid speech than during slower speech and that this gain varies on a slower time scale than the onset or offset of an individual auditory cue. Recall from Section XXIII that a nonspecific gain control signal accompanies each specific cue to regulate the network QT or, equivalently, to renormalize the total operating load on the network (see also Grossberg, 1978e, Section 59). Such a variation of gain with speech rate can partially compensate for a decrease in integration times T_i by increasing λ_i in Equation 54 and decreasing ϕ_k in Equation 56. Thus the effects of a given duration of silence can be interpreted only by knowing the context-sensitive gain that calibrates the processing rates of auditory cues which bound the silence. These properties need to be studied further in numerical simulations.

XLVI. SENSORY RECOGNITION VERSUS MOTOR RECALL: NETWORK LESIONS AND AMNESIAS

This chapter's summary of the temporal coding designs that are presently known is incomplete. One also needs to build up analogous machinery to chunk the temporal order of motor commands and then to show how sensory and motor chunks are interconnected via associative maps. Only in this fashion can a full understanding of the differences and relationships between sensory recognition and motor recall be achieved.

The partial independence of sensory and motor temporal order mechanisms is perhaps best shown through the behavior of amnesic patients (Butters & Squire, 1983). Formal amnesic syndromes that are strikingly reminiscent of real amnesic syndromes can be generated in the networks of the present theory. For example, cutting out the source of orienting arousal in Figure 6.15 generates a network that shares many symptoms of medial temporal amnesia, and cutting out the source of incentive motivational feedback in network models of motivated behavior generates a syndrome characterized by flat affect and impaired transfer from sensory

STM to LTM (Grossberg, 1971, 1975, 1982b). Both of these lesions are interpreted as occurring in formal network analogs of hippocampus and other closely related structures.

Grossberg (1978e, Section 34) analyzes a network (Figure 6.19) in which sensory and motor temporal coding mechanisms are associatively joined to allow updating of internal representations to take place during the learning and performance of planned action sequences. The next section supplements these designs by outlining some related concepts about rhythm.

XLVII. FOUR TYPES OF RHYTHM: THEIR REACTION TIMES AND AROUSAL SOURCES

I believe that humans possess at least four mechanistically distinct sources of rhythmic capability. The on–off rebounds within specialized gated dipole circuits can be used to generate endogenous rhythms (Carpenter and Grossberg, 1983a, 1983b, 1984, 1985), as in the periodic rhythms of agonist–antagonistic motor contractions. For example, suppose that the on-cell of a gated dipole is perturbed to get a rhythm started. A few controlled on-cell inputs at a fixed rate can determine the nonspecific arousal level (Figure 6.21), which then feeds back to maintain an automatic on–off oscillation at the same rate, as in walking, until the arousal level is inhibited. Willed changes in the arousal level can continuously modulate the frequency of the oscillation after it gets going. When successive dipole fields in a network hierarchy interact mutually, they can also mutually entrain one another in a rhythmic fashion (Grossberg, 1978f). A deep understanding of this type of entrainment requires further numerical and mathematical study of the nonlinear dynamics of interacting dipole fields.

In a related type of rhythm generator, source cells excite themselves with positive feedback signals and inhibit other source cells via inhibitory interneurons that temporally average outputs from the source cells. In these on-center off-surround networks, the temporal averaging by inhibitory interneurons replaces the temporal averaging by transmitter gates which occur in a gated dipole. A nonspecific arousal signal which equally excites all the source cells energizes the rhythm and acts as a velocity signal. Ellias and Grossberg (1975) showed that in-phase oscillations can occur when the arousal level is relatively small. As the arousal level is increased, these in-phase oscillations occur with higher frequency. When a critical arousal level is reached, a Hopf bifurcation occurs. Out-of-phase oscillations then occur at increasingly high frequency as the arousal level

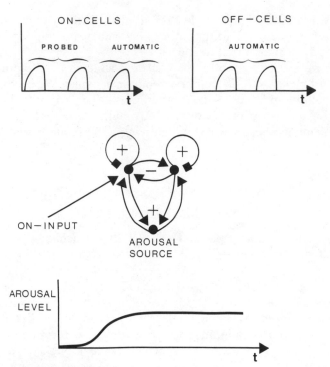

Figure 6.21   A feedback gated dipole as a rhythm generator: A few evenly spaced on-inputs to the gated dipole start an out-of-phase oscillation going between on-cells and off-cells. Both types of cells can activate the nonspecific arousal node which has been sensitized by an act of will. The period of the rhythm sets the average level of arousal, which in turn perpetuates the rhythm until the arousal node is inhibited or further excited to speed up the rhythm.

is further increased. Such results suggest an approach towards understanding how changes in motor gait are controlled by spinal circuits which automatically interpret a simple descending velocity signal by changing both the frequency and the patterning of motor outflow signals to several limbs (Grillner, 1975).

A third type of rhythm occurs when a preplanned "program" of actions is read out of a pattern of temporal order information in STM as rapidly as possible (Section XVI). This type of rhythm also uses nonspecific arousal, in the form of a rehearsal wave, abetted by self-inhibitory feedback that sequentially resets the STM pattern to prevent a single action from being performed perseveratively. Performance of this kind can exhibit at least two properties: an increase in the reaction time of the first item as a function of list length, due to normalization of the total STM activity—

Section XVIII, and a slowing down of the performance of later items, due to the tendency for primacy to dominate recency in short lists (Sections VIII and XXXIV). Sternberg and his colleagues have reported reaction time data of this type during rapid speaking and typewriting of word lists of different lengths (Sternberg et al., 1978; Sternberg et al., 1980). Grossberg and Kuperstein (1986) have used this type of rhythm generator to analyze how a sequence of planned eye movements can be performed under control of the frontal eye fields.

I call the fourth type of rhythmic capability "imitative rhythm." This is the type of rhythm whereby a list of familiar items of reasonable length can be performed at a prescribed *aperiodic* rhythm after a single hearing. It is also the type of rhythm whereby one can think of DA-DA not as a list of four symbols but as DA repeated twice. This example suggests the relevance of interactions between ordered item representations and a rhythm-generating mechanism to the development of simple counting skills (Gelman & Gallistel, 1978). The mechanism of imitative rhythms also uses a nonspecific arousal mechanism. Indeed, all rhythmic mechanisms use nonspecific arousal in some way, and all nonspecific arousal sources elicit rhythm by being interpreted by the field of specific representations that they energize (Section IX). In this sense, all rhythmic mechanisms are structural expressions of the factorization of pattern and energy (Section V).

The intuitive idea leading to a mechanism of imitative rhythm is depicted in Figure 6.22. Each list item is encoded by adaptive filtering and a temporal order representation in STM. Each list item also simultaneously delivers a nonspecific arousal pulse to the rhythm generator. Thus every item excites a specific pathway and a nonspecific pathway in a variant of Figure 6.15. The internal organization of the rhythm generator converts the *duration* of the nonspecific pulse into a topographically organized STM *intensity*. This happens for every item in the sequence, up to some capacity limit. Thus the rhythm generator is a (parallel) buffer of sorts, but it does not encode item information. Rather, it codes rhythm abstractly as an ordered series of intensities. When the rehearsal wave nonspecifically activates the whole field, these intensities are read out in order by a parallel mechanism and are reconverted into durations. A detailed construction of a rhythm generator is given in Grossberg (1985).

Coding a series of durations as a spatially ordered pattern of STM intensities greatly simplifies the efficient learning of aperiodic sequences of actions. For example, a single sequence chunk in $\mathscr{F}^{(4)}$ can simultaneously sample a spatial pattern of temporal order information in STM over a field of item representations *and* a spatial pattern of ordered intensities in the rhythm generator. Read-out from a single sequence chunk can

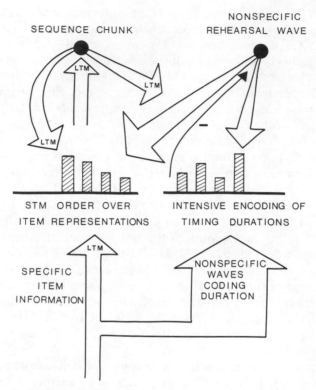

SEQUENCE CHUNK

NONSPECIFIC
REHEARSAL WAVE

LTM

LTM

LTM

STM ORDER OVER
ITEM REPRESENTATIONS

INTENSIVE ENCODING OF
TIMING DURATIONS

LTM

SPECIFIC
ITEM
INFORMATION

NONSPECIFIC
WAVES
CODING
DURATION

Figure 6.22 An aperiodic rhythm generator transforms durations of nonspecific arousal waves into ordered intensities of stored STM activities. Concurrently, the list items that elicited the arousing signals are stored as a pattern of STM temporal order information across item representations. The onset of a sustained nonspecific rehearsal wave transforms the ordered intensities of the rhythm generator back into durations during which the rehearsal wave is inhibited. The result is a series of timed and ordered output bursts from the item representations. Rapid performance of the item representations can occur in response to the rehearsal wave alone even when no inhibiting signals from the rhythm generator are available to modulate performance rate. Both the STM pattern of temporal order information and the STM pattern of timing information can be encoded by a single node, such as the sequence chunk that is generated by adaptive filtering of the STM pattern of ordered item information.

thus recall the entire sequence of items with the correct aperiodic rhythm. For example, a baby may repeat the correct number of sounds in response to an unfamiliar list of words, as well as the rhythm with which the sounds were spoken, even though he or she cannot pronounce the sounds themselves. The ability to imitate the rhythm of one, two, or three sounds is at first much better than the ability to imitate the rhythm or number of a longer list of sounds.

XLVIII. CONCLUDING REMARKS

This chapter illustrates how a small number of network principles and mechanisms can be used to discuss many topics related to the adaptive self-organization of serial order in behavior. Perhaps the most important unifying concepts that arise in this framework are those of adaptive resonance, adaptive context-mediated avalanche, adaptively invariant STM order information in an item field, and an adaptively tuned self-similar masking field. All of these concepts suggest that the functional units of network activity are inherently nonlinear and nonlocal patterns that coherently bind a network's local computations into a context-sensitive whole. The program of classifying the adaptive resonances that control different types of planned serial behavior promises to antiquate the homunculi that burden some contemporary theories of intelligent behavior, and to end Neisser's (1976) nightmare of "processing and still more processing" with a synthetic moment of resonant recognition.

APPENDIX: DYNAMICAL EQUATIONS

A few equations include all the constructions of embedding field theory. Although it is hard work to choose the parameters that characterize specialized processors, these equations provide a guiding framework.

When Equation 6 is generalized to include conditionable inhibitory LTM traces z_{ij}^- as well as conditionable excitatory LTM traces z_{ij}^+, we find (using an obvious extension of the notation) that

$$\frac{d}{dt} x_i = -A_i x_i + \sum_j B_{ji} z_{ji}^+ - \sum_j C_{ji} z_{ji}^- + I_i, \tag{A1}$$

$$\frac{d}{dt} z_{ij}^+ = -D_{ij}^+ z_{ij}^+ + E_{ij}^+ [x_j]^+, \tag{A2}$$

and

$$\frac{d}{dt} z_{ij}^- = -D_{ij}^- z_{ij}^- + E_{ij}^- [x_j]^-, \tag{A3}$$

where $[\xi]^- = \max(-\xi, 0)$. If the inhibitory signals are mediated by slowly varying inhibitory interneuronal potentials x_i^- that are activated by excitatory potentials x_i^+, we find that

$$\frac{d}{dt} x_i^+ = -A_i^+ x_i^+ + \sum_j B_{ji}^{++} z_{ji}^{++} - \sum_j C_{ji}^{-+} z_{ji}^{-+} + I_i^{++}, \tag{A4}$$

and

$$\frac{d}{dt} x_i^- = -A_i^- x_i^- + \sum_j B_{ji}^{+-} z_{ji}^{+-} - \sum_j C_{ji}^{--} z_{ji}^{--} + I_i^{--}, \qquad (A5)$$

In Equation A4, B_{ji}^{++} denotes an excitatory signal from v_j^+ to v_i^+ and C_{ji}^{-+} denotes an inhibitory signal from v_j^- to v_i^+. The other notations can be read analogously. Four types of LTM traces are now possible; for example,

$$\frac{d}{dt} z_{ij}^{-+} = -D_{ij}^{-+} z_{ij}^{-+} + E_{ij}^{-+} [x_j]^+ \qquad (A6)$$

and

$$\frac{d}{dt} z_{ij}^{--} = -D_{ij}^{--} z_{ij}^{--} + E_{ij}^{--} [x_j]^-. \qquad (A7)$$

If interactions can be either shunting or additive, then equation A4 is generalized to

$$\frac{d}{dt} x_i^+ = -A_i^+ x_i^+ + (F_i^+ - G_i^+ x_i^+) \left[\sum_j B_{ji}^{++} z_{ji}^{++} + I_i^{++} \right]$$
$$- (H_i^+ + K_i^+ x_i^+) \left[\sum_j C_{ji}^{-+} z_{ji}^{-+} + J^{-+} \right]. \qquad (A8)$$

Equations A5–A7 have similar generalizations. For example, Equation A6 becomes

$$\frac{d}{dt} z_{ij}^{-+} = -D_{ij}^{-+} z_{ij}^{-+} + (L_{ij}^{-+} - M_{ij}^{-+} z_{ij}^{-+}) E_{ij}^{-+} [x_j]^+ \qquad (A9)$$

If transmitter accumulation rate is slow relative to transmitter depletion rate, then the amount of transmitter Z_{ij}^{-+} generated by the LTM trace z_{ij}^{-+} satisfies

$$\frac{d}{dt} Z_{ij}^{-+} = (N_{ij}^{-+} z_{ij}^{-+} - P_{ij}^{-+} Z_{ij}^{-+}) - Q_{ij}^{-+} Z_{ij}^{-+} \qquad (A10)$$

where Q_{ij}^{-+} increases with x_i^-. The transmitter gating equations of a gated dipole are of this type. Correspondingly, Equation A8 is changed to

$$\frac{d}{dt} x_i^+ = -A_i^+ x_i^+ + (F_i^+ - G_i^+ x_i^+) \left[\sum_j B_{ji}^{++} Z_{ji}^{++} + I_i^{++} \right]$$
$$- (H_i^+ + K_i^+ x_i^+) \left[\sum_j C_{ji}^{-+} Z_{ji}^{-+} + J_i^{-+} \right]. \qquad (A11)$$

If self-regulatory autoreceptive feedback occurs among all the synapses of similar type that converge on a single node, then Equation A10 becomes

$$\frac{d}{dt} Z_{ij}^{-+} = (N_{ij}^{-+} z_{ij}^{-+} - P_{ij}^{-+} Z_{ij}^{-+}) - \sum_k R_{kj}^{-+} Q_{kj}^{-+} Z_{kj}^{-+}. \qquad (A12)$$

The other transmitter equations admit analogous autoreceptor generalizations. Transient properties of transmitters, such as mobilization and enzymatic modulation, may be defined by extensions of these equations (Carpenter & Grossberg, 1981; Grossberg, 1974).

REFERENCES

Anderson, J. R. (1976). *Language, memory, and thought*. Hillsdale, NJ: Erlbaum.

Anderson, J. R. (1982). Acquisition of cognitive skill. *Psychological Review, 89,* 369–406.

Anderson, J. R. (1983). Retrieveal of information from long-term memory. *Science, 220,* 25–30.

Anderson, J. A., Silverstein, J. W., Ritz, S. A., & Jones, R. S. (1977). Distinctive features, categorical perception, and probability learning: Some applications of a neural model. *Psychological Review, 84,* 413–451.

Atkinson, R. C., & Shiffrin, R. M. (1968). Human memory: A proposed system and its control processes. In K. W. Spence & J. T. Spence (Eds.), *Advances in the phychology of learning and motivation research and theory* (Vol. 2). New York: Academic Press.

Banquet, J.-P., & Grossberg, S. (1986). Structure of event-related potentials during learning: An experimental and theoretical analysis. Submitted for publication.

Berger, T. W., & Thompson, R. F. (1978). Neuronal plasticity in the limbic system during classical conditioning of the rabbit nictitating membrane response, I: The hippocampus. *Brain Research, 145,* 323–346.

Butters, N., & Squire, L. (Eds.). (1983). *Neuropsychology of memory.* New York: Guilford Press.

Carney. A. E., Widen, G. P., & Viemeister, N. F. (1977). Noncategorical perception of stop consonants differing in VOT. *Journal of the Acoustical Society of America, 62,* 961–970.

Carpenter, G. A., & Grossberg, S. (1981). Adaptation and transmitter gating in vertebrate photoreceptors. *Journal of Theoretical Neurobiology, 1,* 1–42.

Carpenter, G. A., & Grossberg, S. (1983a). A neural theory of circadian rhythms: The gated pacemaker. *Biological Cybernetics, 48,* 35–59.

Carpenter, G. A., & Grossberg, S (1983b). Dynamic models of neural systems: Propagated signals, photoreceptor transduction, and circadian rhythms. In R. Grissell, J.P.E. Hodgson, & M. Yanowich (Eds.), *Oscillations in mathematical biology.* New York: Springer-Verlag.

Carpenter, G. A., & Grossberg, S. (1984). A neural theory of circadian rhythms: Aschoff's rule in diurnal and nocturnal mammals. *American Journal of Physiology, 247,* R1067–R1082.

Carpenter, G. A., & Grossberg, S. (1985). A neural theory of circadian rhythms: Split rhythms, after-effects, and motivational interactions. *Journal of Theoretical Biology, 113,* 163–223.

Carpenter, G. A., & Grossberg, S. (1986a). A massively parallel architecture for a self-organizing neural pattern recognition machine. *Computer Vision, Graphics, and Image Processing,* in press.

Carpenter, G. A., & Grossberg, S.(1986b). Neural dynamics of category learning and recognition: Attention, memory consolidation, and amnesia. In J. Davis, R. Newburgh, & E. Wegman (Eds.), *Brain structure, learning, and memory.* AAAS Symposium Series, in press.

Carpenter, G. A., & Grossberg, S. (1986c). Neural dynamics of category learning and recognition: Structural invariants, reinforcement, and evoked potentials. In M. L. Commons, S. M. Kosslyn, and R. J. Herrnstein (Eds.), *Pattern recognition and concepts in animals, people, and machines*. Hillsdale, NJ: Erlbaum.

Cermak, L. S., & Craik, F.I.M. (1979). *Levels of processing in human memory*. Hillsdale, NJ: Erlbaum.

Chastain, G. (1982). Scanning, holistic encoding, and the word-superiority effect. *Memory and Cognition, 10,* 232–236.

Cohen, M. A., & Grossberg, S. (1983). Absolute stability of global pattern formation and parallel memory storage in competitive neural networks. IEEE *Transactions, smc13,* 815–826.

Cohen, M. A., & Grossberg, S. (1986a). Neural dynamics of speech and language coding: Developmental programs, perceptual grouping, and competition for short term memory. *Human Neurobiology,* in press.

Cohen, M. A., & Grossberg, S. (1986b). Unitized recognition codes for parts and wholes: The unique cue in configural discriminations. In M. L. Commons, S. M. Kosslyn, & R. J. Herrnstein (Eds.), *Pattern recognition and concepts in animals, people, and machines*. Hillsdale, NJ: Erlbaum.

Cole, R. A., Rudnicky, A. I., Zue, V. W., & Reddy, D. R. (1980). Speech as patterns on paper. In R. A. Cole (Ed.), *Perception and production of fluent speech*. Hillsdale, NJ: Erlbaum.

Collins, A. M., & Loftus, E. F. (1975). A spreading-activation theory of semantic memory. *Psychological Review, 82,* 407–428.

Cooper, W. E. (1979). *Speech perception and production: Studies in selective adaptation*. Norwood, NJ: Ablex.

Cornsweet, T. N. (1970). *Visual perception*. New York: Academic Press.

Crowder, R. G. (1978). Mechanisms of auditory backward masking in the stimulus suffix effect. *Psychological Review, 85,* 502–524.

Dallet, K. M. (1965). "Primary memory": The effects on redundancy upon digit repetition. *Psychonomic Science, 3,* 365–373.

Darwin, C. J. (1976). The perception of speech. In E. C. Carterette & M. P. Friedman (Eds.), *Handbook of perception* (Vol. VII), New York: Academic Press.

Deadwyler, S. A., West, M. O., & Robinson, J. H. (1981). Entorhinal and septal inputs differentially control sensory-evoked responses in the rat dentate gyrus. *Science, 211,* 1181–1183.

DeFrance, J. F. (1976). *The septal nuclei*. New York: Plenum Press.

Dethier, V. G. (1968). *Physiology of insect senses*. London: Methuen.

Dixon, T. R., & Horton, D. L. (1968). *Verbal behavior and general behavior theory*. Englewood Cliffs, NJ: Prentice-Hall.

Dodwell, P. C. (1975). Pattern and object perception. In E. C. Carterette & M. P. Friedman (Eds.), *Handbook of perception* (Vol. V). New York: Academic Press.

Eccles, J. C. (1952). *The neurophysiological basis of mind: The principles of neurophysiology*. London: Oxford University Press.

Eccles, J. C., Ito, M., & Szentagothai, J. (1967). *The cerebellum as a neuronal machine*. New York: Springer-Verlag.

Ellias, S. A., & Grossberg, S. (1975). Pattern formation, contrast control, and oscillations in the short term memory of shunting on-center off-surround networks. *Biological Cybernetics, 20,* 69–98.

Elman, J. H., Diehl, R. L., & Buchwald, S. E. (1977). Perceptual switching in bilinguals. *Journal of the Acoustical Society of America, 62,* 971–974.

Erickson, R. P (1963). Sensory neural patterns and gustation. In Y. Zotterman (Ed.), *Olfaction and taste*. New York: Pergamon Press.

Estes, W. K. (1972). As associative basis for coding and organization in memory. In A. W. Melton & E. Martin (Eds.), *Coding processes in human memory*. New York: John Wiley.

Fisher, R. P., & Craik, E.I.M. (1980). The effects of elaboration on recognition memory. *Memory & Cognition, 8,* 400–404.

Fitts, P. M., & Posner, M. L. (1967). *Human performance*. Monterey, CA: Brooks/Cole.

Foss, D. J., & Blank, M. A. (1980). Identifying the speech codes. *Cognitive Psychology, 12,* 1–31.

Fowler, C. A. (1977). *Timing control in speech production*. Unpublished doctoral dissertation, Dartmouth College, Hanover NH.

Freeman, W. J. (1975). *Mass action in the nervous system*. New York: Academic Press.

Freeman, W. J. (1979). EEG analysis gives models of neuronal template-matching mechanism for sensory search with olfactory bulb. *Biological Cybernetics, 35,* 221–234.

Fry, D. B. (1966). The development of the phonological system in the normal and the deaf child. In F. Smith & G. A. Miller (Eds.), *The genesis of language*. Cambridge, MA: MIT Press.

Fukushima, K. (1980). Neocognition: A self-organized neural network model for a mechanism of pattern recognition unaffected by shift in position. *Biological Cybernetics, 36,* 193–202.

Gabriel, M., Foster, K., Orona, E., Saltwick, S. E., & Stanton, M. (1980). Neuronal activity of cingulate cortex, anteroventral thalamus, and hippocampal formation in discrimination conditioning: Encoding and extraction of the significance of conditional stimuli. *Progress in Psychobiology and Physiological Psychology, 9,* 125–231.

Ganz, L. (1975). Temporal factors in visual perception. In E. C. Carterette & M. P. Friedman (Eds.), *Handbook of perception* (Vol. V). New York: Academic Press.

Gelman, R., & Gallistel, C. R. (1978). *The child's understanding of number*. Cambridge, MA: Harvard University Press.

Gibson, J. J. (1937). Adaptation, after-effect and contrast in the perception of tilted lines, II: Simultaneous contrast and the areal restriction of the after-effect. *Journal of Experimental Psychology, 20,* 553–569.

Grillner, S. (1975). Locomotion in vertebrates: Central mechanisms and reflex interaction. *Physiological Review, 55,* 247–304.

Grossberg, S. (1964). *The theory of embedding fields with applications to psychology and neurophysiology*. New York: Rockefeller Institute for Medical Research.

Grossberg, S. (1967). Nonlinear difference-differential equations in prediction and learning theory. *Proceedings of the National Academy of Science, 58,* 1329–1334.

Grossberg, S. (1968a). Some nonlinear networks capable of learning a spatial pattern of arbitrary complexity. *Proceedings of the National Academy of Science, 59,* 368–372.

Grossberg, S. (1968b). Some physiological and biochemical consequences of psychological postulates. *Proceedings of the National Academy of Science, 60,* 758–765.

Grossberg, S. (1969a). Embedding fields: A theory of learning with physiological implications. *Journal of Mathematical Psychology, 6,* 209–239.

Grossberg, S. (1969b). On learning and energy-entropy dependence in recurrent and nonrecurrent signed networks. *Journal of Statistical Physics, 1,* 319–350.

Grossberg, S. (1969c). On learning, information, lateral inhibition, and transmitters. *Mathematical Biosciences, 4,* 255–310.

Grossberg, S. (1969d). On learning of spatiotemporal patterns by networks with ordered sensory and motor components: Excitatory components of the cerebellum. *Studies in Applied Mathematics, 48*, 105–132.

Grossberg, S. (1969e). On the production and release of chemical transmitters and related topics in cellular control. *Journal of Theoretical Biology, 22*, 325–264.

Grossberg, S. (1969f). On the serial learning of lists. *Mathematical Biosciences, 4*, 201–253.

Grossberg, S. (1969g). Some networks that can learn, remember, and reproduce any number of complicated space-time patterns, I. *Journal of Mathematics and Mechanics, 19*, 53–91.

Grossberg, S. (1970a). Neural pattern discrimination. *Journal of Theoretical Biology, 27*, 291–337.

Grossberg, S. (1970b). Some networks that can learn, remember, and reproduce any number of complicated space-time patterns, II. *Studies in Applied Mathematics, 49*, 135–166.

Grossberg, S. (1971). On the dynamics of operant conditioning. *Journal of Theoretical Biology, 33*, 225–255.

Grossberg, S. (1972a). A neural theory of punishment and avoidance, I: Qualitative theory. *Mathematical Biosciences, 15*, 39–67.

Grossberg, S. (1972b). A neural theory of punishment and avoidance, II Quantitative theory. *Mathematical Biosciences, 15*, 253–285.

Grossberg, S. (1972c). Pattern learning by functional-differential neural networks with arbitrary path weights. In K. Schmitt (Eds.), *Delay and functional-differential equations and their applications*. New York: Academic Press.

Grossberg, S. (1973). Contour enhancement, short-term memory, and constancies in reverberating neural networks. *Studies in Applied Mathematics, 52*, 217–257.

Grossberg, S. (1974). Classical and instrumental learning by neural networks. In R. Rosen & F. Snell (Eds.), *Progress in theoretical biology* (Vol. 3). New York: Academic Press.

Grossberg, S. (1975). A neural model of attention, reinforcement, and discrimination learning. *International Review of Neurobiology, 18*, 263–327.

Grossberg, S. (1976a). Adaptive pattern classification and universal recoding, I: Parallel development and coding of neural feature detectors. *Biological Cybernetics, 23*, 121–134.

Grossberg, S. (1976b). Adaptive pattern classification and universal recoding, II: Feedback, expectation, olfaction, and illusions. *Biological Cybernetics, 23*, 187–202.

Grossberg, S. (1977). Pattern formation by the global limits of a nonlinear competitive interaction in n dimensions. *Journal of Mathematical Biology, 4*, 237–256.

Grossberg, S. (1978a). Behavioral contrast in short term memory: Serial binary memory models or parallel continuous memory models? *Journal of Mathematical Psychology, 17*, 199–219.

Grossberg, S. (1978b). Communication, memory, and development. In R. Rosen & F. Snell (Eds.), *Progress in Theoretical Biology* (Vol. 5). New York: Academic Press.

Grossberg, S. (1978c). Decisions, patterns, and oscillations in the dynamics of competitive systems with applications to Volterra-Lotka systems. *Journal of Theoretical Biology, 73*, 101–130.

Grossberg, S. (1978d). Do all neural networks really look alike. A comment on Anderson, Silverstein, Ritz, and Jones. *Psychological Review, 85*, 592–596.

Grossberg, S. (1978e). A theory of human memory: Self-organization and performance of sensory-motor codes, maps, and plans. In R. Rosen & F. Snell (Eds.), *Progress in theoretical biology* (Vol. 5). New York: Academic Press.

Grossberg, S. (1978f). A theory of visual coding, memory, and development. In E. Leeuwenberg & H. Buffart (Eds.), *Formal theories of visual perception*. New York: John Wiley.

Grossberg, S. (1980a). Biological competition: Decision rules, pattern formation, and oscillations. *Proceedings of the National Academy of Sciences, 77*, 2338–2342.

Grossberg, S. (1980b). Direct perception or adaptive resonance? *Behavioral and Brain Sciences, 3*, 385.

Grossberg, S. (1980c). How does a brain build a cognitive code? *Psychological Review, 87*, 1–51.

Grossberg, S. (1980d). Human and computer rules and representations are not equivalent. *Behavioral and Brain Sciences, 3*, 136–138.

Grossberg, S. (1981a). Adaptive resonance in development, perception, and cognition. In S. Grossberg (Ed.), *Mathematical psychology and psychophysiology*. Providence, RI: American Mathematical Society.

Grossberg, S. (1981b). Psychophysiological substrates of schedule interactions and behavioral contrast. In S. Grossberg (Ed.), *Mathematical psychology and psychophysiology*. Providence, RI: American Mathematical Society.

Grossberg, S. (1982a). Associative and competitive principles of learning and development: The temporal unfolding and stability of STM and LTM patterns. In S. I. Amari & M. Arbib (Eds.), *Competition and cooperation in neural networks*. New York: Springer-Verlag.

Grossberg, S. (1982b). The processing of expected and unexpected events during conditioning and attention: A psychophysiological theory. *Psychological Review, 89*, 529–572.

Grossberg, S. (1982c). A psychophysiological theory of reinforcement, drive, motivation, and attention. *Journal of Theoretical Neurobiology, 1*, 286–369.

Grossberg, S. (1982d). *Studies of mind and brain: Neural principles of learning, perception, development, cognition, and motor control*. Amsterdam: Reidel Press.

Grossberg, S. (1983). The quantized geometry of visual space: The coherent computation of depth form, and lightness. *Behavioral and Brain Sciences, 6*, 625–692.

Grossberg, S. (1984a). Some psychophysiological and pharmacological correlates of a developmental, cognitive, and motivational theory. In R. Karrer, J. Cohen, & P. Tueting (Eds.), *Brain and information: Event related potentials*. New York: New York Academy of Sciences.

Grossberg, S. (1984b). Unitization, automaticity, temporal order, and word recognition. *Cognition and Brain Theory, 7*, 263–283.

Grossberg, S. (1985). On the coordinated learning of item, order, and rhythm. Unpublished manuscript.

Grossberg, S., & Kuperstein, M. (1986). *Neural dynamics of adaptive sensory-motor control: Ballistic eye movements*. Amsterdam: North-Holland.

Grossberg, S., & Levine, D. S. (1975). Some developmental and attentional biases in the contrast enhancement and short term memory of recurrent neural networks. *Journal of Theoretical Biology, 53*, 341–380.

Grossberg, S., & Pepe, J. (1970). Schizophrenia: Possible dependence of associational span, bowing, and primacy vs. recency on spiking threshold. *Behavioral Science, 15*, 359–362.

Grossberg, S., & Pepe, J. (1971). Spiking threshold and overarousal effects in serial learning. *Journal of Statistical Physics, 3*, 95–125.

Grossberg, S., & Stone, G. O. (1986a). Neural dynamics of word recognition and recall: Attentional priming, learning, and resonance. *Psychological Review, 93*, 46–74.

Grossberg, S., & Stone, G. O. (1986b). Neural dynamics of attention switching and temporal order information in short term memory. Submitted for publication.

Halle, M., & Stevens, K.N. (1962). Speech recognition: A model and a program for research. *IRE Transactions and Information Theory, IT-8*, 155–159.

Hary, J. M., & Massaro, D. W. (1982). Categorical results do not imply categorical perception. *Perception & Psychophysics, 32,* 409–418.

Haymaker, W., Anderson, E., & Nauta, W.J.H. (1969). *The hypothalamus,* Springfield, IL: C. C. Thomas.

Helson, H. (1964). *Adaptation level theory.* New York: Harper & Row.

Hoyle, G. (1977). *Identified neurons and behavior of arthropods.* New York: Plenum Press.

Johnston, J. C., & McClelland, J. L. (1974). Perception of letters in words: Seek not and ye shall find. *Science, 184,* 1192–1194.

Jusczyk, P. W. (1981). Infant speech perception: A critical appraisal. In P. D. Eimas & J. L. Miller (Eds.), *Perspectives on the study of speech.* Hillsdale, NJ: Erlbaum.

Kahneman, D., & Chajczyk, D. (1983). Tests of the automaticity of reading: Dilution of Stroop effects by color-irrelevant stimuli. *Journal of Experimental Psychology, 9,* 497–509.

Karrer, R., Cohen, J., & Tueting, P. (Eds.) (1984). *Brain and information: Event related potentials.* New York: New York Academy of Sciences.

Kelso, J.A.S., Southard, D. L., & Goodman, D. (1979). On the nature of human interlimb coordination. *Science, 203,* 1029–1031.

Kennedy, D. (1968). Input and output connection of single arthropod neurons. In F. O. Carlson (Ed.), *Physiological and biochemical aspects of nervous integration.* Englewood Cliffs, NJ: Prentice-Hall.

Kimura, D. (1976). The neural basis of language qua gesture. In H. Whitaker & H. A. Whitaker (Eds.), *Studies in neurolinguistics* (Vol. III). New York: Academic Press.

Kinsbourne, M., & Hicks, R. E. (1978). Mapping cerebral functional space: Competition and collaboration in human performance. In M. Kinsbourne (Ed.), *Asymmetrical function of the brain.* London: Cambridge University Press.

Klatt, D. H. (1980). Speech perception: A model of acoustic-phonetic analysis and lexical access. In R. A. Cole (Ed.), *Perception and production of fluent speech.* Hillsdale, NJ: Erlbaum.

Kuffler, S. W., & Nicholls, J. G. (1976). *From neuron to brain.* Sunderland, MA: Sinauer.

Lanze, M., Weisstein, N., & Harris, J. R. (1982). Perceived depth vs. structural relevance in the object-superiority effect. *Perception & Psychophysics, 31,* 376–382.

Lashley, K. S. (1951). The problem of serial order in behavior. In L. A. Jeffress (Ed.), *Cerebral mechanisms in behavior.* New York: John Wiley.

Lawry, J. A., & LaBerge, D. (1981). Letter and word code interactions elicited by normally displayed words. *Perception & Psychophysics, 30,* 70–82.

Lenneberg, E. H. (1967). *Biological foundations of language.* New York: John Wiley.

Levine, D. S., & Grossberg, S. (1976). Visual illusions in neural networks: Line neutralization, tilt aftereffect, and angle expansion. *Journal of Theoretical Biology, 61,* 477–504.

Levinson, S. E., & Liberman, M. Y. (1981). Speech recognition by computer. *Scientific America,* April, 64–76.

Liberman, A. M., Cooper, F. S., Shankweiler, D. S., & Studdert-Kennedy, M. (1967). Perception of the speech code. *Psychological Review, 74,* 431–461.

Liberman, A. M., & Studdert-Kennedy, M. (1978). Phonetic perception. In R. Held, H. Leibowitz, & H. L. Teuber (Eds.), *Handbook of sensory physiology* (Vol. VIII). Heidelberg: Springer-Verlag.

Lindblom. B.E.F. (1963). Spectrographic study of vowel reduction. *Journal of the Acoustical Society of America, 35,* 1773–1781.

MacKay, D. G. (1982). The problems of flexibility, fluency, and speed-accuracy trade-off skilled behavior. *Psychological Review, 89,* 483–506.

MacLean, P. D. (1970). The limbic brain in relation to psychoses. In P. Black (Ed.), *Physiological correlates of emotion*. New York: Academic Press.

Mann, V. A., & Repp, B. H. (1981). Influence of preceding fricative on stop consonant perception. *Journal of the Acoustical Society of America, 69*, 548–558.

Marler, P. A. (1970). A comparative approach to vocal learning: song development in white-crowned sparrows. *Journal of Comparative and Physiological Psychology, 71*, 1–25.

Marler, P., & Peters, S. (1981). Birdsong and speech: Evidence for special processing. In P. D. Eimas & J. L. Miller (Eds.), *Perspectives on the study of speech*. Hillsdale, NJ: Erlbaum.

Marslen-Wilson, W. D. (1975). Sentence perception as an interactive parallel process. *Science, 189*, 226–228.

Marslen-Wilson, W. D., & Welsh, A. (1978). Processing interactions and lexical access during word recognition in continuous speech. *Cognitive Psychology, 10*, 29–63.

Marvilya, M. P. (1972). Spontaneous vocalizations and babbling in hearing-impaired infants. In C.G.M. Fant (Ed.), *Speech communication ability and profound deafness*. Washington, DC: A. G. Bell Association for the Deaf.

Matthei, E. H. (1983). Length effects in word perception: Comment on Samuel, van Santen, and Johnston. *Journal of Experimental Psychology, 9*, 318–320.

McClelland, J. L., & Rumelhart, D. E. (1981). An interactive activation model of context effects in letter perception, I: An account of basic findings. *Psychological Review, 88*, 375–407.

Miller, G. A. (1956). The magic number seven plus or minus two. *Psychological Review, 63*, 81–97.

Miller, J. L. (1981). Effects of speaking rate on segmental distinctions, In P. D. Eimas & J. L. Miller (Eds.), *Perspectives on the study of speech*. Hillsdale, NJ: Erlbaum.

Miller, J. L., & Liberman, A. M. (1979). Some effects of later-occurring information on the perception of stop consonant and semivowel. *Perception & Psychophysics, 25*, 457–465.

Miyawaki, K., Strange, W., Verbrugge, R., Liberman, A. M., Jenkins, J. J., & Fujimura, O. (1975). An effect of linguistic experience: The discrimination of [r] and [l] by native speakers of Japanese and English. *Perception & Psychophysics, 18*, 331–340.

Murdock. B. B. (1974). *Human memory: Theory and data*. Potomac, MD: Erlbaum.

Murdock, B. B. (1979). Convolution and correlation in perception and memory. In L. G. Nilsson (Ed.), *Perspectives in memory research: Essays in honor of Uppsala University's 500th anniversary*. Hillsdale, NJ: Erlbaum.

Myers, J. L., & Lorch, R. F. Jr. (1980). Interference and facilitation effects of primes upon verification processes. *Memory & Cognition, 8*, 405–414.

Neimark, E. D., & Estes, W. K. (Eds.). (1967). *Stimulus sampling theory*. San Francisco: Holden-Day.

Neisser, U. (1976). *Cognition and reality*. San Francisco: Freeman Press.

Newell, A. (1980). Harpy, production systems, and human cognition. In R. A. Cole (Ed.), *Perception and production of fluent speech*. Hillsdale, NJ: Erlbaum.

Norman, D. A. (1982). Categorization of action slips. *Psychological Review, 88*, 11–15.

Norman, D. A., & Bobrow, D. G. (1975). On data-limited and resource-limited processes. *Cognitive Psychology, 7*, 44–64.

O'Keefe, J., & Nadel, L. (1978). *The hippocampus as a cognitive map*. Oxford: Clarendon Press.

Olds, J. (1977). *Drives and reinforcements: Behavioral studies of hypothalamic functions*. New York: Raven Press.

Osgood, C. E. (1953). *Method and theory in experimental psychology*. New York: Oxford University Press.

Pastore, R. E. (1981). Possible psychoacoustic factors in speech perception. In P. D. Eimas & J. L. Miller (Eds.), *Perspectives on the study of speech*. Hillsdale, NJ: Erlbaum.

Patterson, P. H., & Purves, D. (Ed.). (1982). *Readings in developmental neurobiology*. Cold Spring Harbor, NY: Cold Spring Harbor Lab.

Piaget, J. (1963). *The origins of intelligence in children*. New York: Norton.

Posner, M. I., & Snyder, C.R.R. (1975). Facilitation and inhibition in the processing of signals. In P.M.S. Rabbitt & S. Dornic (Eds.), *Attention and performance* (Vol. 5). New York: Academic Press.

Raaijmakers, J.G.W., & Shiffrin, R. M. (1981). Search of associative memory. *Psychological Review, 88*, 93–134.

Ratcliff, R., & McKoon, G. (1981). Does activation really spread? *Psychological Review, 88*, 454–462.

Reeves, A., & Sperling, G. (1986). Attentional theory of order information in short-term visual memory. Preprint.

Repp, B. (1979). Relative amplitude of aspiration noise as a voicing cue for syllable-initial stop consonants. *Language & Speech, 22*, 173–189.

Repp, B. H., Liberman, A. M., Eccardt, T., & Pesetsky, D. (1978). Perceptual integration of temporal cues for stop, fricative, and affricative manner. *Journal of Experimental Psychology, 4*, 621–637.

Repp, B. H., & Mann, V. A. (1981). Perceptual assessment of fricative-stop coarticulation. *Journal of the Acoustical Society of America, 69*, 1154–1163.

Rescorla, R. A., & Wagner, A. R. (1972). A theory of Pavlovian conditioning: Variations in the effectiveness of reinforcement and nonreinforcement. In A. H. Black & W. F. Prokasy (Eds.), *Classical conditioning II: Current research and theory*. New York: Appleton-Century-Crofts.

Restle, F. (1978). Assimilation predicted by adaptation-level theory with variable weights. In N. J. Castellan & F. Restle (Eds.), *Cognitive theory* (Vol. 3). Hillsdale, NJ: Erlbaum.

Robson, J. G. (1975). Receptive fields: Neural representation of the spatial and intensive attributes of the visual image. In E. C. Carterette & M. P. Friedman (Eds.), *Handbook of perception* (Vol. V). New York: Academic Press.

Rumelhart, D. E., & McClelland, J. L. (1982). An interactive activation model of context effects in letter perception, II: The contextual enhancement effect and some tests and extensions of the model. *Psychological Review, 89*, 60–94.

Rumelhart, D. E., & Norman, D. A. (1982). Simulating a skilled typist: A study of skilled cognitive-motor performance. *Cognitive Science, 6*, 1–36.

Samuel, A. G. van Santen, J.P.H., & Johnston, J. C. (1982). Length effects in word perception: We is better than I but worse than you or them. *Journal of Experimental Psychology, 8*, 91–105.

Samuel, A. G., van Santen, J.P.H., & Johnston, J. C. (1983). Reply to Matthei: We really is worse than you or them, and so are ma and pa. *Journal of Experimental Psychology, 9*, 321–322.

Sawusch, J. R., & Nusbaum, H. C. (1979). Contextual effects in vowel perception, I: Anchor-induced contrast effects. *Perception & Psychophysics, 25*, 292–302.

Sawusch, J. R., Nusbaum, H. C., & Schwab, E. C. (1980). Contextual effects in vowel perception II: Evidence for two processing mechanisms. *Perception & Psychophysics, 27*, 421–434.

Schneider, W., & Shiffrin, R. M. (1976). Automatic and controlled information processing in vision. In D. LaBerge & S. J. Samuels (Eds.), *Basic processes in reading: Perception and comprehension*. Hillsdale, NJ: Erlbaum.

Schneider, W., & Shiffrin, R. M. (1977). Controlled and automatic information processing I: Detection, search, and attention. *Psychological Review, 84*, 1–66.

Schwab, E. C., Sawusch, J. R., & Nusbaum, H. C. (1981). The role of second formant transitions in the stop-semivowel distinction. *Perception & Psychophysics, 29*, 121–128.

Semmes, J. (1968). Hemispheric specialization: A possible clue to mechanism. *Neuropsychologia, 6*, 11-26.

Shaffer, L. H. (1982). Rhythm and timing in skill. *Psycghological Review, 89*, 109–122.

Shepard, R. N. (1980). Multidimensional scaling, tree-fitting, and clustering, *Science, 210*, 390–398.

Smale, S. (1976). On the differential equations of species in competition. *Journal of Theoretical Biology, 3*, 5–7.

Soechting, J. F., & Laquaniti, F. (1981). Invariant characteristics of a pointing movement in man. *Journal of Neuroscience, 1*, 710–720.

Sperling, G., & Reeves, A. (1980). Measuring the reaction time of a shift of visual attention. In R. Nickerson (Ed.), *Attention and performance* (Vol. 7). Hillsdale, NJ: Erlbaum.

Squire, L. R., Cohen, N. J., & Nadel, L. (1982). The medial temporal region and memory consolidation: A new hypothesis. In H. Weingartner & E. Parker (Eds.), *Memory consolidation*. Hillsdale, NJ: Erlbaum.

Stein, L. (1958). Secondary reinforcement established with subcortical stimulation. *Science, 127*, 466–467.

Stein, P.S.G. (1971). Intersegmental coordination of swimmeret motoneuron activity in crayfish. *Journal of Neurophysiology, 34*, 310–318.

Sternberg, S., Monsell, S., Knoll, R. L., & Wright, C. E. (1978). The latency and duration of rapid movement sequences: Comparison of speech and typewriting. In G. E. Stelmach (Ed.), *Information processing in motor control and learning*. New York: Academic Press.

Sternberg, S., Wright, C. E., Knoll, R. L., & Monsell, S. (1980). Motor programs in rapid speech: Additional evidence. In R. A. Cole (Ed.), *Perception and production of fluent speech*. Hillsdale, NJ: Erlbaum.

Stevens, C. F. (1966). *Neurophysiology: A primer*. New York: John Wiley.

Stevens, K. N. (1972). Segments, features, and analysis by synthesis. In J. V. Cavanaugh & I. G. Mattingly (Eds.), *Language by eye and by ear*. Cambridge, MA: MIT Press.

Stevens, K. N., & Halle, M. (1964). Remarks on analysis by synthesis and distinctive features. In W. Wathen-Dunn (Ed.), *Proceedings of the AFCRL symposium on models for the perception of speech and visual form*. Cambridge, MA MIT Press.

Studdert-Kennedy, M. (1975). The nature and function of phonetic categories. In F. Restle, R. M. Shiffrin, N. J. Castellan, H. R. Lindman, & D. B. Pisoni (Eds.), *Cognitive theory* (Vol. 1). Hillsdale, NJ: Erlbaum.

Studdert-Kennedy, M. (1980). Speech perception. *Language & Speech, 23*, 45–65.

Studdert-Kennedy, M., Liberman, A. M., Harris, K. S., & Cooper, F. S. (1970). Motor theory of speech perception: A reply to Lane's critical review. *Psychological Review, 77*, 234–249.

Sutton, R. S., & Barto, A. G. (1981). Toward a modern theory of adaptive networks: Expectation and prediction. *Psychological Review, 88*, 135–170.

Warren, R. M. (1970). Perceptual restoration of missing speech sounds. *Science, 167*, 393–395.

Warren, R. M., & Obusek, D. J. (1971). Speech perception and phonemic restorations. *Perception & Psychophysics, 9,* 358–362.

Watkins, O. C., & Watkins, M. J. (1982). Lateral inhibition and echoic memory: Some comments on Crowder's (1978) theory. *Memory & Cognition, 10,* 279–286.

Weisstein, N. (1968). A Rashevsky-Landahl neural net: Simulation of metacontrast. *Psychological Review, 75,* 494–521.

Weisstein, N. (1972). Metacontrast. In D. Jameson & L. M. Hurvich (Eds.), *Handbook of sensory physiology* (Vol. VII/4). Berlin: Springer-Verlag.

Welford, A. T. (1968). *Fundamentals of skill.* London: Methuen.

West, M. O., Christian, E., Robinson, J. H., & Deadwyler, S. A. (1981). Dentate granule cell discharge during conditioning. *Experimental Brain Research, 44,* 287–294.

Willows, A. O. D. (1968). Behavioral acts elicited by stimulation of single identifiable nerve cells. In F. O. Carlson (Ed.), *Physiological and biochemical aspects of nervous integration.* Englewood Cliffs, NJ: Prentice-Hall.

CHAPTER 7

Cognitive Science and the Study of Cognition and Language*

Zenon W. Pylyshyn

Centre for Cognitive Science, University of Western Ontario, London, Ontario, Canada N6A 5C2

I. INTRODUCTION

The purpose of this chapter is to present, in a general way, some of the principles which characterize a new foundation for the study of cognitive psychology. Although the use of computational models (or "computer simulations") goes as far back as the mid-1950s, and the phrase "information processing approach" has been used since the early 1960s to cover a multitude of types of theorizing, it is only in more recent years that the power of such ideas has begun to be appreciated in its proper context. This phenomenon is part of a broader intellectual movement with serious implications in philosophy, mathematics, linguistics, and even such biological studies as genetics (Monod, 1971) and embryology (Herman & Rozenberg, 1974). The basic notions behind this movement are those of *symbol* and *mechanism*. These ideas are fundamental to the study of mind because they allow for a level of analysis independent of both physical and phenomenological foundations.

The abstract study of cognitive activity from this point of view can be traced back to Alan Turing and other logicians and philosophers in the 1930s and 1940s. It was not until the 1970s, however, that such ideas

---

* This study was originally written in 1975. Because it was widely circulated and quoted as an unpublished manuscript, I have decided to allow its publication in its original form. I still feel that the position I take in this chapter is correct, though in more recent work I have placed much more emphasis on the intentional or semantic property of representations (e.g., Pylyshyn, 1984).

295

began to be articulated in sufficient detail to provide candidate theories of such psychological functions as perception and language comprehension. From the fields of artificial intelligence, formal linguistics, and "information processing psychology" a new collection of ideas and approaches has emerged which promises to form a new field of cognitive science.

In the following pages I examine some of the fundamental premises underlying this approach, because there is always the danger that we may lose sight of the metatheoretical foundations when a new scientific approach enjoys sudden popularity. I confine myself primarily to one particular problem of cognitive psychology and examine how the computational point of view might give a different perspective. That problem concerns the form in which humans represent their knowledge of the world—their cognitive representations. I hope to relate this problem to that of comprehension in general (for a more extended discussion of these issues, the reader is referred to Pylyshyn, 1973a).

We should note at the outset that the problem of cognitive representation goes back, in one guise or another, at least several millenia. Indeed, it was the subject of vigorous and prolonged debate between Platonists and Aristoteleans. While the latter position has enjoyed the edge in contemporary thought, there have been some important exceptions (see, e.g., Weimer, 1973). In any case, the necessity of postulating some sort of representation arises because of the obvious fact that people (as well as most animals and machines) are influenced by factors other than their immediately present environment; we can recall, describe, and reason about objects which are not proximal stimuli. In fact, reasoning is distinguished from motor manipulation by virtue of the fact that the objects on which reason operates are not external physical objects.

Of course, the need for internal objects is more pervasive than the considerations just mentioned might suggest, for we cannot even begin to understand behavior without reference to the internal states of an organism. This situation is in contrast to that which obtains in macroscopic physics (i.e., mechanics), for example, where physical laws are ahistoric in that they apply to the present observable state of a system, irrespective of how the system came to be in that state. In psychology, no description of an observable behavioral state at a particular moment in time is sufficient to establish lawful regularities; one must always postulate some internal, unobservable state as well. Even radical behaviorists recognize this fact in taking the position that behavior depends not only on the current stimulation but also on the organism's past experience (as well as its innate capacities). Such a "history" must, of course, be embodied in some current material state of the organism if it is to have an effect on the organism's current behavior. Nevertheless, it can be studied independently of the particular material forms involved.

Cognitive psychologists are not willing to stop at the point of describing the functional relationship between observable historical antecedents and current behavior. Rather, they want to examine the fine structure of the states themselves. Furthermore, such cognitive states are not the sorts of configurations studied in the natural sciences (i.e., those described in terms of the physical dimensions of time, mass, and length). For one thing, they are highly abstract entities characterized structurally in terms of their function in the cognitive system. Even more important, such states are not taken to be mere descriptions of the conditions that causally determine the behavior of an organism (as in the theory of automata); they are also viewed as representations of the organism's knowledge. In this respect, we can speak of these states as embodying mental representations, and we can use terms such as "believe," "know," "infer," "percept," "image," and so on to refer to aspects of such representations. This is one of the crucial differences between the behaviorists' and the cognitivists' approach to the history embodied in the states of an organism. For the cognitivist, such internal states must be characterized as "models" or "descriptions" in some abstract formal language (for an extended discussion of this approach and its philosophical rationale, see Fodor, 1975).

Because cognitive psychologists want to address such issues as the nature of cognitive functioning (i.e., the rationality of mental functions) rather than its physical and biological embodiment, they use a different theoretical language (e.g., the language of computation) and a more indirect methodology. Contemporary cognitive psychologists typically proceed by constructing a logical surrogate for the flesh and blood organism that is being studied—a surrogate which, on one hand, can be understood in certain ways because it is constructed from simple primitive processes that are known to be mechanistic (in Turing's sense) and which, on the other hand, functions in important respects like the organism being modeled. Admittedly, this general description begs some important questions (phrases like "understood in certain ways" and "in important respects like" need much more refinement), but it must suffice for the time being, since further explication would take us too far afield (see, however, Pylyshyn, 1974).

I begin by examining the question of representation in a somewhat more restricted form. Specifically, I examine the question, What is stored in human memory? Simple as it sounds, this question raises a host of philosophical and conceptual problems for the psychologist.

II. ON WHAT IS STORED: THE CONCEPT OF A SYMBOL

The question of what is stored in human memory is made particularly difficult by an inherent ambiguity with regard to the level of discourse that the questioner may find satisfactory. Depending on the criteria of adequacy adopted, equally correct answers might be "an image of the stimulus," "some unique encoding of the stimulus," "an abstract representation of the concept of the stimulus," "a set of new associative links," "some newly constructed or reorganized neural engram (or cell assembly or phase sequence circuit)," or "some new biochemical structures." If spelled out in sufficient detail, any of these ideas could provide valuable insights into the problem of human memory. The information processing approach is committed to seeking the level of description of a phenomenon at which a mechanistic (in the Turing sense) process is assured. Thus it is appropriate that we begin this analysis of the problem of what is stored by transferring the question to the domain of some mechanism that we appear to understand superficially at least—namely, the digital computer—and examine how an answer to the question might be formulated in this case.

To those for whom the computer is an alien device, the question of what is stored in it may be no less a source of mystery and conceptual difficulty than is the related question regarding human memory. In teaching introductory computer science courses, one notices that many find the statement, "The computer stored the letter A in its memory," comprehensible only in anthropomorphic terms, while others find it difficult not to imagine a photographic image of the letter somehow finding its way into the computer's files. The conceptual difficulties are precisely those encountered in trying to understand human memory storage: Photographs and sound recordings seem to suggest themselves as the most natural paradigm for storage.

The photograph–recording metaphor turns out to be a very misleading one, even for computers. For example, the type of more-or-less isomorphic storage which both photograph and recording provides does not give the storing device access to meaningful units of the stored material. Thus a tape recorder cannot retrieve individual words or sentences, because these are not represented in an integral manner—that is, they have not been explicitly individuated so that they could be referenced as units. Normally, a tape recorder can only be made to retrieve (or otherwise process) arbitrary time segments. Similarly, a photograph does not contain objects but only areas of high and low reflectivity. Objects, words, and similar entities are higher-order abstractions in the sense of being invariant over an unbounded set of purely iconic patterns—that is, there is an infinite variety of light and dark photographic patterns which correspond to the letter A (or to a chair) and a similar unbounded variety of acoustical patterns which correspond to the word *chair*. In this sense, neither words nor letters are available as explicit differentiated parts of such iconic representations.

In the case of storing the letter A in a computer, what is stored must clearly possess this higher-order property of being invariant with respect to such geometrical properties as size, style of typeface, orientation, thickness, color, modality (i.e., input device), and so on. An iconic representation is unique for each instance (token) of the letter and so cannot qualify, since the computer must have access to the *type* A (i.e., the equivalence class of all input signals which we wish to call A), not the *token,* in order to differentiate it from all other characters. In this discussion, the term "token" denotes different occurrences of input events, while "type" denotes a class of functionally equivalent tokens. Thus two tokens represent different types if they are functionally distinct. In computers, functional distinctiveness is a well-defined notion with a fixed meaning. In cognition, however, functional distinctiveness is always understood relative to some domain of discourse. Thus two tokens of the same type in one context may be tokens of different types in another context. For example, a particular word spoken by different people would be tokens of the same type for linguistic purposes but tokens of different types for sociological purposes.)

A camera and a tape recorder are not called upon to perform discriminations on the basis of type; they simply reproduce the original optical or acoustical pattern within the required precision. Even if they were equipped for making comparisons, they could not discriminate the set of inputs which qualify as the letter A from all those which qualify as the letter B without first abstracting from the input the appropriate distinguishing characteristics—that is, without in effect converting them from an iconic representation to a more abstract one which embodies in it the required invariances. Failure to appreciate this fundamental difference between the nature of storage in a camera or a tape recorder, on one hand, and a computer memory on the other can cause a great deal of confusion. The difference can be highlighted by noting that a computer *can* be made to store data in what may be thought of as an iconic manner—say, by converting a photograph into a matrix of relative brightness measures, or by passing an acoustical signal though an analogue-to-digital converter prior to storage. When a letter or word is stored in this manner, however, no process of direct comparison can make the required character or word discrimination. Therefore, a phase of abstraction must still be instituted

Perhaps the intuitively appealing photograph metaphor presents itself because such devices are more familiar to us than computers. At an earlier period of history, photographic images such as those projected by the *camera obscura* were considered magical, for they too abstracted to some degree from the object depicted. The relatively recent invention of perspective in painting, the evidence that certain primitive people find it difficult to recognize familiar objects from photographs, and the peculiar feature of children's drawings wherein important relations are retained at the expense of faithfulness to photographic properties all suggest that the idea of iconic representation is by no means universal or natural (for a more erudite discussion of this point, see Gombrich, 1961, or Goodman, 1968).

Another source of difficulty which we can clarify by transposing from a photograph metaphor to a computer storage metaphor has to do with the idea of storing something abstract, such as a concept or rule. We see in the case of the computer that there is no contradiction in this notion (as many have implied when similar claims are made about human memory). At one level, that of machine hardware, the storage is entirely concrete, being electrical and physical states of machine components. At another level, having to do with the manner in which the representation functions (i.e., the class of external events which are functionally equivalent with respect to the representation), we can speak of the storage of an abstraction or concept. Thus a particular machine encoding of the letter A functions like the concept of the letter A insofar as its only property is that it is different from all tokens of the letters B, C, and so forth. It contains nothing about the size, form, modality, or any other property associated with some particular instance (token) of the letter A.

Turing's great achievement was to show that all one needed in order to account for any known sense of *mechanism* was a device that could distinguish discrete symbol types (i.e., a notion of identical copies of symbols), take on discrete states (which also have this property of the indistinguishability of tokens of the same state), produce indistinguishable copies of symbols, and make transitions from one state to another as a function only of the unique symbol being sensed and its current state. Turing's (1936) discussion of the intuitive motivation for these ideas makes interesting reading for psychologists.

In terms of the question of what is stored, it is both possible and useful to distinguish two parts of the problem. The first part has to do with the material forms of storage—whether it be in the form of relay closures, the magnetization of ferrite cores, or the establishment of new neural circuits—and with the precise physical state that is to represent the particular item to be stored. The second part of the problem has to do with the functional properties which all such forms of storage must have in order to be able to store and retrieve items. The two parts of the problem are quite distinct. Hence we can put aside all considerations of material forms while addressing ourselves to the functional requisites.

Having made this distinction, we may now understand the question of what is stored not as a request for a description of material forms but rather of formal relationships or information structures. Thus when we speak of abstract mental representations, it is in this spirit. We are not denying the existence of corresponding material forms but merely focusing our attention on the functional requisites. Both for the computer and for the mind, the only thing we need to know to answer the question of what is stored is what types of functional distinctions are to be made by the storing mechanism. In the case of a letter, what is stored in the computer can be anything as long as it is unique to that particular type. It is precisely this fact which enables the letter A to be distinguished from the letter B, or the letter C, or any other input character to which the machine is capable of reacting differently. For most purposes, one need not specify anything more unless the questioner is interested in the material forms involved (i.e., in the electronics of the machine).

In the case of a theory of cognitive representations, the theorist determines the functional requirements of the representation, or the boundary conditions, which must be met by any postulated representation. A formal object—which may be a string of symbols, a diagram, a computer data structure, a description of a process, or even a physical object—is then exhibited together with a set of mechanical operations for interpreting the object. Such an object *is* the mental representation (or at least forms part of a theory of the mental representation) in a certain domain. As long as the psychologist has done his or her homework and has produced an object that meets the required constraints, protests that the mind does not really work this way are irrelevant. The only useful interpretation of the phrase "does not really work that way' is that the protester has other evidence in mind which suggests different or additional constraints or criteria, and the formal scheme can be modified to incorporate them. The end result, however, will (by our account) continue to be some formal object independent of biological structures or phenomenological appearances.

III. REQUIREMENTS ON REPRESENTATIONS: ATOMISM REVISITED

A representation must be such that the system will treat representations of tokens of the same type identically and representations of tokens of distinct types differently. I call this requirement the uniqueness–distinctiveness condition. It is only one of many conditions which a representational system must meet. However, it is a necessary condition for defining the building block of cognitive systems—the atomic symbol.

An atomic symbol is a formal entity whose only property is that it is discrete and can be unambiguously "recognized" when it occurs again—that is, from the standpoint of the system as a whole, all copies (tokens) of a particular symbol are indistinguishable from one another yet distinguishable from tokens of every other symbol. Thus the operation of comparing two symbol tokens and taking action which is contingent on whether they are tokens of the same symbol is a primitive operation in all computational systems. Not only is this notion of an atomic symbol the building block of information processing theories, it is also the basis of all mathematics—and in fact of any intellectual activity for which a notational system has been developed.[1] Because this notion implies some kind of atomism, it might seem to be destined to run into the tide of arguments that have been successfully marshaled against atomism by many intellectual schools, including Gestalt psychology. This is not the case, however, since the Gestalt argument, to the extent that it is valid, can only be taken as an indictment of a particular form of atomism—one that tries to build up percepts from sensations or from spatially or temporally local features—and not of the more general claim that the structure of a percept can be described in terms of a structure of discrete symbols. This point is fundamental enough to merit a brief digression.

Gestalt psychologists have enshrined their view in the slogan, "The whole is different from the sum of its parts." But as Minsky and Papert (1972) point out, whether this is true or not depends very much on what one means by both "sum" and "parts." Clearly, there are cases in which a description of a whole in terms of what might be a set of its parts is mistaken. This fact has been amply demonstrated in the Gestalt literature. Nevertheless, to conclude that *no* analysis of a whole in terms of more atomic elements will capture the relevant aspects of the whole is just as mistaken. Even if perception did occur holistically (and what this might mean is far from clear), the fact remains that the whole—the percept— does have structure. So long as the set of percepts has a structure—so

---

[1] Whether one can get away with discrete symbols in all cases or whether certain aspects of cognitive representation are better modeled in terms of continuous "dense" representations is a separate issue which is beyond the scope of this chapter. An idea of the complexity of the issue in the case of artistic depiction may be obtained from Goodman (1968). Asking what it would mean for a mental representation to be "dense" can get one into some rather slippery conceptual issues!

long as one percept resembles another in certain respects and a third in yet other respects—there is no way for a scientist to exhibit this structure without characterizing the individual percepts in terms of relations among more primitive terms. The very notion of structure is predicated on the existence of relations among distinguishable aspects which themselves are unstructured (i.e., which can be represented by atomic symbols). De Saussure (1959) made an observation which has subsequently become a cornerstone of the French Structuralist Movement; namely, that all structures occur in pairs. Relations among distinct entities (paradigmatic structure) imply a set of relations among parts of individual entities (syntagmatic structure).

What has made the notion of atomic elements unpopular in some quarters is that the elementary "parts" in a domain such as perception are rarely simple, physically identifiable or measurable local aspects. Few linguists would question the belief that utterances have a structure which can be described in terms of a small set of phonetic elements. However, no temporally isolated segment of an utterance coextensive with the perception of a phone contains the acoustical invariance needed to identify it as being a particular phoneme. In this case, the whole can be said to be composed of parts, but these parts are not those which temporally local physical measurements can give us. Rather, they represent abstract aspects of the acoustical signal not localized in some brief segment of time.

There are several other undesirable connotations of the notion of primitives or atoms. One is the implication that we are dealing with a set of atoms fixed in advance and that perception or comprehension invariably consists of analyzing the stimulus event as an arrangement (or, even worse, as a vector of indicators) of these primitives. This view has a number of proponents in the social sciences (e.g., in "componential analysis," or in the semantic theory of Katz & Fodor, 1973), in the "feature analyzer" approach to perception, as well as in artificial intelligence, where an attempt is made, for example, to reduce the meaning of linguistic material (particularly verbs) to a structure of semantic primitives (see, e.g., the work of Schank, 1972).

Other approaches emphasize the role of the processes which map representations onto one another. In one approach characteristic of such artificial intelligence work as that of Moore and Newell (1974), as well as of predicate logic formulations, a particular set of primitives, depending on the particular goals of the system at the time the stimulus is encountered. Furthermore, the level to which analysis proceeds on any one occasion is not fixed in advance. Nevertheless, *some* analysis in terms of *some* more primitive atomic elements must always take place. Note that this claim is very different from the claim that a unique or ultimate set of primitive elements exists, or even that a relatively small yet general set of primitive elements can be found in terms of which stimuli are always elaborated to a canonical structure at the time the stimuli are encountered.

IV. STRUCTURE IN LINGUISTICS AND ARTIFICIAL INTELLIGENCE

It may be useful to distinguish among several ways in which the term "representation" is used, since this distinction sheds some light on the question of primitives. When linguists assert that the deep structure of a sentence describes the mental representation of that sentence, they do not mean precisely the same thing that students of artificial intelligence (or cognitive psychology) might mean by a parallel claim that such-and-such describes the mental representation of some piece of knowledge. The difference between the nature of these two claims reveals basic differences in the goals of these two approaches and in the different level of abstraction of their descriptions.

IV.A. The Linguistic Approach

The approach adopted by many linguists—the so-called "competence theory" approach (see Pylyshyn, 1972, 1973a)—attempts to characterize the structure of a set of stimuli (e.g., of the set of sentences in some natural language) as these stimuli are processed by humans. In the case of language, this structure is inferred by appealing to the linguistic intuitions of native speakers. The resulting structures give a formal account of the relationships that hold among parts of a sentence (or other stimulus) and among different sentences. Such a characterization would explicitly exhibit the equivalence of indiscernible stimuli by assigning the same underlying form (i.e., deep structure) to them. It would also account for the relationship among stimuli by explicitly exhibiting similarities and differences among the subparts of their underlying structure.

Since the form of the deep structure reflects the cognitive distinctions that people make among a set of stimuli, it must describe the mental representation of these stimuli. Thus it meets the primary requirement for representations—namely, that no cognitive distinctions be made among the objects of cognition unless the distinguishing characteristics are contained explicitly in deep structure and, conversely, that cognitive equivalences and relationships among stimuli are the result of identical or partially overlapping deep structures.

It should be noted that these requirements are not easily met when we are concerned with infinite classes of stimulus types, as in the case of natural language sentences. Thus the "uniqueness–distinctiveness" condition cannot be met simply by seeking a set of features or even some set of codes for the stimulus set. This is because, in the usual sense of this term, an atomic code is simply the selection of a particular distinct internal object (symbol) from some prescribed or agreed upon set of available objects. Each such code is uniquely associated with a distinct type. A problem arises immediately, however, from the fact that there are an unlimited number of distinct figures or sentences (i.e., an unlimited number of different types), so there must be an infinite number of internal codes. Unfortunately, it is anathema to any empirical theory for it to require an infinite number of different terms or symbols.

As long as we are required to map distinct stimulus types onto elements of a prearranged set of arbitrary codes, we must assume that the organism already possesses an infinite set of internal codes. The only way around this difficulty would seem to be to drop the requirement that these codes are already available to the organism and waiting, as it were, for the incoming stimulus types to be assigned to them (the way the codes for individual characters are assigned in digital computers). But this suggestion leads to a dilemma: How can we map a stimulus type onto a unique code unless the organism already possesses the code? Or, how can an organism perceive a token as an instance of a particular concept unless it already knows (i.e., has a representation of) the concept? In fact, it is precisely because of this difficulty that we must rule out the notion of a code and a coding process of the type depicted in some association theories, in which the code is an available mediator and the coding process is one of invoking the mediator through an existing associative bond. It is also one of the reasons that I have argued against the notion of a gross, uninterpreted representation of a stimulus, called its image, serving as a mental representation (Pylyshyn, 1973b).

There is a way out of this dilemma. For instance, we can think of the representation, not as a prearranged arbitrary code, but rather as a structure which is constructed anew each time a stimulus is encountered. In order to construct such a code-structure, however, each new type cannot be identified or assigned to a representation as a whole; rather, the stimulus must be analyzed into constituent parts and relationships. The representation would then be constructed on the basis of this analysis (for simplicity, we speak of the analysis itself as yielding the representation as its product).

To push this analysis further, we must assume that any stimulus is analyzable at some level of description in terms of some finite set of distinct elements and relations. For example, in the perception of figures, the elements may be angles, lines, arcs, or surfaces. In the case of language, these elements may consist (at the phonetic level) of phonemes or (at the syntactical level) of units such as morphemes or formatives. Each of the infinite set of stimuli can then be analyzed in a finite manner to yield a structural representation which has the properties we require. Such a representation is not at all arbitrary. Indeed, the structure and subparts of the representation, as well as the representation as a whole, are related in a systematic manner to the elements and relations in the stimulus, with the system being prescribed by the way in which the stimulus is analyzed and the representation constructed for each novel stimulus type.

The key idea in the previous discussion is that whenever we have a concept that covers an indefinite number of distinct instances (i.e., contains infinitely many types), we cannot simply "encode" an entire instance in one step. First, we must analyze it in terms of a number of atomic symbols, or primitives. The important requirements which must be met by such primitives are: (1) The primitives must be drawn from a finite (preferably small) set. (2) In specifying a particular pattern of primitives, we uniquely identify the distinctive stimulus type. In other words, the primitives correspond to units which, in various patterns, exhaustively cross-classify a set of types into partially identical subsets. As long as these conditions are met, we have the basis for carrying out the task at hand—namely, the specification of the relation between tokens, analyzed in terms of primitives, and the representation of some particular concept.

Such requirements on primitives are rather powerful. For example, the fact that we cannot assign a stimulus type, which contains an unlimited number of discriminable tokens, to a category without decomposing that stimulus into more elementary aspects means that such properties as "symmetry," "well-formedness," "even number," or "prime number" cannot serve as primitives, since specifying whether or not the stimulus token had any of these properties would not uniquely identify the stimulus type (e.g., there are infinitely many different symmetrical figures). This in turn means that the *computational assignment* of each of the infinite number of distinct stimulus types to these concepts can only be made on the basis of an analysis of tokens into more elementary components.

It is important to realize that there is no mechanical method of assigning tokens of different types to concepts such as those mentioned here without analyzing them in terms of more primitive parts or aspects. Such an analysis is frequently a computationally complex one which can only be specified as a procedure. This point is sometimes glossed over by psychologists. For example, Salzinger (1967) argues against the claim that people learn a grammar in learning a language. His position is that the set of well-formed sentences (if learned at all) represents a "response class" because of the differential reinforcement of elements in that class. However, to claim that strings of words are assigned to the "well-formed sentence" class (or its complement) without benefit of a computational analysis in terms of primitive units is to claim that the brain carries out a task that we know is not mechanically realizable. The real dilemma comes because if one admits that utterances are analyzed into a finite set of basic elements, then at least one of the functions computed over these elements is that described by generative grammar. Of course, Salzinger and other behaviorists would find this characterization unacceptable since it implies that people "know" grammar, at least in the sense that grammar is a way of describing one of the functions that people compute in understanding language.

The previous discussion also bears on an issue on the basis of which we may question the Gestalt dictum that the whole is different from the sum of its parts—namely, the way in which the word *sum* is interpreted. According to the view we have been describing, the sum, or the way in which primitive terms go together to make up the structure of the whole, is a property of the agent that utilizes the representation. It is identified with the computations the agent carries out in constructing the symbol structure from the proximal stimulus. The most abstract characterization of this computation simply gives a formal account of the part–whole relation. In the case of language, such a formal account is called a generative grammar. While it does not describe how this function is computed by humans, or how it might be implemented as an algorithm for a machine, it does tell us what abstract function such a computation must perform. While any number of actual algorithms could compute such a function (and it is the task of the psychologist to find one that meets a variety of criteria of "psychological reality"—i.e., accounts for other psychological evidence), such a characterization, called a competence theory, sets boundary conditions (I have referred to these elsewhere as "requisite computations"—see Pylyshyn, 1972) on the class of formal devices capable of carrying out the required computations.

IV.B. The Computational Approach

As I see it, the computational approach does not quarrel with the requirements on representations described here. It does, however, give less importance to the task of formally characterizing the structure of the percept (i.e., to the competence theory). Because the goal is to understand the way in which representations are constructed and used—both in the performance of the system and in the processes which it carries out—

the structure of the percept itself is considered only one part of a larger problem—namely, the structure of the entire system which deals with representations. As we shall see, this perspective gives the entire enterprise a very different character, though none of its results stand in contradiction to the competence approach.

One way to formulate the basic difference is as follows: In computer science there is a recognition (though not yet well formulated for formalized) of a fundamental tradeoff between the complexity of data structures and that of the processes which operate on them. The distinction is sharp in some systems (e.g., in algebraic languages such as Fortran) and more subtle in others (e.g., in list processing languages such as Lisp). Nevertheless, at every point during the execution of a program, a clear difference exists between what is playing the role of process and what is playing the role of data—that is, between a function and its arguments or between declarative and imperative "knowledge" in the system. While there are contexts in which we want to deemphasize this distinction, and while the roles of data and process are liable to shift readily, it is useful for the present purposes to emphasize the distinction. Thus, when we speak of a representational system Σ, we are speaking not of a single formal object but of the pair $\Sigma = (R, P)$ consisting of a (tentatively) static representational structure R together with a process P which operates on R and provides an "interpretation" of it.

When we speak of requirements such as the uniqueness–distinctiveness conditions or the second-order isomorphism condition, we must interpret these as applying not to some part of R but to the system Σ. This view results in a rather different interpretation of claims such as the cognitive equivalence among stimuli being the result of identical representations of these stimuli. This is true if by "representation" we mean not the particular substructure r into which the stimulus is mapped but the resulting Σ. Two equivalent stimuli need never actually be encoded into a common cononical form r. All we require is that the system treat the stimuli in an equivalent manner in the appropriate context. That is, we require that the (R', P) resulting from one stimulus be functionally indistinguishable from the (R'', P) resulting from the other cognitively equivalent stimulus. Thus, to take an example from logic, suppose that R is the current state of knowledge represented by a set of propositions, P is some deductive proof procedure, r_1 is the predicate logic representation of the proposition underlying one sentence, and r_2 is the representation of the proposition underlying a second sentence. In a predicate calculus representation, the knowledge-base R is changed simply by adding the new proposition r_1 or r_2. Thus, if the two sentences are cognitively equivalent insofar as they assert the same thing, our claim is that even though r_1 and

r_2 may be distinct, $(R \cup \{r_1\}, P)$ should be formally equivalent to $(R \cup \{r_2\}, P)$. That is, the same set of propositions (theorems) should be generated by both.

In general, the problem is more complex than this example suggests. For one thing, it may turn out that the number of steps required to derive some proposition from one of the two formally equivalent systems is greater than that required by the other system. Thus, from some point of view (one of particular interest to psychologists), the two systems are not equivalent. Of course, few systems have the property that new representations are formed simply by adding a new structure. Consequently, the presentation of a new stimulus cannot be automatically identified with the addition of a representational structure r to the database R (although there are many advantages to systems which possess this property, called "modularity"). In fact, the form that the modification of R takes usually depends on the state of Σ at the time the stimulus is encountered (this dependency of the effect of a stimulus on the current knowledge is sometimes called "assimilation"). This form also has a distributed effect on the whole system Σ (this process, by which the organism's state is modified by new stimuli, is sometimes referred to as "accommodation").

In general, the structure to which a certain stimulus gives rise will not only be distributed throughout R but will also depend on what Σ was at the time the stimulus was encountered. Obvious examples include the interpretation of sentences with indexical expressions (e.g., "I am here now") of constructions which depend on a larger context for their interpretation—so-called "diexes" (Fillmore, 1974)—and of sentences which are part of a longer narrative (see, e.g., the empirical work of Bransford & Johnson, 1973, or the theoretical analyses of Winograd, 1972, Charniak, 1972; and McDermott, 1974). Here again, the principle that cognitive distinctions among stimuli arise from differences in the way these stimuli are represented is true only if by representation we mean the representational system Σ. Because of this fact, it is possible for sentences with identical deep structures (in the linguistic sense) to have discernibly different effects on the representational system and, conversely, for sentences with different deep structures to have indistinguishable effects (i.e., to lead to equivalent Σ's).

So far we have argued that the processes which construct, manipulate, and interpret the representation (or, to use a more encompassing term from computer science, which "elaborate" the representation) must not be left out of the analysis of cognitive representation. It might be pointed out, however, that even the general ideas sketched here are not without serious implications. Consider, for example, the question of what constitutes the meaning of an utterance. One of the most influential philosophical books on language and ontology (Quine, 1960) devotes considerable space to a critique of the view that meaning could be some kind of entity. From the computational point of view, however, it makes as little sense to ask what the meaning of an utterance is as to ask *where* it is. The meaning of a sentence is tied to the changes which its reception creates in the representational system. It lies neither in the structure of the sentence itself nor in the change to the representation R, but in the difference it makes to the system (R, P), which, as we have seen, depends on the state of both R and P at the time the utterance is "heard."[2] It is not even in such things as "predispositions to respond" in some particular manner except insofar as this refers to the entire infinite behavioral potential of the system (which is not very illuminating, since whether some particular response is in this set or not is not decidable). In any case, from the artificial intelligence point of view, the meaning of a sentence to an automaton goes far beyond the properties of the particular sentence and is inextricably interwoven with the current goals and state of knowledge of the automaton and the processes for elaboration which the automaton possesses. This may not be a profound insight, but it does help to place into better perspective such age-old questions as, What is the meaning of sentence S?

If we were to examine the natural language understanding system of Winograd (1972) in order to determine the meaning of "Pick up the big red block and place it on the green one" for that system, we would discover a variety of structures: a parsing tree for the sentence (which in its construction involved checking on the existence of the objects referred to); a network of data structures called "object semantic structures," which characterize the objects referred to and which describe procedures for finding such objects (including ones referred to indirectly); another network of data structures called "relational semantic structures," which similarly describe relations among objects mentioned; and a plan for carrying out the command expressed in the sentence by calling on knowledge about "grasping," "picking up," "moving," "placing on top," and so on. Not only is the "meaning" of the sentence distributed among these symbol structures and the various procedures for interpreting these structures, but it is also dynamic. It is an open question where in the process from reception of a question or command to the formulation of a response the system can be said to have extracted the meaning of the sentence.

---

[2] Thus to successfully communicate to another person, a speaker does not simply choose a sentence with the intended meaning. He or she must also infer what the state of knowledge of the listener is so that the intended change in the listener's total representational system (R, P) can be affected.

Before leaving this general discussion of the computational approach to representation, it may be worthwhile to point out that the competence approach mentioned earlier is directed at a somewhat different goal. In keeping with a more structuralist intellectual tradition (see Gardner, 1973), it attempts to give a more formal and more abstract characterization of some part of what we know when we know a language. Clearly, "what we know" includes such structural properties as those described by grammars. That the grammar itself is not found explicitly in our representation of linguistic knowledge (in the sense of R alone) is equally clear by now. Nevertheless, the grammar describes general structural properties that any empirically adequate system (R, P) will implicitly account for. In fact, as noted elsewhere (Pylyshyn, 1973a), the competence theory describes in the most abstract manner one aspect of the function which the system (R, P) computes.

No system can be considered adequate unless it has the power to compute such a function. (One can, of course, argue whether the function is the correct one—i.e., whether the competence theory is empirically valid—but that is a separate issue.) While the competence theory gives an abstract characterization of this function, it tells us little about the particular (R, P) system which computes it. In fact, there is an unbounded number of such systems which are compatible with the competence theory, and additional criteria (both empirical and logical) must be invoked to decide among them. This is a task for both psycholinguists and those in artificial intelligence interested in language comprehension.

V. CONCLUSION: INFORMATION PROCESSING AND ITS ACCULTURATION

We have discussed some of the ideas that form the background of what has been rather loosely referred to in contemporary psychology as the "information processing approach." This approach rests on a foundation which has evolved only relatively recently and so has not yet acquired very deep roots in our scientific culture. The basic concepts are those of a symbol and of mechanism as a symbol-manipulating function. Although these concepts are rather easily accepted in such formal disciplines as logic and computer science, their acceptance into linguistics and psychology has been more painful and even now is only skin deep among most scholars in these fields. The problem is simply that it takes years of acculturation before explanations cast in this framework appear "natural." This uneasiness is often not articulated but shows up in the form of resistance to accepting certain models or mechanisms as being "psychologically real," or to seeing these models as anything more than meta-phors or calculation conveniences. A good example of such resistance from the phenomenological school is contained in Dreyfus (1972; see also the review in Pylyshyn, 1974).

Needless to say, opposition to this approach is not confined to phenom-enologists but is widespread among many psychologists who simply find the notion of symbol structure or mechanism too alien to take as seriously as it is intended. Because the mapping from a program to a physical device (a digital computer) is rather different from that between a program and another physical device (a brain), the latter never achieves the level of "cognitive satisfaction" demanded of explanations. It is possible that we are used to thinking of notions such as symbol and algorithm at too concrete a level (e.g., symbols as binary codes and algorithms as Algol, or Fortran programs which are compiled by a machine into internal machine instructions). In fact, these concepts are logically quite independent of machines (although in practice machines were, and continue to be, indis-pensable for their development), and we might be better off to forget about real machines and to think only in terms of "virtual machines" of unknown physical form which are capable of carrying out certain primi-tive operations. At this level, the comparison between minds and ma-chines becomes more balanced. However, we must leave this topic for another occasion.

REFERENCES

Bransford, J. D., & Johnson, M. K. (1973). Considerations of some problems of comprehen-sion. In W. G. Chase (Ed.), *Visual information processing* (pp 383–438). New York: Academic Press.

Charniak, E. (1972). *Towards a model of children's story comprehension* (Tech. Rep. No. AI-TR-266). Cambridge: MIT Artificial Intelligence Laboratory.

de Saussure, F. (1959). *Course in general linguistics*. New York: The Philosophical Library. (Original work published 1911).

Dreyfus, H. L. (1972). *What computers can't do: A critique of artificial reason*. New York: Harper & Row.

Fillmore, C. (1974). Pragmatics and the description of discourse. In C. Fillmore, G. Lakoff, & R. Lakoff, *Berkeley studies in syntax and semantics* (Vol. I). Berkeley: University of California, Department of Linguistics and Institute of Human Learning.

Fodor, J. A. (1975). *The language of thought*. New York: Thomas Crowell.

Gardner, H. (1973). *The quest for mind*. New York: Knopf.

Gombrich, E. H. (1961). *Art and illusion: A study in the psychology of pictorial representa-tion*. Princeton, NJ: Princeton University Press.

Goodman, N. (1968). *Languages of Art: An approach to a theory of symbols*. New York: Bobbs-Merrill.

Herman, G. P., & Rozenberg, G. (1974). *Developmental systems and languages.* Amsterdam: North Holland, 1974.

Katz, J. J., & Fodor, J. A. (1963). The structure of a semantic theory. *Language, 39,* 170–210.

McDermott, D. V. (1974). *Assimilation of new information by a natural language understanding system* (Tech. Rep. No. AI-TR-291). Cambridge: MIT Artificial Intelligence Laboratory.

Minsky, M., & Papert, S. (1972). Research at the laboratory in vision, language and other problems of intelligence (A.I. Memo 252). MIT Artificial Intelligence Laboratory, Cambridge, MA.

Monod, J. (1971). *Chance and necessity.* New York: Knopf.

Moore, J., & Newell, A. (1974). How can MERLIN understand? In L. Gregg (Ed.), *Knowledge and cognition.* Potomac, MD: Erlbaum.

Pylyshyn, Z. W. (1972). Competence and psychological reality. *American Psychologist, 27,* 546–552.

Pylyshyn, Z. W. (1973a). The role of competence theories in cognitive psychology. *Journal of Psycholinguistic Research, 2,* 21–50.

Pylyshyn, Z. W. (1973b). What the mind's eye tells the mind's brain: A critique of mental imagery. *Psychological Bulletin, 80,* 1–23.

Pylyshyn, Z. W. (1974). Minds, machines and phenomenology. *Cognition, 3,* 57–77.

Pylyshyn, Z. W. (1984). *Computation and cognition: Toward a foundation for cognitive science.* Cambridge, MA: MIT Press, A Bradford Book (1974).

Quine, W.V.O. (1969). *Word and object.* Cambridge: MIT Press.

Salzinger, K. (1967). The problem of response class in verbal behavior. In K. Salzinger & S. Salzinger (Eds.), *Research in verbal behavior and some neurophysiological implications.* New York: Academic Press.

Schank, R. (1972). Conceptual dependency: A theory of natural language understanding. *Cognitive Psychology, 3,* 552–631.

Turing, A. M. (1936). On computable numbers with an application to the *Entscheidungsproblem. Mathematical Society Proceedings, 42,* 230–265.

Weimer, W. B. (1973). Psycholinguistics and Plato's paradoxes of the *Meno. American Psychologist, 28,* 15–33.

Winograd, T. (1972). *Understanding natural language.* New York: Academic Press.

Index